Group Care
for Children

Group Care for Children

Concept and issues

Edited by

Frank Ainsworth and
Leon C. Fulcher

Tavistock Publications
London and New York

First published in 1981 by
Tavistock Publications Ltd
11 New Fetter Lane, London EC4P 4EE

Published in the USA by
Tavistock Publications
in association with Methuen, Inc.
733 Third Avenue, New York, NY 10017

Typeset by Nene Phototypesetters Ltd, Northampton
Printed in the United States of America

British Library Cataloguing in Publication Data

Group care for children. – (Social science
paperbacks)
1. Children – Institutional care
I. Ainsworth, Frank   II. Fulcher, Leon C.
III. Series
362.7'32   HV713

ISBN 0–422–77290–9
ISBN 0–422–77850–8 pbk

Contents

Foreword, by Norman Tutt   vii
Acknowledgements   xi
Preface   xiii

1   Introduction: Group care for children – concept
    and issues   1
    Frank Ainsworth and Leon C. Fulcher

Section I   Group care practice with children

2   Essential components in care and treatment
    environments for children   19
    Henry W. Maier
3   Planned care and treatment: the notion of programme   71
    Leon C. Fulcher and Frank Ainsworth
4   Major approaches to residential treatment   89
    James K. Whittaker
5   New roles for group care centres   128
    Jerome Beker

Section II   Personnel considerations

6   Occupational stress for group care personnel   151
    Martha A. Mattingly
7   Team functioning in group care   170
    Leon C. Fulcher

Section III   Career development and training

8   Patterns of career development in group care   201
    Karen D. VanderVen

9   The training of personnel for group care with children   225
    Frank Ainsworth

Section IV   Research and evaluation

10 Research and evaluation in group care   247
    Chris Payne
11 Cost factors in group care   271
    Martin Knapp

Section V   Conclusion

12 Conclusion   295
    Frank Ainsworth and Leon C. Fulcher

    Index   297

Foreword

Norman Tutt[1]

The idea that children, whose parents are unable or unwilling to care adequately for them within the familial home, should be cared for by the state or voluntary organizations, in small groups by adults who share their lives with the children, has gained considerable currency in the last two decades. The large institutions in which children lived out their lives *en masse*, sleeping in huge dormitories and eating in dining rooms of serried ranks of tables overseen by masters and matrons (which were such a prominent feature of social welfare in the early part of this century), have now been largely discredited and consigned to history. Sepia photographs recording this stage of the child care profession still cast a long shadow over annual reports of voluntary bodies and the corridors of institutions now trying to promote small living groups for the residents.

The promotion of group care has sprung from several converging ideologies, a number of which run, overtly or covertly, through this book. I believe two ideologies have had particular influence. The first arises from work with the adult mentally ill, and is the idea of the therapeutic community. This idea was instrumental in breaking down the belief that therapy was the monopoly of the experts, and instead espoused the view that not only were all ward staff therapists but moreover that patients were capable of offering fellow patients help which could be seen as therapeutic. This movement, led by Maxwell Jones, developed after the Second World War and was regarded by many administrators, traditional clinicians, and nursing staff as something akin to anarchy. However, for many staff who were seeking a theoretical justification for their own beliefs that they should enjoy closer, more informal relationships with the young people in their care, the ideas of a therapeutic community were exciting.

The second ideology arose from the mainstream of child care workers and administrators, stimulated in England and Wales by the

Curtis Committee Report of 1946. This Report accepted that some children were best served by being removed from home, but once removed should as far as possible be cared for within substitute families. This ideology, as well as increasing interest in the fostering of children, led to the development of family group homes in which groups of children and paid adults created at its best an image of the family, but at its worst a parody in which both staff and children were exploited. The family group homes led to serious consideration of how state authorities could create small group living situations for children and adults and yet maintain professional conditions of employment for staff.

By the 1980s the idea of group care is widely accepted in principle and yet its implementation has been slow because of a lack of commitment to provide a full and relevant training for staff. This situation has arisen partly from a lack of certainty over the skills required by staff, but more particularly because of the underlying attitude that the domestic role of caring for children is predominantly a set of feminine and innate skills. The failure to accept feminine skills as being of considerable significance has been commented on in many areas; the belief in innate 'mothering' skills is not only insecurely based, but also irrelevant to the complex tasks of caring for other people's children, particularly when those children manifest disorders of behaviour or development. This book represents an important step towards the fuller acceptance and implementation of group care programmes, since it is one of the first works which attempts to concentrate solely on the mechanics and issues of the practice skills needed for group care, regardless of the agency context. Previous works have either concentrated on the client group (e.g. work with mentally handicapped children or caring for the delinquent child) or the social policy context (e.g. the questions of whether mentally handicapped people are best helped within a hospital or child care establishment, or whether justice or welfare is the 'best' way of tackling delinquency). I would not wish to denigrate any of these works but would question their relevance to the group care worker getting children up in the morning and sharing their lives throughout the day. This book attempts to offer guidance and support to this vital group of workers whose skills will be required whatever social policy is adopted. For example, although current social policy for juvenile offenders stresses decarceration, it is recognized that community-based programmes, whether provided by education, social services, or the justice services, all employ methods of group care and it is clear that if community corrections are to succeed, a highly skilled and committed work force will be essential. Currently these exist in only very limited areas.

Since this book is aimed squarely at practitioners within group care, it can only truly be judged by its success in proving relevant to their experience of the work. Judged by that criterion it proved uncannily successful for me. I was early convinced that group care was a sadly neglected area when, although trained and experienced as a clinical psychologist, I chose to live and work alongside care workers in a boys' correctional institution. In my first week on the staff I was required to take lunch duty and rapidly realized that seven years' training and experience as a psychologist provided little to guide me in my attempt to supervise ninety adolescents at mealtime. Logic told me that psychology – 'the science of human behaviour' – must be relevant to the problem of controlling the behaviour with which these humans were confronting me. Yet I found myself controlled by my feelings of resentment, anger, and frustration, while my behaviour was governed by early memories of how adults had controlled me at school. Later the correctional institution evolved towards smaller group care units but I found myself equally unprepared. The problem of control was lessened but a secondary set of problems was raised when I sat at the dining table sharing a meal with the adolescents. Unprotected by office, desk, case files, test material, and the paraphernalia of clinical psychology, I found myself talking with adolescents, attempting to make sense of their perceptions and experience, and subsequently trying to work with those views in a way which would help the young people's personal and social development. These experiences generated within me a concern for seeking some means of linking theory to improved practice.

Some of these experiences lay dormant until I read this book; they were then reactivated and made me conscious of the exposed and vulnerable position into which most social care workers are forced. They enter the work untrained or with irrelevant training; they are made publicly accountable for their work and yet are not supported by any clearly thought-out theory of practice. This volume encourages the development of greater support. For those readers who feel they have moved beyond direct contact with children and may therefore question the relevance of the book for them personally, I would recommend the chapter by Karen VanderVen which outlines the career levels of social care workers and the feelings experienced by staff in those levels. In her description I found an accurate echo of my own feelings as I moved from social care worker, to administrator, to academic. Such an echo provides an insight into the value of this book in successfully articulating the feelings and training needs of those who undertake a difficult and unattractive task on behalf of society – namely caring for its children.

Note

(1) Norman Tutt is Professor of Applied Social Studies, Department of Social Administration, University of Lancaster, England.

Acknowledgements

As editors we are greatly indebted to Jerome Beker, Martin Knapp, Henry Maier, Martha Mattingly, Chris Payne, Karen VanderVen, and James Whittaker, the contributors to this volume. We came to know the writers as teachers, colleagues, and professional confidants. We increasingly regard them as valued friends. Their willingness to endure the trials and tribulations of authorship at our invitation is more than simply appreciated.

In addition to these obvious acknowledgements, each of the editors in turn would like to make some special mention of some of the organizations and individuals who have helped to make possible much of the work on which this volume is based. Frank Ainsworth would like to record his appreciation to the Nuffield Foundation, whose award of a Social Science Study Fellowship in 1975–6 enabled him to undertake his first North American journey. Acknowledgements are also given to: the University of Dundee, School of Social Administration; the University of Washington, Seattle, School of Social Work; the Central Council for Education and Training in Social Work, London; and Middlesex Polytechnic, Department of Social Work. All of these bodies have provided at various times a diverse experience and an opportunity to travel that has influenced this volume.

In turn, Leon Fulcher wishes to acknowledge appreciation to the people associated with Dr Barnardo's and especially those in the Scottish Division for providing his first opportunity to practise as a social worker in Britain. Acknowledgements are also given to: the Washington State Department of Social and Health Services, Maple Lane School at Centralia; The Lower Columbia Council on Alcoholism, Longview, Washington; and the University of Stirling, Department of Sociology. A special acknowledgement is given to the staff and management of Shawbridge Youth Centres in Montreal, Quebec who have graciously provided research support, co-operation, and encouragement in furthering a comparative study of group care.

At a more personal level, the editors are indebted to their respective wives and families: Brenda, Ewen, and Helen; and Jane, Mark, and Katy. They endured the turmoil, shared the excitement, and have supported us throughout the many months of this project.

Somewhat facetiously, the editors would like to acknowledge the debt they owe to some airline moguls who, by providing an era of low cost transatlantic travel, have facilitated our work.

Finally, acknowledgements are also due to those who have provided administrative, secretarial, and editorial support. Jane Fulcher merits our warmest thanks in this regard. We acknowledge permission given by Jossey-Bass Publications, San Francisco, which allows the reprinting of Chapter 4, 'Major Approaches to Residential Treatment' that originally appeared in James K. Whittaker's *Caring for Troubled Children*.

Preface

For the editors; one British and the other American now resident in Britain, this volume is as much a product of travel as it is of academic contemplation and practice. Travel has involved each editor taking up residence in the other's country as well as many transatlantic voyages. It has also promoted an overview of group care work with children in Great Britain and North America, which gave incentive for our decision to approach other contributors with the idea of preparing this volume. There was also a desire to try and achieve some deeper understanding of, and where possible a synthesis between, the different approaches that are to be found in each country.

An interesting feature of cross-cultural work is that in learning about group care for children in another context, what one acquires is a new way of viewing that with which one is already familiar. This familiarity may all too often result in an unseeing eye. While the obstacles restricting comparison are very real, there has been an attempt to identify some of these where possible and to note parallel histories, alternative political ideologies, and differing cultural norms that prevail. At the same time, however, the volume also includes contributions which focus attention on key issues influencing services for children – across national boundaries.

Bernard Shaw is, of course, quoted as saying that Britain and America are 'two nations divided by a common language'. It is the truth of this comment that compels us to draw attention in this preface to some issues of language and terminology as reflected throughout the volume. We should say from the outset that 'group care' is not a term that is widely used on either side of the Atlantic, although its use is increasingly prevalent. A primary task therefore has been to clarify our use of the term 'group care'. Our second task concerned whether to edit the papers as presented and to use consistent terms and language throughout. There can be little doubt that substantial variations exist in the use of terms on either side of the Atlantic. For example, British writers tend to refer to group care settings for children using terms like 'provision', 'centres', or 'establishments'. Meanwhile, for the same concerns, an American writer is likely to use terms like 'programs', 'facilities', 'cottages', or other words. These variations even extend to issues of national spelling, as with 'programme' or 'program', and 'centre' or center'. In the end, our decision has been to allow each paper to reflect the author's own preference and thereby national differences. We believe it is important for readers to learn to grapple with these differences in their own attempt to acquire a cross- national understanding. Furthermore, to have imposed conformity of terminology and language throughout this volume would have distorted the real position and created a false consensus where none exists. We hope that readers will not find this approach to be too distracting.

Particularly problematic in this regard are the diverse job titles used by group care personnel in each country. There are, of course, a range of historic titles such as Overseer, Houseparent, Housemaster, or Matron that are commonly held. These titles are associated in particular with the older institutional services in the group care field. They stem from the orphanages, almshouses, workhouses, and reformatories of the past. In more recent years there appears to have been a growing divergence in national practices.

In America, a proliferation of new titles are to be found, often borrowed from other professions, including: Child Care Worker, Counsellor, Therapist, Practitioner, and Specialist; or Group Life, Group Care, or Group Worker, Counsellor, Therapist, Practitioner, and Specialist. Further titles will be found to reflect a developmental focus such as in Child Development Specialist. Other titles can be found which may be associated with a theoretical orientation or as related to the location of a group care service within a particular discipline. Child Mental Health Specialists, Teaching-Parents, and Educateurs are all such examples. Generally speaking, however, *Child Care Worker* seems to find most favour. The usefulness of this title seems to be that it allows for all concerned with children's services, and especially group care services for children, to share a common identity, regardless of their theoretical disposition or location of practice. All of the titles are, however, worthy of mention if only to alert the reader to the fact that they refer to a work force that is identified with a growing sense of common purpose in America.

In Great Britain, developments have so far taken a different direction with regard to job titles, seeming to be less ambitious and more common.

In the social welfare sector, the older title of Houseparent still retains a surprising degree of prominence. Matron, a title frequently used in the past, is less common now having been replaced by the rather more neutral, if somewhat euphemistic term Officer-in-Charge. Child Care Worker was an occupational title that gained fleeting popularity in the 1950s and 1960s. This occurred during an era when services were segmented across categories of the population. Then it was possible to acquire specialist qualifications for work with children including those living in institutional, residential, and day care units. The Child Care Worker titles gave way in the 1970s to more general social work titles, including Residential Social Worker. Meanwhile, those personnel engaged in group care work with children across institutional, residential, and day care settings, are now likely to be allotted a title which is prefixed by a reference to setting rather than client population. Thus, in Britain the title most frequently used by group care workers may be *Residential* or *Day Care Worker*. These titles are used within the social welfare services and range across the human life cycle of clients, including children, the adult handicapped, and the elderly.

The reader should also be alerted to the possible different uses of the terms 'social welfare' and 'social services' as found in this volume. In Great Britain, less so than in America, the term 'social service' tends to be used to refer to both nationally promoted welfare programmes as well as local services. Thus, when used by British writers, 'social services' may describe a variety of personal social services that are locally provided for all the population. The term 'social welfare' is also used to refer to the range of personal social services and other support services such as family allowances, supplementary benefits, unemployment benefits, and pensions, to name but a few. 'Social welfare' may also be used to refer to broader notions of social policy and areas of governmental concern.

Some comment is required about our use of the term 'children'. In America, it might have been helpful to have addressed ourselves more specifically to children and youth. Meanwhile, in Britain the appropriate terms might have been children and young people. We have decided to use the one term 'children' as it is a focus around which there is common use. Our intention in referring to children is to include roughly the first and second decades of human development. Our view is that much of the material written here about children in the earlier stages of life also applies to children grown older in the eighth and ninth decades of life.

Finally, it is necessary to qualify our use of the terms 'professional' and 'occupational' when referring to group care personnel. The editors are well aware that some may find these terms provocative. Throughout the volume, we have allowed the terms to be used interchangeably according to the preference of the individual contributor. However, whether referring to occupational craftsmanship or professionalism, the use of both terms implies the following ideal: a disciplined use of knowledge that has been acquired against a backdrop of shared and conflicting values through personal study and practice experience with children who for a time must enter, participate or live in, learn, and one hopes leave group care.

1 Introduction: Group care for children – concept and issues

Frank Ainsworth and Leon C. Fulcher[1]

We approach this volume with two purposes. First, we seek to outline the concept of group care, exploring this concept as it relates to services for children and youth. Second, we have sought to supply papers on a range of key issues which confront group care services for young people. Material is drawn from both British and North American sources which emphasize the usefulness of a group care concept when thinking about and planning services for children and families. Our selection of material for this volume further reflects a commitment to comparative methods of enquiry, and a belief that the comparative approach contributes much to the study of residential, day, and institutional care services. We hope the volume as a whole will demonstrate the value of comparative methods in developing a more concise body of knowledge which can assist practitioners, administrators, and educators alike in their endeavours to improve the quality of group care services.

By way of introduction, we seek here to address ourselves to the concept of group care. We begin with a consideration of group care as *an occupational focus*, identifying those structural and social variables which distinguish this occupational focus from others. Second, we review the development of group care structures in society's response to social problems and human needs, thus identifying group care as *a field of study*. Finally, we present group care as *a practice domain*, showing how large institutions, residential group living, and day care facilities are used to supply services by each of society's major resource systems – health care, education, social welfare, and justice. Our assessment suggests that the time is ripe for the development of a concept which helps to differentiate between group care services and other human services, while at the same time showing how these form an integral part of a larger whole. By examining issues of substance in the provision of group care, we believe it is possible to bridge some of the long-established barriers – some as large as the Atlantic Ocean itself – which have hampered development in this field over the years. Only time will tell whether this belief finds support in the practice community.

Group care as an occupational focus

Conceptualization of services in terms of *Group Care* serves to highlight the varied ways in which interpersonal dynamics and organizational contexts are related. Briefly, the rationale for this concept builds from an appreciation of the organizational pattern around which care services are provided. Such a pattern emphasizes that services are supplied through the medium of group interaction, where individual attention is to some extent subsumed in the requirement for group attention. A group care service can also be identified by the pattern whereby services are supplied within, or in relation to, a defined centre of activity. Such centres can be said to supply services to an identifiable, and usually homogeneous clientele, for periods of more than a few hours per week, increasing to and including 168 hours per week. For the purposes of this volume, attention is drawn to a range of services where the group focus and the shared life-space (Redl, 1959) of children provide the main organizing principles which underlie practice and service design. Group care services require that consideration be given to environmental factors associated with the location of a service centre. Additionally, group care services require that attention be given to the contextual characteristics of a centre and the planned use of physical and social variables which are different from other important approaches to, or patterns of service, such as group work or home-based and office-based family support.

Group care does not therefore only refer to services provided by large institutions or smaller group living centres which can be found throughout Great Britain and North America. It refers also to a range of day-service programmes which use the group and the shared life-space of the group as the primary focus. This means that group care identifies an occupational focus that covers older as well as newer forms of service where nurturing, socialization, and specific therapeutic or learning opportunities are made available to children and families. Interestingly, group care facilities are to be found in each of society's major resource systems. In the health care system, group care workers are usually identified as nurses and the consumers of their services are known as patients. In the education system, group care workers are generally identified as teachers (although all teachers are not group care workers) and their consumers are known as students or pupils. In the social welfare system, residential and day-care workers will be found engaging with residents or clients, whether these be children or adults. Finally, in the justice system, correctional counsellors or officers will be found to assume responsibility for groups of inmates or detainees. In each instance, physical and social care, learning, and guardianship or control feature as distinguishing characteristics, although variations in emphasis will be found within each system.

Because of the manner in which group care services span the four major resource systems on either side of the Atlantic, it is not difficult to see how this field of study has remained fragmented. The extreme visibility of large institutions and the negative evaluation of many forms of institutional care have reinforced the tendency towards fragmentation, with residential group living centres and those which provide day services seeking to avoid any identification with the negative image of institutions. Instead of separating these various patterns of service into an institutional care element and a community care element, we choose instead to see institutional care as reflecting earlier value positions in society's thinking about services for children and families. Equally, institutions can be said to reflect different understandings of how children and families grow and develop. Thus, using a group care formulation, it is possible to see how modifications in the use of institutions, and the development of smaller group living and group day-care services are responses to the changing values, new knowledge and refined methods of intervention which are now available. A principal influence in the movement from larger to smaller facilities could be related to the greater appreciation of processes in child health and development. Another major influence can be identified as economics. As one moves from the occupational focus to explore group care as a field of study, it is possible to identify patterns in the development of group care services across service delivery systems.

Group care as a field of study

We believe it is possible to describe and delineate the field of group care as it spans the major resource systems in Great Britain and North America by considering several different service networks. The first of these has already been mentioned but can be presented diagrammatically as in *Figure 1(1)*.

Figure 1(1)   Span of systems

Health care network	—	Education network	—	Social welfare network	—	Justice network

Note has of course to be made of the fact that these systems are not entirely discrete and that in some situations, client populations may be the same, or there may be considerable overlap. Various patterns of service have evolved that illustrate both overlap and co-operation between systems on behalf of children and families. One example might be a residential group living unit for delinquent youths, located within the social welfare system but accepting entrants from the justice systems (courts) and supplying educational services through an adjoining school programme. Another example might be a day service programme for the developmentally disabled which is sponsored by a health care organization but which offers important educational services to children and welfare services for parents, all as part of the same service.

These illustrations allow us to recognize the extent to which each of the four service systems have come to depend on large institutions as a means of providing services to certain client populations. For example, the health care system contains many large institutions for the mentally ill or retarded. The education system has many large schools, both day schools and boarding schools, which serve normal as well as mal-adjusted, emotionally disturbed children and others with special needs. Services provided by the justice system include a range of reformatory and penal institutions which contain young people. And even the social welfare system has inherited and supplied social care facilities of the institutional type for dependent and delinquent children. A second diagrammatic presentation makes this point firmly *(Figure 1(2))*.

Figure 1(2)   Large institutions across systems

Health care	*Education*	*Social welfare*	*Justice*
Asylums	Day and boarding	Orphanages	Prison
Mental hospitals	schools, incl.	Lodging houses	Reformatory
Hospitals for the	normal, mal-	Emergency care	Detention
mentally	adjusted and	centres	centres
retarded	emotionally-	Community	Training
General hospitals	disturbed	homes	schools
	children		

By outlining the historical development of institutional care services, it is also possible to highlight characteristics of the social policy environment which have influenced the development of group care services as we know them today. Scull (1977) and Seed (1973) have both urged an historical analysis to highlight how the social control of deviance and the economics of social control are related. In this respect, we support a view which identifies the services provided by group care centres as empha-sizing both social care and social control. As mentioned earlier, the emphasis on one dimension or the other will vary as one moves from one service to another. Still, both care and control feature, whether one is looking at a hospital, a school, a children's home, or a detention centre. If one seeks to describe the characteristics of the institutions which have evolved to become modern-day group care services, it is possible to identify at least four eras of social policy influence that have featured in their development. These can be presented diagrammatically as follows *(Figure 1(3))*.

Figure 1(3)   Eras of social policy in the development of institutional services

27 BC (Augustus establishes the Roman Empire)	*Era of exclusion-confinement* – During this period, social policy emphasized the social control of deviants by removing any threatening person or group from community life through death, exile, slavery, or indentured servitude. Deviance is crudely identified as a threat to social order through physical (leprosy), social (witchcraft), economic (slavery) or legal (crime) means.
late eighteenth century (the emergence of the Industrial Revolution)	*Era of institution-building* – During this period, social policy was promoted by social philanthropy and emphasized management of deviants through provision of shelter, food, and work within a moral environment. Distinctions are made between the Mad (insanity and mental deficiency), the Bad (criminals), the Morally Weak (unemployed and the poor) and the Unprotected (orphans and homeless waifs).
mid-1940s (the end of the Second World War)	*Welfare/treatment era* – During this period, social policy is influenced by emerging professional interests which emphasize personal, interpersonal, and family treatment as social remedies for deviance. Specialist services are incorporated into health care, education, social welfare, and justice systems, having a major impact on decision-making.
early 1970s (following enactment of major social legislation in Great Britain and North America)	*Justice era* – During this period, social policy seeks to differentiate between those who should and those who should not be contained in institutions. Closure of institutions is promoted by legislation and agency policy initiatives. Closures are supported by ideological doctrines (religious, professional, and political) which emphasize individual initiative and are reinforced by economic conservatism which seeks to reduce spending in the public services and non-productive sectors. Individual legal rights and the principle of social fairness provide guidelines for responding to social deviance. Death penalties, determinant sentencing, and short sharp shock treatment return to prominence.

One can see from *Figure 1(3)* how social policy can be said to have influenced the development of institutions within the group care field. Large institutions in modern times can be said to incorporate influences from each of the four social policy eras. Of course large institutions, especially those in the health care and justice systems have been severely criticized (Goffman, 1961; Sommer, 1976; Stanton and Schwartz, 1954; Morris, 1978) for their ineffectiveness as care and treatment environments, and for their failure to achieve stated objectives, whatever these might be. However, the same criticisms could be said to have comparable validity for large institutions in the education or social welfare systems.

In response to the rightful criticisms directed towards large institutions, a whole new generation of residential services has emerged over the last two decades or more. The emphasis in this new generation of services has been on the creation of small group living units in the community. Units have been established in existing buildings or specially designed so as to eliminate many of the negative features of institutional life, including block treatment, rigidity of routine, depersonalized care and social distance between staff and residents (King, Raynes, and Tizard, 1971; Tizard, Sinclair, and Clarke, 1976; Mayer, Richman, and Balcerzak, 1978). The new residential group living units provide care, protection, and training which are supplied on a more personalized scale than is to be found in large institutions.

The intention of these smaller group living units has been to promote maximum opportunity for individual attention within the group situation. Using everyday life events as occasions for social learning, group care personnel seek to create opportunities for positive interaction between themselves and their charges, thereby encouraging personal and social development. Care and treatment are achieved through the planned use of educative and re-educative activities which respond to assessed needs of children and families. This development of smaller and more personalized group living services means that another network of services can be identified. *Figure 1(4)* illustrates some of the variations of group living arrangements that are available.

Figure 1(4)   Types of group living

Residential nursery	Family group home	Peer group residence	Group residence	Hostel, refuge or shelter	Grouped, semi-independent living

All of these forms of group living centres can be found, and have been developed to varying degrees, in each of the four service systems that are our concern. They are illustrated in the health care network by hostels for the formerly mentally ill, supervised group homes for the mentally ill, and group homes for the mentally retarded. Education services based on the group living pattern include hostels or group homes for maladjusted or emotionally disturbed children. Meanwhile, in the justice system it is possible to identify bail hostels, after-care hostels, probation hostels, and supervised accommodation schemes which incorporate the residential group living pattern. Finally, in the social welfare system, where the growth of this pattern of service has been particularly extensive, examples of all forms of group living noted in *Figure 1(4)* can be found. Indeed, it has been suggested (Morris, 1978) that the future of social work as a profession lies not in the many individualized therapeutic interventions which are currently emphasized, but in the direction of designing, implementing, managing, and evaluating the range of group care services which are supplied by the social welfare system.

It can be argued that the ability of social welfare networks to develop an extensive range of group care responses has to some measure resulted from this system being the newest of the four human resource systems to which we have been referring. Consequently, this system has not had to operate the same number of large institutions, although it has inherited some from its predecessors. Without the same economic investment in large institutions which commit increasingly scarce resources to inflexible patterns of service provision, the opportunity has been available for devising new patterns of social care. However, the process of 'de-institutionalization', or 'decarceration' as it has also been called, continues throughout all four service systems. This process is constantly being reinforced by imaginative alternatives which are community-based and include group living (twenty-four hour) but also include group activity (eight hour or less) programmes. Both types of programme are mindful of the group focus and the use of life-space in their design, where workers seek to utilize the physical and social characteristics of their centre in a purposeful manner. As such, a range of day services can be said to fall within the group care field, allowing us to identify another network of services, showing how day services exist in each of the four resource systems (see *Figure 1(5)* overleaf).

Finally, it is possible to combine all the illustrations used in this section *(Figure 1(6))* to show how the Group Care field refers to a range of services which supply 168 hours care, fifty-two weeks a year, decreasing through community-based group living to include a variety of day services in co-operation with families. The Group Care field can be shown to span all of the major resource systems in society, reflecting common characteristics which distinguish it from other service areas.

Figure 1(5)   Types of day services across systems

Health care	Education	Social welfare	Justice
Day hospitals	Youth and	Day care/	Community
Day clinics	community	playgroups	service
Health centres	centres	Activity	centres
Day nurseries	Recreation and	programmes	Day and project
	leisure centres	Intermediate	centres
	Day nurseries	treatment units	Intermediate
	Day schools	Day nurseries	treatment
	Intermediate		units
	treatment units		
	Alternative		
	schools		

Figure 1(6)   The group care field across systems

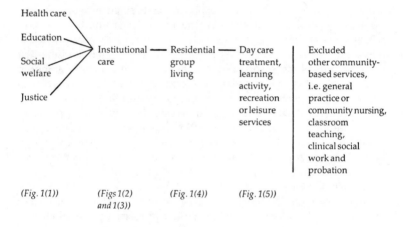

Health care				
Education	Institutional	Residential — Day care		Excluded
	care	group	treatment,	other community-
Social		living	learning	based services,
welfare			activity,	i.e. general
			recreation	practice or
Justice			or leisure	community nursing,
			services	classroom
				teaching,
				clinical social
				work and
				probation
(Fig. 1(1))	*(Figs 1(2) and 1(3))*	*(Fig. 1(4))*	*(Fig. 1(5))*	

In summary then, the Group Care field can be delineated in the following manner. It incorporates those areas of service – institutional care, residential group living (including but not necessarily requiring twenty-four hour, seven days per week care) and other community-based day services (covering lesser time periods) that supply a range of developmentally enhancing services for groups of consumers. The location of a service in the Group Care field results from identifying how each pattern of service places emphasis on shared living and learning arrangements in a specified centre of activity.

Group care as a domain of practice

One particular question worth considering concerns the reasons why Group Care should only now be conceptualized as a separate occupational focus and field of study. Moreover, how does one account for influences which shape such a development? Many of the services listed in our earlier discussion *(Figures 1(2), 1(4) and 1(5))* have existed for years. Yet, it could be said that until recently, group care facilities have been viewed as extensions of a particular specialized service network. Hence, it is not surprising to find that the special and generic characteristics of group care practice across service systems have evaded discussion. Jones (1979) and Wolins (1974) offer some leadership in this area, although both attempts seem to highlight dilemmas facing the development of group care on either side of the Atlantic. Reflecting a British perspective, Jones retains a single profession orientation – that of social work – at the same time that he identifies generic characteristics of the residential setting. Wolins, on the other hand, can be said to retain a single client group focus at the same time that he identifies special characteristics which make group care environments so powerful for children.

Fragmentation of the group care field, across institutional care, residential group living, and day service provisions have further confounded attempts to identify special and generic characteristics in this domain of practice. Additionally, the popular notion of a continuum of services which range from institutional facilities through to community-based agency services, while helpful, has conversely encouraged a superficial dichotomy of interests. This dichotomy has emphasized the differences between institutional and community-based services, rather than drawing attention to their common features. Institutions are generally thought to be outside the scope of community-based services, while day services are almost invariably seen to be community-based alternatives to institutional care. Meanwhile, residential group living features strongly in both institutional care and in the variety of community-based alternatives to institutional care (Mayer, Richman, and Balcerzak, 1978). Still, residential group living, in spite of being heavily embedded in local communities, is often regarded as representative of unwanted institutional services. Thus, child placement policies often distinguish between foster care and residential care (Hazel, 1976), accentuating the virtues of one approach and thereby questioning the other.

It is also important to recognize the extent to which group care services have their origins in the efforts of voluntary and private groups. This history has also contributed towards fragmentation in the group care field. Such a history is especially true in respect of services operating in the social welfare system, and, although less evident now, it also operated earlier in other systems. A distinguishing feature of developments in the voluntary and private sector concerns their emphasis on personal belief, human service, and a commitment to providing group care as a vocation. Until recently, it can be said that personal belief – whether drawn from ideological or religious origins – has provided the prevalent guidelines for group care practice. This contrasts with, although at times it could be said to parallel, the emerging professionalism of group care work, through the influences of nursing, education, social work, penal and correctional training. Thus, it has remained difficult to identify an agreed value base, an occupational identity and particular opportunities for disciplined study and examination in this domain of practice. As Payne points out elsewhere in this volume, reliance on personal belief can easily result in a disregard of knowledge from the behavioural sciences when designing and evaluating group care services. Instead, justifications for group care services have often been developed around philosophical and metaphysical beliefs, thus making it difficult to identify group care as a domain of practice.

However, the growing involvement of national and local government agencies in funding, regulating, and managing all sectors of the group care field has hastened the need to consider group care as a domain of practice. The involvement of government agencies has gained momentum through concerns about institutional abuse which have been drawn to public attention by media exposure of malpractices and through the activities of special interest groups. The economic pressures that surround public funding of group care services have also increased the involvement of government agencies. Calls for fiscal accountability and for the demonstration of service effectiveness and efficiency have increased attention on group care as a costly and complex service structure. In spite of various attempts to close institutions, to care for children with special needs in 'normal' environments, and to maintain children in the mainstream of community life, it is reasonable to believe that institutions will continue to play a part in the structures found in each of society's service systems. In place of outdated practices, institutions are likely to rely on collaborative efforts with smaller group living units and day service centres in responding to the group care demands from those who provide health care, education, social welfare, and justice services.

As a consequence, the emergence of group care as an identifiable domain of practice is now possible. It is less restrictive in focus than others which might be used, in that it does not relate to a single area of service, such as institution, residential group living, or day services. The focus on group care provides a generic basis for practice from which specialist services are subsequently delivered. The generic basis for group care practice allows attention to be given to the organizing principles around which various occupational groups respond to the care and treatment of children. It also provides a broader response to the growing pressure for accountability in the use of public resources, highlighting the need for a variety of responses rather than a superficial dichotomy of institutions and community care. Finally, the identification of group care as a domain of practice offers considerable advantages in the training of personnel. Brief consideration of these advantages can be summarized here.

Fragmentation in this field, as referred to earlier, has made the recruitment and training of manpower difficult. The blend of practice skills which workers require (including those concerned with educative, recreational, counselling, and caring tasks) has not yet received sufficient attention to limit recruitment of untrained or partially-trained personnel throughout the group care services. Unfortunately, such recruitment patterns have been supported by various motives which include attempts to reduce programme costs. Perhaps even more important is the persistent belief that personal attributes of warmth and spontaneity are all-important and are not capable of existing alongside knowledge about and skills in child care. Thus, the development of group care training has been very slow.

Training schemes provided by each of the four sponsoring systems in Great Britain and North America have also given peripheral attention to the characteristics of a group care practice domain. It is, therefore, worthy of note that none of the sponsoring systems at the present time offers training opportunities which locate group care as the focus for their training efforts. However, some minor exceptions can be found to exist at the level of postqualifying or advanced studies. As a whole, most existing training programmes and certainly all those offering first level studies rely on the professional discipline which sponsors the training. Thus, nursing, teaching, social work, and corrections all supply professional or occupational training opportunities which derive from a particular service system. The paradox remains whereby personnel employed in each of the resource systems may be deployed to work in programmes that constitute the group care field. They are thereby expected to provided important services for children with no real basis for the knowledge and skills required in this practice domain.

On acquiring a first-level qualification, if any qualification at all, the likelihood is great that training programmes in nursing, teaching, social work, or corrections will provide minimal teaching on child development. Even that which is provided is likely to be supplied by discipline psychology and not derived from practice activity in the group care domain, hence ensuring an applied focus. While teaching about child development is likely to receive only minimal attention in existing training programmes, even less attention is likely to be given to the importance of context within which practice takes place. Under the existing patterns, preparation of group care practitioners ignores almost entirely such features as group composition, life-space counselling, and the environmental characteristics of a service location – all focal points in our consideration of group care practice.

Such deficiencies in basic practice training are likely to result in a failure to alert personnel to the use of all the physical variables (architecture, use of time, space and objects) and the social variables (events and activities, person-to-person interaction, and personnel teamwork) that constitute all group care programmes. Depending upon how group care programmes have been designed and managed, these powerful environments can encourage growth and development of children; or they can do otherwise. The emergence then of specific training for group care practice is long overdue. In the editors' view, the emergence of group care training is essential in order that these services can be staffed by personnel with knowledge and skills which are relevant to this practice area. More importantly, we believe that children and youth, in their search for social maturity and responsible citizenship, deserve skilled and sensitive assistance from nurses, teachers, residential, and day care workers or correctional counsellors. The generic basis for group care as a domain of practice would not detract from the specialist features of nursing, teaching, social work, and correctional training. On the contrary, we assert that attention to group care as an occupational focus, as a field of study, and as a practice domain would enhance abilities across professional boundaries to supply quality services to children and families.

Issues in group care for children

This volume therefore seeks to offer a series of contributions to the debate about and development of group care. The volume is not intended to provide a total statement about the field, but rather to reflect current thinking and draw attention to major issues affecting the provision of group care services for children. In this respect, the volume should be seen as a contribution to the growing literature that seeks to enhance understanding of group care and promote interest in the positive utilization of these practice settings as resources for children and families.

To this end, the volume is divided into four sections with papers in each section referring to issues that require considerable debate if group care is to continue to develop as a significant practice domain in the human services. The first section, focusing on group care practice with children, is introduced with a paper by Henry Maier which relates knowledge of child development to methods of child care practice in residential group living. We believe this discussion will assist practitioners, administrators, and programme managers in understanding how interventions through everyday life events in group care contexts can further child development. Next, we offer a discussion on the notion of programme in group care service provision, a concept we believe to be inadequately explored on either side of the Atlantic. Dimensions of programme are considered from a comparative perspective, seeking to highlight variables which are different in each national context and those which are common to group care services in both. This section also contains a reprinted paper from James Whittaker's (1979) *Caring for Troubled Children*, that selectively outlines theoretical perspectives that have been used to support residential group living programmes in North America. Even though it has been published elsewhere, this paper is included because it is almost unique in the child care literature in showing how group care programmes can be constructed with due regard to theoretical knowledge. It employs a comparative perspective which lends itself to consideration in the British context, and while emphasizing the residential aspects of group care, we believe that it has considerable relevance to considerations of day service approaches as well. Finally, Jerome Beker contributes a paper which argues for a new view of group care facilities as centres for advanced practice and research. In so doing, he comments on existing patterns of services and offers ideas on how group care centres might contribute more centrally to the education of personnel at the same time as they improve services for children and families. Visionary in concept, this paper provides an interesting contribution to the debate on service organization and the advancement of knowledge and skills in group care practice.

Section II, devoted to personnel considerations, contains two papers which address issues of occupational stress and personnel teamwork in the provision of a group care service for children. Martha Mattingly helps to draw attention to the occupational demands of group care work with children, pointing to the way in which stress and fatigue may result in the premature loss of practitioners from this field of practice. This discussion draws attention to the need to understand stress factors in group care work and to devise means of supporting personnel which will allow them to continue involvement in this very demanding practice domain. Leon Fulcher draws attention to the personnel problems associated with teamwork and team functioning, highlighting how the integrity of a group care service is related to the capacity of teams to adapt successfully to work environments which are both unpredictable and potentially surrounded by turmoil. Positive team functioning is seen to be a significant influence in the management of personnel stress and in the delivery of growth enhancing services for children in group care.

Section III, relating to career development and training, uses an educational theme to draw attention to issues of service design and career planning in group care for children. Karen VanderVen discusses issues of professional development for group care practitioners, identifying how different requirements may feature as being significant as workers move from direct care roles into supervisory and management roles. Frank Ainsworth attempts to clarify the different national positions with regard to the training of group care personnel, offering suggestions concerning the core curriculum required in preparing for work in the group care field with children. In identifying elements in a framework for group care training, content is provided which is seen to transcend national boundaries, organizational arrangements and variations in the occupational title which is ascribed to personnel in various countries.

The final section focuses attention on issues of research and evaluation in group care. While the institutional component of the group care field has been the subject of extensive research and evaluation, generally speaking such endeavours have been undertaken by personnel from academic or occupational disciplines other than group care. Clearly, to qualify as an aspiring occupation or professional group, group care practitioners must respond to the requirement for research and evaluation of their work. And there can be little doubt that research and evaluation must go beyond institutional care provision to give equal attention to residential group living and day services as well. Nor can it be said that research conducted on either side of the Atlantic is known to the practice community in each respective country. Chris Payne's contribution on evaluation is therefore a welcome addition to the sparse comparative literature. The ability of group care personnel to devise research and evaluation approaches or adapt existing methods of enquiry to this field of practice is of particular importance. Finally, Martin Knapp's paper on cost factors in group care offers an example of how understanding from another discipline, that of economics, can be adapted to and offer valuable techniques for use in group care research and evaluation.

Note

(1) Frank Ainsworth is Principal Lecturer in Social Work, Middlesex Polytechnic, Enfield, London, England, and Leon C. Fulcher is Lecturer in Social Work, University of Stirling, Stirling, Scotland.

References

Goffman, E. (1961) *Asylums*. New York: Doubleday.

Hazel, N. (1976) Child Placement Policy: Some European Comparisons. *British Journal of Social Work* **6** (3): 315–26.

Jones, H. (1979) *The Residential Community: A Setting for Social Work*. London: Routledge & Kegan Paul.

King, R. D., Raynes, N. V., and Tizard, J. (1971) *Patterns of Residential Care*. London: Routledge & Kegan Paul.

Mayer, M. F., Richman, L. H., and Balcerzak, E. A. (1978) *Group Care of Children: Crossroads and Transitions*. New York: Child Welfare League of America.

Morris, R. (1978) Social Work Function in a Caring Society: Abstract Value, Professional Preference, and the Real World. *Journal of Education for Social Work* **14** (2): 82–9.

Redl, F. (1959) Strategy and Technique of the Life Space Interview. *American Journal of Orthopsychiatry* **29** (1): 1–18.

Scull, A. (1977) *Decarceration*. Englewood Cliffs, New Jersey: Prentice-Hall.

Seed, P. (1973) Should Any Child Be Placed in Care? The Forgotten Great Debate 1841–1874. *British Journal of Social Work* **3** (3): 321–30.

Sommer, R. (1976) *The End of Imprisonment*. New York: Oxford University Press.

Stanton, A. H. and Schwartz, M. S. (1954) *The Mental Hospital: A Study of Institutional Participation in Psychiatric Illness and Treatment*. New York: Basic Books.

Tizard, J., Sinclair, I., and Clarke, R. V. G. (1976) *Varieties of Residential Experience*. London: Routledge & Kegan Paul.

Whittaker, J. K. (1979) *Caring for Troubled Children*. San Francisco: Jossey-Bass.

Wolins, M. (ed.) (1974) *Successful Group Care*. Chicago: Aldine.

Section I

Group care practice with children

2 Essential components in care and treatment environments for children

Henry W. Maier[1]

I A quick glimpse at life in a residential care and treatment setting

'John and I are going out to kick the ball.'

'Good idea! In a while I'll try to come out too and get in a few kicks. I need a whiff of fresh air too. Have fun,' responded their care worker, Sheila Thomas. She was pleased over her brief conversation with Chris and John. She thought to herself: 'I did it! I was able to allow them to leave with a feeling of my interest in their doings and I managed to omit my usual admonishments about staying out of trouble and wandering away. Still, John and Chris will know that I will be nearby.'

Sheila Thomas, the 35-year-old child care worker of this unit, was jarred out of her reflective mood when she noticed that Matt, in explosive anger, was moving his possessions out of his room. She quickly learned that Matt was at odds with his roommate, Al, whose possessions were mixed up with Matt's. 'If only each child could have his own personal closet space,' thought Sheila. She returned with Matt to their room. She wanted to be certain that she dealt with both of them as she struggled over their differences. The worker felt sure that Matt's outburst was a mere spark of a more persevering rage festering in him and possibly in Al as well. She thought: 'If I could deal solely with Matt, he could be quickly appeased. And it would be so much easier. But neither one of us would then confront his continuous tensions. I also know that I can't fully resolve their difficulties in sharing, but for children at this age I can work on it.'

Sheila Thomas called to the boys outside that she saw they had quite a ball game going; she still hoped to go out later. She also commented on the good play space they had chosen. Sheila congratulated herself for the fact that she managed to point out to Chris and John what they can do rather than a negative message such as 'Keep away from the rose bushes!'

Sheila took a deep breath and moved on into the troubled den, fully aware than an on-the-spot counseling session would unearth more trouble than Matt's immediate complaint suggested.[2] It was also her chance to be an effective care worker rather than a busy guardian. The session was a hot one. It took all her energy to avoid quick solutions. Sheila's counseling session was unlike the ones by social workers or other counseling professionals, where all other activities are assumed to be suspended while client and counselor closet themselves away as if their worlds were confined solely to the interviewing room. On the contrary, life for all three – Matt, Al, and Sheila – goes on. They could hear the television blasting away from the living/dining room. 'Is the television really too loud? Or is the issue instead that there's actually no suitable space for television viewing as long as it has to compete with the continuous clatter of table tennis on the adjacent sun porch? Maybe I should have the courage to fold up the table tennis. Its racket adds more din and confusion than it contributes to the boys' relaxation. We should be able to find a better source for group play and recreation.'

It was hard for Sheila to concentrate on Al's and Matt's dilemma with life vibrating beyond the interview situation throughout the living unit. Yet, she also knew that to deal with problems as they occurred amidst the flow of life was more realistic and opened up avenues to the counseling process as well as enriching their lives immediately. She sat down with the boys and openly empathized with Al and Matt for their uneasiness over living away from home and for having to mingle with so many new faces. Nevertheless, that was the way it was; they had to be at the residential centre. She explored with them how together they could make an undesirable situation more bearable. All three would struggle over the boys' desire to be home and the subsequent anguish of recognizing that their return would not materialize for some time.

Their deliberation was interrupted by severe shouts from the direction of the unit's kitchen.

'Your mother!'

'Your mother, yourself!'

'Your mother loves the bottle more than you!'

A vehement but tearful retort: 'My mother'll fetch me home as soon as she finds a job. You'll see!'

Sheila knew that she could only deal with one situation at a time. Most important in her work was the challenge to handle a single situation fully rather than try to respond superficially to all eruptions. Her thoughts momentarily wandered away: 'Lucky therapists who can deal with one problem at a time in their insulated interview rooms.'

Sheila beamed as if a lightbulb had gone on. 'I am better off here. I can make strides to lessen the boys' unhappiness. There seems to be something in common in the struggles of the kids in this unit and that in itself helps me understand what needs to be done as life goes on.' Turning to Matt and Al she helped these two to explore the confusions and quandaries about their respective home situations. They did seem to be facing many uncertainties and much ambiguous information. Sheila began to respond with greater certainty herself. She could assure them that she or their social worker would try to obtain clear answers as to whether they could count on a visit home soon. She also inquired as to what were the most important questions for them. While she promised action, she also empathized with their sense of hurt and unhappiness for having to live in an institution. She then explored with them what they could do right then in order to ease their immediate life situation. Sheila expected them to continue to be roommates. She voiced her concern over Al's difficulties in getting along with others and Matt's short 'fuse'.

Matt and Al were helped by Sheila with immediate behavioural tasks which each one could manage. Sheila likewise learned what she could do to make unit life more bearable for them. Her focus was upon becoming more adequate rather than avoiding or mitigating more difficulties. Sheila decided to remember: 'Progress also means new troubles. When they'll be ready to play with the others, then their limited social skills and awkward body coordination will require renewed help in getting themselves included in group play.' She smiled to herself: 'I can just imagine that some day I will wish we were back to the days when I had only to deal with individual temper tantrums.'

By this time all unit residents had returned from school. There was neither time for the worker to reflect on her session with these two lonesome roommates nor to have a respite for a cup of tea. She was well aware that each child required her special care. Even if a child in her unit actually presented no difficulties, it still would be a time for child care intervention. Sheila had learned that such a resident may either have adapted too conveniently to institutional life and require urgent assistance with his or her developmental progress or the child might need an advocate on approaching his or her return to regular family life.

At this point the worker was certain that each of the unit's ten preadolescent boys were all troubled children; they required residential care. Sheila made sure that she had individual contacts and brief chats with each about their particular concerns or interests. It was not easy for her to focus upon their concerns. Her head was buzzing with messages, reminders, and tasks she must relay to them. It was very tempting to tell each what he had to do, just to get these concerns off her chest. She was proud that she managed to hold back new demands plus her disappointments over the boys' unfinished jobs. She wanted to be sure to welcome each boy as an individual person of the group rather than as a resident of a joint household. The reminders must wait until a time when re-entry into an unwanted place had been achieved and some of the strain of a day in school had worn off. (Snacks and a period of loafing with few behavioural demands are instrumental for a successful re-entry phase – Maier, 1979 : 162–64.)

The child care worker's concerns for the children in her unit were interlaced with communication among fellow staff members. Sheila had to be sure to brief Tom Smith, the other worker for the afternoon and evening shift. She felt that in the past two hours she had put in a full day's work; yet more than half of her eight-hour working time was still ahead. One of the hardest tasks had to be tackled. She had to list to Tom all the unfinished tasks without becoming defensive, appearing inadequate, or blaming the kids. At the same time it was good to know that there was another adult to share the load. But as she knew too well, another adult also meant more demands by the children and a heightening of rivalry for each worker's time and good will.

As the phone rang again (easily the seventh call since lunch), Sheila's secret response was: 'Let Tom answer it.' She then noticed Tom fully engaged in fixing a boy's flashlight. Simultaneously, other youngsters shared with him their latest jokes. She was pleased to witness the happy bantering; she was also annoyed that she had to jump in again as the unit's phone-answering service. 'Tom should do some of the work here!'

A call from the main office; the dentist in town has an unexpected open hour. He could see Clyde for his emergency appointment. 'Clyde can go on his own. He knows the way to the dentist's office. Shall I give him the bus fare or shall I go with him? It would give us some private time together. He'll have some painful work done. I know he is scared. To call on one of the volunteers wouldn't quite be the same. If I were to go with him I would be with him at a time he needs somebody nearby. It would be quite different from the times I tend to "stand over" him so that he gets on with the tasks at hand. We could also work in some shopping errands; an experience he needs and tasks I have to do anyhow.'

An essential decision has to be made by Sheila. Even if Clyde is capable of going on his own, the worker knows that Clyde will develop more adequately if he has additional caring experiences built into his immediate self-management. Clyde can handle many tasks within the confines of institutional management. At the same time he is trying too hard to manage on his own. He lacks the common experience of turning for support when support is needed. He also has not had opportunities for casual shopping ventures. Sheila's decision to have Clyde go or not on his own is no longer a managerial choice; it has turned into a clinical decision.

In the foregoing pages we have witnessed life on the forefront. We gained a glimpse of a typical afternoon hour at a residential care unit where the child care worker had not a second to spare nor an inch to waste.

Child care, coupled with spatial arrangements, crises handling amidst regular program activities, life events within the centre, and life beyond its walls, all these factors make up the residential service provided to children and youth in care. The nature of the care offered to these children shapes their lives, and the children in turn shape the actual mode of care provided. Moreover, this mutually intertwined caring experience is not merely determined by the interactions between care givers and care receivers. Of equal impact is their physical setting, the material goods at their disposal, and above all, the external forces and institutions which support and negate their efforts. These outside systems, whether they are the child welfare agencies and communal institutions, the neighbourhood and wider community, or the laws and society's conceptions of children's developmental requirements, all serve as salient partners in child care work. These systems define the grand design, the contemporary world scene in which we grow and live.

The subsequent pages of this chapter will cover in detail the very intricate interplay of care giving and care receiving within the context of group settings. The issues before the reader will be covered under the following four major subheadings: (1) the personal ingredients of care giving and care receiving, (2) care giving and care receiving functioning in the physical environment, (3) group living as an everyday life experience, (4) residential life as a prelude to and extension of a child's home and community life.

II Care giving and care receiving as a symphony of human interactions

What constitutes caring?

Care is a very personal experience for both the care giver and the cared-for person. Each needs the other. Each, within the process of caring, becomes more firmly attached and paradoxically takes on a greater range of freedom from the other (Maier, 1980). For instance, a child care worker's efforts in helping Ray, a 9-year-old, to ward off the experience of being teased by the other children in group care, brings this child and his worker closer together. In this example the worker does not express pity to Ray for feeling severely hurt over his peers' teasing. Instead, the worker introduces a new game to Ray and two other boys standing nearby. She invites them to play a game of 'So What?' with her. This worker had just invented the game on the spur of the moment. In this spontaneous game, each one, including the worker, takes alternately the role of teaser and teased. The worker tries to set up a number of playful situations in which she lures each one into participating. While being teased in varying degrees, the teased-one must maintain his 'cool' and remain able to respond matter-of-factly with 'So what?' As Ray experiences the fun of becoming engaged with the peers of his unit, he practises a more effective behavioural response and discovers in his child care worker a person who is interested in him. (Behaviour rehearsals as an interventive method will be more fully taken up in Section IV of this chapter.) Ray experiences closeness to this caring adult and a new closeness to his peers. We note that while this worker consciously refused to curtail the teasing, the mutual playful activity supported Ray.

Curiously, the very feeling of the worker's concern enables Ray to risk more and subsequently to leave the worker and the unit to join the outdoor activities. The worker, in turn, needs special opportunities for becoming close and enmeshed in a child's ongoing life situation in order to be able to enact her genuine care.[3] This particular child care worker is able to validate her role and feel in the groove of *doing* child care work. With her closeness to Ray achieved, the worker also has found an added sense of freedom. She and Ray are perhaps ready to relate to each other on a more meaningful level and to delve into additional difficulties. They might now deal with the immediate object of the boys' teasing: Ray's personal problem of being called 'diaper boy' and 'night floater', reflecting that he wets his bed at the age of 9. Perhaps the worker can now retain Ray's cooperation in conquering his enuresis.

The foregoing incident, an ordinary daily occurrence in residential group life, is not meant to imply that a child care worker's single interventive step can bring about a scenario of successful treatment events. Rather, the example is cited here as an illustration that the minutiae of everyday child care work provide the backbone for change. In the critical incident just cited, the worker might have been very tempted to remind Ray that if he were to stop wetting his bed the teasing would subside – a very logical position, but unsound for Ray's emotional needs.[4] Psychologically, Ray would have temporarily felt even more deserted by the very resource he sought for help. He would have experienced an act of detachment at a moment when he reached out and needed anchorage. We note that the worker skillfully assisted Ray in overcoming some of his personal hurt and isolation while she helped him enhance his personal skills. Little time and energy was allocated to Ray for telling his woes to a sympathetic listener. Instead the worker entered the scene responsively, assuming responsibility in assisting Ray to move beyond the present dilemma. He gained ground in handling conflict without falling prey to others' taunting (a sport typical of this age). As a group care worker the challenge remains to help the children with their effectiveness in meeting daily interpersonal crises rather than to try to avoid or to abolish conflicts. In fact, asking Ray's peers to halt their teasing would mean to ask them to disengage from Ray. The worker's role is to increase the mutual interaction of the group members as well as to include an effective caring concern and a possible program for Ray's efforts to manage a dry bed.

In the preceding case illustration the child and worker became a bit clearer about respective tasks at hand. Simultaneously, they became more attached to each other. Each one needs the other for his or her own competency development and verification: Ray, in the process of relating to peers in conflict situations, and the worker in the process of effective group care. Caring involves a process of being responsive *to* and responsible *for* someone (Wrenn, 1972). It is the activity of being *responsible for* others which differentiates the caring activities of group workers from other caring persons (neighbours, friends, teachers, etc.). It is the worker's role to be a change agent and to impact the children's personal development. The quality of care is not so much a singular question of how the workers feel about the children as it is how they translate their care into actions. What they actually *do* signifies the care they manifest as this is enacted in their role as care specialists.

Gauging temperament

Differences in temperament have become more clearly understood through recent studies in early infant care. Time spent in caring for young infants is viewed as a constant give-and-take between the infant and her or his care giver. In infant tending we witness a blending of the baby's temperament and the care giver's particular disposition at the moment. Infant and care giver jointly find their mutual fit (Lewis and Rosenblum, 1974; Schaffer, 1977). The same holds true for older children and their care givers. In fact, this give-and-take process for tuning in and locating a joint rhythm occurs in the attachment formation in all ages of life (Maier, 1981a). This process of tuning in and finding common strands of attachments is one of the essential features of child care work with all age groups.

Let us start out with an illustrative example. The child care worker Harriet Costigan was having dinner with her table of eight pre-adolescent girls. Early in the course of the meal she nodded to a child across from her to convey concern. Almost simultaneously Harriet moved out of reach all items but fork and plate for Meg, the child on her immediate left. She quickly put the fork in the hand of Meg who had reverted to finger feeding. A girl at the other end of the table had also begun eating with her hands. Harriet noticed it but let it go. She knew that this particular girl was temperamentally a slow-paced but bright youngster who essentially related visually to others. The child's continuous surveillance kept her well appraised of what was going on; however, only strong stimulation would prompt her to act. In contrast, Meg was prone to react to the slightest stimulation with heightened activity. Harriet was wise to remove extraneous items at the moment, lest Meg be sidetracked from eating. Her worker also knew that for this child the fingering of food was not only poor manners, it would also spontaneously escalate to squashing food and eventually to throwing it.

We can better understand the differential handling described above, if we examine recent findings suggesting that persons are born with and are apt to maintain a particular temperament. Different temperaments require different handling. In early infancy, variations in babies' temperaments cause care givers to respond discriminately toward them (Thomas, Chess and Birch, 1968; Escalona, 1968). Follow-up longitudinal research further brings out that specific temperaments persist at least through the childhood years and may even continue throughout a person's life (Thomas and Chess, 1977).

Our personal experiences as well as observations of friends may help us verify that differences in temperament are clearly evident in the way adults participate at social gatherings. Some adults quickly find themselves in the midst of the group, aggressively meeting others. Some conceive of themselves as full participants in the gathering while remaining at a distance, physically removed but visually keenly engaged in the ongoing events. To expand further, in the past ten years we have learned from research on young children's modes of interaction that although there are no classifications of temperament, there is a vast spectrum of temperamental expressiveness. On the one end are children (and possibly adults) who tend to soak up with their senses what is going on around them as if they were 'living radars'. At first impression they appear to be very placid and inactive individuals. However, on further examination they reveal themselves to be active stimulus-scanners. Their eyes are continuously on the go. Their style of relating to the world around them is predominantly visual; they prefer to be a little apart from the events in which they are engaged.

In contrast, individuals on the other end of this temperament spectrum initiate and seem to thrive on continuous physical contact and bodily experience. These bodily active children (or adults) tend to find continuous stimulation in happenings and encounters within their immediate life space. One environmental interaction leads to another. The smallest variation or new stimuli is noted and responded to. These stimulus-impacted youngsters seem to be in perpetual motion and can well be described as the *'go-go children'*.

Findings from the research of both Thomas, Chess and Birch as well as Escalona can be readily applied to the group care scene (Thomas, Chess and Birch, 1964 and 1968; Thomas and Chess, 1977; Escalona, 1968. Also see Segal and Yahraes, 1978:41–51; Cameron, 1978; Schaffer and Emerson, 1964 and Schaffer, 1977).

We learn from these studies that more bodily active infants, the 'go-go children', immediately engage themselves with whatever is within reach. For them each stimulus becomes a call for action. It is not surprising that their care givers, primarily their parents, spontaneously tended in these studies to channel and limit stimuli input. For example, while feeding a baby, the parent was apt to protectively cover the child's hands. In the crib it was common to present them with only one or two toys to avoid overstimulation. While bathing the baby the parent avoided splashing lest the infant start a tidal wave!

By contrast, the infants we have described as 'living radars' adopt a markedly different approach to life events. They take hold of their environment visually. They tend to scan thoroughly their surroundings while also relying upon other sensory (tactile and taste) input. Their actions are typified by focusing, getting hold by sight rather than grasp, using their finger tips rather than gross muscular movements to sense their environment. In turn, their care givers were decisively more apt to increase their stimulation within the field of action. The infants were splashed while bathing. They were cooed to and bodily bounced about. They were deluged with toys and other gadgets in their cribs to enhance the range of life experiences. Parents intensified stimuli input while also granting them a wider buffer zone.[5] In short, these parents had intuitively responded to their infants' major communication style.

What was the eventual outcome of these two groups of children? Differential handling for different kids but satisfactory outcomes for both! Almost all of these children, the 'go-go' and 'living radars' alike, developed into well balanced adults. This satisfactory development was probably enhanced by the care givers' intuitive handling, of accommodating to their infants' temperaments.

The descriptive accounts of these parents' interactions with their young children has relevance for work with older children living in group care settings. Imagine school age children in a group home setting coming into the dining area for their main meal. Some tend to come to the table as if playing a game of rugby. They reach for food while inquiring: 'What's there to eat?' The natural adult response then might be to focus on one thing at a time: 'Sit down!' 'SIT!' 'SIT DOWN!', accompanied by the worker's restraining movements. Simultaneously other children approach the table just as eagerly, perhaps slower in their movements while thoroughly surveying the table. They immediately spot things to their dislike and over distance voice their objections. The worker's reaction would be to ask them to sit down first, simultaneously calling attention to alternate attractions with pleasurable possibilities in order to widen these children's experiential scope (stimuli input).

For child care work the knowledge that children possess different temperaments and that these variations herald specific caring inter-actions can help us recognize the necessity for care givers and care receivers to mutually find their fit. Care workers have to allow them-selves time for discerning a child's temperament. They have to observe and to experience both those children for whom personal involvement requires body contacts and reduction of stimulative input, and those children for whom personal closeness is expressed over distance and requires visual and other stimuli. In short, different strokes for different blokes. Most important, the institutional work settings have to assure the group care staff sufficient time so that managerial tasks do not compete with this kind of selective caring activity.

These recent findings make questionable some of our established emphasis upon standardizing expectations of behaviour and consistent handling of the group of children in care. We have noted that similar treatment of children has a different relevance for each child. If children do vary in temperament, then they logically secure for themselves differ-ent life experiences from their care givers (Brazelton, 1977; Lewis and Rosenblum, 1974). Child care workers can tune in quite readily to their children's particular care requirements. For child care workers to expect of themselves or be required by the program design 'to be laterally con-sistent' is neither a natural nor a desirable objective. Contemporary child development knowledge suggests that the focus in care has to be upon finding a proper enmeshment with the unique child and to proceed accordingly, seeking a mutual fit of that child and his or her care giver rather than trying to adhere to identical behavioural responses for all the children within one group.

Rhythms of care

At moments in which individuals find themselves fully in rhythm with one another – dancing, singing, hand clapping, in sexual activity, in a game of table tennis, in the rapid interplay of ideas in a rap session – these moments of rhythmic exchange provide an experience of close togetherness for the persons involved. Rhythmic activities seem to confirm the experience of repetition and continuity of repetition – and with it a sense of permanency and a promise of predictability (Maier, 1978b:36–43). The individuals participating in rhythmic activity experience a quality of mutual unity and interdependence (Brazelton, Koslowski, and Main, 1974; Lewis and Rosenblum, 1974; Maier, 1978b, 1979; Schaffer, 1977).

In early childhood much of the care givers' and infants' energy goes into a kind of 'dance' where each one tries to fall in step with the other in a cyclical pattern (Hersh and Levin, 1978:3). In this process of mutual inclusion, both search for a way to establish and to maintain a joint rhythm. Rhythmicity is moreover the hallmark of infant toys and activities. Rhythmic experiences, such as rattling a rattle, playing patty-cake, listening to lullabyes, or rocking jointly, bring infant and caring adult into a single frame of joint action. These experiences seem not to be limited to early child developmental periods but tend to be essential for effective interpersonal relationships throughout life. In a number of studies of this phenomenon, rhythmic interactions have been noted as the 'molecules of human behavior' and basic to all human communications (Byers, 1972; Condon, 1975; Maier, 1978b).

In group care individuals are brought together for varying time spans, where each seems to have his or her own rhythm without having been previously 'tuned-up' to the others' style of life. Opportunities have to be created for these participants to discover common rhythms.

Frequently the children themselves create such moments – and occasionally to their caring adults' consternation. Sing-song slogans, for instance, are most contagious for their rhythmic patterns; they tend to be chanted far beyond the outsider's endurance, while the chanters themselves experience a deep sense of unity. It is not surprising in periods of tension that the single rhythmic banging of a spoon at mealtime, perhaps an accidental occurrence, is apt to be picked up in a flash by a whole group. It is the very search for belongingness which makes rhythmic unity such a desirable factor at moments of severe uneasiness in a residential unit. The same contagious ingredients may be observed in the rhythmic chanting or clapping at rallies – and even more so, in demonstrations.

Group care workers can make valid use of this knowledge of the power of rhythmicity. A worker may want to utilize rhythmic interactions as a means for becoming a more vital part of the unit by initiating such exchanges as tossing a ball, singing, dancing, or jam sessions, engaging in a modern 'shake' (the exchange of several rhythmic alternate hand-claps in place of the traditional handshake) or finding a common rhythm in speech, body movements or head nodding. At moments of tension, a familiar record with an inviting rhythm, the tossing around of a quickly exchanged beanbag or a slowly floating balloon can more readily lead to rhythmic togetherness and relaxation than a worker's well meant words of admonishment. In these moments of joint rhythmicity, participants have opportunity to experience a sense of unity and anchorage.

Rituals in many ways constitute an institutionalized form of psycho-logical rhythmicity. Rituals represent a cultural confirmation of a repeated practice, while the participants experience a deep sense of togetherness. In group care, and for children and youth in general, rituals have particular significance as long as they are the children's rituals rather than adult ordained routines. Rituals, more likely than not, arise out of some spontaneously repeated practice. In one group care program, each child gave an old statue in the corner a pat or slap before getting ready for bed. This ritual represented an essential event for the children, eventually becoming just as important as the worker's nightly goodnight bidding or personal pat.[6]

Each institutional unit can probably list its own significant rituals. Examples cannot be cited here. Rituals have to emerge on their own and require the workers' full support as important events in their children's lives, even if they may appear rather ridiculous from the adult's perspec-tive. Conversely, caretakers need to guard against perceiving as 'rituals' such highly desirable routines as teeth-brushing, waiting for everyone to be seated at mealtime, or other behavioural expectations of adults. These are routines and need to be dealt with as such for their practical necessity rather than for any remnant of sacredness pertaining to ritual. Routines serve to accomplish required tasks smoothly with minimal energy and time investment, to achieve temporary order for each person involved. Rather, rituals introduce procedures which prolong or delay the business at hand and lift the activity, establishing it as an event of consequence close to the realm of sanctity.

Dependency has to 'taste' good

'Stay here – so that I can do it myself,' a 3-year old pleaded with his parent. What this young child sensed correctly is a factor of development easily overlooked by adults: close attachment initiates freedom (Maier, 1980). Children in residential care particularly are plagued by uncer-tainty and are often hampered by a severe lack of dependency upon dependable care givers. Children in residential care, as children any-where, require secure dependence upon reliable caring adults in order to develop into dependable adults themselves. A child is, as Alfred Adler has been credited with saying, both the artist and the painting. If children in group care settings could verbalize their psychological state as freely as the 3-year old above, they would be apt to call out: 'I want to count on your being with me so that I can comfortably risk doing without you!' Dependency begets independence (Maier, 1980).

In human development, as recent research findings clearly highlight, a support of dependency and a nurturing of attachment leads to greater readiness to branch out and proceed on one's own. This apparent contradiction can be witnessed in the developmental progression of toddlers. Early in toddlers' development they hold on tightly. The more assured of a stable support, the more ready are these young children to venture on their own. Or, later in life, the more persons are certain of support the more they are ready to risk and to proceed on their own (Sroufe, 1978).

Studies on dependency formation, moreover, reveal that children with highly responsive parents are the ones who are the least fretful. Children securely supported in their dependency strivings are the ones who ultimately achieve secure independence in the very behaviours in which they clamoured for support. (In essence these are children who have been pampered!) Our previous fears of spoiling children and succouring a prolonged state of dependence may not be justified. In fact, children who tend to be so adamant to perform on their own, as well as children who tend to tyrannize their child care staff with suffocating attention-demands, are predominantly youngsters who have suffered from too little attention and meaningful attachments (Segal and Yahraes, 1978). Findings in the past ten years strongly suggest that a lack of dependency support creates greater havoc in a child's development than prolonged dependency itself (Ainsworth, 1972; Ainsworth, Bell, and Stayton, 1974; Brunner, 1970; NICHHD, 1968; and Schaffer, 1977).

In our work with children in group care, dependency support and nurturance are fundamental ingredients of care. They are respectable companions to the conventional basic three: food, shelter and clothing. Children and adolescents in group care settings, often having had scattered experience with having dependency needs met, have yet to experience fully that *being able to depend upon dependence feels good*. Group care programs have to be structured in such a way that child care workers have time, know-how, and above all, immediate support for dependency nurturance.

Dependency support and attachment-fostering efforts are typified by such activities as a child care worker helping a child with bed-making or doing it for the child. The worker may rightly consider it important to do such a task for or with the child, recognizing that the child needs to feel important and wanted. Moreover, bed-making becomes valued as an essential ingredient for comfortable living, and eventually the child will be able to do it independently. The child care workers attending to these child care chores may appear to superiors, peers, etc. to be slaves to the children; they are not. In fact, these workers deserve to be specifically recognized for their involvement and investment in their children's lives (Mehler, 1979). What they are doing is not too different from the common engagement of having a cup of tea prepared and poured or a small errand attended to by a close friend. All these small acts of attention feel good and enriching, even when they could readily have been done by oneself. To feel accepted and to savour such an experience of being attended to is not only pleasant, it is also normal, adaptive, and basic for satisfactory development (Dupont, 1978; Maccoby and Masters, 1970; Sroufe, 1978). (One feels so much freer and less alone, and paradoxically, one can then do much more by oneself.)

Acts of nurturing support and opportunities for added worker–child enmeshment occur throughout the day, often occurring through minute worker–child interplay. They most frequently take place by means of actions rather than words – for instance the worker stopping what he or she is doing while a child is sharing some observation or complaint. Dependency supports also include extra (requested or not) squeezes, pats, or, roughing up a child. (One must, however, be certain that 'roughing up' communicates unmistakenly for both child and worker: 'I like to be with you and care for you.')

Verbal communication can also be utilized toward this end. Workers sharing with children that they thought of them during a separation, or a worker spontaneously expressing good feelings toward a child, communicates caring, of 'being with' the child. For example, 15-year-old Carolyn leaves for school after three days of suspension for fighting, and her worker was heard to comment: 'Carolyn, I'll take a deep breath around nine o'clock this morning, the time you return to your class. Let me know what happens and what you thought and felt. I am sure that you will have some tough moments. Tell me how you managed.' This writer is sure that this kind of interaction and involvement in Carolyn's conflict-prone life has more promise than well meant but distancing remarks like: 'Be good!' 'Stay out of trouble!' Children, like human beings anywhere, need to experience that someone is fully with them even when they are alone. In Urie Bronfenbrenner's cogent words: 'Every child needs at least one person who is really crazy about him (or her)' (Bronfenbrenner, 1977: 5).

Attachment and attachment behaviour

The preceding reference to attachment formation is based upon formulations in which a distinction is made between *attachment* and *attachment behaviours*.

Attachment denotes the affective bonding experience – the feeling of mutual dependence – known or felt by an individual but not necessarily behaviourally expressed. Attachment specifies an experience of interpersonal intimacy and closeness where support has the promise of reaching beyond the present. In a sense, attachment formation is another way of conceptualizing what is generally called: 'developing a relationship'. Attachment emerges when a relationship moves beyond a beginning phase. It is a common event in early child development during the second half of a baby's first year. It is then, at this particular point of development, that stable hierarchies of preferences (attachment) develop. It is also the time when a good deal of trouble starts, such as the child's preference for one parent over the other, or demands for a parent's presence over a previously acceptable babysitter. These manifestations are promising signals that the individual is well on the way in his or her maturing process. These child developmental incidents are matched by similar occurrences in the selective attachments to different workers by the children in group care settings and by evidence of fluctuating feelings as work shifts change or substitute care workers are introduced. Attachments occur and are needed at any point in a person's life (Bowlby, 1969; Bronfenbrenner, 1976; Sroufe and Waters, 1977). After all, one of the signs of maturity is to have the capacity to choose on whom one will depend and to maintain such an attachment over time.[7]

Attachment behaviours, as the words already imply, represent efforts of striving towards attachment but in no way constitute attachment as such. Attachment behaviours signal that the individual's self-management capacity is experienced as unsteady. Attachment behaviours can be described by such proximity-seeking efforts as clinging, staying close, or repeatedly posing self-evident questions (e.g. 'What time is it?' 'When do we eat?') which actually are a cry to be noticed and included. It is useful in practice to be aware of this differentiation and to recognize attachment. Appropriate actions have to be directed toward the process of attachment formation rather than the attachment behaviours themselves. Attachment behaviours, moreover, are intrinsic and natural human reactions and are not merely peculiarities of children in group care settings. Studies of securely attached children bring out that in moments of stress, such as at points of separation, they seek the proximity of the care giver. After reciprocal response of inclusion by the care giver, these children can subsequently handle the separation more competently. In contrast, children with uncertainties in their attachments will either avoid falling back upon their primary care givers or will have added difficulties in facing the changed situation (Kagan, 1978; Sroufe, 1978:56).

Applied to group care this means that such daily care events in attachment strivings should be dealt with as attachment seeking ventures rather than as behavioural expression *per se*. Frequently, when a child screams about other children's behaviour with such penetrating volume that it can be heard in the farthest corner, this call is a cry of loneliness and a sense of desertion rather than a mere act of disruptive behaviour.

Workers may want to conceive of these cries as reminders that the particular youngster needs much active assurance of being included by the worker, possibly right at that critical moment or perhaps later on. The child's loud screams, i.e. the attachment behaviour, is not the point to be addressed. Thus, the tempting reaction of shouting back: 'Stop your screaming!' would need to be swallowed in preference to a caring response which has significance to the youngster.

Theoretical cross roads

The foregoing concern, whether to focus upon the child's specific ongoing behaviour or the individual's assumed basic requirements, is actually a question of theoretical grounding. The previously cited illustrations may serve as an opportunity to highlight the differences and consequences between operating from a behavioural or an interpersonal perspective.

One can delineate the behavioural modification stance in the following: ignoring the child's cry is used as a technique for extinguishing an undesired response, concomitant to this is the reinforcing behaviours (showing attention) when the child is peacefully engaged. While within an interactional perspective in the preceding case example, workers are lauded for their response to the child's cry for assistance and human compassion in a moment of lonely despair. The piercing screams are not conceived of as the central issue but are automatically extinguished once the child feels a stronger sense of attachment. Both perspectives present as the desired end the elimination of undesirable responses and the strengthening of more effective behavioural capabilities. Yet the difference in the value orientation and actual practice activities and potential outcomes are in stark contrast. Within a behavioural perspective the emphasis is upon behavioural modification, as the name of the approach clearly signifies. Within an interactional perspective, the inter-relationship of people, the fostering of attachment and the reliance upon developmental process, move to the centre. Behaviours, in contrast, are envisaged as instrumental rather than as the essence of human existence (Mordock, 1979). In the illustrative example above, workers in this context are expected to relate when needed to the total child rather than to the child's behaviours. Behavioural thinking, in contrast, conceives of the child's behaviour as a manifestation of the child as he or she is.

The behavioural approach in one way is most inviting for its clarity in purpose and apparently simple application in complex situations (Browning and Stover, 1971). Also, a good range of research findings have heralded behavioural management approaches for their proven efficacy. True, behavioural modification is effective as long as specific behavioural changes are conceived as the immediate and ultimate target. The interactional approach has a stronger appeal to persons and institutions with a humanistic orientation. For them, their source of information and verification comes from research on child development within the context of a child's everyday developmental life experiences. Their basic concern centres in providing children with everyday sustenance. The interpersonal approach would maintain that providing a child with the needed support must occur when the child needs it rather than when particular behaviours are acceptable. Strong differences in belief and value systems come to the foreground with this last statement.

Which orientation shall prevail? Both find application within this volume – and more so, both points of view (and frequently a combination of them) are continuously applied in the many practice settings. This writer obviously relies upon an interactional perspective. This perspective is akin to his belief system, and belief systems ultimately determine every person's theoretical bias. Moreover, this position can also be well supported by recent research findings in child development. Findings point out that the *quality* of rootedness in interpersonal attachment determines the nature of behavioural expression and change rather than the behavioural output as determinant of the basic development of human relationship (Brazelton, Koslowski, and Main, 1974; Dupont, 1978; Kirgin *et al.*, 1979; Maier, 1978a; Schaffer, 1977; Segal and Yahraes, 1978). In spite of wide usage of both orientations, there is a decisive difference between them. A behavioural point of view conceives human beings as basically a behavioural apparatus responding to environmental stimulations and reinforcements. An interactional perspective requires one to conceive of human beings as multi-dimensional, as feeling, thinking, as well as behaving persons – acting and responding all in one (Maier, 1976). To put it another way, the essential differences between these two basic alternate conceptions rest between linear, inductive thinking (basic to learning theory formulations) and non-linear, cyclical, deductive thinking (underpinning system theory and an interactional conceptualization).

Attention-seeking/human contact-needing

Let us examine more closely the phenomenon of attention-getting demands, for the previous brief paragraphs on attachment and attachment behaviours have not really addressed the common fear of feeding into attention-getting behaviours. Attention-getting behaviours are part and parcel of children's everyday lives. However, children uprooted from their original living arrangements tend to exhibit such behavioural expressions even more strongly. It is not that they require more attention than other children; rather, as a group they have experienced, thus far, less dependable attention. Attention-getting efforts are actually attachment behaviours, involving strong individual intrusive thrusts directed toward winning fuller inclusion. Thus, the child clinging to the worker, overwhelming as that can be, may be better understood in the light of the child's quest for inclusion rather than as undesirable 'hogging' for exclusive attention.

Wanting attention is basically very human. Who doesn't want, need, and deserve it? In our work with children or youth the salient issue is not the fact that an individual wants attention, although this reasoning is frequently used to explain and by-pass a child's behaviour. Instead, a child's desire for attention has to be understood and addressed as a legitimate expression. To reach out for approval and companionship, to turn toward others when in distress – these are all natural desires and requirements. The writer trusts that these human qualities are also valued by child care staff and their institutional programs (Chess and Hassibi, 1978).

The issue we must concern ourselves with is establishing more secure anchorage for these children and helping them move toward more effective inclusive behaviours. For child care practice the task is thus three-fold: (1) Child care workers demonstrating an open attitude toward the children's desire for inclusion. Children are to be welcomed as vital and full partners in the unit's daily life and into society in general. (2) Workers responding sensitively to the children's urgent appeals for immediate satisfying contacts and clearly acknowledging the stress the child is undergoing. (3) Workers preparing to overlook at the moment the children's unsatisfactory behaviour. Suitable behavioural expressions are taught when appropriate for the child's learning. Sometimes teaching takes place at the critical incident and sometimes later on.

The range of appropriate child care givers' interventions is vast. It may suffice to envision as model a mother's everyday response to the piercing screams of a child whose tower of blocks has unexpectedly caved in. A sensitive parent will respond to the child's frustration rather than to her inconvenience at being called away from her task at hand. She will respond to the child's experience of disappointment rather than to the unpleasantness of the screams. Above all, she will encourage the child to try again, possibly assuring him or her that there is no need to scream so vehemently. Even better, she may not comment at all on the child's vocal outburst of despair (in contrast to trying to extinguish the screams lest the youngster become a screamer). Recent research points clearly to the fact that it is not the children's future behaviour, but their future trust in others and consequent sense of independence that are at stake (Kagan, 1978; Sable, 1979; Segal and Yahraes, 1978).

Bodily comfort speaketh the loudest

'Try out these soft floor pillows,' says a group care worker while handing cushions to a number of 15-year-old girls sprawled out on the floor for an evening of television watching. 'I turned up the heat in the bathroom, so it will be good and warm when you get out of the shower,' remarked another care worker. Concerns for bodily comfort, like straightening out children's blankets at bedtime in order to make them more comfortable for the night or sitting down with a child on the floor so that the youngster can afford a more relaxed bodily posture and eye contact, are common child care activities. But however spontaneous or mundane, this quality of caring is vital and should not be overlooked. Throughout life a sense of well-being and caring is closely related to the degree of bodily security and comfort a person experiences. Moreover, as an individual's bodily comforts are met, so does the person feel welcomed and wanted and more receptive to risk experience beyond his or her immediate bodily demands. Physical sustenance and comfort are thus essential measures of care.[8]

Care giving in many ways is anchored in the personal involvement aspect of the physical care rendered by the care giver. It is the care giver's personal investment which converts physical care into 'caring care'. A worker taking the time to tuck a child into bed, to offer suitable clothing, fix a girl's braids, or rub a youngster's cold hands – these actions deal with transmitting personal physical care and constitute some of the most fundamental components of child care (Maier, 1979 : 161–64).

Because the rendering of personal care of children is so closely associated with the provision of the necessities of life, it is common for child care services to theoretically justify the assignment of both homemaker tasks and child care to the same staff. Actually, budgetary considerations are frequently the basis for this dual assignment. It becomes then questionable what priority is given to the task of relating to the children *per se*.

Theoretically and practically speaking a group care setting is *not* a home. It is true that both family and group care settings are primary group systems. The primary processes are inherent in each, but group care programs are not comparable to family life existence. In order to draw a meaningful line between physical care and physical management functions, it is essential to classify all household functions as management functions; from ordering provisions to seeing that the toothpaste tubes are capped; from washing to the issuing of clothing; from cooking to the serving of meals; from scrubbing to achieving an orderly unit. These management functions need to be carried out by household *maintenance* personnel who can carry them out more efficiently.

With more flexible time at hand and a clearer assignment to assist the children with their most urgent everyday requirements care staff can pursue more readily their primary roles. Staff can then focus on training children in the tasks which must be mastered in order to live effectively as members of a household. Workers and residents together will appropriately take some responsibility for the maintenance of clothing, for joint sharing in some of the preparation and serving of their meals, and for a creative investment in personal care of their place. Maintenance staff just like the administrative staff for each program have to be selected equally for its specifically required capabilities *and* its readiness to be concerned with children's requirements. A cook, bookkeeper, gardener, agency director, or general maintenance person is a vital partner of the total care program. Each one is needed for his or her specialized competency. Each adds his or her vital contribution by which he or she brings to bear in the overall planning and in the interactions with children and staff whatever is essential in the care of children as persons in their own right. In short, the cook, child care worker, executive or janitor is always a person with his or her task speciality *and* a full member of the extended child care team.

Awareness of physical comfort as a prelude for care can be expanded to the way we deal with an individual's personal space, personal belongings, and spatial orientation in general. The child's private place, or drawer, or his or her personal piece of clothing needs to be honoured as part of the individual's special realm, even if the person is not present to claim it (Bakker and Bakker-Rabdau, 1973). We all can envisage instances when household pets have private spaces which are respected. Do we similarly grant to children in our group programs such rights and respect? Do children and adolescents in residential group settings also have a chance to establish territory which is genuinely their own?

Such spaces – private 'corners', beds or other 'mine only' places – have to be indisputably theirs as part of their inalienable rights within their child care arena. It is important to affirm such spaces as duty free regardless of acceptability. Youngsters need to find evidence of their right to exist in difficult as well as in good moments. We are reminded of instances when one child feels hurt that another has taken his or her favoured seat although other chairs are 'just as good'. These are not mere nuisance occurrences. For the child it is an event of personal consequence. Studies of animal and human uses of space clearly suggest to us that invasion of private space is felt sharply as a direct assault to one's body (Bakker and Bakker-Rabdau, 1973; Freedman, 1975). There is a saying: 'Good fences make good neighbours'. This assertion might also apply to children. They too want their territory known and respected. (The concern for private space in the midst of much shared territory in our childcaring institutions and group homes will be more fully reviewed in the next section of this chapter.)

Transitional objects

As a corollary to the above, it is also significant that when children move from one setting to another, they require assistance in making the unfamiliar familiar. Transitional objects – a much loved blanket, cushion, stuffed beast, toy, photo or trinket – serve as linkage transforming a strange place into more familiar surroundings (Winnicott, 1965).[9] The children's treasured possessions, usually a meaningless old tattered object to a casual onlooker, can be vital sustenance for its owner.

It is inherent in the contemporary scene that each child care worker serves also as a personalized transition worker – a person facilitating children's transitions from one life situation to another. Children and youth need assistance with entering, coping and moving forward into a new situation. It follows then, that we need to guard against stripping individuals of their transitional objects as they enter new group living situations. Also, continuing contacts with previously supportive persons provide not only a helping bridge but are essential as transitional contacts for the child.

Behavioural training

The reader may have been puzzled while traveling over the preceding pages that little reference has been made to the training connected with self-management and the maintenance of discipline. These aspects of care are important features of child care. In fact they are so essential that they should be attended to when they have the fullest possible impact.

Children learn most readily from those who have vital meaning for them. They learn from persons like their child care workers whom they recognize as persons to be counted on. They copy those whom they perceive to be on their side, tending to follow those people whose ways of dealing with life issues are most akin to their own. The persons most meaningful for their power, as well as closest to the children's own life situations, have the best chance for influencing the children's behaviour and training. In addition to the primary caring persons, very frequently it is the slightly older siblings and peers or the heroes in stories and on television, a few steps ahead in development, who represent models and idols. They may be almost of equal importance to the central caring figures as well (Bronfenbrenner, 1970; Kessen, 1975; Schaffer, 1977).

Social capability rests upon personal attachment. It is essential to keep in mind that the most potent behavioural training goes hand in hand with a sense of reciprocal closeness and attachment. Effective acquisition of behavioural standards is a consequence of the combination of accepting dependency and wanting to incorporate significant adults' behaviours as one's own (Maier, 1978a : chapter 3). When child caring adults have a sense of close attachment, effective child training starts and more complicated socialization efforts can take their course. While socialization proceeds, children or youth will periodically dip into emotional dependence upon their care givers. These linkages will be both fundamental and freeing. In other words, the fostering of self-management and of enriching children's behavioural repertoires are intimately linked with the formation of close attachment with the care givers (Maier, 1981a).

The preceding pages have essentially taken up the more immediate environment of personal care which has to be provided to children and adolescents anywhere – especially to those in residential group care. The points discussed thus far could well be enumerated as the 'core of care', the essential ingredients for the development of children and youth at home and away from home (Maier, 1979).

III   The language of space – physical arrangements

Spatial arrangements and how they influence daily experience

'We shape our buildings – and they shape us.' This sage comment attributed to Winston Churchill (Proshansky, Ittelson, and Rivlin, 1970:18), also applies to the physical arrangements of residential group care settings. Spatial patterns have the possibility of enhancing or inhibiting activities. The use of residential territory is as much a reflection of the space available as of the quality of interaction between residents and staff (Wax, 1977:51). Only by unusual coincidence will our readers be involved with the design or with the complete rebuilding of a residential setting. Most of us are confronted with the inimitable challenge: in which way can the present setting be adapted within its unalterable limits in order for spatial arrangements to shape service activities in the desired direction?

For the moment let us look in at the age-old phenomenon of children pushing each other as they enter the dining area. This tumbling and shoving is in part a function of age and it is not unusual for a child to thrust forward as if he or she is the only one to find a place at the table, even when customary places are assured. But in part, these scrambles are frequently a matter of the kind of space and timing we offer that take into account sufficient room for children's awkward body movements manifested in moments of hurry and excitement. True, these jostlings can possibly be controlled by continuous supervision and much child care effort. However, the same change in behaviour can be potentially achieved with an alteration in the physical and timing arrangements. A wider 'freeway' at the entrance and between tables is apt to cut down on the pushing and shoving. Such physical alterations can likewise conserve child care staff's energy and avoid an atmosphere of admonishment preceding mealtime gatherings.

Chart of the spatial residential arrangements

Ever present in the dialectic dilemma is the assurance of ample common space while guaranteeing each individual unhampered pursuit of personal interest and associations. Moreover, there is the clear need for continuous proximity of staff while simultaneously assuring the resident a sense of intimacy and private experimentation.

In order to make immediate use of ideas and questions reviewed within this section of the chapter, readers are urged to chart for themselves the physical realities of the residential service program with which they are concerned. On a large sheet of notepaper sketch roughly the groundplan of the residential building(s) and outdoor space of one childcare unit. If the unit is housed on more than one floor, make a diagram for each floor level. Draw in existing walls, steps, doors, windows, built-in closets, major equipment (e.g. refrigerator and plumbing) as well as large pieces of furniture (beds, chests, tables, chairs, couches, television, sewing machine, etc.).

In a study of this diagram of the physical group living environment it becomes important to discern what the spatial set-up allows and encourages, and what it tends to hinder or negate. In which ways do spatial factors impact privacy, supervision, the flow and speed of interactions, spontaneous groupings, access to child care staff as well as contacts with the outside? In such a review, do the findings dovetail with the objectives of the service program? These questions are based upon the understanding that every spatial constellation implicity allows and hampers actions. Indeed, space controls behaviour (Proshansky, Ittelson, and Rivlin, 1970; Sommer, 1969).

Wherever space supports the work endeavoured, the question remains: in which way can spatial factors be altered to even further accentuate this process? Sometimes small spatial alterations bring about substantial changes in the flow of behavioural interactions. For example, care workers frequently maintain an open door while engaged with paperwork in their child care offices. The workers' availability or degree of concentration upon their office tasks can be signaled by the arrangement of their work space as well as their seating position. By arranging their workspace at the far end of the room rather than adjacent to the entrance, their position conveys clearly: 'I am away and at work!' If residents want to establish contact, they are required to come fully into the room while separating themselves from their own peers' sphere of life.

When spatial arrangements are actually impeding or complicating the program, the challenge exists to alter these physical factors. This need becomes particularly urgent when existing arrangements are justified because they have been like that for years! Readers will quickly be reminded of settings (hopefully places of the past) where children are forbidden to run lest plantstands or other cherished mementoes get knocked down. One more illustration: in some programs where the doors of the children's room open to the inside, children are apt to barricade themselves in their rooms when severely agitated and in special need for adult contacts. A small carpentry alteration in the frame and a rehanging of the door may offer possibilities for additional and more promising avenues of intervention. Readers are challenged to review their diagrams and ponder about the residential unit's physical arrangements. Change space, and advance program!

Private space

Territory defines the person. A person's power position and value to an organization can invariably be estimated by the relative space granted as *private* (personal) working domain. Compare the size of the executive's office with those of other offices, the social workers' offices with those of the child care staff. Secretaries frequently protect their desk tops; janitors are intensely possessive about their supply closets; while child care workers guard closely the space allotted for purses, notebooks or other personal belongings. It is not surprising that persons without an office of their own jealously guard that vestige of private territory they *can* claim (Stea, 1970). In applying these observations to work with children and adolescents, we see quickly the importance for children to stake out their territory and the necessity for recognizing their private spaces as personal turf (Bettelheim, 1974). Private space is not only urgently required for a verification of self; private space is also essential for each person as a refuge for contemplation and revitalization of energy (Mehrabian, 1976).

What actually constitutes private space? It is an area recognized by the occupant *and* others as the claimant's full and rightful possession. It represents an area which the occupant can use, arrange and rearrange, or even disregard according to his or her liking. Most important, it is a place where persons have full control over themselves and their immediate environment. The occupant has the sole right to invite or exclude others within this safe place (Bakker and Bakker-Rabdau, 1973). It is a spot where intermittently the individual can be an island to him or herself. In the absence of any such assured sanctuaries, people tend to create their own 'private spaces' by such behaviours as placing themselves behind a newspaper while travelling. Harassed parents may retreat to the bathtub as their sanctum. Children lacking private space of their own tend to seek out the privacy of a swing, toilet, etc.

The wish to be periodically alone and to have space of one's own is not merely a whim of children or adults, it is a human requirement. The latter becomes even more urgent for persons living or working in close proximity with others. (Freedman, 1975). Moreover, at moments of personal tensions and social change, individuals require added privacy and the assurance of ample space of their own.[10] We are reminded of instances of crises when children seek out the assurance and solace of their rooms or wander off the institutional grounds or even run away. Similarly, we witness that when children are tense they require more space between themselves and others, even for instance as they watch television together. Conversely, conditions of sudden overcrowding can bring on intense anxiety, panic behaviours of either fight or flight, or even a suicide (Wax, 1977 : 51–2). The necessity to maintain more space in moments of stress is not necessarily a manifestation of peoples' irritability but rather their very human requirements for larger buffer zones (Horowitz, Duff, and Stratton, 1970). It is an established fact that persons in a schizophrenic state maintain a greater distance from people around them and are in need of more private space for themselves in order to function at all (Bettelheim, 1974 : 136–37; Sivadon, 1970).

What constitutes privacy in the fish bowl of group living?

At this point it might be advisable to pursue further the diagrammed layout of the residential unit. Draw in with contrasting colour or picture mentally for yourself the *private* space granted to child care staff.

This little exercise is apt to reveal quickly whether child care staff have such essential space actually accessible to them. Provision for space is a necessary privilege automatically assured to other professionals in their respective offices. If by chance other professional space is also inadequate, this still does not negate the need for such a refuge at the child care level.

As the next step, shade into the diagram (or visualize for yourself) the *private* space granted each child. Delineate in the children's rooms only those areas as private territory which are distinctly private. Also add in acknowledged 'private space' within the larger residential setting and its neighbourhood.

Children require private corners for their *personal* belongings and for solitary times. It should be noted that protection of personal possessions is primarily an issue of privacy and only secondarily a mechanism for keeping order in the unit. If the concern for order and safekeeping of a child's belongings is a justifiable issue, then some of the belongings may have to be stored selectively in order to safeguard personal possessions and to maintain basic clothing and equipment. To reiterate, a box, a drawer, or a shelf is a must in group care. Moreover, children and youth require territory in their own rooms and in other areas of their group living environment where they can be comfortable and on their own to brood or to gloat, to loaf or to concentrate, to be privately with friends or to indulge in solitary play. Private space also assures the freedom to leave one's project undisturbed for an eventual return.

The sleeping quarters, bed and room, in almost all cultures tend to carry a most personal connotation. For young and displaced people it seems to take on added significance as a vestige for anchorage when their course is unclear. Changes, especially arbitrary or frequent room or bed changes connote a sense of impermanence and casual disregard for the residents' place within the group care setting. The fundamental concern that we may want to bear in mind is that the residents' sleeping quarters are bedrooms belonging to the *residents* as their temporary home base. This principle may contrast to some settings where the rooms *per se* are convinced as belonging to the institutional service rather than an integral arm of the service itself. Special effort has to be directed toward establishing that the children's beds and rooms are not only attractive, comfortable, and practical, but that they symbolize almost more than any segment of the residence the message: 'We care!' (Bettelheim, 1974 : 153). Staff needs continuously to search out whether attention given to furniture, room arrangements, and decorations are really in the best interest of the children or whether these concerns reflect an adult conception of a spick and span and respectable place. A sense of *private* space and personal investment is not fortified by the imposition of adult standards. The reverse seems to be the case: a sense of personal investment and ownership leads to a greater openness to adult suggestions.[11]

The assurance of private space depends much upon marking off respective boundaries. Ownership has to be acknowledged by all parties involved (Bakker and Bakker-Rabdau, 1973). Putting up name plates on doors or posting of signs as 'private', 'stay out', or roping off an area, are effective means of reaffirming established personal space. Such notices are commonly employed by children in their own homes; and readers themselves will recall placards reading 'no entry', 'knock before entering', etc., which were loftily posted on doors. The same holds true for the creation of temporary private spheres within the public life of a group living environment in order that solitary or special sub-group activities can occur legitimately and without interruption. Similarly, children and staff need to map out permissible areas for practising music, physical exercises, for taking a walk, or other recourses verifying the natural desire to be temporarily isolated.

Public space

Every home, as well as each group living situation, has extensive areas which serve as *public* territory. Public territory is the space which can be indisputably used by any one constituent member of the group. During the length of the time a person occupies the particular area it is that individual's 'personal space'. A seat at the kitchen table, provision for privacy in a common washroom, stretching out temporarily on the livingroom couch, are a few examples which assure people of sole occupancy as long as they maintain possession or hold onto the spot by proxy.

But let us go back for a moment to some basic issues. In a group living setting a decision first has to be made about who is to be included in the definition of public. Does public mean the general public? The public of the total organization? Or is public more limited, to mean those associated with a particular group living unit?

Usually space in front of a private home or a children's institution is considered common public space. Anyone has a right to it. But the decision to grant an open range of entry or to permit entrance selectively really rests upon a major policy decision. Are the children's residential units conceived as custodial or service programs? The custodial program can be readily defined and justified as within the community's domain and as everybody's territory. Such a conception fits more into a program which does little more than to warehouse troubled children and is out of step with contemporary thinking (Whittaker, 1979 : 5). In contrast, if we accept the premise in a service program that the group living environment belongs to the residents and the staff specifically associated with the residents' *daily* lives, it follows that others – whether concerned citizens, friendly neighbours, policy makers, or management and other staff participants – only achieve access by knocking and being invited to enter. (Note: invited by the occupants – children and staff – and not by the management or the administration in general.) Although it can be argued that office staff, field-workers, repair specialists, and especially the executive director, are intimately involved in the services rendered to the residents, they would also appropriately get specific permission for entry. (In some instances, when staff persons have become much intertwined with the children's and staff's lives, they may secure spontaneous entry rights for their unique ongoing relationship with the unit's population.)

What about the children's *public* space? If space is public, then there must be access for all. Areas within and outside of the residential unit which are conceived as the children's territory necessarily must be set up as such for the residents' free use. Private claims can only last for the duration of a person's occupancy unless such space has by consensus become an individual's private space. Frequently, individuals will become attached to and are granted specific places as their accustomed spots within public territory. The latter is reminiscent of most homes where a particular place is reserved by 'squatters rights' to a family member or sometimes household pets.

Again, it might be instructive to turn to the previously drawn-up diagram and reflect on the mental picture of a group living setting. Are the areas which thus far have not been marked off as private space actually the children's and staff's *public* territory? Space might be allocated for particular periods of the day (e.g. outdoor area for daylight activities only) or for special ranges of activities (e.g. music corner, fix-it shop or study room). Are these special limitations for public use clearly defined and understood by the residents and staff? It is not unusual that after taking notice of all clearly established public space, there remain areas that lack clear definition. These are the twilight zones, areas of uncertainty and potential conflict with regard to utilization. Frequently the kitchen, workshops, storage rooms, or porch make up these uncertain and conflict-prone territories. Difficulties can be decisively reduced by clearly establishing claims to the area: staff, children with staff, or open to all.

Isolation rooms as a special 'service' space

Some child care programs include as essential for their program the maintenance of an isolation room. Staff finds it necessary to confine children to a special bare lock-up room either to enforce policy of time-out,[12] or such a room may be desperately employed as a recourse when care givers are at a loss (possibly along with the whole treatment field) as to how to deal with a severely troubled child who is completely out of control.

Special caution is necessary here in labeling and using this kind of space. Isolation rooms are frequently euphemistically dubbed 'quiet rooms' when they are in fact punitive and dehumanizing cells. If isolation actually is to serve its intended purpose to separate and calm a distraught child from ongoing agitation, then in most situations the child's own room – a quiet, familiar, and confidence inspiring refuge – is the logical isolation place. Moreover, in the latter setting the child would be encouraged to subsequently use his or her room in moments of severe tension as a safe harbour for finding a personal sense of balance.

Children, as well as adolescents and adults, need people at times of distress; they need people nearby in a place which inspires comfort and that is welcoming. Rarely are isolation chambers conducive for bringing people together. Instead, their naked walls and cold emptiness further arouse a sense of personal negation, social insulation, and individual despair. Isolation rooms have also been justified as a place for children or adolescents to think, to reflect and to come up with a resolve for new ways of handling problematic situations. Since when is being locked up, seated on the floor or on a bare bedstead in an empty room, conducive to thinking? All of us require comfortable settings that transmit encouragement rather than drabness when we feel at odds with the world. Isolation rooms, if used at all, need to convey both personal reassurance and social inclusion for the time the child is temporarily apart from the group.

Let space speak

On the preceding pages the focus has been upon the interplay between physical environment and care and treatment objectives, and upon ways that spatial arrangements can be used by care givers and care receivers for more effective group living. The same perspective can be applied to specific problem situations by evaluating the impact of variables in space that augment or deter human interaction (Goffman, 1971). For instance, the recurrent spilling of trash may easily be a function of space if the trash bin is a long distance from the clean-up place. Without this kind of spatial evaluation, one might easily point to such behaviour factors as a child's clumsiness or personal disregard for people and place.

The message of this section can be summed up with the heading of Fritz Redl and David Wineman's chapter on 'Structure and Strategy of a Treatment Home' in their classic book, *The Aggressive Child* (1957). According to them, residential group care requires 'a home that smiles, props which invite, space which allows' (Redl and Wineman, 1957 : 6), and continuous spatial adaptations which enhance the desired care and treatment.

IV Group living as an everyday milieu experience

Three different perspectives of residential group care

The day-to-day periods of work or play, the association with others, the enjoying of one's own company, the dawdling and daydreaming time, the pursuing of routine tasks; all comprise the minutiae of daily life and are the central components of our primary life experience whether adult or child. These encounters typify life in our respective homes, residential or otherwise. It is within the minutiae of life and not in the big events that one's personal pursuits and direction are determined. For instance, on awakening, the way a person feels about his or her companions, the expectations he or she has for the day ahead, or the impact of events that occur immediately upon awakening all strongly influence the beginning of a person's day.

With such a proposition before us, it is no longer a managerial but a basic care and treatment issue as to whether children in group care should be awakened by a bell, by impersonal calls, or by brief personal attention by the worker. Sensitive decisions need to be made whether messages conveyed to children upon awakening are to be perfunctory greetings, reminders or admonishments about the tasks ahead, or whether messages are to be genuine attempts to connect with children personally, communicating a hopeful vision of the day ahead. Into what kind of space are children awakened – are they surrounded by decorations of by-gone residents, or do they wake up to their own meaningful mementoes?

With this view too, it becomes important to handle with care the minute crises which occur in round-the-clock living – from the onset of the day to falling asleep and beyond. It is important how the worker encounters the youngster who crawls deeper under the blanket when reminded to get up. It is important how one reacts to the small crisis of a teenager missing one of his shoes.

In the last momentary crisis of the missing shoe, we could point to programs which absorb such events as common and of no special relevance. The concerns of such settings would stem from a practical managerial focus. Where is clothing located in readiness for the next morning? Did this boy finally locate his shoe, and did he get off for school in time? In other settings the focus would specifically be upon the staff's handling of this particular situation to forestall future crises of this type. The concern would be primarily with the *behavioural management and maintenance of an overall system* for meeting and overcoming such eventualities. In a third large segment of group care settings, attention would be drawn to the interaction between the staff and the youngster, with major emphasis upon *helping this particular individual in learning to hurdle a problematic daily dilemma*. Each of these three alternative approaches mirrors decisively different views of group care. Let us examine the characteristics and ramifications of each. At this point there can be little doubt about the writer's own strong leaning toward the developmental interaction approach.

The acknowledgement of the writer's predisposition is partially an effort to clarify communication with the reader, but is also an attempt to help the reader identify his or her own perspective. The challenge here is for each of us (and for each group care program) to articulate our own orientation, and our ultimate objectives based on that orientation. Pronouncement of a service's theoretical preference and organizational goals clarifies and gives direction to program development and frees staff for creative and accountable efforts. The alternative is to establish a service's policy by relying on a prescribed set of procedural goals (Seidl, 1977). Procedural accounts do provide staff, especially beginning workers, with direction and security but basically stultify organizational intent, ultimately limiting the care givers' personal investment.

A *managerial program perspective*, which is probably the most common emphasis in our contemporary group care field, requires a clear outline of the major daily program features. In general, this kind of program assures residents of a stable and orderly life experience to which they are expected to adapt. The uncomplicated structure of the service, limited program resources, unsophisticated demands upon residents, and the small staff required render these programs appealing to the public (Burmeister, 1960). The programs' emphases on the children's or youth's adaptation, i.e. fitting into the service, represent the strengths and limitations of this perspective. The structure makes uncomplicated demands at a time when life tends to be most complicated for the child. These services tend to be clear about expectations. However, there is no guarantee that the children's effective adaptation to institutional life will be transferable or applicable to effective living beyond the confines of the program (Durkin and Durkin, 1975).

A *behavioural perspective* and its token economy derivative (Kazdin, 1977), the second previously cited theoretic conception, has attracted interest in recent years, particularly in the United States, and especially in programs associated with correctional endeavours (Phillips *et al.*, 1973; Whittaker, 1979 : 88–98). A behavioural perspective places the accent upon achieving specific accountable changes in children's or youth's ongoing behaviours in order that they can fulfill the expectations of their immediate social environment. Early accounts of behavioural approaches have shown astonishing results (Browning and Stover, 1971; Fixsen, Phillips and Wolf, 1973; Phillips *et al.*, 1973). Subsequent experience with identical techniques, including an adherence to a token economy, has brought out that the results have not been as readily duplicated and the results are possibly attributable to factors other than the inherent reinforcement techniques. It seems to this author (Maier, 1975) and others (Kirigin *et al.*, 1978; Phillips *et al.*, 1973; Whittaker, 1979 : 59 as well as Wolf, Phillips and Fixsen, 1974) that the behavioural approach is valid for its quality to teach *behavioural* training. When the impact is reviewed for its overall effect, however, change seems to have been achieved through the counseling person's powerful continued involvement with the care receivers. The care workers' continued review and negotiations *with* their care receivers about behaviour and about the points earned seem to be a central factor in effecting change, rather than the award or the denial *per se*. Psychologists instrumental in setting up these programs observed that an honest give-and-take and warm relationship is an essential component of every treatment program (Phillips *et al.*, 1973). In short, effective change can be attributed to a combination of the care persons' involvement and the children's actual learning of more acceptable behaviours along with an increased experience of efficacy. In addition, and most essential, effective change has been an outgrowth of a new power alignment. That is to say that care personnel and the children are actually in charge of their own daily life situation as they dispense together the points, tokens, or other rewards. A segment of power has come home into the living unit (Maier, 1975:417–19).

The preceding observations have been introduced to raise questions about group living programs which primarily rely upon a token economy or other forms of purely behaviour modification techniques for their utilitarian appeal. Such programs may create for their residents an artificial system with a heavy stress upon compliance and a barter existence in human relationships. Such an outcome may not be the actual objective of the service, and the service may not provide a style of life which is desirable or advantageous once a person is back in regular community life.

A third variation among basic group care approaches is group living as an *interactional experience*. Learning to live and living to learn could describe its central theme (Maier, 1975). The term 'interactional' in the labelling of this approach implies that it places heavy reliance upon *process* rather than outcome *per se*. This approach also builds upon a developmental perspective. The group living experience, with its continued process of daily interactions focuses on the learning opportunities rather than on problem diffusion. In sharp contrast to the previous two approaches, problems are not avoided but exploited. Difficulties are not seen as obstacles but as sources for learning. Stress is placed upon learning to live within the residence and thus upon acquiring life skills for functioning beyond the confines of institutional services.

Residential group care as an arena for everyday life experience

Children or youth in group living require life experiences within their immediate environment which assist them to feel comfortable but which also challenge and stimulate them. The manner in which such experiences are utilized within the residential community serves to foster continuous development and readiness for life within an ordinary family. Two illustrations might be in order here.

Let us first picture a table of five adolescent girls eating their attractive evening meal. They are rather happy if not boisterous. Such a tension-free mealtime is possibly quite an achievement for the girls and the staff of the unit; but it also can be conceived of as the mere beginning, rather than an outcome, in the staff's and the residents' experience. Staff is challenged to assist the girls to expand their conversation, to have fun together when fun is not easily come by, or to be serious when a wise-crack too quickly glosses over worries and personal tensions.

At another time group care staff is confronted with three girls scream-ing at each other, one being accused of wearing a belt, slip and makeup belonging to another girl and used without permission. The accused girl charges that the other two are 'always doing that' with her belongings. Undoubtedly the girls' unit has an understanding (a policy) with regard to borrowing personal belongings. It can also be readily assumed that such a policy, however well contrived, does not prevent alternate practices. The worker is faced with helping the girls straighten out this violation of their understanding about respecting each other's belong-ings. The managing of this phase of an everyday problem is merely a tangential problem in comparison with the worker's more pertinent task. That task hinges on two principles: (1) What can each one do with her own resources to find pleasure in dressing and makeup? (2) What ways can be examined to facilitate the graceful sharing of wanted items? The latter includes dealing with their mutual feelings about each other, as well as developing the capacity to ask effectively for an item which may or may not be withheld. The emphasis in both of these practice illus-trations is that everyday life events within the group serve to enliven and enrich the youngsters. Such events do not, of course, rule out trouble within this system. Troubles are, after all, the grist for growing.

The developmental aspect of an interactional perspective

An interactional approach in group care, as outlined in the previous paragraphs, builds upon a developmental conception of human beings. The developmental progression of children and adolescents, as well as those with variations in their developmental (designated as 'patho-logical' in other frames of reference) is seen as a continuous cyclic pattern of growth and change, a progression that is relativistic rather than linear. Life is conceived as a process in which the human being is in a continuous search for stimulation, variation, and new experience rather than a homoeostatic balanced, stimuli-free existence (Kuhn, 1970; Maier, 1978b; 1981b). Most important, a non-homeostatic conception challenges us to value people for their capacity to reach out and to develop more fully rather than for their low risk striking for balance (Maier, 1974). With this perspective our work with children or adolescents focuses on what to do in the midst of trouble rather than on how to get the kids settled down. Managerial and behavioural approaches are concerned with problem-avoidance or removal, as if the road of life were free of difficulty. In contrast, group care within a developmental perspective challenges the program to search for content, for forms of interaction which can provide the residents with continued stimulation and learning opportunities. Difficulties are a built-in ingredient and are 'par for the course'.

Normalization principle

'Normalization' of life experience, a powerful notion originating in the Scandinavian countries and introduced as an ideal in the United States in the early 1970s, endeavours to utilize styles by which children or youth can live as typically (culturally normative) an existence as possible in order to establish personal behaviours and life events which are as culturally conventional (normative) as possible (Horejsi, 1979:44-5). Normalization does not mean being 'normal'; rather it connotes that each individual's life ought to be as close as possible to the essence of the life experience of his or her contemporaries. This concept seems so simple and obvious; yet experience has shown that the application of the principles may be a threat to the status quo of any setting (Horejsi, 1979:45). Normalization might mean the establishment of a 'normal' rhythm for the year. For instance: vacations break into routines; seasonal changes bring with them a variety of cultural activities, foods, and alterations in routines. A rhythm for the week underlines a variation between school or work days and rest or leisure days. A rhythm for routines requires a progression where routines do not dominate but are interspersed in a day full of other activities. Clearing the table for instance, is as much a function of anticipating a subsequent activity as of the necessity to get the dishes washed.

The notion of normalization challenges staff, for example, to have a child make purchases at the nearby store even if the desired item (e.g. candy) could be obtained more quickly and economically and with less problem potential right within the premises. Group care units require petty cash not merely for emergencies but for providing the youngsters with expanded learning experiences of attending to errands for everyday items. Toothpaste purchased at a store counter, a mere 'normal' acquisition, has greater meaning to a child than a tube from the supply closet!

Rehearsive practice

Let us turn to another avenue for enriching the life and treatment aspect of residential group life. The author postulates that a pro-active stance is preferable to a reactive posture. To put it in another way, it is more useful actively to pursue creative avenues for change than to attempt to modify procedures in an effort to facilitate smoother outcomes. In fact, as long as much of the work focus is upon overcoming difficulties, a lot of energy goes into impacting children's behaviours at a moment when they are less open to change. A child who is upset about missing belongings, for example, has little interest at that moment in learning how to safeguard and take better care of those belongings. Our attempts to do intensive work for change at such a moment is apt to be singularly ineffective.

The notion of rehearsive practice places the emphasis upon learning when learning has a chance. Rehearsal of new and different ways of managing specific events can be addressed at moments of little stress, in a context of fun and interest-awakening procedures, and above all, in a situation where residents and staff can become fully engaged with each other. During such a period of practice the group care situation becomes the arena where children or adolescents learn not only to do the 'what' of the moment, but the 'how' of the future.

For example, in an institution for adjudicated teenagers some youngsters are on a go-it-yourself schedule. They are asked to manage their own timing for getting up, leaving for school or work, being on hand for meals, etc. Self-management is not a reward for previous good behaviour, but it is rehearsed and learned for life's demands beyond the residential protectory. In this unique practice situation, focus is less upon what these residents can manage and more on what they can eventually learn. In addition, staff may practise with them in spare moments how to deal with such problematic situations as 'arriving breathless but late at work'. Learning occurs with actual rehearsing potential alternatives to such an undesirable but everyday event. It is important to note that more effective behaviour is secured not by talking about these problematic situations but by concretely practising them.

One more illustration: leave-taking and preparation for adapting to a new environment is a factor inherent in the life of each youngster in resi-dential group care (Bale, 1979). Preparations for leave-taking and the actual departure can be faced with a child soon to return home as a real event, and used with the others as an opportunity to rehearse for the eventual day of their departure.

Earlier in this chapter we witnessed the group care counselor prac-tising with Ray and two of his unit mates how the former could discourage teasing by disregarding provoking comments. Ray had to practise these behaviours. Rehearsal practice in a period of, and as part of, an interesting experience made it more possible for Ray to engage himself and to learn. Special situations creating simulated life occurrences are for fun but also for keeps; new ways are practised toward successfully facing previously problematic situations.

A rehearsive approach can also provide workers with a handle for dealing with acquisition of behaviour that ordinarily would not be possible in the 'hothouse' culture of institutional life. It is important to consider the *portability* of the behaviours;[13] in other words, inventing ways of doing things which children can effectively employ once returned to regular community living.

Children in residential care possibly need, even more than other children, to develop and rehearse their power to hold their own at home or at school, as well as within the environments of their group care program. Since institutional programs tend to diminish rather than enhance the residents' power, special rehearsive situations may have to be created in which the residents can practise using their power to hold onto their turf and to impact their own life situations. In a group home in the United States, as illustration, residents agreed to help Carl insist upon his rights whenever he felt slighted. They challenged him to stand up for his rights even if this meant disagreement and the necessity for others, including staff, to alter their own immediate preferences.

Conflict behaviour is another feature which may require special attention by means of the rehearsive approach. In general, in everyday life at home or in group living situations, conflicts tend to be avoided or at best reduced, and to be set aside as quickly as possible. Often this is done with a shift of concern away from the person's intense response to apparent difficulties, diminishing the individuals' opportunity to learn new skills in handling conflict and to work further on the aspects which stirred him. Conflict situations may have to be specially and persistently exploited to assist the youngsters (as well as staff) in developing new ways of dealing with conflict (Maier, 1975: 412–13).

Learning to care for others

Finally, parallel to learning to deal with conflict, children require assistance in learning to demonstrate caring (Kobak, 1979). Children in group care, as probably their contemporaries anywhere, not only need love and affection, but also want and need to love others. Learning to care for others is acquired first by experiencing this care oneself; secondly by having caregiving modelled by esteemed persons; and ultimately by opportunities for providing some care for others. As so much of the residential program is geared toward the provision of care, residential settings have to be vigilant in seizing opportunities where children or youth minister to others. Special opportunities have to be created, such as an individual child fixing a mug of cocoa for him- or herself *and* a friend; sharing the concern of an unhappy roommate by trying to do something for the other – not necessarily to elicit a change in mood but as an expression of compassion.

Learning to care is also fostered by having opportunities for personal enmeshment in the care of dolls, stuffed toys, plants, and pets,[14] and by volunteering for attending to others in distress in and away from the institution. It is amazing how children, severely in want of attachment themselves, can get absorbed by the plight of children in heart-rending distress in distant places. Caring as an expression of love for others (humans, pets, or objects) has to be anchored in individual desires to do something and delivery of the care themselves. In learning to care, the caring process is the central issue. A child becoming concerned over another child in the home community, a frequent occurrence with many young residents, deserves a worker's follow-up. A call, visit, or note by the child to this real or assumed friend, regardless of whether the child's message can effectively offer comfort, is an important opportunity to experience reaching out to another human being. Some children are apt to express their affection to peers, others to younger children, and not surprisingly, many can share with their elders the very kind of care for which they themselves long. All require their respective opportunities (Wrenn, 1972).

Programming and freedom, play and productive work

Play and work, programming, and spontaneity – the many components within one segment of this chapter may seem perplexing. It may help to clarify if we conceptualize that programming deals with the effort of guaranteeing the residents a sound diet of everyday life experience which will hopefully enrich development. The essence of programming is not the scheduling of special events but envisaging and planning a day which promises to satisfy: with adults to support and to guide, with routines which serve to relax, where old ways of doing things are tolerated and new ways are possible, and above all, where life can proceed for fun and for keeps.

Work or play for children, adolescents, and hopefully for adults, involves strong personal investment and opportunities for self-realization. It is essential for children to have ample oportunities for work, activities where they can invest themselves and see the outcome (productivity) of their efforts as useful (marketable) to others. In one program the adolescents are asked to contribute four hours a week of work. Work projects are recommended and posted by the youngsters and staff. Once a resident signs up for a task, a commitment has been established. These teenagers work and frequently they work more than required. Their work assignments are a challenge to them and have value in their own eyes and the eyes of their community. Among some of their tasks are painting, genuine repair work, errands with the maintenance person, and fixing things for elderly neighbours, or cleaning up the sportsfield after a public event. Such tasks are extra; different from the daily chores of cleaning up their quarters, washing dishes, or emptying trash containers which are routines. The routines are necessary and time consuming, but they do not consistute challenge work experience.

Parallel to work, play is children's major avenue for learning, for exploring, for verifying themselves and, above all, for interacting meaningfully with others and environmental events in general. 'Play is active, energetic, creative and imaginative. . . . It is a vehicle by which youngsters learn of their world, of its construction and how they fit into the scheme of things' (Wilson, 1977 : 249). In play children not only deal with their difficulties; play is foremost a vital resource for learning by trial and error, to risk and to do for fun what is either too scary for real or what is better not done or not done yet. It is human to dare oneself and others in play; it is also human to do in play, 'just for fun', all the things which are taboo or at least not quite proper in ordinary life. In play we can win or lose without permanent repercussions; in play one can hurry or dally. In play, moreover, persons can practise and experience essential behaviours which can scarcely be tried out otherwise. Where else but in play can children or adults effectively practise at being outstanding or at playing unashamedly: the fool, to wait and to take turns while on the edge, to outwit, to cheat or to steal within permissible bounds without being caught, to co-operate, to hold back or to give for the greater good. Many forms of play have as a major ingredient a sampling of these: to bluff, to cheat, to steal, to annihilate as well as to share, to team up, or to save the day for all. Consequently, to play 'high court' or Star Wars, Bionic Woman, or Treasure Island can provide a rich give-and-take in fun and learning.

In no way in the light of our contemporary knowledge can this writer reconcile the notion that play serves as a reward for or as reinforcer of good behaviour. On the contrary, play is learning itself. Play provides sustenance for life, including good new problematic behaviours for further learning. The more disturbed or distressed children are, the less able they are to fall back on play as a help-rendering process. In other words, when play is needed most it is least at hand. With such an understanding, play often must be encouraged or induced as an essential ingredient of a child's daily life.

Program planning includes the creation of opportunities for children to do things together, to work, to play, and to fulfill the necessities of daily living (routines) in such a way that the customary procedures do not become routines of the day. Instead, each day's activities stand out for their challenge and adventure, with routines built in as a matter of fact. Program planning serves also the purpose of assuring each child ample private life in the inherent fishbowl existence of group living Simultaneously frequent joint activities will link together the residents of each unit; periodically the unit will be linked with other units of the program, and whenever possible connections will be made with people beyond the institutional barriers.

Provision of activities for children and youth in group care is such a vital area of concern that special attention needs to be called to additional comprehensive resources for this aspect of group care services. Readers may find the following publications helpful. Although some of these resources date back more than a decade, their content is still pertinent: DeNoon, 1965; Nicholson, 1975; Plank, 1973; Redl and Wineman, 1957 : 318–94; Whittaker, 1969; and Wilson, 1977, among others.

. . . And when the expected is not done

What should be our response when clearly enunciated expectations are not fulfilled? Such a question will likely bring forth a flood of answers or at least personal tension. Some readers may respond with the thought: 'Stand firm and make them!' Others may protest vehemently: 'It should not happen!' while many readers may be inclined to respond that 'There must be discipline!'

Perhaps the real concern should be with the fact that our expectations are important. We value what we expect of a child. In other words, the focus should be on the expectation rather than the violation. Focus on the violation ultimately comes to revolve around authority issues and a power struggle over who runs the place (Polsky, 1962); while continued concern with expectations maintains the original concern with what we value to be important.

Let us imagine a group of adolescents who return later than mutually agreed upon from an activity, or who 'forget' to pick up clothing strewn about their rooms. These kinds of situations are in conflict with a set of general expectations. Basic to this conflict is the clarity and degree of importance of these expectations rather than the implied disregard for the adults associated with these expectations. The care workers of the adolescents would have explicitly to convey again that they count on the youngsters' adherence to basic expectations. The expectations still stand regardless of being late or neglecting to straighten out belongings. Most noteworthy, non-compliance does not necessarily alter standards or become an issue of disobedience, rather non-compliance requires a persistence to find ways of meeting these expectations. The focus has to remain upon assisting children *to learn* to do as requested rather than struggling with them over who sets the rules and necessitating the establishment of a way of proving that expectations have been carried out. This latter approach shifts the issue from concern with standards to a power struggle over 'who is on top' (Ebner, 1979).

Let us imagine the rather common occurrence of an adolescent storing her clothing in helter-skelter fashion on the bottom of her open closet in the face of her care worker's explicit demand to straighten out the disorder. The worker is now faced with many alternatives for dealing with this training situation – namely, the care of clothing. Among other alternatives, a worker could take up techniques with this resident demonstrating how she can get it done. A worker could do the job *with* the adolescent to convey the importance of the task. The worker could insist upon priority for this task before time could be given to other activities, or the worker could reiterate her *personal* dismay and with it, her personal concern. The latter would leave the youngster to wrestle with her own conscience over the matter. Incidentally, in the case of a worker with a close attachment with the youngster, more persistent learning would typically occur with the last approach. The youngster's value acquisition would be most intimately challenged by the worker's strong personal appeal, by the worker's identification with her requirements, and in turn, by the girl's identification. We note in this example that the worker does not doubt her authority or power position. In each of the techniques employed, the focus has been on attending to the task.

In the foregoing paragraphs we tried to deal with the ever-present concern for discipline. Emphasis has to be upon assisting a child or youth to fulfill expectations in terms of their actual appropriateness. No direct consideration has been given in the face of non-compliance to what should be done or when and how children should be punished. Concern centres around the critical incident, critical for the child's or youth's learning, rather than the worker's self-esteem and survival (Beker, 1972).[15] The question then shifts from the kind of punishment each piece of violation requires, to what can be done toward the individual's mastery. It is assumed that children and adolescents learn in many different ways. Every possible medium for learning is to be utilized (Whittaker, 1979 : 38) as children and their care givers struggle together. Ways need to be found for learning to live together while living to learn, and for adding new styles continuously to meet and to fulfill tasks yet undone.

V Residential life as prelude and extension of a child's home life

Concurrent work with family and child in group care

Residential care is conceived in general as a temporary measure, even if placement sometimes promises to be for a considerable part of an individual's childhood. A child is placed, assigned, or committed – however the technical language denotes it – as a 'client' of the group care service. The child never *moves* there. Basically, children conceive of their family setting as their home and their home community. Such awareness requires that linkages with the previous home, friends, and other basic community contacts remain part of the child's life while in placement. Moreover, these continuous contacts evolve into participant roles and possibly even recipient roles of agency service in helping facilitate the child's successful return to his or her regular community.

As already implied, children do not lay aside their previous attachments and associations by a mere placement to a new care setting. Old relationships continue; they impact the quality of new ones, especially if these previous associations have been touched by uncertainty and *conflictual* alignment. The notion of a sense of having a past with continuity is essential for the children. Their care giving service needs to work with the children's past alignments and community affiliations as an integral aspect of the children's lives. The same position could be justified on a humanitarian basis; it is their right. Those people who have been intertwined in the child's life have a continuous stake, interest, and commitment; parents, friends, and others cannot be locked out by the altering of a child's care arrangements.

In these days of rapid communication contacts can be maintained by phone, exchange of letters, and face-to-face encounters either by children returning to their home sites or by family and friends dropping in at the group care place. Many child care group settings set as part of their policy the return home of children on weekends or for other regular periods. By means of these contacts child and parent are able to see each other and honour their attachments, however smooth or difficult, so that all can be actively assisted in acquiring skills for dealing with one another. These continued child–parent contacts require active assistance and planning by the group care service. Both parties, separately and together, need to be helped with the progression of their relationship. Counseling by social workers (Magnus, 1974), family therapy for all parties involved (Letulle, 1979), child management and human relationship skill training by the child care workers (Webster *et al.*, 1979), and any or all of these three interventive approaches may be applicable.

Most important in the approach suggested here, there is a shift away from conceiving placement in a linear model. Instead group care and home life are viewed as meaningful and interweaving components. In this framework, when the child returns home for a short or long stay the group care worker's interest, concern, and active involvement will go along. Conversely, while a child is in group care the parent (or parents) wants to know, should know, and is entitled to know of the child's life in the institution.

To facilitate contacts between the children in group care and their families, special thought needs to be directed toward providing an environment which furthers spontaneity and natural give-and-take. Among other factors, these encounters can be enlivened within the group care setting by a comfortable and inviting meeting place. Furniture has to be practical and adaptable for rearrangement to suit the situation. Preferably such a place should also include facilities where people can prepare food right on the spot for eating together. Eating assists with linking people. Often a parent wants to provide and is missed for his or her 'special' cooking. Child care workers might also on occasion join these gatherings. Indeed child, parent(s), and care workers are full partners in residential group care. Parents and care workers need not be competitive as alternate care givers; they are really co-care givers and are actually 'co-parenting' (Berkman, 1979).

'Visiting' home

In preceding paragraphs the author purposely avoided referring to parent's or children's visits. The author has been made aware of the inappropriateness of our use of this term at a time when parents are challenged to become more engaged in long range planning for their children (White, 1979). What do we convey when we urge parents *to visit their children* and schedule children *to visit their homes*?

Incorporation of parents' and others' active assistance into the group care program   In addition to continuous and meaningful contacts between child and parent, group care services may also want to search out ways in which the parents and other relevant home community contacts can be interwoven into the group care's service program. Involvement of parents, etc., in special events as spectators or participants or even as co-sponsors, are all possibilities. On other occasions, some parents, former teachers or friends, can be involved in helping with the painting of a room, a big cookie bake, a canning spree, a fix-the-bicycle day, spring gardening, or an ordinary house cleaning splash. These extra hands undoubtedly will provide a boost, and more important, parents and service become partners. Children and parents can also see and experience each other in different ways while being involved in a joint enterprise. At such work parties it might be even more advantageous when parents and their own children are not working together. Parents can then relate more easily to other children and perhaps a child could learn more easily about his parent's capabilities and contributions through the eyes of other children. Still more natural is the solicitation of family involvement when there can be ordinary give-and-take, such as stopping by spontaneously, thereby encouraging participation and exchange of information by an orderly but basically open-door policy. Parent(s)' and others' participation in parents' groups, advisory councils, service projects, or special task groups of the service, provide other avenues for sharing in the provision and hopefully the direction of the group care service (Whittaker, 1979 : 7 and ch. 6).

Partnership in care and treatment   The essential nature of a continuous partnership of the child, the group care agency, and the client's family or other relevant parties in devising the best care and treatment within the group setting can be well buttressed by recent research. These studies find a positive relationship between parental involvement and effective planning and successful outcome following foster (Fanshel, 1975) and group care (Durkin and Durkin, 1975). Moreover, much effort in residential care work is typically directed to overcoming the residents' unusual susceptibility to undue peer pressure. Such peer pressure is lessened in the face of stronger parental ties (Bronfenbrenner, 1970).

It is important also to point out that a good range of research findings over the past two decades have concluded that the effectiveness of residential treatment is more highly correlated with the amount of help children receive with their post-institutional problems of living than with the nature of their residential experience as such (Allerhand, Weber, and Haug, 1966; Taylor and Alpert, 1973). Post-institutional follow-up work logically requires the joint work of the persons involved in the actual group and home care: the child care workers (Maier, 1975 : 414), family members, social workers, and possibly other key persons (siblings, grandparents, neighbours, teachers, etc.).

A host of questions can be rightly raised whether this broadside approach is feasible at all. Ample case illustrations can be offered in which clients' families have either been perceived as unable or unwilling to cooperate and there will be situations where all efforts will be to no avail. In the majority of situations, however, the clients' families can be involved on some reasonable level, with range and degree of involvement varying greatly. This working partnership typically will not be smooth or complete; it will generally require an all out effort to move along in as active and synchronized a way as possible.

The group care service environment

What has been outlined as a full partnership between clients' home and group service environments can be also repeated as a refrain for the mutual involvement of the group care setting and its peripheral social and physical environment. Regardless of whether it is located in a densely inhabited area or in an isolated country spot, every group care setting has neighbours, a community, institutions, local events, and notable landmarks within its vicinity which make up its living environment.

The group care service, residents as well as all staff members, are in turn actually neighbours, community members, and a decisive service addition to their particular community. (The last point is more fully covered by Jerome Beker in chapter 5 in this book.) The group care service has a host of rich program opportunities in the utilization of neighbours (which in rural settings include the chickens, cows, horses, or pigs). Program is also enhanced by the mere fact of being a constituent part of a community – on a social, economic, and political level, the service has an intrinsic identity as one contributing institution among many others (schools, post office, churches, service clubs, businesses, and so forth). These aspects open up to residential children multi-resources for varied contacts and potential new footholds for a sense of belonging. To cite one illustration: a child writing or dictating a note to someone on the 'outside' requires the purchase of a stamp at the post office. Thereafter, the note has to be mailed. The course of that piece of mail from post office to delivery offers the possibility of establishing a sense of one's place in a regular continuity of the world beyond the child care centre. (Youngsters who have absolutely no ordinary contacts back home to write to still have their present or former social service workers, old teachers, policemen, or others they may recall.)

The environment of the group care setting provides the immediate social realities for program. As such these realities should be utilized and ultimate utilization depends much on the staff's own sense of anchorage in the community. Consequently a service has to expend considerable ingenuity and resource in assisting staff to be and to feel part of the community. This means seeing to it that staff members first feel fully a part of the agency itself, secondly that they have time and resources to become acquainted with the community as part of their work expectations, and lastly that staff members are continuously dealt with not only as constituents of the service but also as members of a joint community.

VI   Concluding summary

Looking back over this chapter we have been drawing an ever widening circle of environments; the rings expand like the rings of a pebble thrown into a pond. With each expansion each ring has become more inclusive, while the centre has become a fuller part of the whole. We started out with an everyday scene of group care. The difficulty of a single child intrinsically drew in other children and their child care workers. In reviewing a number of ordinary struggles which children face in their everyday growing up process, particularly when they have to deal with multi-primary attachment experience, we have been alerted to the pivotal role of the nurturing person. These primary life experiences that we have witnessed are strongly impacted by the spatial arrangements and accessibility to resources. As Bettelheim once wisely proclaimed, 'Love is not enough' (1950).[16] We paraphrase him, 'neither love nor space are enough'. We have learned that even the most caring workers within the most promising setting must be knowledgeable about human development and the application of such knowledge to the everyday care of children.

Curiously enough, much of residential work deals with the contradiction of differentiating and uniting. The moment the child leaves his or her home efforts have to be directed toward his or her return. New associations in the residence must not obliterate past and future ties. Ultimately then, group care extends beyond mere alternate care. It demands joint participation and the caring efforts of all parties in the child's life constellation.

Finally, in our visualization of this full partnership of child (or youth), his or her family and kin, and group care service program, we have briefly acknowledged that the group care service has its own neighbourhood as a vital resource for clientele and staff – and a rallying ground for temporary anchorage. If we place a high value on the child as a full part of this network, we note that the group care service has to ensure that staff themselves experience anchorage and ready entry into active community participation. Assured of these prerequisites, group care staff can venture in similar direction with the children or youth under their care.

Notes

(1) Professor of Social Work, School of Social Work, University of Washington, Seattle, USA.

(2) In earlier literature such counseling sessions have been defined as 'marginal interview'. They occurred 'marginally' to the ongoing casework or psychotherapy (Wineman, 1959). Presently, such counseling is more realistically conceived as part and parcel of the group care and treatment processes.

(3) Feeding, clothing, and attending lovingly to a child's needs are essential parenting features. However, the care worker becomes essentially 'the

professional caring parent' when ordinary parenting does not sustain a child's regular development.

(4) See Morris F. Mayer's dictum that an effective intervention has to meet the dual criteria, 'It has to be logical and it has to be psychologically correct' (Mayer, 1958 : 140).

(5) 'Buffer zone' refers to the personal spatial distance each person requires for his or her sense of personal privacy. These requirements are both idiosyncratically and culturally determined (Horowitz, Duff, and Stratton, 1970).

(6) One may wonder whether an old bust has a place in the livingroom of a residential treatment unit. In this instance, the eleven 13-year-old boys had incorporated this 'built in' piece of sculpture of the founder of the place as a useful feature of their living space.

(7) Credit for this cogent observation goes to a colleague, Monte Berke, Mercer Island Youth Service, Mercer Island, Washington, USA.

(8) Conversely, the negation of physical comfort is a vehement message of non-acceptance. Consider the studies of penal settings, punitive expressions and the accounts of concentration camps. In each of these accounts a restraining or denial of bodily requirements signify the one-down positions, disdain and isolation these captives had to endure.

(9) The Peanuts cartoon of Linus with his blanket is a classic illustration of the human significance of a transitional object.

(10) We need merely to envisage the young people of the 1970s as they wrapped themselves in corners, front entrances, or passages, detached from life around them, as well as these young people's insistence upon 'doing their own thing' amidst the close life of their communal living arrangements.

(11) In fact, children or adolescents rarely destroy things which they conceive as fully their own and they themselves enjoy. It is the author's experience that children at moments of severe anger, including temper tantrums, destroy many valuable items. However, somehow their radio, picture of a genuine friend and cherished pieces of clothing, etc. survive their seemingly blind path of destruction.

(12) See Jon R. Conte's searching cogent monograph on time-out procedures (Conte, 1978).

(13) Appreciation to Ted Teather for introducing me to this descriptive term.

(14) This necessity for caring opportunities suggests that pets, plants, pretty things and pseudo-art objects, brief service projects, etc. are apt to be more than marginal features of a residential treatment program.

(15) Beker (1972) *Critical Incidents in Child Care* is an excellent reader and teaching tool on the manifold individual and group crises which occur in the run of a day, week and month in a residential group care setting.

(16) It is the title of Bruno Bettelheim's first and most impactful publication: *Love is Not Enough*.

References

Adler, J. (1979) The Child Care Worker's Leadership in Group Process. *Child Care Quarterly* **8** (3): 196–205.

Ainsworth, M. D. (1972) Attachment and Dependency: A Comparison. In J. S. Gewirtz (ed.) *Attachment and Dependency*. Washington, DC: V. H. Winston.

Ainsworth, M. D., Bell, S. M., and Stayton, D. J. (1974) Infant–Mother Attachment and Social Development: Socialization as a Product of Reciprocal Responsiveness to Signals. In M. P. Richard (ed.) *The Integration of the Child into a Social World*. Cambridge: Cambridge University Press.

Allerhand, M. E., Weber, R., and Haug, M. (1966) *Adoptation and Adoptability: The Bellefaire Follow-Up Study*. New York: Child Welfare League of America.

Bakker, C. B. and Bakker-Rabdau, M. K. (1973) *No Trespassing: Explorations in Human Territoriality*. San Francisco: Chandler & Sharp.

Bale, T. (1979) Saying Good-bye in Residential Treatment. *Child Welfare* 58 (9): 586–96.

Barker, K. C. (1968) *Ecological Psychology*. Palo Alto, California: Stanford University Press.

Beker, J. (1972) *Critical Incidents in Child Care*. New York: Behavioural Publications.

Beker, J. (1975) Development of Professional Identity for the Child Care Worker. *Child Welfare* 54 (6): 421–31.

Berkman, W. A. (1979) Co-Parenting – An Outgrowth of a Boarding Home Program for Handicapped Children. *Children Today* 8 (4): 10–12.

Bertscher, J. (1973) The Child Care Worker as a Role Model. *Child Care Quarterly* 2 (3): 178–96.

Bettelheim, B. (1950) *Love Is Not Enough*. New York: Free Press.

Bettelheim, B. (1974) *A Home for the Heart*. New York: Alfred A. Knopf.

Bowlby, J. (1969) *Attachment and Loss*, Vols I and II. London: Hogarth Press.

Brazelton, T. (1977) Effects of Maternal Expectations on Early Infant Behavior. In S. Cohen and T. J. Comoskey (eds) *Child Development*. Itasco, Illinois: F. E. Peacock.

Brazelton, T., Koslowski, B., and Main, M. (1974) The Origins of Reciprocity: The Early Mother–Infant Interaction. In M. Lewis and L. A. Rosenblum (eds) *The Effects of the Infant on its Caregiver*. New York: John Wiley.

Bronfenbrenner, U. (1970) *Two Worlds of Childhood*. New York: Russell Sage Foundation.

Bronfenbrenner, U. (1976) The Family Circle: A Story of Fragmentation. *Principal* 55 (5): 11–24.

Bronfenbrenner, U. (1977) The Fracturing of the American Family. *Washington University Daily* 5 October.

Bronfenbrenner, U. (1979) *The Ecology of Human Development*. Cambridge, Massachusetts: Harvard University Press.

Browning, R. M. and Stover, D. O. (1971) *Behavior Modification in Child Treatment*. Chicago: Aldine.

Brunner, J. S. (1970) *Poverty and Childhood*. Detroit: Merrill Palmer.

Burmeister, E. (1960) *The Professional Houseparent*. New York: Columbia University Press.

Byers, P. (1972) From Biological Rhythm to Cultural Pattern: A Study of Minimal Units. Unpublished PhD dissertation, Columbia University, New York.

Cameron, J. R. (1978) Parental Treatment, Children's Temperament, and the Risk of Childhood Behavioral Problems: 2. Initial Temperament, Parental Attitudes, and the Incident and Form of Behavioral Problems. *American Journal of Ortho-psychiatry* **48** (1): 140–47.

Chess, S. and Hassibi, M. (1978) *Principles and Practice of Child Psychiatry*. New York: Plenum Press.

Condon, W. (1975) Speech Makes Babies Move. In Roger Lewin (ed.) *Child Alive*. New York: Doubleday.

Conte, J. (1978) The Use of Time Out Procedures in Group Care Facilities for Children: A Literature Review and Cautionary Note (monograph). Manuscript for publication, School of Social Work, University of Washington, Seattle.

DeNoon, B. (1965) Horses, Bait and Chocolate Cake. In H. W. Maier (ed.) *Group Work as Part of Residential Treatment*. New York: National Association of Social Workers.

Dupont, H. (1978) Affective Development: A Piagetian Model (mimeographed paper). Eighth Annual Interdisciplinary International Conference on Piagetian Theory and the Helping Professions, University of Southern California, Los Angeles.

Durkin, R. P. and Durkin, A. B. (1975) Evaluating Residential Treatment Programs for Disturbed Children. In M. Guttentag and E. L. Struening (eds) *Handbook of Evaluation Research*. Beverly Hills, California: Sage Publications.

Ebner, M. J. (1979) Hard Hats vs. Soft Hearts: The Conflict between Principles and Reality in Child and Adolescent Care and R_x Programs. *Child Care Quarterly* **8** (1): 36–46.

Escalona, S. K. (1968) *The Roots of Individuality*. Chicago: Aldine.

Fanshel, D. (1975) Parental Visiting of Children in Foster Care: Key to Discharge? *Social Service Review* **49** (4): 493–514.

Fixsen, D. L., Phillips, E. L., and Wolf, M. M. (1973) Achievement Place: Experiments in Self-government with Pre-delinquents. *Journal of Applied Behavior* **6**: 31–47.

Freedman, J. L. (1975) *Crowding and Behavior*. New York: Viking Press.

Goffman, E. (1961) *Asylums*. New York: Anchor Books.

Goffman, E. (1971) The Territories of the Self. In *Relations in Public Places*. Glencoe, Illinois: Basic Books.

Goldsmith, J. M. (1976) Residential Treatment Today: The Paradox of New Premises. *American Journal of Orthopsychiatry* **46** (3): 425–33.

Goocher, B. E. (1975) Behavioral Applications of An Educateur Model in Child Care. *Child Care Quarterly* **4** (2): 84–92.

Hall, E. T. (1969) *The Hidden Dimension*. New York: Anchor Books.

Hammond, J. W. (1973) Child Care Workers as Helpers to Parents. *Child Care Quarterly* **2** (4): 282–84.

Hersh, S. P. and Levin, K. (1978) How Love Begins between Parent and Child. *Children Today* **7** (2): 2–6 and 47.

Horejsi, C. (1979) Applications of the Normalization Principle in the Human Services: Implications for Social Work Education. *Journal of Education for Social Work* **15** (1): 44–50.

Horowitz, M. J., Duff, D. F., and Stratton, L. O. (1970) Personal Space and the Body Buffer Zone. In H. M. Proshansky *et al.* (eds) *Environmental Psychology: Man and his Physical Space*. New York: Holt, Rinehart & Winston.

Kagan, J. (1978) *The Growth of the Child*. New York: W. W. Norton; Brighton: Harvester Press.

Kazdin, A. E. (1977) *The Token Economy*. New York: Plenum.

Kessen, W. (ed.) (1975) *Childhood in China*. New Haven, Connecticut: Yale University Press.

Kirigin, K. A., Braukman, C. J., Atwater, J., and Wolf, M. M. (1978) An Evaluation of the Achievement Place Teaching-Family Model of Group Home Treatment for Delinquent Youths (mimeo manuscript). Department of Human Development, University of Kansas, Lawrence.

Kobak, D. (1979) Teaching Children to Care. *Children Today* 8 (2): 6–7 and 34–35.

Kuhn, T. S. (1970) *The Structure of Scientific Revolutions*. Chicago: University of Chicago Press.

Lee, D. (1978) Round-the-Clock Teaching-Parents. *Practice Digest* 1 (3): 14–16.

Letulle, L. J. (1979) Family Therapy in Residential Treatment of Children. *Social Work* 24 (1): 49–51.

Lewis, M. and Rosenblum, L. A. (eds) (1974) *The Effects of the Infant on its Caregiver*. New York: John Wiley.

Lindheim, R., Glasser, H. H., and Coffin, C. (1972) *Changing Hospital Environments*. Cambridge, Massachusetts: Harvard University Press.

Maccoby, E. E. and Masters, J. C. (1970) Attachment and Dependency. In P. H. Mussen (ed.) *Carmichael's Manual of Child Psychiatry*, Vol. 2. New York: John Wiley.

Magnus, R. A. (1974) Parent Involvement in Residential Treatment Program. *Children* 3 (1): 25–7.

Maier, H. W. (1974) A Sidewards Look at Change and What Comes Into View. In *Social Work in Transition: Issues, Dilemmas and Choices*. Seattle, Washington: School of Social Work, University of Washington.

Maier, H. W. (1975) Learning to Learn and Living to Live in Residential Treatment. *Child Welfare* 54 (6): 406–20.

Maier, H. W. (1976) Human Functioning as an Interpersonal Whole: The Dimensions of Affect, Behavior and Cognition. In *Teaching for Competence in the Delivery of Direct Services*. New York: Council on Social Work Education.

Maier, H. W. (1977) The Child Care Worker. In John Turner (ed.) *Encyclopedia of Social Work*. New York: National Association of Social Workers.

Maier, H. W. (1978a) *Three Theories of Child Development* (third revised edition). New York: Harper & Row.

Maier, H. W. (1978b) Piagetian Principles Applied to the Beginning Phase in Professional Helping. In J. F. Magary, M. K. Poulsen, P. J. Levinson, and P. A. Taylor (eds) *Piagetian Theory and the Helping Professions*. Los Angeles: University Press, University of Southern California.

Maier, H. W. (1979) The Core of Care. *Child Care Quarterly* 8 (3): 161–73.

Maier, H. W. (1980) Wanted: Information on the Children in 24-Hour Group Care Services. World Mental Health Conference: *Residential Treatments for Children and Adolescents*. Vancouver, BC: World Federation of Mental Health.

Maier, H. W. (1981a) To Be Attached and Free: The Challenge of Human Development. *Child Welfare* (in press).

Maier, H. W. (1981b) Dependence and Independence Development Throughou the Human Life Cycle: Implications for the Helping Professions. Manuscript for publication, University of Washington, Seattle.

Mayer, M. F. (1958) *A Guide for Child Care Workers.* New York: Child Welfare League of America.

Mehler, F. M. (1979) Houseparents: A Vignette. *Child Care Quarterly* 8 (3): 174–78.

Mehrabian, A. (1976) *Public Places and Private Spaces.* New York: Basic Books.

Mordock, J. B. (1979) Evaluation in Residential Treatment: The Conceptual Dilemmas. *Child Welfare* 58 (5): 293–302.

National Institute of Child Health and Human Development (1968) *Perspectives on Human Deprivation: Biological, Psychological and Sociological.* Washington, DC: National Institute of Child Health and Human Development, Department of Health, Education and Welfare.

Nicholson, M. L. (1975) Child Care Practice and the Passions of Today: Some Propositions. *Child Care Quarterly* 4 (2): 72–83.

Oxley, G. B. (1977a) A Modified Form of Residential Treatment. *Social Work* 22 (6): 493–98.

Oxley, G. B. (1977b) Involuntary Clients' Responses to a Treatment Experience. *Social Casework* 58 (10): 607–14.

Phillips, E. L., Phillips, E. A., Fixsen, D. L., and Wolf, M. M. (1971) Achievement Place: Modification of the Behaviors of Pre-delinquent Boys Within a Token Economy. *Journal of Applied Behavior Analysis* 4: 45–59.

Phillips, E. L., Phillips, E. A., Fixsen, D. L., and Wolf, M. M. (1973) Achievement Place – Behavior Shaping Works for Delinquents. *Psychology Today* 7 (1): 74–9.

Plank, E. (1973) Play Activities. In *Working Within Hospitals* (revised edition). Cleveland, Ohio: Case-Western Reserve University Press.

Polsky, H. W. (1962) *Cottage Six.* New York: Russell Sage Foundation.

Polsky, H. W. and Claster, D. S. (1968) *The Dynamics of Residential Treatment.* Chapel Hill, North Carolina: University of North Carolina Press.

Proshansky, H. M., Ittelson, W. H., and Rivlin, L. G. (eds) (1970) *Environmental Psychology: Man and His Physical Space.* New York: Holt, Rinehart & Winston.

Redl, F. and Wineman, D. (1957) *The Aggressive Child.* New York: Free Press.

Sable, P. (1979) Differentiating Between Attachment and Dependency in Theory and Practice. *Social Case Work* 60 (3): 138–44.

Schaefer, C. E. (1977) The Need for Psychological Parents by Children in Residential Treatment. *Child Care Quarterly* 6 (4): 288–99.

Schaffer, R. (1977) *Mothering.* Cambridge, Massachusetts: Harvard University Press; London: Open Books.

Schaffer, R. and Emerson, P. E. (1964) The development of social attachments in infancy. *Monographs of Social Research in Child Development* 29 (94).

Schwartz, W. (1971) The Practice of Child Care in Residential Treatment. In M. F. Mayer (ed.) *Healing Through Living.* Springfield, Illinois: Charles C. Thomas.

Segal, J. and Yahraes, H. (1978) *A Child's Journey.* New York: McGraw-Hill.

Seidl, F. W. (1977) Conflict and Conflict Resolution in Residential Treatment. *Child Care Quarterly* 6 (4): 269–78.

Sivadon, P. (1970) Space as Experienced: Therapeutic Implications. In Proshansky, H. M., Ittelson, W. H., and Rivlin, L. G. (eds) *Environmental Psychology: Man and His Physical Space.* New York: Holt, Rinehart and Winston.

Sommer, R. (1969) *Personal Space: (The Behavioral Basis of Design)*. Englewood Cliffs, New Jersey: Prentice-Hall.

Sroufe, L. A. and Waters, E. (1977) Attachment as an Organizational Construct. *Child Development* 48: 1184–199.

Sroufe, L. A. (1978) Attachment and the Roots of Competence. *Human Nature* October: 50–7.

Stea, D. (1970) Space, Territory and Human Movement. In Proshansky, H. M., Ittelson, W. H., and Rivlin, L. G. (eds) *Environmental Psychology: Man and His Physical Space*. New York: Holt, Rinehart & Winston.

Taylor, D. A. and Alpert, S. W. (1973) *Continuity and Support Following Residential Treatment*. New York: Child Welfare League of America.

Thomas, A. and Chess, S. (1977) *Temperament and Development*. New York: Brunner/Mazel.

Thomas, A., Chess, S., and Birch, H. G. (1964) *Behavioral Individuality in Early Childhood*. New York: New York University Press.

Thomas, A., Chess, S., and Birch, H. G. (1968) *Temperament and Behavior Disorders in Children*. New York: New York University Press.

Trieschman, A. E., Whittaker, J. K., and Brendtro, L. K. (1969) *The Other 23 Hours*. Chicago: Aldine.

Wax, D. E. (1977) Human Ecological Perspectives Within a Residential Treatment Setting for Children. *Child Care Quarterly* 6 (1): 51–60.

Webster, C. D., Somjen, L., Shoman, L., Bradley, S., Mooney, S. A., and Mack, J. E. (1979) The Child Care Worker in the Family: Some Case Examples and Implications for the Design of Family-Centred Programs. *Child Care Quarterly* 8 (1): 5–18.

White, M. S. (1979) Focus on Parental Visitation in Foster Care: Continuing Involvement Within a Permanent Planning Framework (project under the Child Welfare Services Training Grant Team 9038 T21 – research in progress). School of Social Work, University of Minnesota, Minneapolis.

Whittaker, J. K. (1969) Program Activities. In A. E. Trieschman, J. K. Whittaker and L. K. Brendtro *The Other 23 Hours*. Chicago: Aldine.

Whittaker, J. K. (1979) *Caring for Troubled Children*. San Francisco: Jossey-Bass.

Whittaker, J. K. and Trieschman, E. (eds) (1972) *Children Away From Home*. Chicago: Aldine-Atherton.

Wilson, T. (1977) Creating a Diversified Activity Program in a Small Psychiatric Institution for Children. *Child Care Quarterly* 6 (4): 248–58.

Wineman, D. (1959) The Life Space Interview. *Social Work* 4 (1): 3–17.

Winnicott, D. W. (1965) *The Family and Individual Development*. London: Tavistock Publications.

Wolf, M. M., Phillips, E. L., and Fixsen, D. L. (1974) *Achievement Place: Phase II*. Bethesda, Maryland: National Institute of Mental Health.

Wolf, M. M., Phillips, E. L., Fixsen, D. L., Braukmann, C. T., Kirigin, K. A., Wiher, A. G., and Schumaker, J. (1976) Achievement Place: The Teaching-Family Model. *Child Care Quarterly* 5: 92–103.

Wolf, M. and Proshansky, H. (1974) The Physical Settings as a Factor in Group Function and Process. In A. Jacobs and W. W. Spradlin (eds) *The Group as an Agent of Change*. New York: Behavioral Publications.

Wrenn, C. G. (1972) The Nature of Caring. *The Humanist Educator* June: 167–72.

Wylde, S. R. (1979) Arthur: A Creative Reward Program for Acting-Out Children. *Child Care Quarterly* 8 (3): 220–26.

Yawkey, T. D. and Bakawa-Evenson, L. (1977) Planning for Play in Programs for Young Children. *Child Care Quarterly* 6 (4): 259–68.

3 Planned care and treatment: the notion of programme

Leon C. Fulcher and Frank Ainsworth

Introduction

Programme or *program*,[1] as a term which is used to describe activities in and around a group care centre, is a common expression amongst practitioners, administrators, and educators in North America. The use of this term is much less common in Great Britain. In the United States and Canada, reference to programme may range from descriptions of specific activity with a particular person, as in *individual treatment programme*, to global descriptions of activity with groups or classes of people, as in *residential treatment programme* or *child welfare programme*. There seems to be no generally accepted term in the context of British social care services which could be said to clearly parallel the North American meaning of programme. At times *regime* might be used, or *schedule of activities*, *routine*, *timetable* and *provision*. The term *programme* is used, and increasingly so over the last decade, but there are essential differences which occur in the British use of this term compared with that of their North American counterparts.

Confirmation of this discrepancy can be found in a review of the group care literature published on either side of the Atlantic. Generally speaking, themes in the North American literature assume that *programme* provides a conceptual framework for developing individual and group care experiences (Whittaker, 1969; Pizzat, 1973; and Vinter, 1974). An assumption is made that programme will take account of a variety of influences which interrelate to achieve care and treatment objectives. Alternatively, themes in the British literature incline towards two different levels of consideration. The first focuses attention on social policy and the social administration of services within a health and welfare context (Jones, 1979; Millham, Bullock, and Hosie, 1978).[2] A second theme focuses attention on descriptive accounts of tasks which feature in the provision of direct care services (Beedell, 1970; Berry, 1975; Tizard, Sinclair, and Clarke, 1976; Walton and Elliott, 1980).

Any attempt at a comparative study of group care services for children between Great Britain and North America must acknowledge and account for the differential use of the term programme. We believe that this notion facilitates the more detailed analysis of planned care and treatment in any group care context, and even more importantly, between group care contexts. For this reason, we seek in this chapter to examine the notion of programme in such a way as to make it applicable to group care practice with children on both sides of the Atlantic. Three definitions are identified which allow consideration of promotional, planning, and instructional dimensions of programme. Secondly, consideration is given to what appear to be four levels of programme, ranging from specific accounts of activity to the more global social policy orientation. The social policy orientation is then briefly discussed as a planning dimension of programme in the provision of group care. Finally, a comparative framework is identified which may facilitate a contextual examination of planned care and treatment in group care for children and families.

Dimensions of programme

Programme, in its modern usage,[3] is a term which generally relates to three broad areas of consideration. The first concerns notice of an event and the details which make up the event. This we will refer to as the *promotional dimension* of programme and relates to that which one might receive when attending an event such as the theatre, a concert, or a sports activity. The second definition concerns the world of computer science, systems thinking, and mathematics. This we will refer to as the *planning dimension* of programme. In this sense, programme is used to define a logical sequence of questions which allow for the detailed analysis of complex interrelationships between a range of variables operating in a group care centre. A third area of consideration refers to what we would call an *instructional dimension* of programme and derives from the application of learning principles developed in psychology and education. In this sense, programme is used to identify a sequence of steps which could be followed in the learning of a skill, teaching of a concept, or in altering the frequency of observed behaviour. Both the planning and instructional dimensions of programme reflect modern developments in the world of science, each implying technical expertise and a precise analytical manipulation of particular elements.

Distinct emphases in the use of this term help to accentuate differences which can be found amongst group care practitioners on either side of the Atlantic. North American patterns of practice within the health care, education, social welfare, and justice services have been heavily influenced by the planning and instructional dimensions of programme. In so doing, social care policies and practices reflect the extent to which individualism and liberal philosophy underlie service provision in the United States and to a lesser extent in Canada (Pinker, 1979). Socialization through the primary school, secondary school, and higher education process has been heavily influenced by the application of learning theory, such that learning requirements are identified and these are subsequently developed through programmed instruction. This type of instruction includes precise learning objectives, carefully devised schedules of reinforcement, and systematic monitoring or evaluation of output. Emphasis on verbal skills, social skills, and the development of interpersonal competence are also general features of North American education. In this sense, programme planning and instruction are heavily equated with learning experiences which will 'produce' groups of individuals who have socially acceptable and marketable skills that are suited to a highly competitive socio-economic milieu. In most respects, patterns of group care practice in North America can be said to parallel this philosophy of learning.

Such views of practice, whether they refer to health care, education, social welfare, or justice services, are generally met with disquiet in Great Britain. The notion of programme is met with the suspicion that it implies overt social control and the manipulation of certain groups of society – the young, the old, or the disadvantaged – by other groups of society who hold more power through control of wealth, political position, and resources. By implication, the more powerful group will programme the less powerful groups to 'behave properly' and hence to further the ends of the programmers. Different historical and cultural traditions in Great Britain have emphasized the distribution of wealth and political power as major concerns in social policy. Instead of emphasizing rights for the individual, as in the United States, the emphasis is given more to the balance between obligations and rights. Thus a right leads to obligations and obligations establish rights, thereby establishing a concern for the place of individual welfare within the welfare of the group.

Reflecting this view, a generalization would be to say that educational practices have tended to reinforce attributes such as reasoning ability, analytical capacity, and technical competence, instead of the liberal arts and the development of interpersonal skills amongst graduates. Social reforms since the Second World War, whether inspired by benevolent conservatism or philosophies of socialism, have sought to reduce certain aspects of competition because of the inherent inequality which it is said to perpetuate. The 'unacceptable face of capitalism' is a description which has been used in political circles to distinguish between economic behaviour that is proper and occasions when corporate management exceed the limits of acceptable competition in the market place. It could be suggested that 'doing things in the proper way' is the implicit statement or tradition of social obligation in Great Britain.

Whether the philosophical or ideological principles mentioned above find realization in the practices of health care, education, social welfare, or justice services on either side of the Atlantic, is not for debate here. Rather, the preceding discussion was offered in an attempt to highlight differences in both contexts. An oversimplification would be to say that the emphasis in North America is on 'the means of production' with the belief that in getting the means right, the ends will be justified. In Great Britain there is an emphasis on 'the ends of production' with the belief that in properly identifying and agreeing to ends, means can be left to take care of themselves. We argue that orientations dominant in each national or regional context offer an important perspective to the others, each reflecting fundamental limitations in the extent to which planned care and treatment services have developed.

In North America, there has been a seeming disregard for the political and ideological implications of group care programming. In the pursuit of increasingly complex or refined models and techniques of treatment planning, very little attention is given to the implications of defining a social problem in such a way as to conclude that educational psychology or social treatment programmes are required. In Great Britain, the limitations are in many respects reversed. By concentrating on the historical development and on the broader questions of legitimacy for care and treatment provision, there remains a considerable reluctance to develop clear and concise expectations of individual and small group behaviour in the daily provision of group care services. The preoccupation with tasks in the delivery of services is very likely to be an extension of the social policy orientation which is dominant. Thus, to define tasks is to assume that the aims of a service are clear and that the justification for such aims is sound. Little attempt has been made to question this assumption in the professional development of group care personnel in Great Britain. Our view is that neither the planning and instructional dimensions of programme which are prevalent in North America, nor the social policy and promotional dimension of programme, which is somewhat more prevalent in Great Britain, can be ignored in the development of effective and humane programmes of group care for children and families.

By way of summary then, we have argued that an appreciation of the various uses of the term programme is an essential prerequisite for the comparative study of group care services on both sides of the Atlantic. It is a persistent theme which influences practice, yet its meaning is derived from various, and at times, competing views, opinions, and theories. Views which support the notion of programme attain considerable influence whether they are vaguely held, insecurely based or informed by research. As a notion which is quite central to the provision of group care services, the term programme can refer at one and the same time to four levels of consideration: (1) an individual plan for a child; (2) an activity for a group or an individual; (3) the service provided by a group care centre; and (4) the legislative, regulatory and funding arrangements whereby services are supplied to families and children through government intervention at various levels and through involvement of voluntary or private groups. It is to the fourth level of consideration, the organization and social policy context, that we now turn.[4]

Social policy: a planning dimension of programme

The historical development of services for handicapped people in Scandinavia serves to highlight the social policy dimension of programme. Grunewald (1972) identified four stages of development from which to review this history. The first, or *diagnostic stage*, featured identification of particular problems that occurred amongst a specific group of individuals. From such a social diagnosis came the formulation of plans to meet particular needs. The second stage, that of *specialization*, followed from the belief that particular needs are best met by special solutions which are tailored to meet those needs. Grunewald (1972:10) asserts that social policy activities during this second stage led to centralization of services in Scandinavia and the domination of services by specialists or professionals to whom the consumers of services subordinated themselves. The third stage of development, that of *differentiation*, occurred when social policies recognized that a particular service cannot be standardized for all recipients.

Grunewald considers that the Scandinavian countries are presently in the third stage of social policy development, that of differentiation, while other countries close to Scandinavia are mainly in the specialization stage. Our own view is that services in North America, ranging across a variety of handicapping conditions, are also mainly in the specialization stage. In some instances, however, especially in rural areas, development of services may still be at the diagnostic stage. The fourth stage of development, what Grunewald considers to be the last stage, is a composite one characterized first by *decentralization* of services, then provision for *integration* of services for the handicapped with those similar services which non-handicapped individuals receive in the community. We might describe this stage as reflecting a social policy of *normalization*.

Grunewald indicates that certain other developments must have taken place before the normalization of services can occur. Such developments include the provision of enough trained personnel who can offer services in a given geographical area, a transportation system for the handicapped, and a general state of readiness and relative open-mindedness among the population. If this hypothesis is correct, then initiatives taken by some social services departments over the past few years in Great Britain are worthy of consideration here. For example, some departments have sought to develop foster care services and thereby to reduce the volume of placements for children in residential and institutional care centres (Hazel, 1979). Such initiatives have supported a view that children should normally live in family-like environments and that all forms of service should support children living in their own or another family unit wherever possible (Strathclyde Regional Council, 1978). Residential care is viewed as a short-term, back-up service that is directly involved in supporting families, foster families, and children who are beginning to live independently in the community. This is the philosophy or ideology of professional service which is maintained through such a programme of social policy initiatives.

However, it should also be noted that regional policies advocating a reduction in residential care services and an increase in foster care provision come at a time when cutbacks are being demanded in the public service sector in Britain. Central government policies, in pressing for cuts, support a view that national and world inflation can be overcome by reducing public spending and controlling the money supply; by stimulating development in the private enterprise sector; and by encouraging personal initiative and innovation in order to bring about a prosperous and healthy society. Whether one supports such a government programme or not, such policies are themselves based on a philisophy or ideology of government. Hence, public spending cuts provide an additional social policy dimension to our consideration of services for children and families. Programmes are altered through a funding programme which realigns priorities for spending and which promotes development in the private sector.

Taken together – a policy calling for the reduction of institutional services and a policy calling for public expenditure cuts – both influences can be expected to contribute to a climate of uncertainty, apprehension, and frustration amongst personnel and consumers across the range of service systems. It is in this sense that we establish the clear relationship between the social policy dimension of programme and the other three dimensions referred to earlier. As social policy alters the proportion of beds in residential care as compared with day care or foster care places, so the service provided by a group care centre changes.

Often change is reflected in *reactive* or accommodative responses by personnel and clients, as the service provided by a group care centre changes through externally controlled processes. As the overall centre changes, so do the activities which are made available for groups and individuals over the days and weeks. Enthusiasm may wane. Undercurrents of tension and rumour amongst personnel are almost inevitably mirrored within the consumer group, and it is in this sense that individual plans for particular children are left open to question. Falling numbers in personnel, client referrals, or both, if even in the short-term, will substantially influence the programme of activities which can be provided in a group care centre. At the same time, a rapid increase in client referrals to a day centre without an increase in the number of personnel recruited to function in that day care staff team, will substantially influence the programme of day care activities provided. As the basic ingredients of a group care programme reduce to a weakened common denominator – that of managing turmoil – then other programme dimensions begin to suffer. The range of nurturing care opportunities may become narrowed; socialization experiences may be reduced, increasing the likelihood that negative socialization experiences will replace positive ones (Polsky, 1962); and specific therapeutic intervention experiences, including behaviour control issues, become increasingly paramount in the programme of activities offered. As these features of a group care programme suffer, then individual care and treatment programmes for especially vulnerable children may become open to question, were reasoned professional opinion sought and heeded. The dangers involved in restricting our conception of programme in group care practice should now be obvious. It is perilous to ignore the influences of social policy in planning group care programmes. We turn now to consider a comparative framework, which outlines eleven variables which facilitate a contextual exploration of group care programmes.

A comparative framework for the study of group care programmes

Problems of methodology in comparative research provides a useful starting point for the concluding section of this chapter. To put it another way, how does one know that what is seen on a visit to a residential centre in the State of Kansas or the Province of Manitoba has any comparison with a residential centre in Yorkshire? There are certain rules which must be followed if one is to avoid making simplistic and superficial statements about such visits. To begin with, one must be very cautious about evaluating whether one centre is better than the other. Similarly, one must be sure to question whether these centres perform a comparable function within their respective geographic areas. Some consideration should be given to the question of 'facts' and of the determination about which facts to observe (Holt and Turner, 1970).

The basis around which one seeks to 'understand' the significance of certain observations is also fundamental. Here, the criteria which are used to explain variations in practice are clouded by the absence of any global theory which informs group care work. This means that what one practitioner 'sees' in each centre may not be what another will see. We remind the reader that this was our primary reason for reviewing uses of the term programme, as orientations to planned care and treatment in different centres are likely to vary enormously. Furthermore, differences are likely to go well beyond the simple contrast between one theoretical orientation and another. For our purposes, it is not sufficient to compare all centres which work with children or delinquents. Nor is it sufficient to compare centres which work with adolescent boys in the United States, Canada, and Great Britain. Our concern is to overcome three problems in comparative research (LaPalombara, 1970).

First, we have tried to find a level of explanation which is applicable on both sides of the Atlantic. Second, we have attempted to select factors which will facilitate comparison, including cross-cultural comparisons and comparisons between various group care services within the same geographic context. Finally, we have tried to take account of the accessibility of information and its level of comparability. The history and meaning of certain information within its particular political or social climate has been a major concern. We have benefited greatly from the work of others in this field (Wolins and Gottesmann, 1971; Wolins, 1974; Vinter, 1976; Mayer, Richman, and Balcerzak, 1975; Millham, Bullock, and Cherrett, 1975; Millham, Bullock, and Hosie, 1978; Hazel, 1976; and Rushforth, 1979). It is our view that the furtherance of comparative research will offer an important way forward in the development of group care programmes for children and families.

Using a comparative framework, it is possible to identify at least eleven variables around which the study of group care programmes might proceed. The first of these concerns a *social mandate and focus* variable which determines to a large extent the type of population that will be found in a group care centre. Here the focus is on the legal commission to act as a care-giving service, usually involving a charge or command from a superior official or judge to an inferior, ordering him to act. The framework of legislation which empowers a group care centre to act is a feature of this programme variable. Whether a service is mandatory or voluntary is frequently a concern, although certain parallels can be drawn between a judge who commits a child to an institution for a period and a parent who assigns responsibility for the care of their child to a group care worker for the day. In each group care programme, there is an element of transferred authority to act, and, by definition, an object of transfer – in this case a child. By using social mandate and focus as a key variable for comparison, it is possible to construct specific hypotheses which will facilitate group care research.

A second variable around which comparative study might develop concerns *siting and physical design of centre*. The focus in this instance is directed towards the actual building which houses a group care centre, its location in relation to the general population and those distinguishing characteristics which give the building a history and public image. The converted manor house in the country or a cottage, built within the grounds of an institutional campus, offer different opportunities for group living as contrasted with the opportunities available when the centre is purpose-built in the midst of a large housing scheme. Features such as proximity to social amenities; the extent to which a facility can be made secure; and the extent to which the architectural design supports programme activity for a particular clientele: all are worthy of consideration. The uses of space inside and around a group care centre are also significant features. Furthermore, the boundaries between private and public space, as discussed by Maier in chapter 2, are important. The older the building, the more likely it is to have its ghosts. This characteristic is frequently encountered when an old boy or girl returns for a visit. The ghosts become evident in a former resident's stories, especially when none of the current group of staff or children actually shared experiences with the story-teller. One institution with which we have had contact is housed in a building that dates from the fifteenth century when it served as a priory for religious brothers. That it continues as a group care centre after five centuries means that the cloistering effect built into the building is still evident in its twentieth-century variation with adolescent girls (O'Toole, 1980). However, even purpose-built centres can be found to have the wrong purposes built into them. Hence our concern for a siting and physical design variable in the development of group care programmes.

A third variable which may be used for comparative study concerns *personnel complement and deployment*. One is invited here to consider the total number of people who are recruited to work in a group care centre; the various titles, roles, and configurations of status that can be identified; and the way that personnel are scheduled to work in the centre over the course of a day, week, or month. One of the common features of all group care programmes is the staff rota or schedule. It often becomes the focus for discussion amongst a group of children as they try to find out which staff will be taking them swimming or to the pictures. It is always a focus for discussion amongst staff when someone has failed to turn up for their shift or when a supervisor has rearranged the schedule. Through the more detailed analysis of group care staff rotas, several interesting features of programme can be illuminated. Some rotas have been fixed by union–management contract while others are negotiated or renegotiated weekly. Still other rotas might highlight only those periods when members are allowed time-off as could be found in a religious community for the handicapped. An interest in personnel and the patterns around which they are deployed can be met with varying levels of suspicion on the part of staff. Little wonder when one considers how influential the rota can be in shaping the life-style and personal life of workers. It is all too easy for one to view programme as something which is only about children. When one considers too, the requirements for personnel support amongst the stresses of group care work, the case is quite strong for examining personnel complement and deployment as important influences on group care programmes.

The fourth variable involves *patterns in the use of time and activity* in group care programmes. In group care, the timing of activities is of considerable significance if daily and weekly rhythms are to be established and maintained, thereby facilitating opportunities for child development (Maier, 1977). It might be argued that the same importance can be attributed to the timing of activities for staff. While the child care opportunities and principles contained in an exploration of 'the other 23 hours' are important (Trieschman, Whittaker, and Brendtro, 1969), such an exploration should also extend to a consideration of the 168 hours of a residential group care week. This allows one to consider routines of the day or week; differences between weekdays, weeknights, and weekends; and transition periods within a day or week, when certain activities may be of particular importance. Using a 168 hour time frame, it is possible to draw comparisons between the working week of residential care and day care centres, allowing one to consider more closely how a day care service might supplement and support family life for a child (Garland and White, 1980). Variations in activity over the seasons of a year are also worthy of consideration, highlighting as they will just how different a group care programme can be as it moves from summer, through autumn, winter and spring. Careful consideration of patterns in the use of time and activity should offer positive advantages in the development of planned care and treatment programmes for children and families.

Admission and discharge practices make up the fifth variable. Here, the focus of attention is on the way that new members join into the life of a group care centre and also on the way that people come to leave. Often there is little conscious attention given to the admission and discharge practices used in a centre. It is also essential that staff look at and prepare for the eventual departure of the child from the earliest days of his involvement. It is possible in some centres for one child to leave the programme in order to make room for another, hence one would expect to find some overlap between the two membership rituals. Rituals of this sort might be identified as being planned, as when working with a regular admissions day, or unplanned, as when responding to demands for twenty-four-hour emergency care. The admission process may be very selective with carefully negotiated discharge procedures. On the other hand, admissions may be open to a wide-ranging group of clients and discharge may be the same for everyone or left open to individual needs. The contrast in programmes between a residential treatment centre and a drop-in emergency centre will highlight the variations outlined above. The extent to which practices are made formal, such as with a case conference or review board, is another consideration. In contrast to the formal practices, an informal pattern might be identified when a child absconds as an alternative to discharge. Rites of initiation, rites of passage, graduation rituals, termination rituals, rites of excommunication, and last rites are all important features of social groups in any culture. Little wonder then why a consideration of admission and discharge practices offers a useful basis for programme planning in group care communities.

The sixth variable to be considered involves *social customs and sanctions*. Social customs are the usual ways of behaving or acting that one might identify as a participant-observer in a group care centre. There may be public customs and private customs, as might be found when observing children and staff together and when observing them while separate from each other. Interactions between residents and staff of Cottage Six at Hollymeade offer a useful example of this overt and covert dimension (Polsky, 1962). When considering sanctions, one would look to the rules or the laws of a group care centre. Associated with rules are the sanctions which are imposed as penalties for disobedience. Sanctions also serve to reward members for obedience, such as when sanctioning a special treat. Sanctions may suggest an economic or political act by an authority to coerce another or a group into conformity with certain norms of conduct. Here the focus is upon social order and methods of social control, allowing certain parallels to be drawn between the microcosm community of a group care centre and the community at large. Special attention must be given to the positive customs and sanctions, as well as attending to the negative ones. Both feature greatly in the life of any group care programme.

Social climate of the centre is a seventh comparative variable which might be used in examining group care programmes. As compared with earlier variables, this one is far more abstract and difficult to identify than the others. However, it is grounded in the experience of every direct care worker or supervisor who is able to sense the tone of a group by testing the social atmosphere which pervades a group care centre. Moos (1976:330–31) discusses social climate in terms of the 'personality' of an environment, and has devised a methodology for measuring it. He has noted a relationship dimension which refers to the extent to which people are involved in the environment, the extent to which they support and help one another, and the extent to which there is spontaneity and open expression amongst them. Moos' personal development dimension refers to aspects of personal growth and self-enhancement as they occur in an environment, and these are thought to vary somewhat among different environments depending on underlying purposes and goals. A system maintenance and system change dimension is thought to remain fairly similar across all environments. Aspects such as orderliness, the clarity of expectations, the degree of control, and the responsiveness to change are all thought to be features of this third dimension of climate. While including this variable in a comparative framework for the study of group care programmes, it is worth noting that the research evidence which supports its inclusion is still inconclusive, especially as concerns cross-cultural study. However, such evidence as is available supports grounded practice to the extent that we believe social climate can be assessed and is an influence in the work of any group care centre.

The eighth variable involves *links with family, school, and community*. At one level, a simplistic counting, or census approach to observing and recording contacts with 'outsiders' would establish a baseline against which more rigorous study might proceed. Identifying the times when 'outsiders' are most likely to visit, along with clarification of which 'outsiders' come at which times, offers further clarification of the extent and means whereby important 'outsiders' are engaged in the work of group care. In identifying the links which build up between a group care programme and the social supports which exist outside the centre, an inevitable question emerges. It concerns the activities of 'insiders'. When looking at this programme variable, it would seem increasingly that an assessment is required of both: the involvement of 'outsiders' (an ideal) and the real or imagined tensions which are experienced amongst the 'insiders' (a reality), often resulting from planned and unplanned involvement of 'outsiders' in an active group care programme. Through initiating such an assessment, one is forced to consider the extent to which interpersonal politics and intrigue (for both good intrigue and bad exist in all work groups) endorse or restrict collaborative practice which crosses the boundaries of a group care centre and its community. Through comparing planned and unplanned involvement of 'outsiders' in group care programmes – with a high and low-involvement measure of programme participation by 'outsiders' – one may find a practical framework against which to assess performance effectiveness of the service with children and families. In a similar way, such exploration facilitates study of inter-disciplinary boundaries which operate as a multi-disciplinary group care regime determines the pattern of programme involvement of 'outsiders'. For a variety of reasons, a study of links between group care centres and family, school, and other community members is important.

The ninth variable concerns *the criteria used for reviewing and evaluating performance*. Whether these criteria, and the practices which develop, are imposed by external sources, such as the legal framework, an administrative policy, or by judicial mandate, or whether they are imposed according to the actions and decisions reached by an individual or a staff group, some criteria will nevertheless appear, whereby review and evaluation of social behaviour is carried out in every group care programme. The criteria which might be used may range from vague comparisons of one child being like so-and-so to quite elaborate attempts to evaluate psychosocial development and behavioural competence. Time or length of stay is frequently a controlling variable, such as would be the case in weekly, three monthly, or six monthly reviews. Meetings of one sort or another are often used to evaluate performance of group members, such as might be found in a therapeutic community meeting .or an inter-disciplinary review. Programmes vary in the extent to which staff make all decisions, or where there is sharing which occurs between children, families, and staff around the timing of key decisions. It is reasonable to suggest that some theory, ideology, philosophy, or value orientation will be found to underpin review and evaluation in a group care programme. In this respect, attention to behavioural schedules or points might suggest an orientation which stresses social learning; group evaluations might suggest aspects of a therapeutic or religious community orientation; while a case conference discussing clinical symptoms might suggest a medical orientation. Whether the criteria used in reviewing and evaluating performance are made explicit, or remain implicit in the operation of a group care programme, such criteria are nevertheless important when comparing one programme and another.

The tenth variable, *theoretical or ideological determinants,* is reflected in the criteria used for review and evaluation of group care programmes.

This variable refers to the technical, moral, and philosophical justifications which are used by the 'producers' of programme, to account for their activities with the 'consumers' of programme. Instances will vary whereby this variable is found to influence programmes. The justifications given by a junior member of staff to a supervisor concerning actions with children, may be framed in very personal terms which reflect basic attitudes and moral values. Equally, these same justifications may refer to religious beliefs, theoretical orientations, or political philosophy. Beit-Hallahmi and Rabin (1977) have used this variable in exploring the group care kibbutz as a child-rearing environment. Their findings suggest that the influence of collectivist ideology, which formed the basis for the kibbutzim movement, is closely related to the child-rearing practices found in these social laboratories today. By contrast, studies of group care centres in Great Britain have tended to rely on other variables to describe and explain differences in approach, except when referring to the social policy dimension of practice. However, studies in North America have frequently sought to use theoretical models to explain whether one programme was any more effective than another. Whittaker, who follows in chapter 4, offers a helpful discussion of four theoretical orientations which have influenced group care for children in the United States.

The last variable to be considered here involves *cost factors* in group care. Ordinarily, attention to cost factors has referred to aspects of budgeting, cost accounting, and patterns of spending in the operation of a group care programme. However, thanks partly to the work of economists and others associated with the Personal Social Services Research Unit at the University of Canterbury at Kent, further dimensions of costing can now be identified. Working over the past few years, the PSSRU has developed a 'production of welfare' model which can be used in examining the costs involved in supplying group care services. Using this model as the basis for enquiry, social costs might be identified to the extent that a community makes use of a group care service resource and the extent to which the service, in turn, makes use of community resources. Opportunity costs might be identified to the extent that resources are available within a day or living unit programme to provide activities which will stimulate and enable growth and development amongst, and on behalf of a service consuming group. Personal costs might be assessed to the extent that nurturing care, socialization experiences, and specific social learning opportunities are of personal benefit to a child and his family. Martin Knapp, writing in chapter 11, provides a helpful introduction to additional ways of looking at cost factor analysis in group care.[5] Consideration of the 'production of welfare' model for costing group care services would seem to be worthy of attention. It helps to open the way to much more discriminating and deliberate attempts to consider the economics of group care for children and families.

Conclusion

In summary, we have tried to identify differing patterns of use and problems of definition when looking to the term *programme* as a conceptual reference for planned care and treatment in group care. Considering both sides of the Atlantic, three definitions of programme were identified, referring to a promotional dimension, a planning dimension and an instructional dimension. Next, we identified four levels of consideration whereby the term programme is used in group care for children and families. These included: an individual plan for a child; an activity for a group or an individual; the service provided by a group care centre; and the legislative, regulatory, and funding arrangements whereby services are supplied to families and children through government intervention at various levels or through involvement of voluntary and private groups. Closer attention was given to the social policy which surrounds and influences programme planning in group care. Finally, a comparative framework was provided which may facilitate the study of group care programmes on both sides of the Atlantic. Eleven variables were identified around which the comparative study of programmes might proceed. These were:

 (1) social mandate and focus
 (2) siting and physical design of centre
 (3) personnel complement and deployment
 (4) patterns in the use of time and activity
 (5) admission and discharge practices
 (6) social customs and sanctions
 (7) social climate of the centre
 (8) links with family, school, and community
 (9) criteria used for reviewing and evaluating performance
(10) theoretical or ideological determinants
(11) cost factors.

Some of these variables are drawn from a social policy perspective, while others rely heavily on anthropology, industrial relations, or sociological perspectives. Compatability is also sought with developmental perspectives in psychology and social psychology. Throughout, we have tried to avoid imposing a particular theoretical structure on group care practice. Instead, we have tried to identify common features which transcend all group care centres. We acknowledge, however, that to avoid naming any particular theory of group care is by definition a reliance on some other theoretical base, or perhaps more correctly, a basis in philosophy or ideology. We argue for an orientation which draws broadly from a range of perspectives when seeking to apply theory in the development of group care programmes. Furthermore, we believe that inductive learning and practice wisdom should go hand in hand in the practice of group care. The human drama of caring is very powerful, often reflecting both destructive and creative forces at play in the lives of the actors. We have tried to show how considerations of planned care and treatment in group care must pay attention to a greater variety of variables than have generally been used to date. To stay with our theatrical metaphor: actors, supporting actors, staging, lighting, and props are just as important as the lines of a script in determining whether a performance is understood and well-received by the audience. We believe that the same features apply when studying the drama of life in any active group care programme.

Notes

(1) We offer both principal spellings of the term, because spelling offers the first clue as to which side of the Atlantic the term relates when discussing services. As this paper has been written while located in Great Britain, it conforms to the British conventions concerning spelling.
(2) Discussions with Decky Watson, Director of Social Work Courses at Stirling University, have helped to clarify the social policy dimension of welfare and social work practice as it differs between North America and Great Britain. By and large, when considering the professional education of social workers and other human service personnel, there is no real counterpart in North American colleges and universities for the significant contribution made to professional training in Great Britain through the academic study of social policy and administration. The Department of Social Services Administration at the University of Chicago is an interesting exception, although social services administration is a more restricted component of the broader study of social policy and social administration found in Britain.
(3) The reader is referred to three dictionaries – *Chambers' Dictionary*, *Oxford Dictionary* and *Webster's Dictionary* – to find reference to three derivations of this word. The 1962 Chambers publication identifies programme as an obsolete Scottish word. The 1976 Oxford publication identifies the word as coming primarily from the United States and the international language of computers. Meanwhile, the American publication identifies the word as emerging from the French and Greek derivations. Our professional experience over the past twelve years or more has taught us a good deal about our native tongue, English. Natives are tolerant and frequently amused to find mere social scientists asserting that American, Canadian and English are not necessarily the same language. Similarly, Scottish-English, Irish-English,

Welsh-English and English-English vary considerably within a geographic area much smaller than most states and provinces in the United States or Canada. South African-English, Australian-English and New Zealand-English vary again. Having discovered the obvious, we do feel that sufficient other social work and group care practitioners have also made this mistake, thus warranting this footnote. Language is intimately wound up in culture. In developing a language for group care practice, we believe that cultural dynamics are more important than words.

(4) Urie Bronfenbrenner (1977) has identified four systems of influence which assist considerations of the experimental ecology of human development. These four systems of influence – the microsystem, the mesosystem, the exosystem, and the macrosystem – have certain parallels with the four dimensions of programme outlined in this chapter. The social policy dimension as we refer to it is probably to be located between Bronfenbrenner's exosystem and macrosystem, incorporating elements of both. In other respects, it would seem appropriate to separate out certain elements from his exosystem and make elements of his macrosystem more distinct.

(5) Martin Knapp's chapter in this volume is also *Discussion Paper No. 141* to be produced by the Personal Social Sciences Research Unit at the University of Canterbury at Kent.

References

Beedell, C. (1970) *Residential Life with Children*. London: Routledge & Kegan Paul.

Beit-Hallahmi, B. and Rabin, A. I. (1977) The Kibbutz as a Social Experiment and as a Child-Rearing Experiment. *American Psychologist* **32** (7): 532–41.

Berry, J. (1975) *Daily Experience in Residential Life*. London: Routledge & Kegan Paul.

Bronfenbrenner, U. (1977) Toward an Experimental Ecology of Human Development. *American Psychologist* **32** (7): 513–31.

Garland, C. and White, S. (1980) *Children and Day Nurseries*. London: Grant McIntyre.

Grunewald, K. (1972) The Guiding Environment: The Dynamic of Residential Living. In V. Shennan (ed.) *Subnormality in the 70's: Action for the Retarded*. London: National Society for Mentally Handicapped and World Federation of Mental Health. Also in D. M. Boswell and J. M. Wingrove (eds) (1974) *The Handicapped Person in the Community*. London: Tavistock Publications.

Hazel, N. (1976) Child Placement Policy: Some European Comparisons. *British Journal of Social Work* **6** (3): 315–26.

Hazel, N. (1979) New Patterns of Placement for Adolescents: Professional Fostering and Other Experiments. *The Third Aberlour Trust Lecture*. Stirling, Scotland: Aberlour Child Care Trust.

Holt, R. T. and Turner, J. E. (eds) (1970) *The Methodology of Comparative Research*. New York: Free Press.

Jones, H. (1979) *The Residential Community: A Setting for Social Work*. London: Routledge & Kegan Paul.

LaPalombara, J. (1970) Parsimony and Empiricism in Comparative Politics: An Anti-Scholastic View. In R. T. Holt and J. E. Turner (eds) *The Methodology of Comparative Research*. New York: Free Press.

Maier, H. W. (1977) The Core of Care. *The First Aberlour Trust Lecture*. Stirling, Scotland: Aberlour Child Care Trust.

Mayer, M. F., Richman, L. H., and Balcerzak, E. A. (1975) *Group Care of Children*. New York: Child Welfare League of America.

Millham, S., Bullock, R., and Cherrett, P. (1975) *After Grace – Teeth*. London: Human Context Books.

Millham, S., Bullock, R., and Hosie, K. (1978) *Locking Up Children*. Farnborough, Hants: Saxon House.

Moos, R. H. (1976) *The Human Context: Environmental Determinants of Behavior*. New York: John Wiley.

O'Toole, M. (1980) Group Care Practice Study. Unpublished paper, Department of Sociology, University of Stirling.

Pinker, R. (1979) *The Idea of Welfare*. London: Heinemann.

Pizzat, F. J. (1973) *Behavior Modification in Residential Treatment: Model of a Program*. New York: Behavioral Publications.

Polsky, H. W. (1962) *Cottage Six: The Social System of Delinquent Boys in Residential Treatment*. New York: Russell Sage Foundation.

Rushforth, M. (1979) *Committal to Residential Care: A Case Study in Juvenile Justice*. Edinburgh: Scottish Office Central Research Unit.

Strathclyde Regional Council (1978) *Officer/Member Report – Child Care*. Glasgow: Social Work Committee.

Tizard, J., Sinclair, I., and Clarke, R. V. G. (1976) *Varieties of Residential Experience*. London: Routledge & Kegan Paul.

Trieschman, A. E., Whittaker, J. K., and Brendtro, L. K. (1969) *The Other 23 Hours*. Chicago: Aldine.

Vinter, R. D. (1974) Program Activities: An Analysis of Their Effects on Participant Behavior. In P. Glasser, R. Sarri, and R. Vinter (eds) *Individual Change Through Small Groups*. New York: Free Press.

Vinter, R. D. (1976) *Time Out: A National Study of Juvenile Correctional Programs*. Ann Arbor, Michigan: University of Michigan.

Walton, R. G. and Elliott, D. (1980) *Residential Care: A Reader in Current Theory and Practice*. Oxford: Pergamon Press.

Whittaker, J. K. (1969) Program Activities. In A. E. Trieschman, J. K. Whittaker, and L. K. Brendtro *The Other 23 Hours*. Chicago: Aldine.

Wolins, M. and Gottesmann, M. (1971) *Group Care: An Israeli Approach*. New York: Gordon & Breach.

Wolins, M. (ed) (1974) *Successful Group Care*. Chicago: Aldine.

4 Major approaches to residential treatment

James K. Whittaker[1]

Several cautions are in order before reading the following paper. First, the review of theoretical approaches *is* selective: within each of the major headings, the work of many additional contributors could have been included. While the limits of space prevailed, the approaches considered are at least representative of the *major* sets of ideas that have influenced residential treatment in North America over the last ten or fifteen years. Secondly, the term 'perspective' is used advisedly since there is a continuing lack of any overall theory of residential treatment – a theory which is likely to be constructed slowly, piece by piece from the ground up, rather than rendered – whole cloth – from some yet to be discovered body of knowledge. This is essentially a vote for *induction* over *deduction* to answer the single most important question for residential treatment so well put by Quay in a recent review (1979 : 409): namely, the need to identify the critical independent variables in a residential treatment setting. Finally, it would be misleading to suggest that the question of theory for residential treatment is, at present, uppermost in the minds of American residential care staff or senior administration. Several other issues demand more immediate attention. The first is, simply, *cost* – or, more accurately, cost benefit. We have moved beyond the dramatic case illustration (e.g. that one could provide tuition and maintenance at the most exclusive boarding school *and* the twenty-four hour per day services of a psychotherapist more cheaply than the present costs of some residential centres) to the point where many funding authorities have simply put a lid on the amount they will spend for residential child care and are more carefully linking funding with severity of the child's disturbance. Highest hit are those establishments with higher staff ratios (hence, a higher cost of care) who face increasing pressures to keep bed spaces filled with more severely disturbed children. A second major cluster of issues concerns *institutional abuse* and *neglect* and *permanency planning*. In the past year alone, two national studies and two separate Congressional investigations in America have uncovered major abuses in the substitute child care system. In addition to actual physical and psychological abuse, they include: inappropriate (often premature) placement, inadequate case planning and review (resulting in 'drift'), lack of proper staff training and absence of continuity e.g. follow-through with natural families, liaison work with schools, and other informal helping networks. While such issues may not seem directly related to the question of theory, they are very much related to the question of purpose in residential treatment and will thus lead, ineluctably, to the principles, concepts, and constructs that will inform any new conceptualization of residential practice.

Two final caveats are also in order in approaching the paper which follows: first, it will be obvious to both British and American readers that the focus is on residential treatment for troubled children – not the broader spectrum of group care services encompassed by this volume. In part, this has to do with the fact that in most of North America the placement of choice for the dependent or neglected child would be family foster care. With some few regional exceptions, the community 'children's home' has pretty much disappeared from the scene or has been transformed into a treatment oriented group residence. In fact, while other forms of group care for children – shelter care and respite care, for example – have begun to flower in the last few years, it is probably safe to say that to the extent that North America has contributed anything to group care theory and practice, it has been precisely in this area of residential treatment. Finally, the paper deals only in part with the general body of outcome research on residential treatment, in large part because it tells us precious little about the specifics of the treatment model being tested. The interested reader will find more complete reviews of the outcome literature in Whittaker (1979:186–204), Durkin and Durkin (1975) and Quay (1979).[2]

'How can these children be helped?' is a question that has vexed child welfare professionals and lay citizens for well over a century. While most nineteenth-century programs for troubled children stressed moral conversion as a necessary requisite for change, there was, even then, a recognition of the enormous power of the total living environment as a potent force in changing children's attitudes and behaviour (Whittaker, 1971a). Exactly how one identifies all the powerful forces in a group living situation and redirects them towards therapeutic goals – in essence, creating a therapeutic milieu – is a question for which we still have no definite answer. That we continue to struggle after so many efforts by talented and dedicated theoreticians and practitioners is testimony to the complexity and difficulty of the problem. To understand our present situation a little better, this chapter will explore the seminal influences on the development of milieu treatment for the troubled child and his family and critically review existing approaches to the therapeutic milieu.

Psychoanalytic approaches

In the early 1930s, a young autistic girl was brought to Sigmund Freud for treatment; Freud referred the child to his daughter, Anna, who specialized in child psychoanalysis. Anna Freud determined that the child was in too regressed a condition for psychoanalysis and that what she really needed was a totally psychoanalytically oriented living environment. She suggested a young art student couple who had a burgeoning interest in psychoanalysis and education. The young couple agreed and took the child into their family for what was to be a six-year stay. Thus, the lifelong work of a pioneer in the residential treatment of severely disturbed children – Bruno Bettelheim – was launched. (Anna Freud continues her lifelong work at the Hampstead Child Therapy Clinic in London.)

The group that was to have the most profound and lasting influence on the development of milieu treatment in the United States included a large number of refugees from Nazi persecution, who came to this country from Germany and Austria in the late 1930s and early 1940s. They were strongly influenced by psychoanalysis – particularly in its applications to education – and by the power of the group association; and their collective contribution literally *was* the literature on milieu treatment for children from the 1940s through the 1960s. These pioneers included Bruno Bettelheim (1950, 1955, 1967, 1974; 1948, with Emmy Sylvester); Fritz Redl (1959, 1966; 1957, with David Wineman); Susanne Schulze (1951); Gisela Konopka (1946, 1954); Morris Fritz Mayer (1960; 1971, with Arthur Blum); and Eva Burmeister (1960). While their adherence to Freudian concepts varied in degree and while the children with whom they worked ranged from autistic to delinquent, they all attempted to apply basic psychoanalytic principles to the child's total living environment. Of this distinguished group, two individuals – Bruno Bettelheim and Fritz Redl – stand pre-eminent. Their work spans the continuum of childhood disturbance from the solipsistic retreat of the autistic child (Bettelheim) to the acting out of the preadolescent delinquent (Redl). (No attempt will be made here to summarize the contribution of all the individuals mentioned here. The reader is urged to consult the original sources for a fuller explanation. Other contributions include Noshpitz,

1962; Goldfarb, Mintz, and Stroock, 1969; Cummings and Cummings, 1963.)

The two critical forces in the development of psychoanalytically oriented milieu treatment for children in the United States consisted of the contribution of the group already mentioned and the concurrent influence of the child guidance movement, with its emphasis on individual psychotherapy as the treatment of choice for the disturbed child and the psychiatric team as the preferred model of organization.

Bruno Bettelheim   Bettelheim's contribution to the treatment of severely disturbed children was moulded by two major life influences: psychoanalysis and his experiences as a prisoner in the Nazi concentration camps of Dachau and Buchenwald. From psychoanalysis, he gained an understanding of the elaborate unfolding of the human personality, in all its vicissitudes; from his prison experiences, he discovered the resiliency of the human spirit in overcoming the most degrading environments.

From 1944 to 1973, he was director of the University of Chicago's Sonia Shankman Orthogenic School for emotionally disturbed children – a school that continues in the mould he cast. His books and articles cover a wide-ranging sphere of interests, including the concentration camp experience, prejudice, child development, and communal child rearing. Most pertinent to our discussion here are the volumes directly based on his experiences at the Orthogenic School: *Love Is Not Enough* (1950), *Truants from Life* (1955), *The Empty Fortress* (1967) and *A Home for the Heart* (1974). Bettelheim's (1974 : 5) self-appraisal of his work is as follows:

> '*Love Is Not Enough* was meant to suggest that a consistent therapeutic philosophy, with careful thinking, planning, and acting on it, has to underpin that tender care which is necessary if one is to help a psychotic person gain mental health. . . . The book illustrated this principle by describing big and small events alike as they followed each other in the course of the day, in the life of those whom the institution served.
>
>   The next book, *Truants from Life*, contained only a short statement on the overall treatment success as of that time; the essential content consisted of four long case histories. It was hoped that these would show how – and why – the personalities of these children unfolded during the years they lived at the institution. From their quite different life histories and their various pathologies (severe delinquency, anorexia, institutionalism, and childhood psychosis), the reader could see how a unified philosophy, and an institution based on it, is helpful in restoring mental health. . . . Many years later, *The Empty Fortress* was to

present a more complete discussion of the therapeutic results of the Orthogenic School for the most severe form of childhood psychosis – infantile autism. *A Home for the Heart* was written to make this particular form of total therapy useful to others by detailing what it consists of, and by telling the story of the staff, because they are all important for its success.'

It is difficult if not impossible to capture what is essential in these volumes, for it is the anecdotes and images that remain imprinted on the mind of the reader. For example:

Bettelheim explaining that, in order to protect his child patients, no parent was ever admitted to the school's living area (1974 : 210).

Bettelheim cajoling an adolescent anorectic girl to drink a glass of milk and then securing her commitment to enter treatment (1974 : 176).

Bettelheim's gentle description of the disturbed child's slow transition from dreams to waking (1950 : 83).

Bettelheim's account of Paul, who progressed from 'wild critter' to university student (1955 : 153).

Bettelheim – who, it will be remembered, once described mothers of autistic children as 'feral mothers' (1959) – passing off behavioural approaches to infantile autism as reducing children to the level of 'Pavlovian dogs' (1967 : 410).

Bettelheim's uncanny sense of the effect of architecture on human behaviour (1974 : 130–180).

Bettelheim's detailed account of a staff member's living quarters – well organized in the northern half, disorganized in the southern half – as representative of her early unresolved years in the Deep South and her present well-integrated life in the North (1974 : 299).

While there is much of value and sheer brilliance in Bettelheim's work, it is a difficult approach to put into operation. To be sure, his clinical accounts are fascinating descriptions of what disturbed behaviour is like, though in my judgment many are based on false assumptions and sheer speculation about the origins of childhood disorders. Bettelheim's purposeful isolation of parents from the treatment environment – in the face of recent studies indicating the cruciality of the transition from institution to community (Allerhand, Weber, and Haug, 1966; Taylor and Alpert, 1973) and the potential for involving parents as full participants in the treatment process (Schopler and Reichler, 1971a) – indicates a rigidity of position apparent in other areas of his model; for example, in his refusal to analyze fairly the more recent behavioural approaches to childhood psychoses. I can still recall his response at a professional meeting some years ago to a questioner who asked (quite innocently) how the recent experiments in behavioural therapy with psychotic children should be 'answered'. Bettelheim responded: 'Freud said it long ago – there will always be dogs barking at the wheels of the caravan, but the caravan rolls on.' I can remember, as a young practitioner at the time, wondering if the dogs were, in fact, trying to communicate something to the caravan driver – perhaps a loose wheel – or a road missed? On a conceptual level, his model of milieu treatment is really no model at all but, rather a collage of case vignettes, clinical observations, and descriptions of routine – fascinating to read in part, difficult to comprehend as a unified whole. In fact, there is such an inordinate amount of idiosyncrasy (and I intend no derogation here) in his work – for example, his extreme 'protection' of the milieu against visitors and parents – that one is left wondering whether his methods could be applied successfully elsewhere.

On the positive side, Bettelheim's passion for detail is reflected in every clinical account. His respect for the individual is a theme that recurs throughout his work, and his attention to the therapeutic impact of the events of daily living – the rules, the routines, the games and activities, and the struggles – helped to turn an entire mental health profession's attention from the therapy room to the life space.

On the whole, however, a reader is forced to conclude reluctantly that the essential ingredient in Bettelheim's model of milieu treatment is Bettelheim himself. His is the omnipresent force – fathoming the depths of a child's behaviour; challenging a staff member to look into himself; nurturing a frightened child in the night; stoutly defending his model against all who would challenge it. Arrogant, cryptic, challenging, engaging – in writing as in person – Bettelheim and his work stand permanently intertwined: exciting to experience, impossible to duplicate. Bettelheim concluded his last book on milieu treatment expecting and welcoming challenge: 'I hope the reader will try to discover where I have gone wrong, but not be satisfied merely by registering a negative, but try to understand why and how it all could be done better. If he does this, he will have paid the author the highest compliment possible' (1974:14). That is the challenge, the great stimulus, which Bettelheim's work presents: to find a better way. Whatever eventually becomes of his ideas, Bettelheim will always be viewed as a pioneering force in the development of milieu treatment.

Fritz Redl   What the contribution of Bruno Bettelheim represents for the psychotic child, the work of Fritz Redl represents for the delinquent. A psychologist and psychoanalyst, Redl came to the United States from Vienna in 1936, strongly influenced by Freud and by the work of August Aichorn (1935) with delinquent adolescents. He was keenly interested in the interplay between individual and group dynamics and in the group's potential as a medium for changing delinquent behaviour. Redl settled in Detroit, where he was founder and director of the Detroit Group Project and Pioneer House – a small, community-based residential program for hyperaggressive, acting-out preadolescents. He also directed a special residential unit at the National Institute of Mental Health in Bethesda, served as consultant to several of the larger psychiatric children's hospitals in the country, lectured on an international scale, and was a professor of behavioural sciences at Wayne State University. His writings span nearly fifty years and cover the fields of child mental health, special education, group dynamics, and milieu treatment for behaviour-disordered children. His two books on the Pioneer House project with David Wineman – *Children Who Hate* and *Controls from Within* (published as a single volume in 1957) – stand as singular classics in the literature of milieu treatment. His other books include *Mental Hygiene in Teaching*, with M. Wattenberg (1959), and *When We Deal with Children* (1966). Two of Redl's contributions to the theory of mileu treatment are his analysis of the essential ingredients in a therapeutic milieu and his development of the life-space interview.

In a brilliant synthesis of organizational, group, and individual dynamics, Redl provided the field of child mental health in the 1950s with a conceptual screen for viewing all the diverse elements in a therapeutic milieu. He also developed the various 'tools' to be used in changing children's behaviour. Central here was his concept of the *life-space interview* (LSI), a set of action-based interview strategies designed to help child care workers deal with real-life problems of children when and where they occur. *Life space* refers to the total physical, social, psychological, and cultural 'space' surrounding an individual at any given point in time. The focus (and often the locus) of the interviews is the child's own natural milieu, and most deal with specific behavioural incidents. The strategies include 'emotional first aid' – techniques designed to help a child weather a behavioural storm and return to the life space; and techniques for exploring a more chronic pattern of behaviour in relation to the child's overall treatment goals. Basically, the life-space interview was developed for two reasons: (1) the inadequacy of the reality-detached, fifty-minute therapy session as a device for dealing with the problems of behaviour disordered children living away from home; and (2) the need for a specialized set of techniques for child care workers and house-parents to provide what Redl called 'therapy on the hoof'. (The life-space interview concept has been expanded and applied to a variety of educational and treatment settings. See Long, Morse, and Newman, 1971 : 442–52, 473–91.)

The impact of Redl's work is difficult to assess. Though it opened its doors over thirty years ago, Pioneer House foreshadowed many of the innovations in community-based child treatment: low visibility, strong community ties, focus on teaching specific behavioural skills, and involvement of child care staff as on-line therapists (Redl and Wineman, 1957). I have suggested elsewhere (Whittaker, 1970a) several possible reasons why Redl's model was not widely adopted – generally having to do with its 'folksy' terminology (some of the techniques are labelled 'massaging numb value areas', 'new tool salesmanship', 'draining frustration acidity'), unlikely to appeal to the scientifically minded professional, and a falsely imputed view of the model as overpermissive. (For Redl's thoughts on this issue, see Redl, 1966 : 355–78.)

A third and more plausible reason has to do with the traditional structure of institutional facilities for emotionally disturbed children in this country. Many residential facilities are organized more around the needs of the professional groups who run them than around the needs of the children they are designed to serve. Thus, we have a 'medical model' of residential treatment, which is usually just an extension of the psychiatric team from child guidance. In this system, child care workers are used to care for and often live with the children, but their function is not usually seen as 'treatment' *per se*. A variation on the medical model is the 'social work' model of residential treatment. Here the same kind of role rigidity is maintained, despite a shift in the status hierarchy. Typically, psychiatric social workers are responsible for the treatment of the children – usually in office interviews – though they may make use of psychiatric and psychological consultants. In the period 1950–1970, numerous specialities were elevated to professional status; but in some ways this practice worked to the detriment rather than the benefit of the children in care. In the course of a single week's time, the disturbed child might be expected to see his psychotherapist, group therapist, family caseworker, occupational therapist, recreational therapist, music therapist – and so on. The life-space model of treatment rejected such specific role definitions in favour of a far more generic approach. It was a model of treatment developed from the problems posed by the children in care and not from the needs of any single professional group. Herein probably lies a reason why the model has been adopted so infrequently: it wreaks havoc with the traditional notions of 'who does what' in a residential treatment centre. In addition, the life-space model contains a built-in threat to the therapist who is accustomed to working only in the sanctity of his or her office and in the context of the fifty-minute hour. Dealing with problems in the life space is akin to working in a fishbowl: both successes and failures are clearly visible to all.

Despite these and other problems in adaptability, Redl's work has contributed significantly to the theoretical development of milieu treatment in two important areas. His was the first and – at the time – most sophisticated attempt to provide a taxonomy of aggressive behaviour in children. For Redl, there never was simply an 'aggressive child'; instead, there was a complex interplay of personality facts and group dynamics located in a particular space-time context that combined to produce a specific behavioural result. In many ways, his work foreshadowed the efforts of Wahler, Patterson and other applied behaviour analysts in identifying the structural aspects of deviant child behaviour (Wahler, House, and Stambaugh, 1976; Patterson *et al.*, 1975). Second, his model stood nearly alone for many years as a testimony to the belief that success in milieu treatment is directly related to the ability of programs to incorporate child care workers as primary agents of therapy. While many clinicians paid lip service to the importance of child care staff, Redl built a model of treatment around them. He developed specific techniques – such as the life-space interview – for managing children's behaviour as well as for teaching alternatives. He recognized the power of the peer group as a potential force for positive change and developed a conceptual scheme for observing and intervening with group behaviour. His model recognized the importance of activities in a therapeutic milieu, and he helped to elevate program activities to the status of a 'full-fledged therapeutic tool'. His notions on the use of punishment and on preadolescents – contained in works written in the 1940s and early 1950s – remain valuable today.

In my opinion, Redl's work retains its viability because many of his concepts can exist apart from the psychoanalytic foundations on which they were originally conceived. Much of what Redl had to say about the techniques for the management of surface behaviour in children can be translated without damage to a social learning framework (Redl and Wineman, 1957 : 395–486). The life-space interview material, although procedurally primitive, continues to provide a useful framework for organizing therapeutic conversations with children and can serve as an adjunct to individual behavioural programs designed to build new behavioural repertoires or extinguish old ones. Perhaps more than any other single theoretician of his time, he contributed to our understanding of what actually makes a milieu work.

The child guidance movement and residential treatment

If the 'life-space' model of Redl was slow to catch on in the children's institutional field, a more traditional child guidance approach, stressing individually oriented child therapy, spread rapidly. By the mid-1960s, nearly 70 percent of all child caring institutions provided individual treatment by psychiatrists, social workers, or other professionals; for institutions serving delinquent and emotionally disturbed children, the figure was closer to 90 percent (Pappenfort, Kilpatrick and Roberts, 1973). Treatment typically consisted of ego-supportive casework provided by a therapist who was structurally unrelated to and often physically removed from the child's living space. This division of labour in child treatment has impeded attempts to change existing child care institutions and create new decentralized services. I have elsewhere (Whittaker, 1970c, 1971b) described the effects of the child guidance movement on the children's institutional field in the early part of this century and will provide only a brief summary here.

As early as 1920, the organizational requisites for the new mental hygiene technology were becoming clear: a psychiatric team composed of psychiatrist, clinical psychologist, and social worker operating out of a single clinic. This pattern of organization, with the subsequent addition of other clinical specialists, would constitute the basic pattern of service in child guidance for years to come. Soon the child guidance model – organized around the 'psychiatric team' – became the paradigm for institutional treatment. It would be overstating the case to say that the majority of institutions for dependent and delinquent children incorporated the child guidance model in the 1920s – in fact, only a small minority would do so – but this particular form of organization for treatment did come to be recognized as the most appropriate one for the children's institution. What seemed to be working in the larger community should certainly be efficacious in the institution, so the logic ran. Just as the child guidance model provided a new organization for treatment, the growing popularity of Freudian psychology would provide a new technology for treatment.

By the end of the 1920s, certain institutions – among them, the Children's Village, Dobbs Ferry, New York; the New England Home for Little Wanderers, Boston; the Jewish Protectory and Aid Society's Hawthorne Cedar Knolls School, New York; and the Whittier State School in California – had developed their clinical programs to the point where they became models of how the new treatment organization and technology could be adapted for use in an institutional setting. These institutions roused professional interest throughout the country and attracted many visitors from children's agencies, who were anxious to see how the psychiatric team would function in an institutional setting.

One important drawback of the infusion of this new structure was the distance that was created between the members of the psychiatric team and the other members of the institutional staff. This fact may be demonstrated in the development of the role of the psychiatric caseworker. In the attempt to establish social work as a scientific discipline, and to relate the social worker's function on the psychiatric team to that of the psychiatrist and the clinical psychologist, social workers had to be disassociated from other – 'nonprofessional' – health care workers. Thus, in many institutions the department of social service became something apart from the department of child care. Social workers, like their professional colleagues in psychiatry and psychology, recognized the importance of the work of cottage personnel but clearly saw them as operating on a different level. This sense of division comes through in descriptions of various institutional staff training conferences held during this period. The flow of information was downward from the professional staff (who presumably had the expertise in mental hygiene and treatment concepts) to the line staff (who did not). The social worker preferred to advise the psychiatrist of a 'social knowledge and technique which he usually lacked' than to spend her time consulting with the line staff on matters of child care and managament (Taft, 1919).

Thus, toward the end of the 1920s a treatment structure separate from the group living, or cottage, structure was developed in children's institutions. The separation was enhanced by the fact that the treatment of choice for the newly classified 'emotionally disturbed' child took place mainly in a carefully structured therapy session with a professional psychotherapist. Cottage staff and other institutional personnel were viewed as important supportive figures, but not as the primary therapeutic agents. The fruits of this separation would be felt for many years to come.

Conclusions Psychoanalytic theory contributed much to the early development of milieu treatment, both as a screen for assessing disturbed behaviour and as a framework for organizing therapeutic interventions. The theory is of limited usefulness today, however, for explaining the disturbed behaviour of children or for treating it in the context of a therapeutic milieu. In diagnosis, highly individualized explanations of disturbed or delinquent behaviour – which placed the blame on faulty super-ego or ego development – appear now to have little validity, ignoring as they do environmental, sociocultural and physiological influences. In fact, the whole taxonomy of psychodynamic constructs adds little to our understanding of what specifically we mean by 'delinquent', 'emotionally disturbed' or 'malajusted' behaviour. The vocabulary of psychoanalytic theory interposes a layer of confusing and vaguely defined terminology between the troubled child and his behaviour and provides little practical help to the child care worker attempting to change the behaviour; it also increases the likelihood of reifying internal, pathological personality states that have no empirical basis. Finally, the overwhelming predisposition of psychoanalytic theory toward functional or psychogenic explanations of disturbed child behaviour places unwarranted blame on parents as the cause of their child's disorder and has tended to subordinate alternative explanations – neurobiological, sociocultural – in favour of the family etiology hypothesis.

In the area of treatment, a similar argument can be made. To the extent that some psychoanalytically based approaches to milieu treatment remain viable – the work of Redl, for example – they are useful *in spite of* their psychoanalytic underpinnings and not because of them. The structural implications of the infusion of psychoanalytic treatment into the therapeutic milieu have been particularly unfortunate. The concept of the role of child therapist as a professional separate and apart from the child's living space has had a profoundly retarding effect on the development of the milieu as a means and a context for therapeutic gain. Since the therapist was isolated from the actual behaviour in the ward or cottage, his view of the child was derived from information collected in the artificial environment of the fifty-minute therapy hour. To compound the problem, the individual therapist was often the person responsible for directing the child's total treatment plan – including supervision of line child care staff, who had an infinitely greater knowledge of the child's behaviour in a more nearly real-life context. Small wonder that the forces actually governing the course of a child's progress in residential treatment often had less to do with the formal structure of treatment authority and more to do with informal, covert systems. It is no accident that Polsky's classic *Cottage Six* (1962) – which showed that the dominant force in a treatment institution for delinquent adolescents was a powerful delinquent subculture, in part reinforced by the houseparents for purposes of control – deals with an institution where the psychiatric caseworker was both physically and functionally removed from the cottage culture. (As if to symbolically underscore this point, it has been disclosed that the actual 'Cottage Six' was the most physically distant from the building where individual casework took place.) Equally unfortunate is the fact that the child's individual therapist was often the parents' only contact with the treatment centre. Thus, critical information about the child's actual progress in acquiring skills for living was transmitted secondhand, if at all.

My intent here is not to impugn the motives of individual therapists or to question the efficacy of individual psychotherapy as a therapeutic tool appropriate for some children. Many therapists have been sensitive to the problems mentioned here, and there is a small but significant literature on the problems of adapting individual psychotherapy to a therapeutic milieu (Noshpitz, 1971; Brodie, 1972). These attempts, however well conceived, miss the major point: *a truly therapeutic milieu cannot be organized around the concept of individual psychotherapy as the central mode of treatment delivered by a therapist who is both physically and experientially removed from the child's natural life milieu.* This is the dilemma facing many existing child treatment programs today. Even when desirous of change, these programs find themselves saddled with an organizational structure that simply will not permit the decentralization of clinical authority from the therapy room to the life space. At the very least, an analysis of the structural and functional effects of the infusion of psychoanalytic concepts into the children's institutional field should forewarn us about the *carte blanche* acceptance of any theoretical system or pattern of organization until we have examined fully the possible unanticipated consequences of our actions.

Behavioural approaches

Behavioural approaches to milieu treatment are a relatively new phenomenon when compared to their psychoanalytic counterparts. In the children's field, as in the mental health field generally, behaviour modification entered through the 'back door' with those children for whom more traditional approaches had failed: notably, autistic children (Lovaas, 1967; Wolf, Mees, and Risley, 1964) and older, case-hardened delinquents (Cohen and Filipczak, 1971). In the early 1960s, pioneering work was undertaken by a group of psychologists and educators at the University of Washington, who attempted to apply the principles of behaviour analysis in a natural setting – in this case a campus preschool. These early studies focused on the effects of teacher attention in maintaining problem behaviours in children. In a series of experiments, the investigators demonstrated that such diverse behaviours as regressed crawling (Harris *et al.*, 1964), socially isolate behaviour (Allen *et al.*, 1964), excessive crying and whining (Hart *et al.*, 1964), and excessive scratching (Allen and Harris, 1966) were directly controlled by their immediate consequences in the environment – in this case the attention of adults. Attempts to alter these behaviours through a selective process of withholding and dispensing social reinforcement were successful and acted as a catalyst for a series of research endeavours designed to demonstrate the practical value of a behavioural approach in a wide variety of child caring agencies: schools, residential treatment centres, juvenile courts, and group homes. As with the psychoanalytic approach, individual behaviourists differed in style and emphasis, but their efforts were founded on a commonly agreed-upon set of principles, from which their strategies evolved:

(1) A child's psychological nature is his behaviour; directly observable and measurable actions constitute the sum and substance of person-

ality. The behaviourist rejects the notion of inner personality states such as id, ego, and superego.

(2) Behaviour is largely controlled by the environment and, in the case of operant or active behaviour, is either strengthened, maintained, or diminished by its immediate effects on the environment. Therefore, if the reinforcers for any given behaviour can be identified and brought under control, the behaviour itself can be similarly controlled.

(3) The symptom of the troubled child is the entire problem; it is not simply an external manifestation of some underlying disease process, psychoneurosis, or character disorder. If the acting out of the delinquent, or the bizarre behaviour of the psychotic child, is stopped, then the basic problem of delinquency or psychosis has been solved.

From an etiological point of view, the behaviourist looks to the child's prior learning history for diagnostic clues: how were negative behaviours elicited? How are they being maintained? What sorts of reinforcers are operative for this particular child? Treatment typically involves four stages: (1) identification and specification of the problem behaviour; (2) determination of the controlling conditions: patterns of reinforcement, learning history, environmental factors; (3) specification of pro-social behavioural goals; (4) application of any of a number of behavioural techniques, either singly or in combination, followed by a precise evaluation of progress.

These techniques often include the contingent use of both positive and negative reinforcers to simultaneously accelerate desired behaviours and decelerate undesirable ones. Behavioural treatment may occur as the result of an individual behaviour modification program or a specially constructed learning environment. (For a programmed introduction to behavioural theory and technology, see Patterson and Gullion, 1968.) Some of the more important behavioural contributions to milieu treatment for disturbed and delinquent children are the Achievement Place project for juvenile court-referred preadolescents (Phillips *et al.*, 1973a), the former National Training School program for adolescent delinquents (Cohen and Filipczak, 1971), and the work of Browning and Stover (1971) at the Children's Center in Madison, Wisconsin – a residential centre for psychotic and behaviour-disordered children.

Achievement Place   Achievement Place – a family-style, community-based treatment home for delinquent youths – grew out of the joint efforts of a group of concerned citizens, juvenile court professionals, and behavioural psychologists from the Bureau of Child Research at the

University of Kansas at Lawrence. The goal is to teach youths the basic skills – social, academic, self-help, and prevocational – that will help them out of trouble with their families, their teachers, and the law (Phillips *et al.*, 1973a). Central to the model is the teaching interaction created between the youths and their 'teaching parents' – a professional couple, specially trained in the techniques of behaviour analysis and intervention. Training for staff includes intensive classroom and practicum experience and may culminate in a master's degree offered through the University of Kansas. In Achievement Place, the youth progresses through a series of behavioural programs, which gradually allow him or her more freedom and privileges as behaviour improves. Behaviour is carefully recorded in school, in the living environment, and on home visits, and the progress of an individual youth is continuously monitored. The power of the peer group is tapped through a self-government system, including an 'elected manager'; and a consumer review of program effectiveness is integral to the model.

An interesting finding occurred when the investigators attempted to replicate the initial Achievement Place project in a second home – and failed. Though they had recreated an identical point system, they had overlooked the subtle but extremely important social reinforcement that occurs between houseparent and youth around the dispensing of points. In fact, the point system could work at peak effectiveness only in the context of a warm, open and giving interaction: 'Many clinical colleagues have told us all along that "relationship" is an essential component of any therapy. We are now convinced that they are right' (Phillips *et al.*, 1973a:107).

In contrast to earlier efforts at establishing behavioural programs for delinquents, Achievement Place attempts to describe and objectify the social processes that can enhance or inhibit the token economy: individual relationship, peer group process, and the specific teaching of social skills. The Achievement Place model has now been replicated in a number of communities, and adaptations of the model have been used in institutional as well as community-based settings. While results are far from complete, the positive aspects of the model appear to be these:

(1) Achievement Place is a *communicable approach* to delinquency treatment; it represents perhaps the most precise and detailed behavioural model of community-based treatment for delinquents in existence today. Training and program development procedures are well articulated, and a number of specific training tools have been developed. (The model is currently being implemented and training materials developed in many sites around the country, but particularly at Boys Town in Nebraska.)

(2) Achievement Place appears to work – at least insofar as a limited follow-up would suggest. On the criteria of recidivism, school attendance, and school grades, the early graduates of the program appear to be doing better than similar cohorts of youth exposed to probation or a traditional delinquency institution.

(3) Costs are low when compared to those of institutions: $5000–$8000 (compared to $20,000–$30,000) for capital outlay, and $4000–$5000 (compared to $6000–$12000) for yearly operating costs (Phillips *et al.*, 1973a : 106). Since the costs of institutional care are themselves low in comparison to the costs of private residential treatment, the savings may be even greater.

(4) Achievement Place is a true community-based program – low in visibility, high in connectedness to other community systems: school, family, vocational, recreation, peer group – and could well be justified on humanitarian grounds alone.

Areas of continuing concern include the following:

(1) While the initial results of the program are impressive, they are not based on a systematic comparison with other types of treatment. Since youths were not randomly assigned to the project, preselection factors may have favoured those youths judged most likely to succeed in a community setting. Such a judgment – however sound clinically – would violate the principle of random assignment necessary for a true comparative study. Moreover, while the present comparison with a delinquency institution and probation makes sense – both are traditionally used services for such youths – a more telling comparison might include other carefully specified community-based approaches – including nonresidential alternatives. Both of these concerns may be addressed in the more comprehensive external evaluation currently under way.

(2) The teaching parent concept – while an exciting one – raises again the question of the enormous problems encountered in recruiting, training, and holding on to effective houseparents. Turnover is evidently a problem in the Achievement Place project, and alternate staffing approaches would warrant consideration.

(3) Questions have been raised about the appropriateness of the Achievement Place model for other than small, semirural communities with fairly homogeneous populations and commonly shared lifestyles. How successful the model would be in a culturally diverse, urban environment remains to be seen.

(4) Cost comparisons need to be more fairly assessed. Phillips *et al.*, (1973a) compare the cost of institutional care with an Achievement Place home, neglecting to control for the array of services contained

in the institution's budget – school and social service, to name two – and provided free to Achievement Place by other community agencies. The whole cost of training the teaching parents and supporting the consultant staff – provided for on a National Institute of Mental Health grant totaling nearly $1,000,000 – is not readily apparent in the budget figures. In fairness, these may reflect more start-up costs than ongoing program costs.

In sum, the Achievement Place model represents an innovative and exciting approach to community treatment which has managed to improve as a result of its failures. The commitment to comprehensive evaluation at all levels of the program significantly increases the likelihood that the questions raised previously will ultimately be answered.

The National Training School project   Cohen and Filipczak (1971:xix) report on an experimental behaviour modification program for juvenile delinquents at the former National Training School in Washington, DC. Under federal grants, a pilot program was established in the mid-1960s, the object of which was to positively expand the academic and social repertoires of forty-one incarcerated adolescents through the use of a specially designed learning environment. A point system – or token economy – was used to deliver reinforcement for appropriate classroom and dormitory behaviour. The goal of the program was to increase the academic behaviours of all students and to prepare as many as possible for return to the public school within one calendar year. Points gained in the classroom could be redeemed for cash or used to buy a variety of privileges, including better food, certain program activities, and more comfortable accommodations within the program. Evaluation indicated significant gains in both IQ and educational behaviours during the period of institutionalization. Data on recidivism of the students indicated a slower rate of return to the juvenile or adult justice system than for the group of National Training School graduates as a whole.

The importance of the postinstitutional environment as a support system is stressed by the authors as an important factor in determining ultimate community adjustment. The crucial nature of the postinstitutional environment was also stressed in research conducted at the Robert F. Kennedy Youth Center (KYC) in Morgantown, West Virginia – the federally sponsored successor program to the old National Training School in Washington, DC. There a sophisticated behavioural program developed by Herbert Quay at Temple University was used to type delinquents into categories and to provide a total learning environment in the institution. An in-depth analysis of fifty KYC releases revealed that the differential training program at KYC was no more successful in promoting in-program success or twelve-month postrelease success than were the programs at two traditional training schools (Cavior, Schmidt, and Karacki, 1972). The analysis suggests that what happens to the delinquent adolescent following release is as much dependent on the kind of support and assistance he receives in the community as it is on the treatment he receives in the program. These findings coincide generally with the conclusion of two other studies (Allerhand, Weber, and Haug, 1966; Taylor and Alpert, 1973), which indicate the enormous power of the postinstitutional environment in determining the ultimate suceess of residential treatment programs for emotionally disturbed children.

The Children's Center   The work of Browning and Stover (1971) at the Children's Center in Madison, Wisconsin, is significant because it introduced the concept of an experimental-clinical approach to milieu treatment for young disturbed children – based in part on the use of the single-subject design (see Whittaker 1979 : chapter 8) – and because the authors outlined the organizational barriers to implementing a behaviourally oriented treatment program in a residential setting.

The problems encountered involved program design and staff attitudes and reaction. Specifically, it proved difficult to design a program that was balanced (one that stressed equally the acceleration of desirable behaviour and the deceleration of undesirable behaviour), that offered continuous positive social reinforcement, and that elicited increasingly complex behaviours. Staff problems were even more numerous. First of all, they generally felt that behaviour modification techniques were 'unnatural'. In addition, they did not always carry out the program's requirement. Sometimes they failed to reward newly acquired behaviours (so that the children lapsed into old behaviour patterns to receive attention), or they had difficulty in 'reading' correct responses and often reinforced the wrong response or delayed reinforcement, or they would settle for less than the agreed-upon criterion response (given their relatively low expectation of what the children were capable of). Again, poor interstaff communication was a real problem in effecting a successful behaviour modification program. Finally, the authors found limitations to the generalization of effects and in providing a treatment environment that gradually approximated the home setting. They concluded that one should not assume generalization but, rather, should work to ensure that what is learned in one setting is elicited and maintained in another.

Browning and Stover's observations are similar to those of Repucci and Saunders (1974), who introduced a behavioural model into a state training school for delinquents, and form the nucleus of a growing literature on what might be called the sociology of behaviour modification in residential settings. Other behavioural contributors whose work has significant implications for the development of milieu treatment are Lovaas (1967) and Kozloff (1975) with autistic children; Schopler and Reichler (1971a) and Johnson and Katz (1973) on using parents as developmental therapists for their own children; Rose (1972) on the behavioural treatment of children in groups; Goocher (1975) on a behavioural approach to child care work; and Wahler (1975) and Patterson *et al.* (1975) on behavioural interventions with troubled children in their own homes.

Conclusions It is probably only a slight overstatement to say that the most significant advances in milieu treatment for troubled children over the last decade have come about as a result of the introduction of behavioural technology to the life space. The impact is not unlike that of psychoanalytic theory in earlier decades. Although it is too early to assess the overall impact of behavioural approaches on milieu treatment, the following observations appear to be justified on the basis of available evidence:

(1) Behavioural approaches provide a systematic and effective means for teaching alternative behaviour to troubled children.
(2) The behaviourists have helped immensely in specifying such important but ill-defined treatment variables as relationship, role modelling, and teaching interaction.
(3) The behavioural model is a communicable model – easily understood by line staff – which increases the probability of consistency in treatment between different staff members.
(4) The behavioural approach has helped child care professionals focus on the specific behaviours that are causing the troubled child or his family difficulty and then devising equally specific strategies for dealing with them.
(5) The behavioural approach does not assume an 'illness model' of childhood disorders but, rather, focuses on specific steps that may be taken to 'unlearn' old behaviours while adopting new ones.
(6) The behavioural approach lends itself particularly well to comprehensive evaluation; goals are clearly specified in advance, and treatment procedures are explicit.
(7) Individual behavioural programs are often difficult to establish – particularly for many of the complex interpersonal behaviours.
(8) The organizational context is a critical intervening variable in determining the success or failure of a behavioural approach to child treatment. This is particularly true in residential setting.
(9) Token economies apparently are subject to the same market forces

as money economies and must be carefully monitored to avoid such things as inflation and recession.

(10) Helping the child make the transition from the artificial environment of the behavioural treatment program to his home community is a difficult problem – particularly if control of environmental reinforcers is limited.

(11) Behavioural programs are easily sabotaged – either unwittingly or purposefully – by staff members who may be unclear on or in disagreement with basic program objectives.

(12) The early stereotype of behaviour modification as 'cold', 'mechanical', and 'Machiavellian' continues to exist in many communities and represents a problem of considerable magnitude for staff training and community acceptance.

While behaviour modification is not a panacea for child treatment, as many of its earliest and most vocal proponents argued, neither is it the cruel and barbarous method that some of its early critics held it to be. Behavioural modification will most certainly play a prominent role in any future development of a model of milieu treatment for troubled children.

Guided group interaction approaches

Guided group interaction approaches stress the importance of the milieu as a total system in influencing behaviour. As a social system, the child caring institution has held a particular fascination for social scientists. Jules Henry's (1957) description of the culture of interpersonal relations in Bruno Bettelheim's Orthogenic School was followed by studies of the conflict betwwen houseparents and social workers (Piliavin, 1963), socialization of residents in an institution for retarded children (Dentler and Mackler, 1961), and the interpersonal behaviour of children in a residential treatment centre (Raush, Dittman, and Taylor, 1959). Though its focus was an adult mental hospital, Goffman's (1962) classic study of the 'asylum' had major implications for the children's field in its description of how institutional structure and processes sometimes were at total odds with the formally stated treatment objectives of the institution.

In 1962 the sociologist Howard Polsky published a small book, *Cottage Six*, which directly challenged current notions of what constituted quality residential treatment for delinquent adolescents. As a participant-observer, Polsky joined a cottage of delinquents in an institution that prided itself on the sophistication of its clinical services. In fact, 'Hollymeade' had pioneered in the introduction of mental hygiene concepts in an institutional setting. Each boy received frequent – sometimes daily – individual therapy from a trained psychiatric caseworker in an office physically removed from the culture of the cottage. The remainder of the youth's day was supervised by a set of cottage parents – largely untrained and effectively removed from the clinical decision-making process in the institution.

Polsky concluded that the supposedly disorganized world of the adolescent delinquent was, in fact, centred around an elaborate diamond-shaped power structure, made up of the various subgroupings within the cottage: 'leaders', 'status seekers', 'con artists', 'isolates', 'bushboys', and 'scapegoats'. A delinquent subculture – which stressed intimidation through physical coercion, toughness, and a code of silence – flourished within the cottage and endured, even though the central actors changed periodically. In spite of the contribution of highly skilled individual therapists, the critical force in determining the individual youth's course of rehabilitation was the delinquent subculture of the cottage. Cottage parents – largely untrained and overworked – often bought into or tolerated the delinquent subculture for the purpose of controlling the group. Because of the house staff's inability to deal effectively with this delinquent subculture, individual boys felt abandoned to it. Polsky (1962:149) explains:

> 'In the family the child is not exposed to a father and a mother, but to their interaction, their "family culture". In the institution, the youngster is barred from extensive interaction with the professional staff culture, yet he is expected to achieve the latter's goals. In the cottage, hard-pressed cottage parents are outnumbered by delinquent youths. Many boys improve in spite of the negative peer culture; others fail because of it.'

If the behaviour of an individual delinquent is in fact maintained by a delinquent subculture, then effective rehabilitation should involve the peer group as an integral part of the treatment process. For example, the Achievement Place project has developed an elected manager system, which harnesses the power of the peer group toward positive ends. Another approach to delinquency treatment that focuses exclusively on the nurturance, development, and utilization of a positive peer culture is *guided group interaction* (GCI)[3] – a method of counseling developed after the Second World War for use with recalcitrant prisoners in army disciplinary barracks. Though they originated in total institutional settings, GGI groups have also been used in community-based day treatment programs and group homes (Empey and Lubeck, 1972; Flackett and Flackett, 1970). Pilnick (1971) defines guided group interaction as follows: 'Guided group interaction is a process of group treatment which directs the dynamics and strengths of the peer group toward constructively altering and developing the behavior of the group members'.

According to Empey and Lubeck (1972), the basic objectives of guided group interaction are to question the utility of persistent delinquency, to provide behavioural alternatives, and to provide recognition for a youth's personal reformation and for his willingness to help reform others.

In guided group interaction, the peer group acts as a positively reinforcing agent in helping the youth develop positive prosocial values; in addition, strong sanctions help to ensure conformity to group norms. In many institutional settings, for example, the group alone decides what privileges an adolescent may enjoy within the residence and when he is ready to return to the community.

The group itself is seen as the primary vehicle for change, and members are responsible for helping each other resolve problems both in and out of the group meeting. In addition to the highly structured group session – which occurs daily for a period of approximately one and a half hours – the members are usually together in work, school, and recreation as well. Through the process of group decision making and task assignments, many situations arise which require some members of the group to help others who cannot 'handle the situation'. This process builds the self-worth of the individual member and the confidence of the group as a positive force for changing behaviour. Typically, groups are composed of seven to eleven adolescent members and an adult leader. The daily session begins with a reporting of problems by each member. While there is some variation among individual practitioners, the following list is representative (Vorrath and Brendtro, 1974:76): low self-image, inconsiderate of others, inconsiderate of self, authority problem, misleads others, easily misled, aggravates others, easily angered, stealing, alcohol, or drug problems, lying, fronting (trying to be something you are not: clown, tough guy, dumbbell).

Every aspect of the physical structure of the meeting room is arranged to provide for maximum eye contact: individual group members sit in a semicircle, and the group leader sits behind a desk or table, apart from the group but ready to influence the interactions as he deems necessary. The role of the group leader is pivotal; he alternately supports, confronts, interprets, and summarizes the interactions of the members and maintains a 'presence' even when he is away from the treatment setting. For example, in an institutional setting the group leader may drop in at unexpected times and thus keep current on behaviour that occurs outside of the group sessions. Vorrath and Brendtro describe the group leader's primary verbal behaviour as 'questioning', which serves the purpose of stimulating the group toward the solution of problems. Each session follows a strict agenda: reporting problems, awarding the meeting, problem solving, and leader summary.

Since many groups are formed in delinquent institutions, a primary source of reinforcement is the almost universal desire to return to the community. A central function of the group is to make it impossible for a member to leave the setting through delinquent means, such as 'conning'. The leader does not attempt to provide answers for the group but forces decisions back to the members. Final authority does rest with the leader, particularly with respect to discharge. Members therefore become dependent on one another, and 'helping' is encouraged outside as well as within the daily group sessions.

The effectiveness of GGI remains open to question. Early experiments with GGI (McCorkle, Elias, and Bixby, 1958; Weeks, 1963) yielded no statistically significant differences in the recidivism rates of graduates of the GGI program and those of the regular reformatory. More recently, Empey and Lubeck's (1972) study compared graduates of a community-based GGI program with those of a traditional delinquency institution; again, there were no significant differences between the recidivism rates of the experimental and control groups. Although there was no assess-ment of long-term outcomes, the data suggested that the experimental program, which was much shorter and thereby less costly, was at least as effective as the control program (Sarri and Selo, 1974:278). Stephenson and Scarpitti (1974), in a review of several institutional and community-based GGI programs, found that the GGI graduates fared somewhat better than the traditional reformatory graduates but not as well as youths on parole. Their overall conclusion (1974:189) was as follows: 'Taken together, the evidence from these studies is not impressive with respect to the general efficacy of guided group interaction when compared with alternative programs of correction'.

Vorrath and Brendtro (1974:150–51) report on an unpublished study from the Minnesota Department of Corrections' Red Wing Institution (where the senior author initiated a GGI program), which purports to show a 'success' rate of over 80 percent and a drop in recidivism from the previous 50 percent to 18 percent in a two-year follow-up of graduates of the program. What these results demonstrate is open to question, since a methodological comparison with several similar studies revealed that the Minnesota study ranked 'poor' in four areas and 'fair' in two others (Sarri and Selo, 1974:268).

While generally inconclusive, studies of GGI as a treatment tool with delinquent youth suggest the following strengths and limitations:

Strengths

(1) For those older adolescents whose delinquent behaviour originates and is maintained in the peer group, GGI presents a potentially

powerful technique for going to the heart of the delinquent subculture and orienting it in a positive direction.

(2) With its daily meetings, peer confrontation, and focus on present problems, GGI significantly lowers the probability of the delinquent's being able to 'con' his way through the treatment program.

(3) In an institutional setting, GGI can link school, cottage, and community behaviour in a way that helps to ensure improvement across systems. It is a positive approach that stresses 'growth' rather than illness and is, in many respects, a true 'self-help group'.

(4) GGI is less expensive than traditional training school programs when used in a community-based setting.

(5) Group leaders do not require extensive graduate professional education and are often selected for training from the ranks of line child care staff.

Limitations

(6) Some critics have argued that GGI is to a large extent based on personality rather than method. Some programs have centred around a single messianic leader, who brooks no compromise with the 'rightness' of the model. Harstad (1976) suggests that GGI is not more widely used because its promoters have turned off prospective users through simplistic, overbearing, and insulting presentations.

(7) Relatively little has been written about the method itself. The literature is sparse, and few formalized training programs for group leaders exist. Thus, agencies desirous of trying out the model often find that they have to buy into a long-term consulting contract to receive the necessary staff training.

(8) GGI is presented as a total approach to youth treatment, and its use as an adjunctive therapy has been discouraged in favour of an 'all-or-nothing' approach. This would seem to render useless the notion of differential diagnosis and treatment for the youthful offender.

(9) As a way of organizing a total therapeutic milieu, GGI leaves much to be desired. With so much power invested in the group leader and so much action taking place in the group meeting, other staff – notably child care workers – can begin to feel that they are little more than caretakers.

(10) The data – as with most total-treatment approaches – are at this point unclear. The present literature is particularly limited in two important areas: For what type of youthful offender does GGI appear to be most effective? What organizational structures

provide maximum enhancement for the GGI approach?

(11) GGI is less effective with the younger troubled child, for whom the peer group is less powerful, and for psychotic children or severely emotionally disturbed children.

Educational approaches: Project Re-Ed

Project Re-Ed (Hobbs, 1966) was designed to create a total living and learning environment for the troubled child and stresses the teaching of competence across the total spectrum of the child's development as the fundamental purpose of the helping environment. There is also in Project Re-Ed a theoretical eclecticism not found in the approaches previously discussed. While I am aware that many additional educational approaches to child helping exist – particularly in the literature of Western and Eastern Europe, the Soviet Union, and Israel – I believe that this particular approach has the most direct and immediate bearing on the development of community-based group care settings for troubled children in the United States. (For some additional examples of educational approaches, see Wolins, 1974; Makarenko, 1955; Guindon, 1970; Wolins and Gottesmann, 1971.)

This pioneering program began as the result of a cooperative effort of the National Institute of Mental Health, Peabody College, and the states of Tennessee and North Carolina to provide a new kind of institution to help emotionally disturbed children. Re-Ed programs have been established in several locations in Tennessee, and there is one centre in Durham, North Carolina. The critical influences on the program's originator, Nicholas Hobbs, and his associates have been described as follows:

> 'Robert LaFon and Henri Joubrel of France introduced the staff to the idea of the *éducateur* and the small residential school. Catherine McCallum in Scotland provided the example of the 'educational psychologist' trained on the job to work with disturbed children. Campbell Loughmiller's ideas on camping for disturbed boys profoundly altered the character of Re-Ed as did the Peace Corps and the Outward Bound Schools of England. The intellectual heritage of Dewey, Rogers, Wolpe, Skinner, and Barker (all together!) is apparent in the program.'
> (Bower *et al.*, 1969 : 9)

The Re-Ed model combines special education and group living in a small, community-based program. Staff consist of teacher-counselors – former classroom teachers with special training in program activities and life-space intervention. In his introduction to the project, Hobbs (1964) cites several governing assumptions and biases:

A learning bias   The task of reeducation is to help the child learn new and more effective ways of construing himself and his world and to learn habits that lead to more effective functioning. We assume that the child is not diseased but that he has acquired bad habits. . . . Our effort is to initiate a learning process that will come to fruition in the weeks and months and years after the child's experience in a Re-Ed school. Reeducation is a problem in learning to learn.

A time bias   A child is most likely to get referred to a mental health facility at a time of crisis. . . . Improvement thereafter may often be expected. . . . To provide nothing more than a benign sanctuary for a child at a time of crisis is a worthy endeavor. The reeducation process claims time as an ally, not just as an effect to be bettered.

A growth bias   We do not assume some mystical growth force as an explanatory principle, but simply note descriptively that children (in the middle years) are still open to experience and change, with surplus energy to support the operation. A broken bone knits more rapidly at six than at sixty; we assume a comparable viability in the psychological domain.

A social systems bias   We are trying to move beyond concepts of individual adjustment, beyond concern for family–child relationships . . . to a program of intervention that constantly assesses and tries to change in appropriate ways the child . . . and all of the special people of importance or potential importance in his world.

A bias away from 'dynamic psychology'   With no clear advantage to be gained from the use of a therapeutic strategy (psycho-analytically oriented psychotherapy) that calls for a high level of psychological sophistication, we have chosen the simpler course: we are impressed enough by the complexity of the simplest seeming solutions to helping the disturbed child.

An adiagnostic bias   The formal psychiatric diagnosis is of little value in the process of reeducation. We have not been able to specify differentiated treatment procedures for differential diagnoses, nor have we observed thus far any relationship between diagnosis and responsiveness to the school program.'

From this base, Hobbs identifies a number of core components of the reeducation process: developing trust, gaining competence, nurturing feelings, controlling symptoms, learning middle-class values, attaining cognitive control, developing community ties, providing physical experience, and knowing joy.[4]

In the Re-Ed model there are two teacher-counselors for each group of eight children housed in a community residence. Teacher-counselors have already taught in public school and have had additional training consisting of a period of course work and a practicum. One teacher-counselor is primarily a daytime formal teacher; the other is an after-school informal counselor who works with the group as a whole. All decisions concerning actions to be taken toward the child are in the hands of the teacher-counselor. The average length of stay for children is six months.

Evaluation consists mainly of parent and teacher ratings. While results were tentative, they generally showed favourable improvements in school performance and behaviour at the time of graduation and an eighteen-month follow-up. Before Re-Ed, approximately 75 percent of the children were rated as having severe emotional or behavioural problems in school; after Re-Ed, approximately 75 percent of the children were rated in the normal range or as having mild problems (Bower *et al.*, 1969). A follow-up study (Weinstein, 1974) indicates marked improvement in comparison with untreated controls, but further analysis is required before the effect of the project can be assessed with certainty.

Any assessment of the Re-Ed program must begin with an assessment of Hobbs himself. On rereading his work today, one is even more impressed with what he had to say in the early 1960s and the eloquence with which he said it. His conception of the philosophical base of Re-Ed preceded by at least a decade the most cogent and articulate arguments in favour of community-based services for troubled children. Re-Ed appears to capture in a single setting what is most desirable in those services: low visibility, a total-systems focus, strong linkages with school and family, time-limited intervention, a 'growth' perspective, and a simplified organizational structure. Moreover, Re-Ed has received accolades from its panel of consultants (Bower *et al.*, 1969) and from the Joint Commission on Mental Health of Children (1970:44), which gave unqualified endorsement to the program and urged its expansion nationwide:

'Because of its proven effectiveness, in terms of both cost per child served and success in restoring the child to home, school, and community, the Commission recommends that the Re-Ed model be adopted and extended as one of the many needed kinds of services for emotionally disturbed children. Specifically, the Commission recommends that funds be made available to any state, community agency, or nonprofit corporation for the construction and operation of residential schools for emotionally disturbed children, patterned after the Re-Ed plan. Funds should be sufficient to establish at least 100 schools with at least one school in each state to serve as models for other programs.'

With all this favourable publicity, it is puzzling that the Re-Ed concept has not made greater inroads into the fields of child mental health and juvenile corrections. While severe cutbacks in federal funding for children's programs and the vested interests of the existing mental health professions in maintaining the status quo in services must surely be counted as partial answers, there remain, on closer observation, some serious and unanswered questions about the Re-Ed model itself. First, although the model is detailed and eloquent on a philosophy of education for troubled children, it is woefully short on specifics. What specific skills must a teacher-counselor acquire in order to help children alter old behaviour patterns and adopt new ones? What are the essential components in the group living process, and how do they relate to the major presenting problems of the children in care? While certain program elements – such as wilderness camping and program activities – are mentioned, it is not clear whether these are seen as primary or secondary formats for teaching or whether they apply equally to all children. Second, while I share Hobbs' bias about the inadequacy of psychoanalytic theory in explaining the behaviour of troubled children and would second his strong emphasis on teaching competence, I part company with his 'adiagnostic' bias. If his major point is the damaging effects of labels and the inadequacy of present diagnostic schemes (see Hobbs, 1975a, 1975b), then the answer must surely lie in the direction of devising *more precise* diagnostic criteria, which yield specific behavioural objectives. How does one operate 'adiagnostically'? Does he ignore the complex array of bio-psycho-sociocultural forces in which the troubled behaviour originated and through which it is being maintained? Does not an 'ecological' approach demand a precise and systematic assessment of the child-in-environment? How does the teacher-counselor decide what will produce change in a given child and what particular response he should make, given a universe of possible choices? These are important questions for any demonstration effort to attempt to answer, and they are absolute prerequisites to the sort of nationwide dissemination envisioned by the Joint Commission on Mental Health of Children. In short, Re-Ed is, at the level of philosophy, entirely communicable and extremely compelling. At the level of actual practice, as reported in the literature, it is slightly better than primitive.

A related question concerns the selection, education, and duties of the teacher-counselor – patterned closely on the European model of *éducateur*. There is in the writings of Hobbs – as in many other proponents of the *éducateur* concept – an almost infinite optimism about the positive potential of bringing together 'naturally' talented counselors and children with problems. For example, witness Hobbs' (1964:14–15) emphasis in the following description of the Re-Ed process:

'Techniques are important but they are clearly not all, *nor are any particular procedures essential to the process of reeducation.* The heart of Re-Ed is the teacher-counselor, a decent adult; educated; well trained; able to give and receive affection, to live loose and to be firm; a person with private resources for the nourishment and refreshment of his own life; not an itinerant worker, but a professional through and through; a person with a sense of the significance of time, of the usefulness of today and the promise of tomorrow; a person of hope, quiet confidence, and joy.'

This is a beautifully and simply expressed statement about the kinds of qualities one hopes to find in a child care professional. But is there something required beyond 'joy' and 'decency'? I am reminded here of the criticism that my late colleague McNeil (1969 : 17) – himself no stranger to the world of troubled children – offered in response to another version of the *éducateur* model:

'What is critically absent in the role specification of the *éducateur* is the "O" in the familiar S-O-R (stimulus-organism-response) formula of the learning theorists of a half a century ago. The *éducateur* stimulates the human organism via arts and crafts and vigorous activity, and, perhaps, he can subjectively sense positive response to these efforts. But this is a blind, mindless effort to gloss over the reality of the perceptual, motivational, emotional, and cognitive human transaction that occurs in the mysterious "black box" called psychic life. What seems lacking is a workable description of:
(1) What kind of child with what kind of problem?
(2) What developmental life conditions and experiences have produced this child-with-a-problem?
(3) What life forces exist at this moment?
(4) How is change produced in human beings, and what skills are needed to bring it about?'

Other questions remain as well: What specific skill training does the teacher-counselor receive for working with families of troubled children? Does the Re-Ed model envision other professional pathways to the teacher-counselor role, or must all staff come from the profession of education? What is the turnover rate for teacher-counselors, and what organizational requisites are necessary to make this form of service delivery work at optimum efficiency? What sort of ongoing training, consultation, and ancillary support services are required by the teacher-counselor, and how are they woven into the fabric of the Re-Ed program? In short, while the concept of the teacher-counselor raises some exciting possibilities for the future development of community-based services, it also raises some important educational and organizational questions, which remain unanswered. At the time of its inception in the early 1960s, the Re-Ed program represented a bold and innovative departure from traditional child mental health services. Hobbs and his associates answered resoundingly in the negative to the supposition that emotionally disturbed children could not receive education for living in a short-term, noninstitutional, growth-oriented residential school staffed by specially trained teachers. The results of the first stage of their project are now available, and it remains for us to examine through future research and demonstration efforts what implications they contain for the future of residential child care.

(1) At the level of philosophy, the Re-Ed concept – as articulated by its originator, Nicholas Hobbs – presents us with an eloquently written brief for the community treatment of troubled children, a brief that foreshadowed by at least a decade the arguments for deinstitutionalization.

(2) Re-Ed proposed a bold restructuring of mental health services for troubled children in need of care away from home. Among the more significant aspects of the service package are its short-term nature, low community visibility, commitment to the development of the child, and educational emphasis.

(3) Re-Ed's conception of the 'teacher-counselor' represents a pioneering attempt to translate the European concept of the *éducateur* to the American scene.

(4) At the level of program detail, the Re-Ed model is less fully developed. Procedures are not clearly apparent; indeed, one gets the impression that *no* procedures are critical to this approach – leaving an enormous problem when it comes to replication and evaluation.

(5) The role of the teacher-counselor needs further amplification with respect to skill training, selection, professional background, development of a career ladder, and place on the mental health team.

These limitations notwithstanding, the work of Hobbs and his colleagues in Project Re-Ed constitutes a bold and innovative approach to reaching troubled children in their home communities. As a theoretician, Hobbs was ahead of the field by at least a decade, and many of his ideas as embodied in Project Re-Ed deserve reexamination today.

A final personal reflection: the other 23 hours

Inevitably, the foregoing review led me to examine the seminal influences on my own thinking about the therapeutic milieu and, more specifically, the thinking behind an earlier collaborative effort, *The Other 23 Hours* (Trieschman, Whittaker, and Brendtro, 1969). That volume written primarily as a practice manual for child care workers, attempted to provide a reasoned conceptual and practical approach to the care and treatment of emotionally disturbed children in residential centres during the hours of the day not spent in individual therapy. Our effort differed from Project Re-Ed and many of the other previously mentioned approaches to milieu treatment in two significant ways. First, the book reflects less a single demonstration effort and more the collective experience of the authors in a number of different treatment settings – notably the Walker School in Needham, Massachusetts, and the University of Michigan Fresh Air Camp. Second, we were not attempting to create a new model of service delivery for troubled children; rather, we were interested in examining how the events of daily living in a therapeutic residence – the rules, routines, games, and personal encounters – could be used to teach children something about the reasonable limits of their present behaviour, while at the same time providing them with opportunities for growth and change. We hoped to develop a set of 'lenses' for examining the events of daily life and a set of guidelines for managing them that would be useful for the line child care worker faced with tasks of nurturing, teaching, and disciplining the disturbed child in 'the other 23 hours'.

To this undertaking we brought a diverse array of professional experiences and theoretical biases; our backgrounds were in clinical psychology, social group work, education, and psychology. We pooled a collective experience that included child psychotherapy, behavioural modification, special education, and group treatment. The work of Redl and Wineman (1957) had a seminal influence on the development of the book and reinforced our common belief that the theoretical framework used in milieu treatment had first to be translated in terms that made sense to the child care worker operating alone in the life space with a group of disturbed children. In fact, our approach derived not from any single theoretical perspective – though psychoanalytic ego psychology, in particular, the later work of Robert White (1959, 1960) on 'competence' provided a unifying theme for much of what we finally developed. Rather, we used as primary data our own experiences and those of other child care workers in intervening with behaviour in the life space. While we continued to be interested in the *why* of behaviour, we were much more concerned with what to do about it – a concern that was continuously reinforced by child care staff who needed daily help in managing and redirecting the often noisy and troublesome behaviour of the children in our care, as well as in providing them with constructive alternatives for the future. This essentially pragmatic approach to child care work yielded a result that was neither theoretically 'pure' nor empirically tested and in no sense constituted a fully developed model of milieu treatment. We did produce a set of observations and suggestions that seemed to help child care workers and other professionals make some sense of the behaviour of the troubled child in 'the other 23 hours' while at the same time expanding their range of options for what to do about it.

Three central ideas emerge from the book. First, the therapeutic milieu is conceived of as a 'living and learning' environment where the events of group living – the rules, routines, activities, and behavioural interchanges – become formats for managing disruptive, troublesome, and maladaptive behaviour, as well as for teaching prosocial alternatives (Trieschman, Whittaker, and Brendtro, 1969:1–51). Because children learn in different ways, the milieu must incorporate many different teaching formats that accommodate to the different styles of learning: We believed that child care counselors, who work with the children around the clock, should be the major agents of therapy and that a therapeutic milieu should not merely help children gain insight, or manage their behaviour, but should help them build competence (and confidence) in a wide range of areas.

A second contribution was the development of the concept of 'relationship' as it informs the teaching context. In our scheme (Trieschman, Whittaker, and Brendtro, 1969:57), each element of a relationship – social reinforcement, communication, and modeling – facilitates a specific learning process: reward and punishment learning, insight learning, and identification-imitation learning, respectively. Using this framework, we offered suggestions for establishing 'relationship beachheads' (see Brendtro, 1969) and for overcoming certain barriers to relationship formation. Our intention here was to identify the processes of social interaction that occur between child care worker and child and that can have a profound effect on the success of treatment – a fact graphically illustrated in the failure of the initial attempt to replicate the Achievement Place project mentioned earlier (Phillips *et al.*, 1973a).

A third contribution of the book was its conceptualization and development of the various formats available for teaching alternative behaviour: mealtimes, bedtimes, wake-up, and program activities. In each of these sections, we attempted to demonstrate the function of the routine, or activity, in developmental terms as well as its specific strengths and limitations as a format for teaching alternative behaviour. The final section of the book dealt with understanding and dealing with temper tantrums, observing and recording the behaviour of children in the life space, and avoiding some of the roadblocks to therapeutic management.

While *The Other 23 Hours* continues to provide a useful framework for understanding and intervening in the therapeutic milieu, certain shortcomings are more apparent today than they were at the time of publication.[5] First, while the theory base of the book is presented as essentially open and eclectic, it relies far too heavily, in my opinion, on psychoanalytic ego psychology for its justification. The interposition of the term *ego* between the behaviour that needs to be changed and the formats available for teaching reflects, I believe, the authors' classical training and the theory available at the time the book was written. I do not mean here to denigrate the function of cognitive process or to downgrade the enormous heuristic contribution of ego psychology to the development of a theory of human behaviour. I do suggest that we are still far from having a coherent, unified theory of milieu treatment and should therefore avoid overreliance on any single theoretical schema, particularly one with such shaky empirical underpinnings. At another level, the book suffers from the same procedural primitivism for which I criticized other approaches to milieu treatment. This is a problem for residential treatment as a whole and is reflected in the available evaluative research, which, if it indicates change in the dependent variable at all, is unable to provide a precise definition of the independent variables responsible for the change.

A second and obvious flaw in the book is the absence of any clearly articulated procedures for evaluation of the individual case or of the total program. The evaluative component is critical to any approach to milieu treatment today, not only because it is the only way in which we will ultimately arrive at a theory of changing children's behaviour but also because it may be necessary for the very survival of the program. Finally, the book suffers from an insufficient treatment of the important elements in the child's total life system. Notable here for their absence are sections on the importance of classroom education and the importance of working with parents.

Despite these and other shortcomings, I still agree with the essential conception of the milieu as a medium for competency acquisition that makes use of a variety of formats for teaching alternative behaviour and which weighs equally the cognitive and affective as well as the behavioural components of the change process.

One can come away from a review such as this with the feeling that we really know nothing about what 'works' in residential treatment. Such is not the case. Each approach to residential treatment has, in its own way, furthered our knowledge of one or another important aspect of the therapeutic milieu. We know, for example, more than we used to about the relative potency of insight versus behavioural approaches with particu-

lar levels of troublesome behaviour. Research studies and painful experience have convinced us of the enormous power of the peer group as a
potent intervening variable in changing individual and group behaviour. We know that models of treatment organization that are functional
in a clinic setting may not be at all appropriate when extended to a
24-hour-a-day program. Finally, we realize more than ever the critical
importance of aftercare services as a follow-up to residential treatment
and the notion of taking a total ecological approach to helping troubled
children and their families. Future models of residential treatment will
most certainly be built on the foundations laid by Aichorn, Bettelheim,
Redl, Hobbs, and the many other contributors who have gone before.
Perhaps the most important lesson to be learned from a review of this
type is that no model of residential treatment should be based solely on
theoretical presuppositions but should instead begin – as did the
contributors cited above – with the real-life problems of the children
coming into care.

Notes

(1) Professor of Social Work, School of Social Work, University of Washington,
    Seattle, USA.
(2) The following appeared in James K. Whittaker, 1979, *Caring for Troubled
    Children: Residential Treatment in a Community Context*. San Francisco: Jossey-
    Bass, pp. 43–83, and is reprinted here with permission of the author and
    publisher. (Available also in the United Kingdom from Jossey-Bass Ltd.,
    28 Banner Street, London EC1Y 8QE.)
(3) Vorrath and Brendtro (1974) and others make a point of distinguishing their
    positively oriented peer approach (positive peer culture) from the original
    guided group interaction method. While the new emphasis on the positive
    aspects of the peer process is both understandable and laudable, the two
    labels describe, for all intents and purposes, the same phenomena and will
    therefore be used interchangeably.
(4) This last component appears to have been borrowed directly from the Maxim
    Gorky labour collective for delinquents, which existed in the USSR in the
    1920s under the direction of Anton Makarenko (see Rhodes and Tracy,
    1972 : 420–33).
(5) In the years since the publication of the book, I have benefited immensely
    from discussion of many of these issues with my colleagues, Albert Triesch-
    man and Larry Brendtro. While their views, and mine, have changed since
    the book was published, I must, in fairness, take full responsibility for the
    following criticism.

References

Aichorn, A. (1935) *Wayward Youth*. New York: Viking Press.

Allen, K. E. and Harris, F. R. (1966) Elimination of a Child's Excessive Scratching by Training the Mother in Reinforcement Procedures. *Behavior Research and Therapy* 4: 79–84.

Allen, K. E., Hart, B., Buell, J. S., Harris, F. R., and Wolf, M. M. (1964) Effects of Social Reinforcement on Isolate Behavior of a Nursery School Child. *Child Development* 35: 511–18.

Allerhand, M. E., Weber, R., and Haug, M. (1966) *Adaptation and Adaptability: The Bellefaire Follow-up Study*. New York: Child Welfare League of America.

Bettelheim, B. (1950) *Love Is Not Enough*. New York: Free Press.

Bettelheim, B. (1955) *Truants from Life*. New York: Free Press.

Bettelheim, B. (1967) *The Empty Fortress*. New York: Free Press.

Bettelheim, B. (1974) *A Home for the Heart*. New York: Knopf.

Bettelheim, B. and Sylvester, E. (1948) A Therapeutic Milieu. *American Journal of Orthopsychiatry* 18 (2): 191–206. Also in H. W. Polsky, D. S. Claster, and C. Goldberg (eds) (1970) *Social System Perspectives in Residential Institutions*. East Lansing: Michigan State University Press.

Bower, E., Laurie, R., Strutter, C., and Fetherland, R. (1969) *Project Re-Ed*. Nashville, Tennessee: George Peabody College.

Brendtro, L. K. (1969) Establishing Relationship Beachheads. In A. E. Trieschman, J. K. Whittaker, and L. K. Brendtro (eds) *The Other 23 Hours: Child Care Work in a Therapeutic Milieu*. Chicago: Aldine.

Brodie, R. D. (1972) Some Aspects of Psychotherapy in a Residential Treatment Center. In J. K. Whittaker and A. E. Trieschman (eds) *Children Away from Home: A Sourcebook of Residential Treatment*. Chicago: Aldine.

Browning, R. M. and Stover, D. O. (1971) *Behavior Modification in Child Treatment*. Chicago: Aldine.

Burmeister, E. (1960) *The Professional Houseparent*. New York: Columbia University Press.

Cavior, E. C., Schmidt, A., and Karacki, L. (1972) *An Evaluation of the Kennedy Youth Center Differential Treatment Program*. Washington, DC: US Bureau of Prisons.

Cohen, H. L. and Filipczak, J. (1971) *A New Learning Experiment: A Case for Learning*. San Francisco: Jossey-Bass.

Cummings, J. and Cummings, E. (1963) *Ego and Milieu*. New York: Atherton Press.

Dentler, R. A. and Mackler, B. (1961) The Socialization of Retarded Children in an Institution. *Journal of Health and Human Behavior*, 2: 243–52.

Durkin, R. P. and Durkin, A. B. (1975) Evaluating Residential Treatment Programs for Disturbed Children. In M. Guttentag and E. L. Struening (eds), *Handbook of Evaluation Research*, Vol. 2. Beverly Hills, California: Sage Publications.

Empey, L. T. and Lubeck, S. G. (1972) *The Silverlake Experiment*. Chicago: Aldine.

Flackett, J. M. and Flackett, G. (1970) Criswell House: An Alternative to Institutional Treatment for Juvenile Offenders. *Federal Probation* 34: 30–7.

Goffman, E. (1962) *Asylums*. Chicago: Aldine.

Goldfarb, W., Mintz, I., and Stroock, K. W. (1969) *A Time To Heal*. New York: International Universities Press.

Goocher, B. (1975) Behavioral Applications of an Educateur Model in Child Care. *Child Care Quarterly* **4** (2): 84–92.

Guindon, J. (1970) *Les Étapes de la Rééducation* (Stages in Reeducation). Paris: Editions Fleurus.

Harris, F. R., Johnson, M. K., Kelley, C. S., and Wolf, M. M. (1964) Effects of Positive Social Reinforcement on Regressed Crawling of a Nursery School Child. *Journal of Educational Psychology* **55**: 35–41.

Harstad, C. (1976) Guided Group Interaction: Positive Peer Culture. *Child Care Quarterly* **5** (2): 109–20.

Hart, B. M., Allen, K. E., Buell, J. S., Harris, F. R., and Wolf, M. M. (1964) Effects of Social Reinforcement on Operant Crying. *Journal of Experimental Child Psychology* **1**: 145–53.

Henry, J. (1957) The Culture of Interpersonal Relations in a Therapeutic Institution for Emotionally Disturbed Children. *American Journal of Orthopsychiatry* **27** (4): 725–35.

Hobbs, N. (1964) The Process of Reeducation. Unpublished paper, George Peabody College, Nashville, Tennessee.

Hobbs, N. (1966) Helping Disturbed Children: Psychological and Ecological Strategies. *American Psychologist* **21** (12): 1105–151.

Hobbs, N. (1967) The Reeducation of Emotionally Disturbed Children. In E. M. Bower and W. G. Hollister (eds) *Behavioral Science Frontiers in Education*. New York: John Wiley.

Hobbs, N. (1975a) *The Futures of Children: Categories, Labels and Their Consequences.* San Francisco: Jossey-Bass.

Hobbs, N. (ed) (1975b) *Issues in the Classification of Children: A Sourcebook on Categories, Labels, and Their Consequences* (2 vols). San Francisco: Jossey-Bass.

Johnson, C. A. and Katz, R. C. (1973) Using Parents as Change Agents for Their Children: A Review. *Journal of Child Psychology and Child Psychiatry* **14**: 181–200.

Joint Commission on Mental Health of Children (1970) *Crisis in Child Mental Health: Challenge for the 1970s.* New York: Harper & Row.

Konopka, G. (1946) *Therapeutic Group Work with Children.* Minneapolis: University of Minnesota Press.

Konopka, G. (1954) *Group Work in the Institution.* New York: Association Press.

Kozloff, M. A. (1975) *Reaching the Autistic Child in a Parent Training Program.* Champaign, Illinois: Research Press.

Long, N. J., Morse, W. C., and Newman, R. G. (1971) *Conflict in the Classroom* (second edition). Belmont, California: Wadsworth.

Lovaas, O. I. (1967) A Behavior Therapy Approach to the Treatment of Childhood Schizophrenia. In J. P. Hill (ed.) *Minnesota Symposium on Child Psychology.* Minneapolis: University of Minnesota Press.

McCorkle, L. W., Elias, A., and Bixby, F. L. (1958) *The Highfields Story.* New York: Holt, Rinehart & Winston.

McNeil, E. (1969) The European *Éducateur* Program for Disturbed Children: A Response. *Forum for Residential Therapy* **2** (1): 15–20.

Makarenko, A. S. (1955) *The Road to Life: An Epic of Education.* Moscow: Foreign Languages Publishing House.

Mayer, M. F. (1960) The Parental Figures in Residential Treatment. *Social Service Review* **34** (3): 273–85.

Mayer, M. F. and Blum, A. (eds) (1971) *Healing Through Living: A Symposium on Residential Treatment*. Springfield, Illinois: Charles C. Thomas.

Noshpitz, J. D. (1962) Notes on the Theory of Residential Treatment. *Journal of American Academy of Child Psychiatry* **1** (2): 284–96.

Noshpitz, J. D. (1971) The Psychotherapist in Residential Treatment, In M. F. Mayer and A. Blum (eds) *Healing Through Living: A Symposium on Residential Treatment*. Springfield, Illinois: Charles C. Thomas.

Pappenfort, D. M., Kilpatrick, D. M., and Roberts, R. W. (eds) (1973) *Child Caring: Social Pollicy and the Institution*. Chicago: Aldine.

Patterson, G. R. and Gullion, M. (1968) *Living with Children*. Champaign, Illinois: Research Press.

Patterson, G. R., Reid, J. B., Janes, R. R., and Conger, R. E. (1975) *A Social Learning Approach to Family Intervention*. Eugene, Oregon: Castalia.

Phillips, E. L., Phillips, E. A., Fixsen, D. L., and Wolf, M. M. (1973a) Achievement Place: Behavior Shaping Works for Delinquents. *Psychology Today* **7** (1): 74–80.

Phillips, E. L., Wolf, M. M., and Fixsen, D. L. (1973b) Achievement Place: Development of an Elected Manager System. *Journal of Applied Behavior Analysis* **6** (4): 541–63.

Piliavin, I. (1963) Conflict Between Cottage Parents and Caseworkers. *Social Service Review* **37**: 17–25. Also in H. W. Polsky, D. S. Claster, and C. Goldberg (eds) (1970) *Social System Perspectives in Residential Institutions*. East Lansing: Michigan State University Press.

Pilnick, S. (1971) Guided Group Interaction. In R. Morris (ed) *Encylopedia of Social Work* Vol. 1. Washington, DC: National Association of Social Workers.

Polsky, H. W. (1962) *Cottage Six – The Social System of Delinquent Boys in Residential Treatment*. New York: Russell Sage Foundation.

Quay, H. C. (1979) Residential Treatment. In Quay, H. C. and J. S. Werry (eds) *Psychopathological Disorders of Childhood* (second edition). New York: John Wiley.

Raush, H. L., Dittman, A. T., and Taylor, J. J. (1959) The Interpersonal Behavior of Children in Residential Treatment. *Journal of Abnormal and Social Psychology* **58**: 9–26.

Redl, F. (1959) The Concept of a 'Therapeutic Milieu'. *American Journal of Orthopsychiatry* **29**: 721–36. Also in G. H. Weber and B. J. Haberlein (eds) (1972) *Residential Treatment of Emotionally Disturbed Children*. New York: Behavioral Publications.

Redl, F. (1966) *When We Deal with Children*. New York: Free Press.

Redl, F. and Wattenberg, M. W. (1959) *Mental Hygiene in Teaching*. New York: Harcourt Brace Jovanovich.

Redl, F. and Wineman, D. (1957) *The Aggressive Child*. New York: Free Press.

Repucci, N. D. and Saunders, J. T. (1974) Social Psychology of Behaviour Modification: Problems of Implementation in Natural Settings. *American Psychologist* **29**: 649–60.

Rhodes, W. C. and Tracy, M. L. (1972) *A Study of Child Variance*. Ann Arbor: University of Michigan Press.

Rose, S. D. (1972) *Treating Children in Groups: A Behavioral Approach*. San Francisco: Jossey-Bass.

Sarri, R. C. and Selo, E. (1974) Evaluation Process and Outcome in Juvenile Corrections: A Grim Tale. In P. O. Davidson, F. W. Clark, and L. A. Hammerlynch (eds) *Evaluation of Community Programs*. Champaign, Illinois: Research Press.

Schopler, E. and Reichler, R. J. (1971a) Parents as Cotherapists in the Treatment of Psychotic Children. *Journal of Autism and Childhood Schizophrenia* **1** (1): 87–102.

Schopler, E. and Reichler, R. J. (1971b) Psychobiological Referents for the Treatment of Autism. In D. W. Churchill, G. D. Alpern, and M. K. Demyer (eds) *Infantile Autism: Proceedings of the Indiana Symposium*. Springfield, Illinois, Charles C. Thomas.

Schopler, E. and Reichler, R. J. (1976) *Psychopathology and Child Development: Research and Treatment*. New York: Plenum.

Schulze, S. (ed.) (1951) *Creative Group Living in a Children's Institution*. New York: Association Press.

Stephenson, R. M. and Scarpitti, F. R. (1974) *Group Interaction as Therapy: The Use of the Small Group in Corrections*. Westport, Connecticut: Greenwood Press.

Taft, J. (1919) Relation of Personality Study to Child Placing. *Proceedings: National Conference on Social Welfare* **46**: 595–98.

Taylor, D. A. and Alpert, S. W. (1973) *Continuity and Support Following Residential Treatment*. New York: Child Welfare League of America.

Trieschman, A. E., Whittaker, J. K., and Brendtro, L. K. (1969) *The Other 23 Hours: Child Care Work in a Therapeutic Milieu*. Chicago: Aldine.

Vorrath, H. H. and Brendtro, L. K. (1974) *Positive Peer Culture*. Chicago: Aldine.

Wahler, R. G. (1975) Some Structural Aspects of Deviant Child Behavior. *Journal of Applied Behavior Analysis* **8** (1): 27–43.

Wahler, R. G., House, A. E., and Stambaugh, E. E. (1976) *Ecological Assessment of Child Problem Behavior*. Elmsford, New York: Pergamon Press.

Weeks, H. A. (1963) *Youthful Offenders at Highfields*. Ann Arbor: University of Michigan Press.

Weinstein, L. (1974) *Evaluation of a Program for Re-Educating Disturbed Children: A Follow-up Comparison with Untreated Children*. Washington, DC: US Office of Education, Department of Health, Education and Welfare.

White, R. W. (1959) Motivation Reconsidered: The Concept of Competence. *Psychological Review* **66**: 297–333.

White, R. W. (1960) Competence and the Psychosexual Stages of Development. In M. R. Jones (ed.) *Nebraska Symposium on Motivation*. Lincoln: University of Nebraska Press.

Whittaker, J. K. (1970a) Developing a Unified Theory of Residential Treatment. *Mental Hygiene* **54** (1): 166–69.

Whittaker, J. K. (1970b) Training Child Care Staff: Pitfalls and Promises. *Mental Hygiene* **54** (4): 516–19.

Whittaker, J. K. (1970c) Planning for Child Care Institutions. Unpublished doctoral dissertation, University of Minnesota.

Whittaker, J. K. (1971a) Colonial Child Care Institutions: Our Heritage of Care. *Child Welfare* **50** (7): 396–400.

Whittaker, J. K. (1971b) Mental Hygiene Influences in Children's Institutions: Organization and Technology for Treatment. *Mental Hygiene* **55** (4): 444–50.

Whittaker, J. K. (1979) *Caring for Troubled Children: Residential Treatment in a Community Context*. San Francisco: Jossey-Bass.

Wolf, M. M., Mees, H., and Risley, T. (1964) Application of Operant Conditioning Procedures to the Behavior Problems of an Autistic Child. *Behavior Research and Therapy* **1**: 305–12.

Wolins, M. (ed.) (1974) *Successful Group Care: Explorations in the Powerful Environment*. Chicago: Aldine.

Wolins, M. and Gottesmann, M. (1971) *Group Care: An Israeli Approach*. New York: Gordon & Breach.

5 New roles for group care centres

Jerome Beker[1]

When the irresistible force meets the immovable object, prudence suggests that we seek an alternative resolution that allows us to disengage without sacrificing legitimate and significant objectives.[2] This has relevance to the context of group care, since it is hard to say which is now more pervasive, the demand that institutional group care and treatment programs be abolished or the evidence that such programs will continue to exist.

Cyclical though it may be, much of current professional and lay opinion holds that for reasons intrinsic to institutional and other group care services, these kinds of programs have failed to realize their objectives, are intrinsically cost-ineffective, are too expensive – whether effective or not – and deprive young people and their families of their rights. There is even broader agreement that these observations reflect the reality of most contemporary group care, which some view as the result of operational failures rather than as intrinsic to group care settings. Propelled by frequently undifferentiated concern for economy and by all too frequent, often widely publicized incidents of abuse, increasing pressures have arisen to abandon institutional group care in favour of less expensive, less 'restrictive' alternatives in juvenile corrections, rehabilitation, treatment, dependency, retardation, and the like.

The future of group care

Although many young people have been 'deinstitutionalized' as a result of these factors, the numbers of those in residential programs do not seem to decrease. New models of group care have begun to emerge, but there appears to be little prospect of significantly reducing the numbers of youth for whom we will need to provide residential programs in situations other than family settings. Some recent research even begins to suggest, contrary to most current thinking, that incarceration is a more effective antidote to juvenile crime than the less restrictive options (Murray and Cox, 1979), a view that might, in the current political climate, stimulate a return to the acceptance of such alternatives, including mandatory sentencing and the like. Increasingly influential views of the rights of minors, that are altering the traditional role of the juvenile court in favour of more formal legal approaches, may tend to push the field in the same direction. For better or worse, group care is very much a phenomenon of the present and the future as well as the past.

The essential question, then, is not how group care can be destroyed or enshrined. It is how group care – as a means of helping people – can be enhanced, used as appropriately and effectively as possible, and its non-helping consequences reduced or eliminated. A detailed analysis of the sources of difficulty is beyond the scope of this chapter, but it seems reasonable to conclude that the more that group care settings are integrated within the broader community in responsible roles, the more possible it should be to avoid the negative, 'institutionalization' phenomena that have been identified by Goffman (1961) and others. Wolins (1974:288), for example, reports on the basis of extensive research that 'social integration within the large milieu appears to mark the successful program'. It seems essential, therefore, that we explore available models suggesting how this might best be accomplished.

The continuum of care

Many current attempts to respond to these issues emphasize the importance of providing a continuum of operationally linked services ranging from most to least restrictive, to which clients can be assigned and among which they can be transferred as appropriate to their needs, resources and development (Whittaker, 1979). In this context, residential and community-based services represent different elements of a comprehensive system of services rather than a service dichotomy. Few would disagree that, other things being equal, we would for many reasons prefer that young people remain at home as much as possible. But we recognize that other things are not always equal, and the continuum of care concept enables us to envisage an integrated range of services attuned to the changing individual needs of the client.

Since child and youth services both in Great Britain and North America are typically fragmented among categories of clients served (e.g. disturbed, delinquent, and dependent), a pluralistic view of 'continua of care' would be a more accurate representation. In the United States, for example, the child welfare system, the mental health system, the developmental disability system, and the juvenile justice system are largely parallel, with few readily negotiable 'crossover' opportunities. Therefore, a young person who becomes involved with one is likely to have difficulty in making a transition to another continuum that might be more appropriate. For the purposes of the discussion that follows, the single continuum concept is clearer and is retained, but it should be remembered that the actual situation is more complex. We will return to this point later.

Since its roots lie in the search for community-based alternatives to institutional care and in such concepts as 'least restrictive alternative', the continuum of care has been depicted as just that, a bipolar continuum *(Figure 5(1))*. Legalistically and programmatically, this is a useful schema because it provides a view of the range of available options and a convenient (although sometimes oversimplified) depiction of the relative restrictiveness of each. It is less useful, however, as a representation of the organizational structure required, if such a system is to be able to work effectively in meeting the changing needs of individual clients. Viewing the configuration of agency resources as a wheel or star with the individual agencies (or programs in a multifunction agency) on the circumference permits easier portrayal of the essential communication links. *Figure 5(2)* suggests a schema that might lend itself more readily to the necessary interaction and coordination in the service of the client.[3]

Figure 5(1)   Illustrative continuum of care and treatment in child and youth services

Most restrictive
| Institutional incarceration
| 'Open' institution
| Community group home
| Foster home placement
| Day treatment
| After-school program
| In-home assistance
| Family counseling
| Group or individual counseling
| Parent education
| Leisure-time services
Least restrictive

Note: Other options are also available in some situations, e.g. five-day placements, weekend placements, sleep-in centres, respite centres for parents, 'crash pads', and the like. The sequence on the continuum may vary depending on the nature of particular programs.

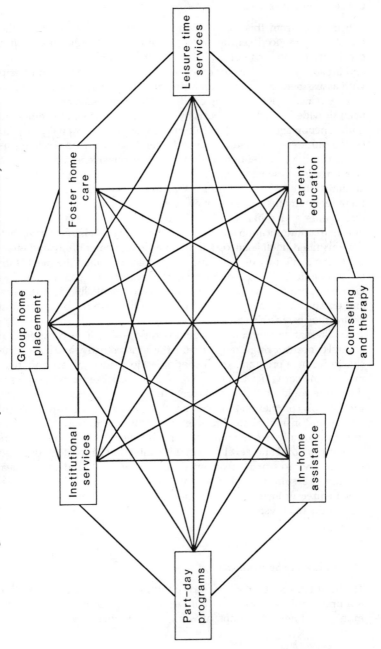

Figure 5(2)   Communication patterns in a model continuum of care in child and youth services

Coordination of services

Still missing from this formulation is the coordinating function, the broadly experienced central service equipped to handle intake with sensitivity to the range of available resources, to provide consultation and broader perspectives for other than routine situations, and to help with assessment, program monitoring and the re-assignment of clients among available services as needed. Traditionally, such assistance has been provided on a limited basis by central or administrative offices in multifunction agencies and by informal contact or, occasionally by joint or community-sponsored intake and referral services. As mechanisms for facilitating intervention decisions and responsiveness to changing client needs, these have tended to be inefficient; to be more attuned to administrative tasks and concerns than to program and individual treatment requirements; to be relatively isolated and inaccessible to prospective clients and other 'outsiders'; and often to serve as barriers to effective communication among the services *(Figure 5(3))*. Nor have they demonstrated notable success in helping to implement fully and effectively the continuity of care concept, particularly when the need is for sensitive and timely re-assignment of clients across the continuum. This is to be expected, since these mechanisms are essentially administrative and organizational and typically lack direct ties with the programs and clients they ostensibly exist to serve.

An alternative would be to view the service system as comprised of several concentric rings, ranging from the least restrictive and least intrusive preventive programs on the periphery to residential care and treatment at the core *(Figure 5(4))*. Increasingly specialized services toward the centre could, in this model, provide both the needed interventions for the most complex and difficult problems as well as a constant flow of energy and insight about effective intervention to those working with less dramatically needy young people and their families. If they were reconceptualized and developed in this context as Centres for Advanced Practice and Research, residential centres would stand in an ideal position to assume this role and function, thus facilitating their effectiveness in direct group care and treatment as well as catalyzing the effectiveness of the total system.[4]

The health care field: an analogy

The health care system provides a roughly analogous model *(Figure 5(5))*. Routine health care takes place in normal living situations in the community: at home, at school, at work, and the like. A wide variety of

Figure 5(3)   Likely communication patterns in a continuum of care with a central coordinating service

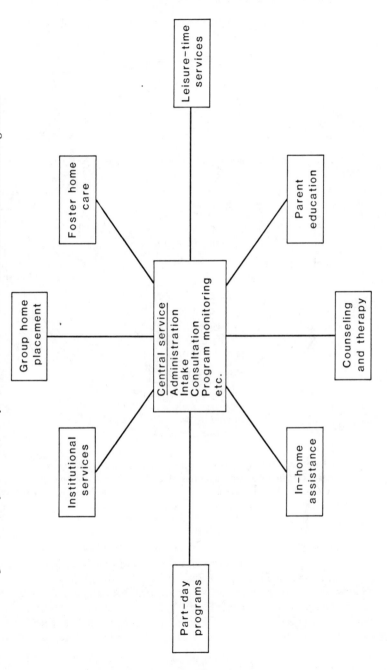

Figure 5(4)   A concentric portrayal of the continuum of care in child and youth services

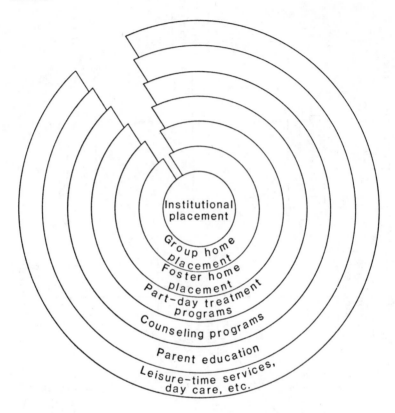

Institutional placement

Group home placement

Foster home placement

Part-day treatment programs

Counseling programs

Parent education

Leisure-time services, day care, etc.

Note: The 'notch' in the figure portrays the possibility of direct access for consumers/clients to each layer of service, with decreasing frequency closer to the core, but usual access would be through the outer layer to the inner ones. (Referrals may also skip particular layers of service.)

preventive efforts include, for example, media publicity and other approaches to citizen education and a variety of group-based efforts to deal with potential health problems, such as AA, Weight Watchers, and Smoke-Enders. For minor or beginning health problems, we usually consult a physician or a clinic. The next step may involve tests and consultation with a specialist. Local hospitals provide in-patient care when needed, for more or less routine or clear-cut situations. However, when the diagnostic and treatment resources of these agencies are insufficient, contact is usually made with a teaching hospital so that its broader range of expertise and other resources can be brought into play. If circumstances indicate, the case may then be referred back to local facilities for treatment, but the system (at least in theory and certainly in many cases in fact) provides an opportunity for access to the needed level of service. At the same time, it provides less sophisticated services for routine cases which do not need such intensive consultation and intervention; such cases would otherwise flood the system. In addition, contact with the teaching hospital and its resources makes available, at least ideally, a steady flow of expertise that informs and energizes the health care system at all levels and health care throughout the population.

Typically, the diagnostic process at each 'layer' of service *(see Figure 5(5))* involves a decision regarding where the patient can best be served and is followed by referral when that seems indicated. Such referrals are not normally seen as failures by those involved – there are, of course, exceptions – but as effective utilization of available resources to meet specific needs. The more highly specialized settings and personnel also provide continuing education services for the less specialized ones, not only to broaden and deepen their treatment competence, but also to increase their diagnostic sensitivity and their awareness of appropriate resources for referral. This occurs at every layer of the hierarchy, e.g. physicians educating the public about the symptoms of possible heart attacks and the cancer danger signs, and programs provided by teaching hospitals for medical specialists in all fields. To paraphrase the classic prayer, good medical practice requires the knowledge and skill to treat effectively what one can treat, the security and information to refer appropriately elsewhere what one cannot, and the wisdom to know the difference.

Contrasts with child and youth services

The predominant flow of clients in child and youth services is quite different. Rarely does anyone progress systematically by referral through the system, from leisure-time services and day care, for example, to a clinic setting, to day treatment, to a residential program if that seems indicated – all as the result of orderly, client-centred diagnostic decisions beginning with early identification of and response to troubled or troubling behaviour.[5] In many cases, referral for more appropriate service is unduly deferred by the staff due to inertia, or actively resisted as carrying some onus of personal or program failure. Not infrequently, little happens until dramatically needy behaviour results in immediate referral, perhaps even for institutionalization, with-

Figure 5(5)   A concentric portrayal of the continuum of care in health care

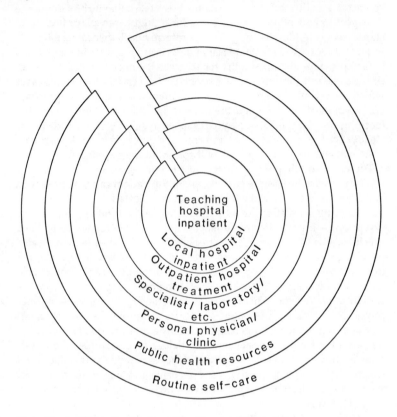

Teaching
hospital
inpatient

Local hospital inpatient

Outpatient hospital treatment

Specialist / laboratory / etc.

Personal physician / clinic

Public health resources

Routine self-care

Note: The 'notch' in the figure portrays the possibility of direct access for
     consumers/clients to each layer of service, with decreasing frequency closer
     to the core, but usual access would be through the outer layer to the inner
     ones. (Referrals may also skip particular layers of service.)

out adequate exploration of less restrictive alternatives. Such referral
decisions are often externally imposed through the justice system or
otherwise. As a result, residential settings are used to meet a largely
undefined combination of sometimes conflicting needs involving social
control, in addition to developmental support and treatment. Economic
and other sanctions tend to demand that residential facilities be kept as
full as possible and not reduce the numbers in programs oriented to
social control. Because of this, internal monitoring cannot, under current

conditions, be depended upon to reject inappropriate referrals or to assure that clients are promptly referred to less restrictive alternatives when that course is indicated on the basis of their current needs and capacities.

The contrast is perhaps clearest in the context of persons viewed as untreatable', those whom we do not seem to have additional ways to help (Hirschbach, 1980). In the health care system, such individuals tend to be referred out, to be sent to less specialized hospitals, to custodial facilities, or to their homes. In child and youth services, however, the more intractable the case, the more likely is a referral for long term placement in a nominally treatment-oriented residential facility. There may be young people who need to be in such 'protective custody' for their own protection and/or that of society, but an institution that views this as its primary function – and, therefore, pays less attention to fostering developmental progress – is hardly equipped to take the lead in designing and implementing creative approaches to treatment for those who could more readily be helped. This situation has some of its roots in the use of the institution as an instrument of social control, as mentioned above; others lie in the conceptual confusion that has developed among treatment, developmental, and custodial functions and processes in residential programs (Durkin and Durkin, 1975).

This is not to imply that institutions serving delinquents or other categories of young people who are frequently referred for reasons of social control cannot serve community needs in the expanded ways that have been proposed. It has frequently been observed that institutional populations tend to be more alike than different whether they are labeled as delinquent, dependent, mentally ill, or categorized in other ways. The programs are generally similar as well, and all should be characterized by a focus on setting and meeting developmental objectives on an individualized basis, regardless of the population or primary referring system involved. More broadly, there is need for close integration of the juvenile justice system with other youth-serving structures (e.g. mental health, social service, special education). Thus, the proposed model can be developed largely irrespective of the institution's nominal target population, provided its program focus, its interrelationships with other youth-serving activities and the expectation and demand systems within which it functions are appropriate.

The limits of the analogy

The model of the health care system with the teaching hospital at its core has emerged in the context of rapidly expanding technology, which has resulted in explosive increases in the demand for a variety of expensive, sophisticated medical equipment, and technical knowledge and skill. Private physicians and local hospitals, serving a relatively limited number of patients, simply cannot afford to acquire and maintain such equipment and expertise; nor can they keep up with the geometric rate of change in these areas. The situation in child and youth services, where technology is generally less of a factor, is not fully parallel. In many cases, the developmental needs that bring young people to us require gradual, humanistically-oriented, close interpersonal intervention rather than an external, technology-based 'quick fix'. Nonetheless, the need for coordination and a means of bringing the most sophisticated understandings to bear on the needs of each individual is analogous in the two systems.

In health care, the coordination/linking function often remains with the referring physician, whereas referrals in child and youth services usually leave the case essentially closed as far as the referring agency is concerned. Collaboration among agencies around broader program concerns is also typically minimal, although efforts to establish effective inter-agency consultation or 'networking' for youth advocacy and other purposes are increasing (Center for Youth Development and Research, 1978). On the other hand, the health care system, with the teaching hospital at its core, has facilitated the implementation of ever-expanding medical knowledge and technology. It has also been able to hand over much of its preventive and healing capacity through 'health advocacy' efforts at levels successively closer to the 'grass roots', and thus to influence the direction of health policy, health programs, and practices in the community, and the everyday lives of the population. Not only is the teaching hospital embedded in the health care system, but the system which it serves is increasingly embedded in the wider community. Referral and coordination may remain largely the task of the local physician, but the physician is typically involved in the professional network centred around the teaching hospital.[6]

In contrast, the developmental flow of institutional group care and, for that matter, child and youth services in general, has been in the direction of isolation rather than integration, at least until the relatively recent emergence of deinstitutionalization ideas and pressures. Political sensitivities and considerations of treatment objectives and philosophy combined to establish the largely isolated, total institution (e.g. Goffman, 1961) as the predominant setting for group residential care and treatment of children and adolescents. This model was assumed to provide the best possible combination of necessary rehabilitative services, nurturance for the youth involved, efficiency, and protection for the public. The model was almost unquestioned (and largely unseen), at least by the lay public, until recent years.

Thus, both those associated with institutions and those who are not tend not to view their roles as closely integrated and interdependent, and movement toward a model such as that proposed above will require major restructuring of such habitual perceptions and expectations. It will be necessary to reduce the isolation and stigma normally associated with the institution by narrowing the social distance between its residents and staff on the one hand, and the community on the other. This is, of course, in harmony with current ideas and trends in response both to developmental and treatment considerations and to the more clearly political and fiscal concerns that have mobilized opposition to such programs, and represent in one sense an extension of that thinking.

The process of change

That such a rapprochement has begun seems evident in changing ideological positions in institutions as well as in changing practices. For example, the belief in twenty-four hour consistency as absolutely essential in residential programs may be giving way to the idea that a relatively independent school program can help youngsters learn how to function 'outside' and how to use resources from the living situation more effectively (Eisikovits and Eisikovits, 1980). Community service departments are being established in many settings, sometimes in function only but often in form as well, to maintain contact and to work with former residents, to involve volunteers, to interpret the agency to the community, and to foster and enhance agency-community contacts in other spheres. Thus, the institution itself is opened to the 'fresh air' (and difficulties) of public scrutiny, perhaps leading to more careful internal practices, to cooperation in providing community services where appropriate, to greater public understanding of necessary costs, to increased public participation and the like.

The community school movement as a model

The 'community school' movement provides a model of a somewhat analogous evolution. Over the years, local schools developed into largely 'closed' settings, not welcoming public involvement and participation and not providing much beyond classroom learning from 9 a.m. to 3 p.m., although they began as true expressions of the community. Professional and political factors later combined to 'close' them to 'outsiders', but the trend in recent years has been to open the schools to the public, providing the school together with some of its personnel as a community centre. Adult education, health and nutrition programs, cooperative day care, and many other activities are increasingly school-based; lay aides from the community work in regular classrooms; school personnel work with community groups; and programs for students range far beyond the classroom through extended field experiences, work-study arrangements, and the like. The process of opening the schools to the community has not always been a smooth one and is far from complete, but it seems to be addressing the needs of both in generally constructive ways.

Similarly, looking at the institution and the community today, we can see that there is a mutuality of need and potential. The community, to a much greater extent than the institution, functions in the 'real' world, as reflected in its interpersonal atmosphere, its reward system, the availability of role models and the like. It can provide a balancing, normalizing environment for those who are accustomed to institutional settings, whether as residents or as staff. The institution, on the other hand, has and can provide direct access to a variety of kinds of expertise that can enhance many aspects of community life as well as residential child and youth services. Most apparently, those personnel employed in the institution know more about many of the kinds of troubled youth in the community and their developmental needs than do most people – even allied professionals – particularly in the nonurban areas where most institutions are located. They also know much about developmental needs in general, group processes in classrooms and elsewhere, and community and social problems (e.g. alcohol and drug abuse) that communities and their social agencies could usefully apply to their own problems. All this needs to be harnessed for mutual benefit.

Implications for group care centres

Such concepts as networking, integrated services, and the continuum of care have been introduced in the human services in recent years, in recognition of the consequences of fragmented disciplines and programs in terms of service gaps, wasteful duplication, unserved or inappropriately served populations, and other factors. This has not, however, had much impact on the institution, except in the course of implementation – so far, very limited – of the notion of the continuum of care (e.g. Whittaker, 1979), whereby referrals to and from institutions are more closely linked to the availability of appropriate 'less restrictive' alternatives. A much more profound application of the networking concept entails integration of the institution with the total human service system and the community as a whole, along the lines and for the reasons that have been described above in relation to the teaching hospital and the health care system.

The proposed recasting of institutions as Centers for Advanced Practice and Research will, however, require an additional major step. This involves their assumption of a leadership role in the child and youth services system and the acceptance of a degree of responsibility for its overall functioning, at least in the modelling sense that marks the relationship of the teaching hospital and the overall health care system. This is not, of course, a role to which most institutions will automatically be summoned by the community, nor one for which many institutions are equipped and ready in terms of ideology or personnel. Rather, the process will begin as an evolutionary one, with exemplary models emerging here and there, where fortunate combinations of institutional and community skill, sensitivity, and awareness of each other's needs and resources permit. Sophisticated efforts will be built on the foundations established by more modest ones, some of which are already beginning to appear.

Emerging patterns of integration

The most concrete and obvious level of integration is represented by collaborative efforts using resources shared between the residential centre and the community to provide programs for institutional residents and community youth (whether on a joint basis or not) in such areas as education, recreation, employment, and clinical services. Many examples exist already, such as institutional populations attending public school in the community, special 'on grounds' schools serving community youngsters with special needs, and the like. Such programs begin to stretch the inside/outside boundaries but usually do not breech them except for the youngsters involved; they do not bring the two spheres directly to bear on each other in an organic way.

Another level of interaction involves the establishment and recognition of the residential centre as a source of consultation or technical assistance available to the community in meeting its needs and dealing with its problems. Thus, for example, the residential centre might provide educational programs for local parents and professionals on a continuing basis, even as it provides ongoing inservice training for its own staff. In the same sense, its library and its professional staff may serve as a resource and provide consultation on community youth problems and related areas to the surrounding community as they do to the internal community. This consultation or technical assistance can be conceptualized and implemented more broadly as an effort to reach out to assist the community in identifying and conceptualizing problems as well as in solving them.

As relationships and trust are established and confirmed through these processes, joint planning, and shared responsibilities can be developed. The research capacity of the residential centre can begin to address community needs. In these ways, new roles can be helped to emerge through which the centre may find itself at the heart of the development and implementation of preventive and other services designed to equip children and youth for a future in the community. One effect will be to open the institution to new expectations of itself, as traditionally internally-oriented thinking gives way through the exchange of ideas to broader perspectives.

With their own ideas expanded in these ways, and with a clearer, fuller, and more appropriate identity, residential centres will be in a position to assume broader and more central community responsibilities. They can begin to be perceived as, and begin to function as, Centers for Advanced Practice and Research analogous to the teaching hospital. What will be required, however, are new patterns of resource allocation to support this role and much clearer understanding and more effective implementation of residential services for children and youth, community service networks, and services to young people in the community. Such centres are not substitutes for what we need to know and do, but they may provide a more effective way to organize for the task.

The process

Tradition, stigma, and a variety of vested interests (Albee, 1980) have exerted powerful influences on maintaining the status quo; other political pressures, funding limitations and program failures have pressed toward restrictive change, often toward closing institutions completely. Given these countervailing pressures, how can progress be made toward a more rational, appropriate, and viable role for institutions as Centers for Advanced Practice and Research in the context of their physical and social surroundings, their objectives, and the needs of our youth?

The primary initiative will need to be taken by the institution to reshape its self-image and to redirect some of its energy in these directions. To do so credibly, it will need to rethink its staffing procedures and priorities, job descriptions, and supervisory expectations. Child care workers and others have begun to accept roles in the community, but almost always in the context of working with youngsters who have been institutional residents and their families. Increasing efforts will need to be made with people who would previously have been defined as outsiders, not subject to the efforts or the direct influence of the institution.

Communities will need to begin to view the institutions in their midst as positive resources rather than as psychologically distant entities unrelated to their daily lives (except when vandalism caused by runaways or similar events force them to take note). The impetus for such change can be expected to develop from the imbalance between community needs in meeting the still increasing problems of young people and the ever-tightening availability of community resources, but only if institutions present themselves as available, appropriate, and competent alternatives. This will require the kinds of community links that can support and enhance existing services while easing a heritage of stigma. It will require efforts to change the community's perceptions not only of the institution, but also of young people, their needs, and how these needs can best be met. It will require the development of collaborative efforts to share the institution's resources with the community in the context of a wide and growing range of community needs. It will require not only competence, but also efficiency in delivering essential services: two elements of organizational functioning for which institutions have not been noted in the past.

Support from outside groups

Relevant governmental and nongovernmental bodies (e.g. state and federal funding agencies, community chests, and private foundations) can play useful supportive and even leadership roles, although their efforts and influence sometimes tend to be conservative. Whether as the result of political pressure or their own convictions, however, such groups have from time to time actively and persuasively supported the demonstration of new approaches to difficult problems. There should, therefore, be opportunities for communities and institutions, who are open to the development of such a role for the institution, to attract the needed credibility, political support, and/or financial resources for demonstration projects. The effective involvement of the media and appropriate citizens' advocacy organizations should also be explored. Since the process involves not only changing the image of the institution and establishing a new role for it, but also changing the way the community and its helping professionals organize and deliver a wide range of services for children and youth, such support and assistance will be essential.

Operating principles

The success of such an effort will depend heavily on the ability of the child and youth services system in general, and the institutions involved in particular, to organize their efforts in accordance with several key concepts and operating principles that have often been difficult to establish in such circles in the past. Most crucial of these is a developmental perspective: the view that necessary interventions should focus on providing opportunities for growth-enhancing experiences that may be needed to supplement the resources already available to the young person involved. This is in contrast to traditional 'correctional' or 'treatment-oriented' approaches, where the focus tends to be on the youngster's 'problem' that needs to be eliminated. Although these are not mutually exclusive, undue emphasis on the latter may limit the effectiveness of institutional and other child and youth services personnel. In particular, it may limit their ability to work successfully with youngsters in more favourable developmental circumstances than those with which the worker is professionally familiar, or with his or her regular clientele as they progress. The developmental perspective can be viewed as a normalizing focus as contrasted to a problemizing one.

Second, the successful development of the system along the proposed lines will require new comfort in bridging established boundaries. Although some progress in this direction has been made between institutional and the other child and youth services which form the continuum of care described above, structural rigidities remain firm in many instances across the mental health, juvenile justice, and social welfare systems. Once a youngster has been identified as a delinquent (a 'bad kid', for example), he or she is likely to encounter formal and informal admission requirements and exclusions that make it difficult for him to go where he needs to in order to receive appropriate help if that is outside the juvenile justice system. However, as child and youth services personnel become increasingly familiar with the range of resources available beyond their own agency and its accustomed partners, they will be better able to match referrals to client needs and to advocate for appropriate changes in their agency's acceptance criteria and for new linkages and new services where gaps exist.

The immediate question for the worker, at least on the surface, is a simple one. Where, and with what kind of supervision, should this youngster sleep tonight? Where should he or she eat, and with whom? What can be done to help him or her to get 'back on the track' in a developmental sense? And on a longer range basis, what kind of plan can be made to help the youngster re-establish (or establish) a reasonable developmental progression, and how and under what auspices can it best be implemented? The situation is more complex, however, since proposed programs that cross agency boundaries frequently require policy changes or internal and external re-alignments. Typically, any re-alignments of service will require changes in policy which determine reimbursement for service and whether such services can be offered at all. Still evolving conceptions of the rights of children and youth, their families and others concerned also to some extent limit and direct the nature of such interventions. The necessary changes will, therefore, need to be pursued on a variety of levels.

Bridging boundaries in this sense refers not only to the complex of social agencies itself, but at least as importantly to other resources in the community. This is a logical concomitant to the 'least restrictive alternative' continuum, providing a context of normalization even if on an externally planned basis until the young people involved can manage their lives more independently. The involvement of the family as (potentially if not currently in fact) a youngster's major resource is being emphasized in this context, and will be influenced by broadened concepts of family and neighbourhood involvement in child rearing that are on the horizon (Bronfenbrenner, 1979). Child and youth services will, therefore, increasingly require the full partnership of parents and the community, and personnel will be needed who can work comfortably and effectively in this context.

Reconstituted as Centers for Advanced Practice and Research, group care centres will need to incorporate these dimensions into their programs and into the awareness and skill of their personnel. The old concept of the institution as a 'laboratory of living', frequently cited but typically more honoured in the breach than in the observance, can be implemented in such centres as a source of knowledge and understanding about the establishment and maintenance of a growth-enhancing milieu. These insights and methods can then be expanded to apply to the families and communities that will continue to provide the primary environment for the overwhelming majority of our children and youth. Building on these approaches and the continuing development of intensive treatment techniques for particular problems, such centres can serve as a wellspring and provide the impetus for enhancing developmental influences in the institution, in other child and youth serving agencies, and in the family and the community.

Notes

(1) Professor and Director, Center for Youth Development and Research, University of Minnesota, Minneapolis St Paul, USA.

(2) The author wishes to acknowledge with appreciation the support of the Agricultural Experiment Station of the University of Minnesota (Project No. 56-14, Publication No. 11,471, Scientific Journal Series) and the assistance and suggestions offered by Frank Ainsworth, Margaret Atkinson, Mike Baizerman, Harold Beker, Zvi Eisikovits, Paula Simon, and Ruth Teeter.

(3) It should be noted that the designations of points on the continuum are, in each of the figures, arbitrary and hypothetical. For example, a particular group home may be more 'community-based' and less 'restrictive' than a particular after-school program. The purpose here is to illustrate the range of

and some possible points on such a continuum, not to indicate where specific categories of service fit, since the latter may vary widely from agency to agency and from place to place.

(4) The emerging roles of public and private organizations involved in purchase-of-service arrangements in child and youth services (e.g. county social service departments, local school districts, and insurance companies) will require new accommodations as well. Prompt attention needs to be given to developing approaches through which such roles can be integrative rather than serving as an additional source of fragmentation in service and accountability.

(5) Leisure-time programs (e.g. 4-H, boys' and girls' clubs and scouts) and day care are included in the continuum as reflecting developmentally oriented, preventive services that should be integrated with other elements of the child and youth services system. The desired ideal is *not* that one should use *none* of the services offered; it is that everyone should use what he or she needs, a model currently more closely approached in education and health care than in child and youth care services. This perspective may help to reduce the stigma generally associated with involvement at any level of the continuum of child and youth care when leisure time and day care services are not viewed as an integral part of that continuum. The schools can function effectively as part of the continuum as well, and they do so in many instances.

(6) The point here, of course, is not to ignore the failures of a health care system that has proved itself to be less than fully responsive to health care needs, but to highlight ideal and actual modes of functioning that may be instructive in the search for ways in which it might be possible to organize child and youth services for more effective service delivery.

References

Albee, G. W. (1980) Social Science and Social Change: The Primary Prevention of Disturbance in Youth. *Proceedings of the Gisela Konopka Lectureship* (Occasional Paper No. 2). St Paul, Minnesota: Center for Youth Development and Research, University of Minnesota.

Bronfenbrenner, U. (1979) *The Ecology of Human Development: Experiments by Nature and Design*. Cambridge, Massachusetts: Harvard University Press.

Center for Youth Development and Research, University of Minnesota (1978) *Youthwork Coalitions*. St Paul, Minnesota: The Center.

Durkin, R. P. and Durkin, A. B. (1975) Evaluating Residential Treatment Programs for Disturbed Children. In M. Guttentag and E. Struening (eds) *Handbook of Evaluation Research*, Vol. 2. Beverly Hills, California: Sage Publications.

Eisikovits, R. A. and Eisikovits, Z. C. (1980) Detotalizing the Institutional Experience: The Role of the School in the Residential Treatment of Juveniles. *Residential and Community Child Care Administration* 1 (4): 365–73.

Goffman, E. (1961) *Asylums*. New York: Doubleday.

Hirschbach, E. (1980) Children Beyond Reach? Unpublished manuscript, Youth Horizons, Montreal.

Murray, C. A. and Cox, L. A., Jr (1979) *Beyond Probation: Juvenile Corrections and the Chronic Delinquent.* Beverly Hills, California: Sage Publications.

Whittaker, J. K. (1979) *Caring for Troubled Children: Residential Treatment in a Community Context.* San Francisco: Jossey-Bass.

Wolins, M. (1974) *Successful Group Care: Explorations in the Powerful Environment.* Chicago: Aldine.

Section II

Personnel considerations

6 Occupational stress for group care personnel

Martha A. Mattingly[1]

Introduction

The traditional clinical professions such as medicine, nursing, education, psychology, and social work as well as the emerging child care profession have focused primarily on the welfare of the patient-client. While the well-being of the practitioner has long been generally and implicitly addressed in the training and supervision of human service providers only recently have serious efforts been made to identify the problems confronting these workers and to reflect on their consequences. It is interesting to note that while child care is a young emerging profession it has been in the forefront of these efforts (Mattingly, 1977a).

The concept of occupational or job stress has developed slowly over the last twenty years and efforts in this area have gained momentum with the current concern with the quality of working life. In general, occupational stress refers here to workers' physiological and psychological responses to situations perceived as potentially disruptive (McLean, 1974). Disruptive situations may be either desirable or undesirable. Such positive changes as going on vacation, receiving a promotion or raise in pay, or learning a new and more effective child care technique produce stress. However, the concern here will be with the negative stress, which arises from those situations perceived as undesirable, painful, and challenging to the ability of the worker to cope effectively.

The 'burn-out syndrome' is an extreme response to occupational pressure. It has been described as primarily an experience of exhaustion resulting from excessive demands on the worker's energy and resources accompanied by a dehumanization of the caring process (Freudenberger, 1975, 1977; Maslach, 1976; Maslach and Pines, 1977; Mattingly,

1977b). The burn-out syndrome appears to be widespread among human service workers whose work requires intense interpersonal involvement (Hall *et al.*, 1979; Maslach and Jackson, 1979; Mattingly, 1979; Pines and Kafry, 1978; Pines and Maslach, 1978; Seiderman, 1978; Shubin, 1978; White, 1978; Yager and Hubert, 1979). In addition, symptoms of combat neurosis,[2] an extremely similar if not identical phenomenon, have been identified in some teachers in inner-city schools (Bloch, 1978).

The problem of job stress and burn-out is of special concern in professional child care work. In recent years child care workers have made enormous strides both towards professionalization and towards improvement of the quality of care expected for children. Advances have been made in the design and availability of training. Child care workers, other related professionals and advocates have become active both in organizations and issues concerned with the child care worker's ability to render appropriate care. But if the field is to thrive and mature, it is essential that there be a substantial cadre of experienced, educated, and committed practitioners. Retention of workers (The New Child Care Worker, 1974) and the quality of care provided by many long term workers are well-known problems in the field. Part of this is due to rather widespread poor selection procedures, training, salaries, and working conditions. A significant contribution, however, also comes from the physical and psychological exhaustion experienced by child care workers in the caring process. The result appears to be high staff turn-over, potential apathy, and frustration for continuing workers, and the loss of some especially able practitioners who are concerned with their effectiveness with children. It is important to keep in mind that there are effective long term workers who do not report serious personal damage from stress.

While the child care profession, as well as many workers and agencies, have begun to address the issues of job stress and worker burn-out, some resistance to its discussion is still occasionally encountered. Such considerations arouse painful memories, a sense of vulnerability, and issues of responsibility many would like to avoid. It can bring agencies and systems face to face with the need for changes it may be more comfortable and convenient not to confront. And finally it can bring the profession face to face with an enormous problem requiring attention.

The profession's willingness to confront these issues raises the hope that effective ways to cope with the stress of group caring work can and will be found. The benefits will be reaped by group child care professionals who will be able to work with greater dignity and to mature in the skills of their chosen profession. The ultimate beneficiaries will be the children.

A reflection on sources of stress in child caring work

'Burn-out' is frequently used as a catchy phrase to explain various sorts of frustration and fatigue. In order to come to grips with the problem of stress it is necessary to identify sources of stress. Each person, of course, experiences stress in an individual manner and needs to consider his/her own situation. This reflection is drawn from the literature, the personal experience of the writer, and the generous sharing of many child care workers who expressed their frustration and pain.

Agency attitudes and policies contribute to the stress experienced by child care workers. The effects of an agency as a closed system are frequently seen (White, 1978). Many agencies have enduring traditions which come from more autocratic times. Others are parts of large and cumbersome bureaucracies which have lost the ability to be flexible and responsive. Workers can begin to assess the particular structure of their agency and its relationship to the stress they experience.

An effectively closed system is characterized by a sense of isolation and rigidity. Such an agency is isolated from professional and community resources and has a major, usually unspoken, goal to remain hidden and unchanged. There is an excessive emphasis on presenting a favourable public impression, protecting the agency from criticism, and accounting for aspects of the agency which are not central to the quality of service rendered, e.g. the linen inventory, maintenance records, and groundskeeping staff. Such agencies tend to protect themselves by a screening procedure for new staff and consultants which assures maintenance of the preferred agency attitude. This may result in the rejection of sophisticated applicants as overqualified, unlikely to work as good team members, or not familiar with 'our' problems.

Events which create conflict and disequilibrium tend to be dealt with by denial and retreat to the agency ideology. Problems are identified as arising from discrete issues and persons. The ecology of the agency is not made a focus for review. A high turnover rate for child care workers may be dealt with by proclaiming that no one can do such difficult work for more than two years. Crisis management issues are considered client problems without consideration of deficits in the program of care and treatment offered. Persons who begin to raise issues related to the agency are frequently identified as inept and unsuited for this type of work. Supervision is often defined as an accountability review. The result is a rigid and inflexible setting which diminishes the role of the worker and truncates the support system an agency can be expected to provide.

Morale and job satisfaction tend to decline steadily from the top to the bottom of an agency hierachy. Morale among child care workers is directly related to their perceived ability to influence the decisions affecting their work (Shamsie and Lang, 1976). Within agencies child care workers are frequently perceived as among the least valued of employees. The common low level of financial compensation is the most substantial evidence for this perception. Currently the child care worker may not only find himself a devalued and perhaps dispensable, easily replaced employee but is also subject to the current increasing awareness of the central role of the child care worker in providing quality care for children. Thus while being told of his importance, and encouraged toward professional associations and training, he is deprived of the economic and psychological circumstances necessary to engage in an exciting and productive career.

Workers enter the field of child care with a variety of motivations. For the most part they are dedicated, concerned persons who wish to offer themselves and their resources to assist children in their development and rehabilitation. Dedication, concern, and idealism are essential for all caring work. In fact, these qualities may be the source of the motivation and energy for difficult caring tasks (VanderVen, 1979). Concerned child care workers support the growth of each child from their own resources and talents. However, there is an inescapable stress producing conflict between the worker's commitment to give and the reality that frequently he cannot give enough. Each person's emotional resources are limited. The refreshment provided by family, friends, colleagues, and personal interests are often insufficient. This conflict is a particular hazard for the beginning worker but one with which all caring persons struggle throughout their careers.

The idealism and dedication which characterize the decision to engage in caring work are severely challenged by numerous physical and psychological assaults on wellbeing and self-esteem. Upon entering the field, workers usually perceive themselves as concerned and helpful persons whom clients and society will value. By way of contrast workers are confronted by assaultive youth, messy and aggressive children, and ungrateful families. The nobility of caring work turns out to be a myth. Successful workers develop a personal durability as they integrate the idealistic view of caring for children with the everyday realities. However, no matter how skilled and sophisticated the worker, a kick in the shins, broken glasses, an insult, and a child's lack of progress are all assaults on self-esteem which threaten workers' perceptions of their helping ability.

Experiences which enhance workers' sense of effectiveness are quite random and inconsistent. In many instances they cannot remain involved with a child for a sufficient period to see productive growth and the resolution of major difficulties. The limitations imposed by agency structure or funding sources, special client needs, and changes in family circumstances or attitudes may result in the termination of the worker-client relationship. Perhaps a seed has been planted that will bear fruit in the future. Perhaps not. The worker has been interrupted in the middle of something and is denied the rewards of a job well done.

Many child care workers still unfortunately lack the professional knowledge which would allow them to assess the effectiveness of their everyday practice. Supervision is frequently neither rendered by persons skilled in child care nor readily available. Much supervision is almost exclusively problem or deficit focused. Colleagues may also not be able or willing to provide feedback on the quality of work. This problem is likely to also be especially severe for supervisors and administrators. Thus the person is left without a realistic evaluation of the quality of work.

The child care worker also must process an enormous amount of information with great speed. In the many hours of direct child contact the worker maintains a disciplined alertness and vigilance to the children and the setting. Masses of verbal and non-verbal behaviour, the sounds and conditions of the environment, the program of the day, and the history and treatment plan for each child are registered in awareness. Situations must also be dealt with on many levels at the same time. In fact, the very basis of child care practice is the use of the everyday environment to support each child's growth while completing the tasks essential for organized living. The child care worker practises in a 'pressure cooker' characterized by rapid decision making and intense sustained interaction.

The conflict between client-care and custodial managerial requirements is inescapable and includes such things as food preparation, acquiring a good community image with well-dressed and comported children, and maintaining a full census so that the agency and the establishment can survive financially. The nature of clinical child care rarely permits the isolation of these concerns. Rather the conflict is embodied in everyday decisions and interactions. It can be anticipated that as professional child care workers have increasing participation in agency decisions this inevitable conflict will become more acute.

Daily practice is most often open to the view of superiors, colleagues, children, and occasionally to parents and the community. There are few places to hide errors and bad days. There is no tape recorder to turn off or office door to close. In addition the child care worker serves as a model for the children in his care both by his behaviour and attitudes. The children are affected by how the worker expresses anger, solves problems, has fun, and deals with the disliked carrots. The worker's task is difficult. To pretend or 'put on' attitudes and feelings is ineffective.

Rather the worker is called upon to be a fully human person, honest in interactions, and concerned with personal behaviour and attitudes.

Child care workers are called upon to be empathic with a person at a different developmental level from themselves (Olden, 1953). There is a professional commitment to place one's personal experience of child-hood in the service of children in need and to engage, as it were, in an empathic tension. Workers must remain fully adult, not identifying with the child or allowing the child to be an inappropriate participant in their own psychological conflicts, while being in touch with childhood per-ceptions and feelings. Negative emotions such as anger, guilt, and potential loss of control are almost common. These are not congruent with the image of a helper of children and frighten many workers particularly at the beginning of practice.

The worker who lives as well as works with the children served con-fronts additional hazards. Agency requirements vary greatly but three and a half to five days a week at the facility are not unusual. This may require continuous responsibility for the children or include inter-spersed off-duty periods in which the worker may or may not be required to remain on the premises. The live-in worker's 'amorphous omnipresence' (Grossbard, 1960) provides limited opportunities for withdrawal, psychological repair, and personal recovery. Interpersonal interactions are also very intense. Living quarters may allow for the con-stant intrusion of children's noises. Personal phone calls and visits as well as the security of personal possessions may be severely limited. Off-duty time is open to interruption by both children and staff for insub-stantial reasons such as finding a lost shoe or confirming the time of a parental visit. The live-in worker's perpetual exposure to the stressful environment tends to intensify all the stress producing influences (Reed, 1977).

The child care worker must also sustain his professional identity with limited reinforcement from social and community sources. The common characteristics of babysitter, disciplinarian, and self-sacrificing martyr reflect the impoverished and inaccurate understanding of professional child-care work. Thus the child care worker is denied realistic psy-chological support from these sources and must continue to re-establish for himself 'Who am I?' and 'What do I do?'

Burn-out: experiences and signals

Exposure to potentially harmful levels of stress is an inevitable part of child caring work. A debilitating and painful response to these pressures is the burn-out syndrome which is a phenomenon of physical and psy-chological exhaustion. Some basic components of burn-out which occur with regularity have been identified and measured (Maslach, 1976; Maslach and Pines, 1977), viz. emotional exhaustion, depersonalization, and lack of personal accomplishment. In addition, each person's stress response has a unique individual pattern of symptoms, behaviours, and attitudes. Since most child care workers are young adults some of the traditional symptoms of stress may be masked (Hewitt, 1979). Thus any particular 'burning-out' worker may experience only part of what is described here.

Burn-out frequently begins as a vague suble experience of discontent. The worker begins to have doubts about his caring work. He may feel inadequate to and overwhelmed by the tasks which confront him and feel a growing unconfortable rigidity in his thinking and behaviour. He may be irritable, labile in moods, less empathetic, and behave – on occasion – in ways which are not congruent with his values or self-image as a helper of children. This experience is frequently confronted alone and the worker often comes to the conclusion that he is unfit for the work he has chosen. A severe fracture of professional identity is a common result.

As the pain and confusion increase the worker may try to discuss these feelings with supervisors, colleagues, and friends where an attitude of denial may be the response. Some talented workers report that their clinical work, though somewhat less flexible and creative, remains of very good quality during a burning-out process. These persons seem to have the ability to isolate the effects of the stress they experience from clinical work. Their pain is not apparent and their feelings are likely to be ignored.

In response to the 'burning-out' worker, supervisors and colleagues may adopt a traditional inner psychic view and insist that the worker must deal with the personal problems which are obviously the source of the difficulties. The necessity for a critical self-reflective attitude has been emphasized in the training of the professional child care worker. Thus he may be predisposed to engage in an energy consuming self-review and perhaps seek professional assistance. This effort even further depletes the worker's already meager energy (Freudenberger, 1975). Workers report that even skilled psychotherapists often do not recognize the stress arising from the caring commitment. A note of caution is required here. Some workers have personal problems which interfere with caring work. These need to be identified and dealt with. However, the customary and uncritical assumption of the inner psychodynamic view of the worker's distress effectively excludes consideration of the full circumstances of engaging in a caring commitment. Thus many, if not most, workers are denied the support and assistance to which they are entitled from agency and colleagues.

The worker may reject the suggestion that he work on his personal problems. Then he confronts the experience that something frightening is happening. The sources he knows about are unable or unwilling to help. Many workers have expressed a serious concern about 'going crazy'. This arises from the major discrepancy between the painful personal experience and the lack of interpersonal validation for the experience.

A diminishing distinction between the time and place for personal life as well as a diminished distinction between the psychological needs of the worker and child may signal 'burn-out'. This merger between the worker and the agency is a particular hazard for young workers. The structure of formal training which frequently demands an almost total commitment and the enthusiasm of beginning workers both contribute. The staff member may find it difficult to stop working. Careful consideration may reveal that over a period of time the worker has stopped taking lunch hours and breaks. If relief personnel are available for these periods the person may just 'hang around'. He may also 'hang around' at the end of the work period and on days off, perhaps working, perhaps not. He may be enthusiastic when called upon for overtime and emergency duty and volunteer to provide extra services on his own time. There may be frequent requests to invite children home. These behaviours and attitudes may signal that the worker lacks the energy and motivation to develop and sustain a rewarding personal life. Thus he relies on the agency increasingly to meet personal needs. Again a note of caution. These comments are not intended as guidelines for worker behaviour. The caring commitment and personal interest may lead workers to appropriately offer personal time, skills, home, and family to assist a child. Excessive agency regulation of these matters is usually not helpful to stress management. Rather it may be a manifestation of the generally high level of stress in the agency and a lack of trust in supervisors' and workers' competence and judgment (Reed, 1977). These comments are intended to identify a hazard and encourage reflection on the personal meaning of such behaviours and attitudes.

Rigid and inflexible attitudes with a stubborn resistance to change are also part of the 'burn-out' phenomenon. As the worker's interaction with his setting becomes more stressful, personal resources are diminished and exhaustion approaches. Workers may find themselves without the flexibility needed to be confident and effective. The worker may retreat to a position in which he 'knows it won't work' or 'has already tried it before' when innovations are suggested. Attempts at change are broadly resisted. The burning-out worker literally cannot depart from the usual work pattern and experiences proposed innovations as personally unmanageable (Freudenberger, 1975).

Rigidity is also frequently reflected in the worker's vocabulary.

Language may become more evaluative and distancing, with the use of stereotyped phrases and words. This is particularly, but not exclusively, evident in regard to perceptions of the client (Maslach, 1976; Maslach and Pines, 1977). Stereotyping statements can be simple such as 'quiet child' and 'disruptive child' or they can be very sophisticated such as in repeated referrals to unresolved Oedipal conflicts or separation issues. The worker is exhausted and does not possess the energy necessary to process the complex data of the situation. Partial perceptions are channelled into preconceived categories. This allows the exhausted worker to garner his psychological energy and continue to serve his clients.

Burning-out workers are also vulnerable to a substantial misevaluation of their abilities and prerogatives. Some workers grow increasingly unsure of themselves. They become overly concerned about personal deficiencies and may imagine errors in practice. They may become unduly apologetic to colleagues, supervisors, and children and request additional supervision designed to elicit approval and reassurance. These workers underestimate themselves.

Overestimation was graphically described by one burning-out worker. A serious ice storm struck the area on an evening when her group was scheduled for an off-campus activity which was particularly valued by children and staff. In spite of warnings in the news media she loaded the van and started down a long treacherous hill. At one point when the van had slid off the road, she sent a very disturbed child out to evaluate the situation. Finally after surmounting numerous hazards the group arrived safely at its destination. Only months later was this exceptionally well-trained and experienced worker able to analyze this situation. She had felt almost completely directed by the predetermined schedule which called for this particular activity on this particular evening. This well-trained and experienced worker dangerously *over-*estimated her ability to surmount real hazards and seriously misjudged the evaluative capacity and ability of her child-helper. One need only reflect for a moment on such considerations as safety for young, retarded or disturbed children, suicide supervision, and confronting violent youth to be struck by the dangers for both child and worker which can result from this problem of misjudgement.

Trust in one's colleagues and reliance on their skills, goodwill, and ability to help evaluate one's work are perceived by child care workers as a major source of support (Maslach, 1976; Nelson, 1978). The loss of trust in other members of the working team and the assumption of a self-sufficient attitude often result from overestimation. 'If I want it done right I'll have to do it myself', 'If only Johnny had been assigned to me, all that trouble wouldn't have happened'. Such thinking further isolates the burning-out person from the support of colleagues and requires the exhausted worker to expend even more energy.

It is not unusual for several members of a work group to burn out simultaneously. The staff support system begins to deteriorate and group collusion becomes a predominant feature of staff relationships. Staff meetings may become brief and/or be cancelled frequently for superficial reasons. Meetings which are held may be stereotyped and repetitive. Participants frequently express the feeling of having attended the same meeting before, perhaps even many times. On occasion staff and committee meetings may become preoccupied with numerous details and become very long yet unproductive. Worker interactions, both professional and social, are marked by urgent, compulsive, repetitive displays of feeling. Stories comparing hazards, noble feats in the face of danger, and bizarre or amusing client behaviour are told unendingly. Short term tension reduction and a personal sense of relief may result. All of these interchanges are characterized by a non-attentive attitude in which participants do not focus on client concerns or listen effectively to one another. Collusive relationships become dangerous when they substitute for genuine concern for colleagues.

Excessive stress is also likely to be manifested in physical symptoms. With almost startling regularity health problems begin or intensify during the burning-out process. No particular health problems have been identified as closely associated with the burn-out process in child care workers, probably because of their young average age. Workers are most often just aware of an increase in illness and medical contacts. Sometimes the problems are difficult to diagnose and seldom is there opportunity for discussion about the relationship between job-stress and health difficulties. An increase in accidents and injuries has also been speculated as well as an increase in the use of escape routes such as food, tobacco, alcohol, and other mood altering or tranquilizing drugs (Freudenberger, 1977; Maslach, 1976).

Stress resistance and recovery

The caring commitment makes many demands upon the energy and resources of group care workers. It is generally thought that many effective workers feel driven from the field in a state of exhaustion and confusion. Others become the exhausted, cynical, and apathetic 'walking wounded'. An increase in workers' capacity for stress resistance and recovery can preserve their freedom to sustain a caring commitment and/or to follow the directions of their personal development. Each person can imagine a special setting and wish to be magically transported. The proverbial south sea island with its white sand, gentle winds, and waving palms presents an idyllic relaxed image. But effective stress management depends rather on a thoughtful and disciplined process. With careful attention individual workers, professional groups, and agencies can develop practical and helpful plans.

An articulated level of personal awareness is essential for all interpersonal helping work (Freudenberger, 1977). Reflection can begin with a consideration of personal motives and needs in relation to caring work. Why am I doing this? What do I need from the work? What are my rewards? Vague notions and traditional cliches, such as 'I like children' or 'I just enjoy helping' do not constitute the results of a serious reflection. It is sometimes useful to think about particular clients and situations which have been especially rewarding or unpleasant. A meticulous detailed description will highlight important dimensions which affect the worker's practice.

It is also helpful to identify and perhaps even to describe in writing areas of particular competence. It may be that there is only limited external help available for this process in that supervisors and co-workers might not be sufficiently skilled in group care work to highlight competence. Even the professional literature is limited and often not widely known. The lack of clarity or misunderstanding about areas of personal competence serve to deprive workers of substantial and realistic experiences wherein self-esteem and professional effectiveness can be rewarded.

The structure and quality of personal life is a major factor in the ability to manage stress effectively. Patterns which once were useful may become detrimental as personal circumstances change. Some unproductive habits were probably established by accident. Group care workers are frequently tempted into junk food meals and irregular eating. The ever-present coffee pot, cups of tea, or soft drinks are invitations to excessive caffeine consumption. Appropriate amounts of sleep and general health care are also important but often neglected. Nutrition and sleep habits may require additional attention when live-in schedules, rotating shifts, and split shifts result in disrupting living patterns.

Rewarding personal activities need to be identified and planned for. Often the efforts of group care workers to establish a profession and participate in training intensifies this problem. During any serious professional training period the demands are such that personal interests are frequently set aside in order to fulfil training requirements. Also the excitement engendered in a beginning period of work can pre-occupy the young practitioner. Thus during an intense period of training, professional activity, and enthusiastic work involvement, a worker's participation in rewarding personal activities may have been severely limited. In seeking to restore a balance between personal and professional activity, previous interests should be considered as well as explorations of new directions resulting from personal growth and maturation. Traditional hobbies are, of course, possibilities but developing new career interests, or writing a book might also be refreshing. The possibilities are limited only by the scope of imagination.

It is a common experience for workers to be pre-occupied with work-related thinking and feelings and/or to feel continuing tension long after leaving the work site. Effective transition allows the worker to put aside job concerns and to engage more fully in personal life (Maslach, 1976). The process of worker transition has received little attention and perhaps is assumed, mistakenly, to occur automatically. Each person can identify his/her own style of transition but must recognize that the same procedure may not always be effective. Workers have shared the following: settling the concerns of the day by talking about them, a rigorous closure on work which avoids any discussion of it, changing clothes, physical exercise, shopping, being along, listening to music, playing a musical instrument, blocking work-related thinking by engaging in cognitive activities not related to work, having a drink in a social circumstance. The transition process is especially difficult for persons who end the work period at odd times such as early morning or late at night and those with rotating shift schedules (Kroes, 1977). Only by developing and maintaining effective transition patterns can the benefits of personal life make a full contribution to stress-management. This area cannot be too greatly emphasized.

Group care workers frequently feel exhausted by the end of their work period. It is difficult to muster the necessary energy and enthusiasm for the physical exercise which contributes to one's general state of health and frequently provides a sense of wellbeing. Thirty minutes of vigorous exercise three times a week is commonly suggested. It is important to keep in mind personal preferences, health concerns, and the reality of what is available. Resistance to regular physical activity can sometimes be seen in unrealistic planning and the expectation that it will be enjoyable. Particularly at the beginning there will be no perfect day and it will not 'feel right'. Many workers find that after the exercise habit is instituted, it becomes genuinely enjoyable and a highly valued period in the personal schedule. In addition it is helpful to develop personally compatible and practical relaxation techniques which can be used when needed. Various practices, if properly employed, can serve this function (Benson, 1976). Formal meditation techniques, prayer and other religious exercises, solitude, listening to music, and soaking in the tub have been suggested.

Vacation or holiday time, now almost universally available to child care workers, is an important asset to be used in behalf of personal refreshment and growth. Much has been written about the difficulties many persons have in using holiday time effectively. Again personal reflection and understanding are important. Some persons prefer short vacations to long ones. Some prefer high levels of planned recreational activity; others prefer a restful, more spontaneous pace. An effort should be exerted to understand personal style and needs and then to coordinate these with family and friends.

As was already discussed, rigid and inflexible attitudes, stereotypic thinking, perceptual rigidity, and diminished creativity are part of the stressful experience. Exercises and activities which employ imaginative thought will aid cognitive and perceptual flexibility. In this regard the arts, e.g. drama, music, and painting are well known. Small personal exercises can also be developed. For example, imagine that you can fly. What would it feel like? Cold? Hot? Windy? Would you fly on a carpet, in a personal carrier, or like Superman? Where would you go? Or imagine you have just become a millionaire. Each person can, no doubt, create various exercises of personal interest. It has also been suggested that participation in a pre-constructed phantasy in which the participant is successful is useful at stressful points in the work day. Standke (1979) presents the example of thinking about climbing a difficult hill during which obstacles are overcome. Perhaps in the future workers will take 'phantasy breaks' by withdrawing briefly to a quiet, comfortable area to develop a scene in imagination. This technique, while requiring further investigation, has the advantage of being usable in close proximity to the occupational stress.

In addition, imaginative exercises can be used by personal or professional groups and agencies to facilitate the creative exploration of problems and solutions. One such exercise suggests that participants have unlimited resources and can redesign their current agency or plan a new one. Participants are encouraged to share ideas as they occur without evaluating their practicality. Some notions are refreshingly phantastic: close the agency and buy everybody a family, fund research in self-esteem transplants, buy a politician, send the difficult kids to the moon, buy a plane and have seasonal programs in different parts of the world. This exercise (Kroes, 1977) helps to free participants from their everyday concerns. Among the absurb suggestions are usually embedded kernels of creative ideas which can then be used as a basis for a second stage of discussion which addresses the issues in a more realistic fashion.

Support from family, friends, colleagues, profession, agency, and community is an important contribution to workers' caring commitment. Since there are such widespread misconceptions of group care work, extra effort is required to give family and friends a more accurate understanding. Perhaps a visit to the agency or a planned discussion will allow them to respond more effectively. A spirit of trust and generosity can develop in colleagueal relations. Group care workers should be available to associates with an attitude of willingness, confidentiality, and concern. Even though professional workers are clinically trained listeners, the telling of intriguing tales, attitudes of denial, or uncritical encouragement frequently predominate. Each worker has the right as well as the need to turn to colleagues and expect to be respectfully heard. Co-workers should be assisted in taking earned compensatory time, sick time, vacations, and other benefits without being made to feel guilty for abandoning clients and fellow workers. To be sure, inappropriate and unreliable workers appear in agencies from time to time. These persons require supervisory attention but should not be permitted to create a distrustful atmosphere. Off-duty time should be fiercely guarded. All workers are responsible for the protection of off-duty colleagues and should expect the same consideration in return. Participation in a professional association can also provide the opportunity to develop support between colleagues, keep up with new ideas, create and sustain a professional identity, and influence agency and community perceptions of group care workers.

A well-managed agency contributes to stress-management (Ayres, 1977). Job descriptions should exist for all positions. Personnel policies including such items as benefits, grievance procedures, and general agency procedures should be available. In the past many agencies were quite lax about these. Pressure from funding agencies and a general concern with accountability have resulted in most agencies having such documents available. However, availability is only the first step. These documents need to be reviewed for their reality and implementation. Do job descriptions provide accurate guidelines so that agency and workers share a common and appropriate view of workers' duties? Can compensation time really be taken by the worker who has earned it? Can sick time be used when needed? Can vacations be planned in advance with a consideration of the needs of both clients and workers? Or are the specifications of these items mere papers written to satisfy regulating bodies but with little relationship to the realities of work?

Appropriate task related policies and procedures also facilitate stress-management by freeing the worker from unimportant or inefficient decision-making and coordinating complex agency enterprises. Creative energy is then available for matters which require it. Policies and procedures should be reviewed in this light and revised or eliminated if they are not facilitating. Workers frequently feel that direct care of clients as well as their information and insights are not valued by the agency. Participation in those aspects of agency and client planning that are relevant to direct care work can provide for an appreciation of the complex caring system, a sense that caring work is taken seriously, and give the agency the benefit of the workers' knowledge and creativity.

Scheduling is another issue which is critical for agencies and also has a major impact on the personal life of workers. Group care, particularly of residential clients, presents the difficult problem of planning for continuous attention to client needs. Work patterns seem, all too often, to be determined by administrative convenience and a wish not to be accused of unfairness. The resulting patterns frequently are unrelated to the needs of the client or the client care worker. For example, excessively long periods of on-duty time, such as ten days on and five days off, may be scheduled. In this case the worker may spend most of the off-duty period simply recovering from exhaustion and repairing personal relationships. Another destructive pattern, particularly when the duty is twenty-four hours, is four days on-duty and four days of off-duty. This does not allow for any consistency of specific days of the week off-duty. Thus the worker is effectively excluded from almost all organized activities, e.g. classes, choirs, and sports groups which usually meet on regular days of the week. The rotating shift may also create additional problems of disrupted personal schedule and physiology.

Scheduling also needs to provide for 'time-outs' which allow a brief withdrawal from especially stressful situations. Time involved in direct client contact is related to the worker's level of stress (Maslach, 1976). Variation in work diminishes the impact of client contact and if well planned such variation can add novelty and challenge for the worker. For example, direct care work might be combined with planning in-service training, ordering supplies, or participating in other administrative or case management duties. Discussions of scheduling in group care work up to now have been simplistic and little has been done with flexi-time, compressed time, and job sharing which have been successfully enacted in other areas of employment including those responsible for continuous client care (Cohen and Gadon, 1978). Creative experimentation is badly needed.

Appropriate supervision provides an assessment of work including recognition of strengths, identification of weaknesses with assistance for their correction, and a supportive forum for expressing and dealing with the intense feelings which arise in group care work. It requires a supervisor who is clinically skilled in group care work and who has a balanced sensitivity for the client, the worker, and the agency. Regular effective supervision, encompassing all these factors, is rarely available on a regular basis. The supervisory process often must be initiated by the worker (Mattingly, 1977b; Nelson, 1978). The availability of supervision is also influenced by budget constraints. Workers, professional groups, and agencies all have potential influence in assuring that effective supervision is readily available to increasing numbers of group care workers.

Professional group care workers should also be engaged in a continuing effort to identify both new directions and unsatisfactory aspects of their practice. The inadequate preparation of some workers, changes in client population or alterations in services delivered will also result in the discovery of areas requiring training. For example, the reception of increasing numbers of aggressive clients may require the acquisition of appropriate management skills. Provision of services to adolescent parents may motivate the traditional youth worker to acquire information about parenting and early childhood. Unfortunately, much reflection and supervision may only serve to identify vague problematic areas yet fail to clearly specify learning needs so that appropriate information and training can be sought.

It is important to recognize that philosophical, ethical, legal, and theoretical information are also essential to effective group care practice and should be kept in mind when formulating study plans. Workers and/or agencies can then develop specific study plans. Individual workers frequently have professional study plans which are independent from the agency. This allows the plan to be tailored to personal style and interest as well as to focus on skills and knowledge relevant to future career plans. An effective study plan must be realistic in terms of the time and energy available. It needs to be concrete, embody the principles of effective educational design (VanderVen and Mattingly, 1979), and have a timetable including a termination point. This allows participants to experience the pleasure of completion and accomplishment. Some suggested formats are: reading, asking a skilled or knowledgeable worker to teach others, a small study group, an agency in-service program, the programs of professional associations, and educational institutions.

Group care worker associations can encourage training programs to include a range of clinical and indirect skills which will allow for reasonable flexibility in choosing the type of client and setting for work. In addition, professional associations can provide a forum for the discussion of occupational stress and encourage its inclusion in pre-service and in-service training. This will provide workers with an understanding of the stressful conditions they are likely to encounter and increase their ability to cope effectively (McLean, 1974).

Conclusion

Group child care workers, along with many other human service personnel, have made substantial progress in exploring the stressful nature of their work. The topic appears with increasing regularity in in-service training and the programs of professional associations. Agencies are sometimes willing to engage in self-review and to promote appropriate discussion. Individual workers, with or without agency support, can engage in effective personal planning. Thus both workers and agencies can move beyond the isolation, confusion, pain, and helplessness which have all too frequently characterized the process of burning-out.

The somewhat dramatic images called forth by the term 'burn-out' can, however, contribute to its use as a vague term for dissatisfaction or frustration. The systematic study of occupational stress for care givers has only just begun. The experience has not yet been fully described. The situations which care givers find distressing have not been adequately identified. Only a little is known about the conditions which aggravate or attenuate the process. Effective long term workers, supervisors, and administrators have not been studied. Further specification of the stress and burn-out process will allow workers and agencies to plan more precisely. The result, hopefully, will be an increase in workers' effectiveness and satisfaction with substantial benefits accruing for children, youth, and families.

Notes

(1) Associate Professor in Child Development and Child Care, School of Health Related Professions, University of Pittsburgh, Pittsburgh, USA.

(2) Combat neurosis refers to the pattern of physiological and psychological symptoms which were originally identified in military casualties as resulting from exposure to the severe environmental pressures of combat.

References

Ayres, P. R. (1977) Staff Stress in Day Care: The Director's Role. Unpublished master's thesis, University of Pittsburgh.

Benson, J. (1976) *Relaxation Response*. New York: Avon.

Bloch, A. (1978) Combat Neurosis in Inner-City Schools. *American Journal of Psychiatry* **135** (10): 1189–192.

Cohen, A. R. and Gadon, H. (1978) *Alternative Work Schedules: Integrating Individual and Organizational Needs*. Reading, Massachusetts: Addison-Wesley.

Freudenberger, H. J. (1975) The Staff Burn-out Syndrome in Alternative Institutions. *Psychotherapy: Theory, Research and Practice* **12** (1): 73–82.

Freudenberger, H. J. (1977) Burn-out: Occupational Hazard of the Child Care Worker. *Child Care Quarterly* **6** (2): 90–9.

Grossbard, H. (1960) *Cottage Parents: What They Have to Be, Know, and Do*. New York: Child Welfare League of America.

Hall, R. C. W., Gardner, E. R., Perl, M., Stickney, S. K., and Pfefferbaum, B. (1979) The Professional Burn-out Syndrome. *Psychiatric Opinion* **16** (4): 12–17.

Hewitt, L. H. (1979) Work Characteristics, Quality of Supervision and Job Stress in Child Care. Unpublished master's thesis, University of Pittsburgh.

Kroes, W. H. (1977) *Society's Victim – The Policeman*. Springfield, Illinois: Charles C. Thomas.

McLean, A. (1974) Concepts of Occupational Stress. In Alan McLean (ed.) *Occupational Stress*. Springfield, Illinois: Charles C. Thomas.

Maslach, C. (1976) Burned-out. *Human Behavior* **5** (September): 16–22.

Maslach, C. and Jackson, S. (1979) Burned-out Cops and Their Families. *Psychology Today* **12** (12): 58–62.

Maslach, C. and Pines, A. (1977) The Burn-out Syndrome in the Day Care Setting. *Child Care Quarterly* **6** (2): 100–13.

Mattingly, M. A. (ed.) (1977a) Symposium: Stress and Burn-out in Child Care. *Child Care Quarterly* **6** (2): 88–137.

Mattingly, M. A. (1977b) Sources of Stress and Burn-out in Professional Child Care Work. *Child Care Quarterly* **6** (2): 127–37.

Mattingly, M. A. (1979) Stress in Work with Children. *Children in Contemporary Society* **12** (2): 21–4.

Mattingly, M. A. and VanderVen, K. D. (1979) Meeting the Treatment Needs of Children through Educational Preparation of Child Care Practitioners. *Proceedings of the Fifth Annual Inter Association Child Care Conference*. Valley Forge, Pennsylvania.

Nelson, J. E. (1978) Child Care Crises and the Role of the Supervisor. *Child Care Quarterly* **7** (4): 318–26.

Olden, C. (1953) On Adult Empathy with Children. *Psychoanalytic Study of the Child* **8**: 111–26.

Pines, A. and Kafry, D. (1978) Occupational Tedium in Social Services. *Social Work* **23** (6): 499–508.

Pines, A. and Maslach, C. (1978) Characteristics of Staff Burn-out in Mental Health Settings. *Hospital and Community Psychiatry* **29** (4): 233–37.

Reed, M. J. (1977) Stress in Live-in Child Care. *Child Care Quarterly* **6** (2): 114–20.

Seiderman, S. (1978) Combating Staff Burn-out. *Day Care and Early Education* Summer: 6–9.

Shamsie, J. and Lang, G. (1976) Staff Attitudes and Management Styles in Psychiatric Hospitals. *Canadian Psychiatric Association Journal* **21**: 325–28.

Shubin, S. (1978) Burn-out: The Professional Hazard You Face in Nursing. *Nursing* **8** (7): 22–7.

Standke, L. (1979) The Advantages of Training People to Handle Stress. *Training/ HRD* February: 23–6.

The New Child Care Worker: An Agent in Delivery of Human Services: The Future Professional. Unpublished paper presented by staff of N. J. Pritzker Children's Hospital and Center, Chicago, Illinois, at the 1974 American Orthopsychiatric Association Annual Meeting.

VanderVen, K. D. (1979) Developmental Characteristics of Child Care Workers and Design of Training Programs. *Child Care Quarterly* **8** (2): 100–12.

White, W. L. (1978) Incest in the Organizational Family: The Unspoken Issue in

Staff and Program Burn-out. Unpublished paper presented at the 1978 National Drug Abuse Conference, Seattle, Washington.

Yager, J. and Hubert, D. (1979) Stress and Coping in Psychiatric Residents. *Psychiatric Opinion* **16** (4): 21–4.

7 Team functioning in group care

Leon C. Fulcher

I Group care workers discuss their work

The example which follows is drawn from an in-service training course which was offered to group care teams working in a residential school for delinquent adolescents. This team of nine workers was assigned to a living unit for twelve boys and included six basic grade care staff, a senior care worker, the unit supervisor, and a residential treatment supervisor who carried management responsibility for the team's work. Only the teacher and night staff were missing from this training session. As part of the introductory process, workers were asked to reflect back over the past seven days and try to identify the greatest frustration they had encountered on the job during that time. Team members were also asked to think back over the same seven day period and identify the greatest satisfaction they had encountered on the job. Each member of the team was asked to share his or her examples with the group, thus providing a focus for discussion early in the course.

Frustrations reported by this team covered a wide range of issues. One member mentioned the amount of written work required on the job, and the difficulties associated with getting everything done within the time constraints of a working day. Another mentioned having only two sets of keys when there are three workers on the floor, thus emphasizing keys every time you turn around. A third mentioned the washing machine breaking down, while her colleague referred to the snack time routine which had collapsed into chaos. Being off work with a work-related injury, but very much wanting to be back at work was another frustration put forward. A basic-grade worker mentioned the frustration of not being able to attend the staff meeting because no relief workers were available to cover the staff meeting time that he worked each week.

The supervisor complained of meetings which tend to prevent him from spending time in the living unit, while the residential treatment supervisor referred to paperwork looming on her office desk. Having to wait beyond the end of shift at midnight for a team member who had failed to turn up was voiced as another frustration, and this view was echoed by various members. Several members commented on how easy it was to pinpoint frustrations in their group care work; some jokingly wondering if they had to be limited to only one frustration, as two or three extras wanted airing. Overall, themes of job frustration provided by this group of workers encompassed a wide range of practical issues which confront group care teams as they seek to provide a continuous service, week in and week out, for troubled and troublesome children.

Team members experienced more difficulty in identifying job satisfactions which they had encountered in the preceding week. However, one team member reported great job satisfaction at now being able to attend team meetings which he had previously been prevented from doing because of scheduling difficulties. A second worker reported how good she felt when a particular boy asked for her involvement in an activity. Another child sharing his letter from a first-ever pen pal featured highest on a third worker's list. A recently appointed worker mentioned how he thought he was beginning to recognize a pattern of behaviour being presented by one of the boys and then taking this up with the lad, thereby receiving confirmation of observation skills as a group care worker. A basic-grade worker talked somewhat philosophically about finally getting the frustrations untangled in the unit and feeling that the atmosphere had calmed again. Another colleague mentioned that he was feeling a rapport with other members of the team, and how nice it felt to come off a shift feeling good about how the day had gone. Being pleasantly surprised and hopeful at the performance of a new manager at various meetings in the agency over the past working week, was also referred to as an important job satisfaction. The residential treatment supervisor, just back from holiday, commented on how satisfying it was to work with this team.

Taken overall, the satisfactions and frustrations of the job for this particular group care team reflect a wide range of personal and professional considerations. More importantly for our purposes here, the themes reported were drawn by group care personnel from the events of one working week. This team was considering its work in relation to one specific group care unit which plays a small part in a large social service agency. The agency, in turn, services a large metropolitan area. In the discussion which follows, we will refer back to this team from time to time, to provide a practical reference point for our discussion. However, before posing some questions about the nature of teamwork and about why there need be concern with teamwork in the study of group care services, it is important to supply additional details about our colleagues above who provided us with this glimpse into their working lives.

One interesting feature of this team concerned its composition. Within the group were both men and women with ages ranging between early twenties and early fifties. The supervisors were qualified and several members of the team held undergraduate degrees. About half had families of their own. Some were married, some single; some had been married before, while others had never married. Almost half of the group were engaged in a job of work that was different from the career for which they had originally prepared. Team membership incorporated at least five cultural affiliations. Several of the team members could be described as 'veterans' or 'journeymen' in the trade, whilst about as many others could be described as 'rookies' or 'apprentices'. Some 'apprentices' to the group care field came as skilled craftsmen from other occupations. Several team members came with a career pattern which spanned a range of trades, professions, and experiences, including substantial experience of parenting their own families. All of the group were eager to explore the work they were doing and spoke quite openly with each other as a group.

The work task (or tasks!) allocated to this group of workers was to operate a specialist, short-stay unit for adolescent boys who were just arriving at the school. The team listed three objectives as the focus for their work. They sought to help boys to settle into the school and to initiate preparations for which of the various living units a boy should be assigned during his stay. The team was expected by the parent organization to supervise and constructively occupy children who were awaiting a suitable placement or who were placed with the agency on an emergency basis by judicial mandate. One function of the service this team provided could be described as reception and assessment. Their service involved collaboration of some kind with fourteen other group care teams, together encompassing nearly 150 people. The unit was identified as a central resource as it received children from, and placed them across, the range of services supplied by the parent organization. Collaboration with social workers, teachers, psychologists, nurses, doctors, recreation personnel, maintenance staff, and police was also required, along with supervising visits from families.

The legal and agency backdrop against which this team operated had recently altered. In the two years prior to this course, the team had had to adapt to new juvenile justice legislation which was enacted by government. The new statutes emphasize the process of law and the legal rights of children. The new code replaced statutes established early in this century that were based on the principle of *in loco parentis* responsibilities inherent in the state. All social service and child welfare personnel working in this region of the country were expected to change their patterns of work in order to respond to new policies and procedures set down in the modernized statutes. Enactment of this legislation reoriented work within a large new administration which had been established slightly earlier by other legislation. Reorganization of social services had been fashioned around economies of scale. New staff were recruited who supported the new legislation, to work with personnel who held seniority of service under the old legislation.

Partially in response to the new legislation, the parent organization had redesignated the purpose around which this team and their work site would be used. Whereas the team now worked with boys on a short-term basis, twelve months earlier they had been working with girls on a longer-term basis. Most of the team members had 'lived through' both changeover processes. All agreed that the past two years had been pretty rough and that some team members had left their jobs because of the strain. One or two ventured a fatalistic remark about the possibility of it happening all over again under the new administration. Most of the group were committed to their jobs for the long term as they held neither the training qualifications nor the option of moving to new employment because of family commitments and the level of unemployment in the area.

The foregoing example was selected as it offers a composite picture of the variety of issues which can confront group care teams in their work. Within the example can be found many issues of central importance to the consideration of team functioning, both within and outside the group care sector of employment. As Maier states in chapter 2,

'the care offered to children shapes their lives, and the children in turn shape the actual mode of care provided. Moreover, this mutually intertwined caring experience is not merely determined by the interactions between care givers and care receivers. Of equal importance is their physical setting, the material goods at their disposal, and above all, the external forces and institutions which support and negate their efforts. . . . Whether these outside influences are the child welfare agencies and institutions, the neighbourhood and wider community, or the laws and society's conceptions of children's developmental requirements, all serve as salient partners in group care work.'

A prevalent assumption in group care work is that some level of co-operation and collaboration is required between personnel, in order to provide a 'good enough' service for children and families. Such team-work principles have also extended to the invitation for parents to join with group care staff as partners in the helping and learning process

(Whittaker, 1979). But what of the assumptions about teams and the teamwork which is required to provide such a service?

II   Why be concerned with the formation and operation of work teams in group care?[1]

When beginning to think of team functioning as an important concept in the provision of a group care service, one is reminded of the poster which hung in the office of a twenty-four hour emergency care centre. The poster illustrated a group of workers caught in the middle of marsh-like terrain, surrounded by reptiles. The saying at the bottom offered a feverish warning: 'When you're up to your neck in alligators, it's hard to remember that the original aim was to drain the swamp!' Such are the myriad of influences which can make teams function at less than their potential, that task achievement in group care work is too frequently left open to question.

In her study on the functioning of social systems as a defence against anxiety amongst nursing staff in a general hospital, Isabel Menzies (1970) describes the development within social organizations of a structure, culture, and mode of functioning as being influenced by a number of interacting factors. Crucial among these factors were:

'the primary task of assignment, including such environmental relationships and pressures as that involves; the technologies available for
performing the task; and the needs of the members of the organization
for social and psychological satisfaction.'   (Menzies, 1970:8)

Later work extended these considerations to an exploration of task and anti-task dynamics in the functioning of adolescent institutions. Task was taken generally to incorporate activities which an 'enterprise must perform in order to survive' (Menzies, 1977:13). Menzies identified

'a danger of primary task being implicitly redefined when the task as
originally and perhaps more realistically defined becomes too difficult,
or when societal pressures against task definition are too great. In
other words, task may implicitly slip over into anti-task'.   (1977:16)

The conclusions which are drawn from this now classic work stress the importance of effective management as a major staff support system in taking responsibility for positive task performance amongst group care teams.

Building from Menzies' pioneer research, six questions can be iden-
tified which seek to differentiate more clearly between the task and anti-task variables of structure, culture, and mode of functioning in the operation of group care teams. An assumption is made that team func-

tioning is a multi-faceted construct and that no all-embracing theoretical framework is available which readily explains variations between one team and another. Therefore, in posing six questions about teamwork, an attempt will be made to offer some theoretical material with which to examine team functioning over the course of time. Our purpose here is to outline possibilities, at the same time that we try to translate theory into practical terms. However, given our current state of the art in group care, it could be said (and often is) that theory is irrelevant when standing on the firing line with children. This suggests that another qualification is warranted before we proceed. I assume that practitioners will assess contributions from theory to the practice of group care as being irrelevant unless the material relates to specific situations in the work environment and is also felt by practitioners to address dilemmas facing them in the course of a working week. This is not altogether easy, but it does seem to offer direction when trying to bridge that theoretical gulf which separates training from practice. In ideal terms, we believe practice should inform theory. Our experience in group care leads to the conclusion that theoretical ideals are often a long way from trying to be good enough in practice.

1 WHO Cares? – *Team Functioning as dependent upon the composition and internal organization of work groups*

WHO team members are, their particular life histories, style of working, and status are all important variables to consider in a discussion of teamwork. We begin with this focus since it seems to be the most commonly voiced explanation for teamwork troubles given by group care personnel. Themes such as personality clash, wrong personality, and over-involvement in the work are all fairly commonplace in discussions with group care workers.

On the one hand, members may be considered as replaceable and expendable objects, as may have seemed the case in an infantry platoon during the First World War. Or, team members may be viewed as highly valued and skilled participants in a complex task. The Special Air Service rescue team which entered the Iranian Embassy in London in 1980 releasing threatened hostages offers an example of teamwork where valued team members achieved objectives well beyond the capacity of individual members. The NASA ground teams that escorted man to the moon and back again offer a large scale sample of how contributions offered by team members can be skilfully orchestrated to attain almost unbelievable objectives. In the provision of a group care service, the assignments to which personnel are posted, like the examples above, cannot be carried out by one individual. The task must be shared with other individuals, requiring at a minimum, some elementary level of collaboration or teamwork.

The literature provides an ever-increasing discussion of the occupational stresses of group care work. Mattingly (1977), Freudenberger (1977), Menzies (1970, 1977) and Dunham (1978) summarize work carried out on both sides of the Atlantic considering the impact of prolonged exposure to the stresses of group care work. Whether one is concerned with job satisfaction or the quality of working life for group care personnel, such concern is directly related to the quality of service provided by a group care centre. For similar reasons, the personality and character of each member of a staff team is worthy of consideration in discussing teamwork. Children in receipt of care make very careful discriminations between each member of a staff team, and might well become unsettled when relief staff – who are unknown to them – take charge. That individual staff are blamed for many work-related problems further confirms the importance of asking WHO Cares? when thinking about teamwork. However, other factors may be equally important, if not more so than composition. *Internal organization of a work group* is just such a factor.

Any attempt to understand or to predict the behaviour of teams must take account of the way in which mental processes of members are modified by the very fact of being members of a team. Writing shortly after the First World War, one of the founding fathers of social psychology, William McDougall (1920:21) made the following observations:

> 'It is a notorious fact that, when a number of men think and feel and act together, the mental operations and the actions of each member of the group are apt to be very different from those he would achieve if he faced the situation as an isolated individual. Hence, though we may know each member of a group so intimately that we can, with some confidence, foretell his actions under given circumstances, we cannot foretell the behaviour of the group from our knowledge of the individuals alone.'

This means that one must be prepared to study the interactions between members of a team and also the influence between a team as a whole and each member. Patterns of team organization must be considered alongside the influence that patterns of organization have on the life of the team.

McDougall postulated that groups differed greatly from one another in respect of the kind and degree of organization they possess. This means that the simplest forms of human group might have little or no organization. In other groups (or teams), individuals have certain determinate relations with one another which have arisen in one or more of three ways (McDougall, 1920 : 21–2). First, certain relations may have been established between the individuals before they came together in a team, and these previously recognized relations will continue to play a part in determining their collective deliberations and actions. Second, if any team enjoys continuity of existence, certain more or less constant relations, of subordination, deference, co-operation, leadership, and so forth, will inevitably become established between members. Finally, a team may have a continued existence and a more or less elaborate and definite organization independently of the individual members. In such a case individuals may change while the formal organization of the team persists. Each person who joins is received into some more or less well-defined position within the team and these formal positions determine in great measure the nature of individual relations to other members of the team and to the team as a whole.

One can identify in McDougall's formulations a framework which helps to explain the formation and operation of group care teams over the course of time. McDougall's early work on instinctual behaviour and the link between physiological influences and social behaviour received almost universal rejection by his contemporaries. However, while acknowledging these criticisms, the later clarification of McDougall's work (McDougall, 1932) involving 'individual propensities' and an outline for a theory of learning, has to date received very limited attention, especially by the social sciences. Meanwhile, findings in the medical field of neurophysiology (Weil, 1974) now suggest that cognitive selection of behaviour is both physiologically-based and environmentally-influenced, and that particular patterns of behaviour are used, learned, and re-used by a person to respond to certain physiological, environmental, and social stimuli.

To translate this into practical terms, a staff member – in deciding what to do in a crisis – is influenced by a personal experience of physical and nervous tension which results from physical changes like increased heartbeat and glandular secretion of adrenalin which results from activity in the brain. During the few seconds between deciding what to do and doing it, the staff member will be influenced by how he feels, what is going on around him and the social drama which unfolds through the social interactions between himself and the children. The act of engaging the crisis (the response) requires that anxiety or stress-induced tension (the internal stimuli) and the assessment of what the crisis is about (the external stimuli), be directed towards a group of children (the interpersonal stimuli) in such a way as to reduce tension and hopefully allow learning to result from the event. For the most part, this process is carried out with almost instinctual speed, hence there may have been some justification for McDougall's use of the term 'instinct' when trying to describe a physiological basis for understanding social behaviour.

When it is applied to a consideration of work groups, this formulation facilitates examination of the contributions which individuals make in teams and of the limitations which team structure imposes on the participation of individuals. Cartwright and Zander (1968) and Davis (1969), amongst others, provide further confirmation of McDougall's proposition that group structure – or certain recurring and expected patterns of interpersonal behaviour – is of considerable influence in determining group performance. It is in this sense that we can explore team functioning as dependent upon the composition and internal organization of work groups.

2 HOW Do We Do This Work? – *Team Functioning as dependent upon leadership and decision-making in work groups*

HOW team members are expected to carry out their assignment is a second dimension of teamwork. As was seen in the initial example, certain matters such as the attendance at team meetings at the end of a shift, feeling good about the hard day's work, or support from qualified supervisors might be influential issues in that team's functioning over the course of a week. Perhaps the metaphor of a relay team will help to describe how one shift hands over the 'baton' of responsibility to another, for running the next lap in an athletics event. A distinguishing characteristic of group care teams, like other production teams, is that it is continuously engaged in some way with the assembly line or the recipients of care. At one extreme, group care personnel are expected to supply a 168-hour service, fifty-two weeks a year. In a day care service, the 'production' period may be reduced to a few hours a day or week. It is in this sense that our relay team metaphor might have relevance. Some group care teams may be functioning in 'sprint' or 'middle-distance' events, such as might have been the case with our nine workers in the reception/assessment unit. On the other hand, teams may be functioning in 'marathon' or 'endurance' events, presenting different demands and varied stimulation for team members. A group care team providing for children with profound mental handicaps might at times feel as if they are participants in an endurance test.

Whatever the event – a handover of duty, being on-call, or being off-duty – all imply some level of co-operation and transfer of responsibility in a work event. As in the relay race, group care personnel frequently carry their own 'baton' of responsibility, sometimes in the form of a key. Perhaps responsibility rests simply in the title of staff, volunteer, or parent, and this distinguishes one worker from another. In all cases, responsibility is transferred from one team member to another, and then back again, throughout the course of a working week. This means that any consideration of teamwork must also look at leadership and deployment of teams, patterns of decision-making, and a consideration of HOW teams go about their work. Because leadership and personal incompetence are so frequently put forward as the reason for teams not functioning adequately, it cannot escape our attention in an exploration of group care teams. In any consideration of *leadership*, the basic important question concerns the extent to which one believes that individual influence shapes team activities and outcomes; or alternatively, whether team activities and outcomes are associated more with contextual influences, and individual influences, while important, are not all that important in determining the shape of things.

Various theoretical reasons have been noted for expecting that individuals would have less effect on organizational outcomes than would an organization's context (Pfeffer and Salancik, 1978 : 9–10). In relation to group care organizations, these reasons include the following theoretical justifications. First, both personal and agency selection processes are likely to lead to similarity amongst organizational leaders. This in turn restricts the range of skills, characteristics, and behaviours of those likely to achieve positions of importance in group care organizations. Second, even when a relatively prominent position in the organization has been achieved, the discretion permitted to a given individual is limited. Decisions may require the approval of others in the organization; information used in formulating the decisions comes from others; and some persons may attempt to pressure or influence others in their work roles. All these social influences further constrain the individual's discretion. Finally, it is simply the case that many of the things that affect group care teams and agencies are not controlled by participants within the organization. Considering all these factors, it is not likely that group care administrators would have a large effect on the outcomes of most agency activity.

Pfeffer and Salancik (1978) argue that the conditions under which there would be greater or lesser administrative impact is an important issue, and have developed a *resource-independence perspective* of organizational analysis. They argue that on research evidence presently available, administrators and supervisors may be much less influential than is reflected in the literature on organizational behaviour. The prevailing theme in this literature is said to derive from an internal view of organizations, and that what is required is an orientation which also takes account of the extent to which organizations are dependent on external resources. An appreciation of at least three concepts is required as a prerequisite to the understanding of a resource-dependence perspective. These are the concepts of: (a) organizational effectiveness; (b) organizational efficiency; and (c) the symbolic role of management. It may be helpful to summarize these concepts here.

Effectiveness of an organization is defined as its ability to create acceptable outcomes and actions (Pfeffer and Salancik, 1978:11). Caution is urged against confusing effectiveness with efficiency. Effectiveness is measured by the ratio of resources used compared with the outcome produced. Meanwhile, efficiency involves doing better what the organization is currently doing, and is an *internal standard* of performance. Effectiveness represents an *external standard* concerned with how well an organization meets the demands of various groups that are interested in its activities. Often the call for effectiveness is translated by managers and workers into an internal plea for efficiency of operation. However, the acceptability of an organization and its activities is ultimately judged by those outside the organization. An extreme example from the broad spectrum of group care structures might be drawn from the Nazi work and death centres in the 1940s (Heimler, 1963). Slaughter was carried out very efficiently and the 'service' was deemed to be quite effective by the leadership of Germany. However, these extermination centres were judged to be an abhorrence by the external world and subsequently individual officers and executioners were convicted for their effective and efficient work. Briefly put, an external orientation for studying the behaviour of organizations places much emphasis on the turbulent environment within which organizations function. We shall consider this dynamic later in our discussion, but first, one other concept, the symbolic role of management must be introduced.

Pfeffer and Salancik (1978:16) have noted with others (e.g. Kelley, 1971; Lieberson and O'Conner, 1972) that individuals apparently desire a feeling of control over their social environments. The tendency to attribute great effect to individual action, particularly actions taken by persons in designated leadership positions, may be partially accounted for by this desire for a feeling of personal effectiveness and control. Thus, one function of the team leader or manager is to serve as a symbol, or a focal point for the organization's successes and failures. By symbolic reference, a leader may come to personify the organization, its activities, and its outcomes. The writers claim that endowing leaders with an aura of power enhances individual feelings of predictability and control, giving observers an identifiable, concrete target for emotion and action. People want to believe in the effectiveness of leadership and personal action, and to say that managers serve as symbols is not to deny their importance. The sacking of an unsuccessful football coach, a supervisor, or an agency executive provides an emotional release, or catharsis, which is too real to dismiss as being unimportant. Those who remain in the organization are left with the hope that things will be improved, thus reaffirming a belief in the importance of individual action. The manager or team leader who serves as a symbol exposes him or herself to personal risks. They become accountable for things over which they have limited control, and personal careers and fortunes may suffer as a consequence.

Thus one can see how important it is to consider the effect of external influences as well as internal ones in the operation of group care teams. Evaluation of effectiveness and efficiency are directly related to this consideration, as is a reconsideration of the symbolic role in leadership. HOW team members go about their various assignments is just as important as considering WHO is given which assignment in the team. However, some aspects of teamwork are perhaps less open to scrutiny than others, for many of the reasons outlined above.

3 WHERE Do We Start? – *Team Functioning as dependent upon characteristics in the work environment*

WHERE work teams are located within an organization and its personnel charts and WHERE they are deployed to assume work assignments in a particular work site constitute further influences on teamwork. Most group care teams will be found towards the bottom of organization management charts, or at least experience tends to support such a view. However, the siting of work teams on organizational charts is not really the central issue for consideration here, important as it is. Instead, the primary concern is with an actual workplace to which team members are assigned. Such a workplace, its siting and physical design will impose particular demands on the capacity of personnel to perform. When personnel live on the premises of a group care centre, even greater demands are imposed, often blurring the boundaries between personal and professional activity. A group care team whose workplace is situated in a highly populated area have opportunities which vary enormously from say our nine staff members who worked in a semi-isolated workplace, sheltered away from public amenities and supplied almost exclusively by institutional services. Families and friends of children in care are also influenced by WHERE a group care centre is situated, and the involvement of visitors has a direct bearing on the work carried out by personnel. Any consideration of teamwork must therefore account for influences imposed by the workplace and its environment.

The events encountered by a work team in a group care environment do not present themselves with neat labels and interpretations. Rather, team members and the children with whom they work give meaning to the events. It is in this sense that Weick's (1969) concept of 'the enacted environment' can be applied to our consideration of work teams in group care. A prevalent view is that group care environments are created by the adults and children who frequent them. Further, as group care environments are created and used, the system of referring agencies adapt to and endorse these service environments as being of assistance to clients. Weick postulates that as human actors, the personnel and children who inhabit an environment do not just *react* to their environment. In many ways they can be said to *enact* it.

The use of this term enactment can be found to have two general meanings. The first is 'to decree by legislation or policy directive', while the second meaning is 'to re-create or represent something as by staging a play'. Both processes are involved when interpreting events in a group care environment. Personnel are 'directed' to a particular workplace, and there, along with other personnel who have been similarly directed, they engage children and are engaged by children in activities which are both 'play' and 'drama'. Maier (1975) describes this process as 'learning to learn and living to live'. But the question of what a group care environment is, is meaningless without reference to the focal organization, and more precisely, to the individuals who plan and carry out the activities which take place there.

Weick (1969:65) identifies several properties of an enacted environment, each of which has relevance for our consideration of group care. First, in the process of enactment, the creation of meaning has to do with remembering and paying attention to events which have already occurred. Second, since the attention is directed backward from a specific here and now in time, whatever is occurring at the moment will influence what the person or persons discover when they reall experiences. This means that team attention is directed backward from a given point in time, and whatever past experiences are fixed upon, these become the basis from which further action or enactment takes place. For example, when an experienced worker is faced with a difficult situation to do with a group of older children, she or he is likely to refer back to previous encounters which resemble this one (even if through an instantaneous mental process) to obtain cues on how to enact the new drama. Maier (1978) has considered this process in relation to the application of Piagetian principles in professional helping. Goffman (1974) refers to it as a person framing their experience in such a way that it makes sense and informs their action.

Another group care worker facing a difficult situation helps us to clarify a third property which Weick (1969) postulates to be central to the process of enactment. This is that memory – be it memory retention, recall, or reconstruction – influences the meaning workers convey to experiences. A middle-aged woman, who is a single-parent mother of adolescent boys, was hired to work as a group life counsellor in a school for delinquent girls. She reported for her first day of work, dressed in a skirt and high-heeled shoes which seemed befitting the professional status accorded to counsellors. On arriving at the school, this woman was directed to one of the living units and soon found herself locked into one of the first secure treatment units for girls in the United States. Within minutes of being locked into this work environment, a riot broke out injuring the supervisor. Our new worker lost her high-heeled shoes and barely managed to alert security in time to obtain back-up support. The experience had a telling effect on her subsequent performance. Some years later, while working again in the same unit, the same worker exuded tension and an increased authoritarian response at the slightest indication of horseplay by the girls.

The fourth property of enactment is clarified as we continue the same example. Only when this staff member's authoritarian response occurred in the centre did the various stimuli for that response become identified. Weick's explanation of this last property is that 'an action can become an object for attention only *after* it has occurred' (Weick, 1969 : 65). While the staff member was acting in an authoritarian manner and thereby changing the tone of the environment, the reasons for her action were not entirely clear. Thus, in the early days of her return to working in the secure unit, it was not unusual for someone to ask 'What is she on about?'. Later, through supportive supervision, this same staff member was able to develop alternative responses for dealing with tense situations. She also became much more sensitive to her own ability to influence events without resorting to authoritarian means.

As our concern is with finding explanations for variations that can be found in the functioning of group care teams, the notion of an enacted environment has several attractions. In that the discussion so far has been concerned with the process whereby individuals give meaning to certain events, so this process becomes complicated further when shifting attention from the individual worker to the work team. In a team context, collective rather than individual influences control the interpretation of meaningful events which occur in the active group care environment.

However, characteristics of the work environment include more than just the meaning which team members give to events. There are also structural variables, or the staging, lighting, and props around which human drama and play is enacted. The siting and physical design of a centre plus the spatial arrangement of rooms and furnishings all play a fundamental part in determining how a group care environment is enacted. Earlier in this volume, Maier discussed the uses of public and

private space in group care centres. Moos (1976:111–26) has also identified three aspects of the environment – distance, spatial arrangement,
and amenities – which have been found to influence human behaviour.
Therefore, starting with structural characteristics in the environment
and drawing from the enacted environment formulations advanced by
Weick (1969), it is possible to see how team functioning in group care
work can be influenced by the work environment. WHERE such
environmental milieux are situated, and the extent to which they
impose restrictions on the interaction between personnel and children,
provides a starting point for this enquiry.

4   *WHEN Are You On Duty? – Team Functioning as dependent*
upon human development processes in personnel (and – in the
case of group care service personnel – developmental characteristics
of the client group)

WHEN team members are expected to work constitutes another important area for discussion. Here one might consider the hours of work,
patterns of on and off-duty, length of service, and benefits which have
accrued for working over a particular period of time. Immediate details
are available in the first instance by examining the weekly or monthly
work schedule which is available in some form within every group care
centre. Explorations into the impact of shift-work, of on-call duty, and of
over-time duty in group care work are likely to highlight factors which
are similar to those identified in the goods-producing and service-
producing sectors of employment (Faunce and Dubin, 1975; Agassi,
1975; Ginzberg, 1975; and Reed, 1977). When personnel report to work
and return home again focus attention on the interaction between
working life and personal life. When personnel stay in tied accommodation, or live on the premises, the boundaries between working life and
personal life become even more blurred as when a worker 'comes home
to work' after a quiet evening with friends. A night shift worker once
described an occasion when he had stopped off for a beer after a long
'day' at work. The cleaning lady in the bar gave him the number for
Alcoholics Anonymous because she thought that anyone drinking at
7.30 in the morning must have a drink problem!
    A consideration of when personnel work also requires clarification of
career patterns in what Levinson *et al.* (1978) describe biographically as
an *adult life structure*. Variations can be expected between the newly
qualified young person entering work in a group care centre, and, say,
the team member in his late forties, already a grandparent and working
in a second or third career. This is not to suggest that one or the other
person is likely to make the better member of a group care team. Instead,

it is to suggest that certain developmental influences may help to shape or frame the functioning of group care teams over time. Caution is required when one takes account of the criticisms levelled at the ego psychology assumptions used by Levinson and his associates, criticisms relating to the subjectivity, the speculative nature, and biographical foundations inherent in the psychosocial orientation. Others, however, including Maier, Ainsworth, and VanderVen in this volume, have supported this view in their considerations of personal and professional functioning amongst group care personnel (see also Weber, 1961; Menzies, 1970; Maier, 1977).

The concept of life structure is seen as providing a way of looking at the engagement of an individual in society (Levinson *et al.*, 1978 : 42). The basic pattern or design in a person's life has been considered from three perspectives. The first involves the individual's sociocultural world or the preconditions for his action. The second includes aspects of self, such as patterns of thinking, feeling, and action along with personal values, beliefs, and an unconscious dimension. Finally, there is an individual's participation in the world, focusing on the landscape, the cast of characters, and the variety of resources and constraints out of which man fashions his life.

When an external event has a decisive impact, one may wish to consider how processes in the self may have helped to bring it about and to mediate its effects. Similarly, when an inner conflict leads to dramatic action, it may help to consider how external influences may have touched off the conflict and determined how it would be played out. Working along these lines, Holmes and Masuda (1974) and Harrington *et al.* (1977) have demonstrated how certain correlations can be drawn between significant life events and illness susceptibility, while Brown and Harris (1978) have shown that significant life events influence different people in different ways. Thus, one might seek to question how various aspects of a person's world influence the formation of a life structure and shape its change over time.

Levinson and his associates found that occupation and marriage/family are usually the most central components in shaping the basic pattern or design of a man's life. It is through participation in these two social arenas that a person engages most directly with the world. An occupation is one of the primary factors determining income, class, prestige, and a place in society. Family life, on the other hand, connects one to various other components of life, including a family and class of origin, ethnicity, and occupation. Several studies of group care work with children have shown where high staff turnover, limited career mobility, and restricted training opportunities leave personnel in a disadvantaged occupational position (Cawson, 1978; Millham, Bullock, and

Hosie, 1980; Newman and Mackintosh, 1975). In terms of family and domestic life, it could be said that group care work influences life style in at least two ways. First, shift-work poses an influence on family life, just as it does for all shift-working personnel. Second, there is the additional influence of close emotional involvement between a worker and the children or colleagues with whom they work. These emotional demands can all too easily pose a threat to family life at home. It is in this sense that a framework for adult development (Levinson *et al.*, 1978 : 57) might be applied to an assessment of teamwork. Furthermore, events such as marriage, divorce, change of occupation, death of a family member, birth of a child, and loss of a job, may be assumed to be important influences in the life histories of men and women working in group care.

General caution should be heeded when blaming teamwork problems on a team member who is 'going through the menopause' or because another couple of staff are 'having an affair' in their personal lives. However, WHEN people work and how long they have been working – both in the overtime sense and in the career sense – are important influences to consider when thinking of teamwork. It is in this respect that Maier's developmental assertion (in chapter 2) might be amended to read '. . . the care offered children shapes their lives, and the children in turn shape [the lives of the caregivers and] the actual mode of care provided'.

5   WHAT Are You On About? – Team Functioning as dependent upon work orientation

WHAT personnel believe teamwork to be, and WHAT managers believe to be the ingredients of successful teams constitute other dimensions worth considering. There would seem to be a prevailing belief amongst human service organizations that teamwork is a 'good thing'. This belief is generally supported by a growing body of research and academic opinion (Brieland, Briggs, and Leuenberger, 1973; Barker and Briggs, 1968, 1969; and Emery, 1977; among others). One prevailing orientation promotes a view of teamwork which emphasizes decision-making by consultation, democratic principles of membership, personal and group accountability, group sanctions, collaboration, co-operation, and the use of initiative. Another orientation, perhaps best described as 'Machiavellian', tends toward some form of dictatorship, whether benign, ruthless, or otherwise. This orientation is likely to emphasize decision-making by hierarchical directive, feudal principles of membership, superior/subordinate accountability, reward by promotion, punishment by blocked promotion or alteration of work hours, role demarcations, and the tendency of team organization to inhibit worker initiative.

In group care work, attitudes to and expectations of teams will also incorporate various theoretical assumptions about the primary task of work. A behaviourist orientation (Pizzat, 1973) is likely to emphasize quite different aspects of teamwork than would be the case of a group care team operating according to a Rudolph Steiner philosophy, emphasizing as it does the spiritual, physical, and social rhythms which are naturally healing for a child (Weihs, 1971). The orientation that is dominant in the functioning of group care teams is likely to play an important part in determining how teams go about their work. Any attitudes, beliefs, ideologies, theories, philosophies, or creeds which are used to justify and promote group care activity will be experienced first hand by children in care. As such, a consideration of work orientation is fundamentally important to the provision of a group care service.

Russell's (1975) enquiry into the variety of attitudes held by workers about their employment and job satisfaction provides a useful starting place. The work orientation variable represents the extent to which workers list their wants and expectations in order of priority relative to their employment. Russell challenged Herzberg's (1968) two-factor theory of job satisfaction which postulated that factors leading to job satisfaction are separate and distinct from the factors that lead to job dissatisfaction (Russell, 1975 : 301–02). Herzberg's differentiation of factors resulted in the two-factor analysis of job satisfaction delineated according to *job content factors* (motivators) and *job context factors* (hygiene). Job content factors included the needs for recognition, achievement, possibility for growth, advancement, responsibility, and the work itself. Job context factors include salary, interpersonal relations (team and supervisors), technical supervision, company policy and administration, working conditions, factors in personal life, status, and job security.

Herzberg's motivator-hygiene theory is claimed by Russell to have resulted in inconclusive research evidence. He argues that the way in which workers perceive their work as satisfying or dissatisfying will be directly related to the values which are given to various aspects of the job and its environment. Russell proposed that job satisfaction was a positive function of workers attaining their priority work needs. Further, workers' expectations of their priority work needs were a function of their orientation to work. This sociological perspective implies that workers can be responsive to *both* intrinsic and extrinsic rewards. Similarly, both types of rewards may be reported by workers as satisfiers and dissatisfiers at the same time (Russell, 1975 : 306). Support for this assertion derives from findings which show that workers who are instrumentally oriented (e.g. a labourer on an assembly line) derive their work meaning from extrinsic rewards (e.g. money), whereas workers who are expressively oriented (e.g. many group care workers) derive their work meaning from intrinsic rewards (e.g. feelings of satisfaction from relationships with children).

Heimler (1975) has also developed a satisfaction construct which in some ways can be said to parallel Herzberg's work on job satisfaction. However, Heimler postulated that the absence of satisfaction is not the same as dissatisfaction.[2] He argues instead, that an alternative construct, frustration, is required in considering the emotional significance of work (Heimler, 1969). Thus, job satisfaction *and* job frustration should be identified at one and the same time, along with some recognition of how satisfactions and frustrations in life outside of work influences a person's capacity for work. Heimler further postulated that orientations to life satisfaction are socially and culturally defined within five broad areas of social functioning, including: work life, financial life, life with friends and peers, family life, and personal life. Similarly, orientations to life frustration were seen to be socially and culturally defined, being expressed through: activity, health, influence, moods, and habits. Heimler (1975, 1979) concludes that some economic distribution of energy is required throughout the various areas of satisfaction and frustration, and that some relative balance will be found between satisfactions and frustrations. Thus, the greater the frustration and the lower the satisfaction, the more likely it is that a worker's job performance will become known to both team members and the supervisory process.

Russell's (1975) work orientation variable allows one to extend traditional considerations of job satisfaction to include Heimler's justification for examining both satisfaction *and* frustration amongst workers. When applied to the practices of group care teams, work orientation is likely to be reflected in different patterns of satisfaction and frustration all within the same group of personnel. Such indeed was found to be the case in our original example. In this sense we can postulate that a coalescence of themes between satisfactions and frustrations amongst a group of workers will influence their pattern of team functioning over time. Work orientation can be expected to exert an influence both at an individual and at a team or organizational level. WHAT team members believe their work to be about, and the importance that is given to certain aspects as compared with others, will provide some indication of their work orientation. This dimension of teamwork has received very little attention in the group care literature.

6 WHAT's It FOR? – *Team Functioning as dependent upon the organization and social policy environment*

Finally, when looking at teamwork in group care, it is also important to ascertain FOR WHAT reasons teamwork objectives gain support. Some might suggest that teamwork ensures continuity of production, or continuity of service, so that a consumer group can rely on that service. Others might say that a reasonable level of consistency in performance is also required by a consumer group, and that teamwork is required to achieve such consistency. Efficiency and effectiveness are other goods or service-producing arguments referred to earlier, but are equally important here as arguments which support a policy of teamwork.

In group care work, these variables are likely to involve many issues which are external to the actual workplace and lifespace of a group care centre. The enactment of legislation which reorganized social services in 1968 (Scotland) and 1970 (England and Wales), and the later reorganization of local government administration in 1974–75 offer British examples of how changes in the organization and social policy environment might influence personnel. Alterations in children's legislation, plus similar reorganization of health and welfare administration in many regions of North America, have had parallel results there. Jobs have often been refashioned and redefined within a very short period of time (as was the case with the staff in our example), and very little is known about the impact this has on children and staff whose lives are thus rearranged, by forces well beyond their influence.

The rise of evaluation research to a place of prominence in academic and service-producing organizations, as discussed by Payne in chapter 10, gives further substance to a resource-dependence view of organizational functioning. As human service organizations seek to survive (and more optimistically, to gain confidence in their capacity to work with children), so these organizations must now be more watchful of the turbulent social policy environment within which they operate. A social policy environment would here incorporate political and economic policies at regional, national, and international levels. Emery and Trist provided one of the earliest and most influential attempts to describe characteristics of the organizational environment (Pfeffer and Salancik, 1978:63). In discussing the four types of environment within which organizations have functioned, Emery (1977) has summarized characteristics of the first three environments in order to focus particular attention on the fourth. Emery is particularly interested in the problems of adaptation and organization survival while operating within the turbulent environment of our modern age.

In Emery's summary (1977:8–11) of environmental types, Type 1: *random, placid environments* were characterized as having similarities with an organization being dropped for the first time into a tropical jungle without a survivor's handbook for that region. Trial and error were the required activities and responsibility for survival was left simply with the resources available within the organization. Type 2: *clustered, placid environments* were characterized as being a development beyond Type 1 where some ordering of relationships between organizations can be found, allowing organizations to seek survival by reaching out into the environment for what it needs and to avoid those elements which offer a threat. Type 3: *disturbed, reactive environments* brings us more closely to the type of situation that is still quite prevalent in many areas of the world. Here various organizations emerge in direct competition with other organizations. Tactics and strategy emerge as one organization seeks to discover the intentions and capabilities of its competitors and thereby plot its survival. Type 4: *turbulent environments* were characterized as resulting from both the competition for survival as found in Type 3, and from processes that are set off in the environment itself, such as the oil crisis and dependence on political stability in the Middle East. With shifts in the ground, the ground-rules change in unpredictable ways. Emery (1977:10) believes that the turbulent environment is the most complexly textured of all the environments. *Adaptive behaviour* is now all that is possible as organizations seek to continue operating and paradoxically, adaptive responses are actually required, as distinct from mere survival tactics.

Turbulent environments are of particular concern in our thinking of teamwork in group care centres. Such centres are frequently characterized by high uncertainty, complexity, and unpredictability. The traditional focus of Emery's work has been directed towards the world of international industry and commerce, although such a perspective can also be shown to have considerable relevance to our discussion of group care teams. The critical consequence for organizations operating in a turbulent environment is the degree of complexity reflected in their task. It can be said that the more complex the task, the greater the degree of uncertainty and unpredictability for both personnel and administrators. This happens in relation to the uncertain expectations which will be required of members in an organization if they are to collaborate with others (e.g. parents, volunteers and others) in their service-producing work. The central question is therefore how group care teams can adapt to these anticipated uncertainties, and moreover, how they can avoid *maladaptive responses* by developing constructive approaches in the face of unpredictable demands.

Maladaptive responses occur when an organization does not acknowledge the difficult conditions under which its staff work. One approach is to ignore the complexity of the environment so that the agency responds in a way which would only be adequate for a less complex environment. To strive for the 'good old days' is an example of this maladaptive response. Another approach is to ignore certain aspects of the environment, thereby directing the organization's attention towards coping with only one part or one aspect of the environment. To define a problem as strictly an educational problem, a social service problem or a health problem is an example of this response. Emery (1977) distinguishes between three forms of maladaptive behaviour which can be commonly found in organizations functioning in turbulent environments (see also Emery and Emery, 1973). These are superficiality, segmentation, and dissociation. Elsewhere (Fulcher, 1979), we have considered how these maladaptive responses could result in the need for an employment manifesto amongst group care personnel. However, for our purposes here, it is important to consider both maladaptive and adaptive possibilities.

The first pattern of maladaptive response, *superficiality*, occurs when the deeper roots, or the wider implications of a task which brings work groups together, are denied. On a personal level, it occurs when an individual denies feelings and attitudes which are basic to his pattern of functioning. The characteristic attitude in this instance is *intolerance* where one wishes that an increasing number of people just did not exist. 'They', 'He' or 'She' become the target for why things are not working in a team. Little attempt is made to ask 'Them' about how working relationships could be improved. Emery (1977 : 33–4) lists three attitudes which are associated with this pattern of maladaptive response. These are paraphrased as follows: (a) instead of the critical 'Is this necessary?' there is acceptance that 'this is the way things are'; (b) instead of pursuing 'what should be' there is the admonishment to be 'grateful for small mercies'; (c) leisure is not pursued as free uncommitted time but as relief from bad feelings. Such attitudes can be seen as a denial of individual character, whether of a person or an organization, and constitute a tactical retreat from an environment that is seen to be too uncertain or complex.

Segmentation or fragmentation is the second way that group care teams can maladjust to a turbulent work environment. In this instance, sub-goals become goals in their own right, and various goals are pursued independently of any real or apparent purpose. The social field is transformed into a set of social fields, each integrated in itself but poorly integrated with each other. In this instance, work groups often move beyond superficial explanations of their tasks, but come to overemphasize the differences between members, simplifying their choices between 'Ours' and 'Theirs'. In this pattern, the characteristic attitude is *prejudice* with the expectation that 'people ought to stay in their place' Thus, as an organization seeks to move beyond a superficial response to a turbulent environment, it can easily fragment into parts pursuing their own ends, and factions interact without respect to the teamwork demands which are required in the primary task. While segmentation can be said to draw members to a closer identification of what 'They' believe is important, in some respects this pattern of response is more intractable than the others which are more visible. In fragmented teams, turbulence in the work environment and in team relationships is likely to result in an escalated 'cold war'. Periodic episodes of fury and feud erupt as team members struggle to influence the course of events in a complex and largely unpredictable group care environment.

Dissociation, the third way of simplifying an overcomplex environment, is essentially an individual, passively-adaptive response and develops from what happens at a social level rather than at the organizational level. Here, individuals try to reduce the uncertainties in their work environment by denying the relevance or usefulness of others as colleagues or partners in the tasks which they seek to perform. The characteristic attitudes in this pattern are those of *indifference* and *cynicism* as members take up the stance 'somebody else will take care of it'. It is not so much the complexity and uncertainty of the work environment *per se* that encourages this kind of passive adaptation. It is the increasing unpredictability of what might follow from involvements with others. As workers withdraw from public commitments, the reasons for their behaviour are less available and thus less open to the understanding of others. They are compelled to judge each other in terms of the external and visible characteristics of their behaviour. The relationships between team members become superficial, less dependable, and more prone to intrigue.

It will be very surprising indeed if group care personnel and administrators have not had experiences with colleagues who demonstrated these various approaches in their work: the worker who sees things only his way and cannot tolerate alternative views; the worker who gets on with the job, perhaps managing fairly well, but ignoring or even resisting the idea that what he is doing may have an adverse effect on other people; or, there is the worker who refuses to look at how his contribution to the team effort may be putting extra demands on others, and moreover, how this performance may be viewed by the organization at large. These three patterns are not mutually exclusive but each becomes a critical feature to consider when exploring the intricacies of group care work environments.

In spite of the influences which easily bring about maladaptive responses, there are some factors which can help bring about active adaptation to work demands in a turbulent environment (Emery, 1977: 67–123). To do so, team members are required to look beyond a superficial assessment of what is required to perform assigned tasks. They are required to avoid an over-reliance on power and influence as the means by which their will, and hence their view of what is right, is imposed on other team members. Further, they are required to willingly invest some level of personal commitment in their job and in work relationships, although such commitment need not imply a total commitment. Quality of working life is directly related to a quality of life outside of work, and both of these pursuits will be influenced by the way that working lives are organized and by the ideals that are sought through work and outside work. Thus one can claim that the living and learning environments of group care work are particularly susceptible to a lack of social and emotional wellbeing amongst workers. The way that administrators and policy-makers establish, fund, recruit, and deploy group care teams will go a long way to determining whether they are able to actively adapt to the demands imposed by turbulent environments. Emery (1977) suggests two ways that this can be done.

First, teams can be organized and deployed in such a way as to see each part as replaceable. As and when one part fails or ceases to function, another takes over. Special controls are required to determine if the parts are performing satisfactorily, and extra controls are required to keep track of the controllers. This pattern of organization is inherently prone to errors and considerable time is required to learn new ways of working. Armies are an example of this pattern.

Alternatively, organizations might seek to adapt by striving for teams which build the element of diversity into their membership, while also ensuring that considerable overlap of skills is available within each team. At any one time, some of the skills which are available within the 'resource pool' will not be required. As and when one team member is unavailable to perform, there are other members who can step in and continue supporting a team effort. In this way, team performance is less dependent on key individual members. All members cannot function exactly alike, but their collective performance is greater than the sum of the parts. So long as a member retains any of their capabilities to function satisfactorily, they are of some value to the team. A winning football team gives an example for this pattern of team organization, especially when noting the importance of reserves who can come off the bench to score goals.

In each pattern of organization it is possible to identify a set of ideals which will be conveyed implicitly through a team's performance in a turbulent environment. In the first pattern – which emphasizes replaceable parts – teams are prone to struggle blindly on, believing that a particular way of doing things will be successful. They are prone to believing that ample resources and more trained personnel will bring about a successful achievement of the primary task. Hard work and commitment is believed to be associated with success, and success, with having their good efforts recognized and rewarded. Participation in this type of adaptive team is likely to require heavy commitment and it is not always easy to know when contributions are 'good enough'.

In the second pattern of organization design – where diversity of skills in a team is more important than the individual parts – Emery (1977) suggests that people are implicitly making choices amongst ideals. Members can seek a sense of *teamness* rather than always trying to do their own thing. They may seek mutual help and *nurturance* rather than always imposing their own will on the team. They might strive to include the ideal of *humaneness*, along with the usual criteria for determining task effectiveness and efficiency. And though it may be a difficult notion to grasp, work environments which nurture a sense of teamwork and which emphasize humane relationships performing a collective task, offer people a more enjoyable environment to be in. If people enjoy their work and the other people in their work environment, then *enjoyment* becomes a force for creativity and purposeful action in their lives. It is in this sense that quality of working life gains substance. If people do not enjoy working with children, then the consequences for those children will be substantial.

While the idea of an organization and social policy environment is more abstract that the other dimensions of teamwork to be considered earlier, it may well be one of the most important influences. The significance of this dimension is that it is primarily an external influence to the functioning of group care teams. FOR WHAT ends, do group care workers and organizations pursue teamwork practices? The answers to such a question are likely to be fundamental to the quality of services provided for families and children. The functioning of group care organizations in the 1980s would seem to be especially vulnerable in the turbulent environment which prevails.

III   Summary and conclusions

Several issues have been shown to relate to our original question, WHY be concerned with the formation and operation of work teams in group care? These issues involved a consideration of WHO team members are and the possibility that team functioning will vary as the result of composition and internal organization of teams. HOW teams are expected to carry out their assignments gave rise to the possibility that team functioning is shaped by leadership and decision-making influences in work groups. WHERE team members are assigned to work gave rise to a consideration of enacted environments, and the possibility that team functioning is influenced by characteristics in the work environment. WHEN team members are expected to work, and the career patterns which emerge over their working lives gave rise to the possibility that patterns of functioning are related to human growth and development processes. Amongst group care teams, an added feature involves taking account of characteristics in the client group as an interpersonal influence which may shape adult development. WHAT personnel and administrators believe teamwork to be, gave rise to a work orientation hypothesis which considers both job satisfaction and frustration Finally, the importance of asking FOR WHAT ends teamwork objectives gain support in group care resulted in a formulation which accounts for the way in which personnel teams are dependent upon the organization and social policy environment.

As was seen in our original example, it is the persistence of group care teams to continue functioning when members change, and when tasks or assignments are reallocated, that encourages further study in this area. An attempt has been made to show how the functioning of group care teams and the functioning of children in the care of those teams are interrelated parts of a whole. This means that one feature of the service cannot be explored in isolation from the other. Our conclusion is that future research and evaluation endeavours will need to take greater account of personnel influences which have been largely neglected to date in explorations of the group care field.

Notes

(1) The writer is indebted to several people for helping to clarify some of the ideas presented in this chapter. Among these, I would like to pay particular acknowledgement to Steve Bordwell, Gale Burford, Max Flood, Geoff Myer, Steve Regis, and Chris Turner.

(2) Weil (1974) summarizes medical research in the field of neurophysiology which shows how different cognitive and behavioural responses result from pleasure and unpleasure stimulation in the limbic system of the brain. It would appear that certain parallels can be drawn between these findings and Heimler's (1975) satisfaction and frustration constructs.

References

Agassi, J. B. (1975) The Quality of Women's Working Life. In L. E. Davis and A. B. Cherns (eds) *The Quality of Working Life*, Vol. I. New York: Free Press.

Barker, R. L. and Briggs, T. L. (1968) *Differential Use of Social Work Manpower*. New York: National Association of Social Workers.

Barker, R. L. and Briggs, T. L. (1969) *Using Teams to Deliver Social Services*. Syracuse, New York: Syracuse University School of Social Work.

Brieland, D., Briggs, T. L., and Leuenberger, P. (1973) *The Team Model of Social Work Practice*. Syracuse, New York: Syracuse University School of Social Work.

Brown, G. W. and Harris, T. (1978) *Social Origins of Depression: A Study of Psychiatric Disorder in Women*. London: Tavistock Publications.

Cartwright, D. and Zander, A. (1968) The Structural Properties of Groups: Introduction. In D. Cartwright and A. Zander *Group Dynamics* (third edition).
London: Tavistock Publications.

Cawson, P. (1978) *Community Homes: A Study of Residential Staff.* London: Her
Majesty's Stationery Office.

Davis, H. (1969) *Group Performance.* London: Addison-Wesley.

Dunham, J. (1978) Staff Stress in Residential Work. *Social Work Today* 9 (45): 18–20.

Emery, F. and Emery, M. (1973) *Participative Design.* Canberra: Australian
National University, Centre for Continuing Education.

Emery, F. (1977) *Futures We Are In.* Leiden, The Netherlands: Martinus Nijhoff.

Faunce, W. A. and Dubin, R. (1975) Individual Investment in Working and
Living. In L. E. Davis and A. B. Cherns (eds) *The Quality of Working Life,* Vol. I.
New York: Free Press.

Freudenberger, H. J. (1977) Burn-out: Occupational Hazard of the Child Care
Worker. *Child Care Quarterly* 6 (2): 90–9.

Fulcher, L. C. (1979) Keeping Staff Sane to Accomplish Treatment. *Residential and
Community Child Care Administration* 1 (1): 69–85.

Ginzberg, E. (1975) Work Structuring and Manpower Realities. In L. E. Davis and
A. B. Cherns (eds) *The Quality of Working Life,* Vol. I. New York: Free Press.

Goffman, E. (1974) *Frame Analysis: An Essay on the Organization of Experience.* Cambridge, Massachusetts: Harvard University Press.

Harrington, R. L., Koreneff, C., Nasser, S., Wright, C., and Engelhard, C. (1977)
Systems Approach to Mental Health Care in a Health Maintenance Organization Model,
Three Year Report. Washington, DC: National Institute of Mental Health.

Heimler, E. (1963) Children of Auschwitz. In G. Mikes (ed.) *Prison.* London:
Routledge & Kegan Paul.

Heimler, E. (1969) *Mental Illness in Social Work.* Harmondsworth: Penguin Books.

Heimler, E. (1975) *Survival in Society.* New York: Halsted Press.

Heimler, E. (1979) On the Emotional Significance of Work: An Audio-taped Interview (27 September). Department of Sociology, University of Stirling.

Herzberg, F. (1968) *Work and the Nature of Man.* London: Staples Press.

Holmes, T. H. and Masuda, M. (1974) Life Change and Illness Susceptibility. In
B. S. Dohrenwend and B. P. Dohrenwend (eds) *Stressful Life Events: Their Nature
and Effects.* New York: John Wiley.

Kelley, H. H. (1971) *Attribution in Social Interaction.* Morristown, New Jersey:
General Learning Press.

Levinson, D. J., Darrow, C. N., Klein, E. B., Levinson, M. H., and McKee, B.
(1978) *The Seasons of a Man's Life.* New York: Ballantine Books.

Lieberson, S. and O'Connor, J. F. (1972) Leadership and Organizational
Performance: A Study of Large Corporations. *American Sociological Review*
37: 117–30.

Maier, H. W. (1975) Learning to Learn and Living to Live in Residential Treatment. *Child Welfare* 54 (6): 406–20.

Maier, H. W. (1977) The Core of Care. *The First Aberlour Trust Lecture.* Stirling,
Scotland: Aberlour Child Care Trust.

Maier, H. W. (1978) Sensori-Motor Phase Knowledge Applied to Beginnings in
Professional Helping. In J. F. Magary, M. K. Poulsen, P. J. Levinson, and P. A.

Taylor (eds) *Piagetian Theory and Helping Professions*. Los Angeles: University Publishers.

Mattingly, M. A. (1977) Sources of Stress and Burn-out in Professional Child Care Work. *Child Care Quarterly* 6 (2): 127–37.

McDougall, W. (1920) *The Group Mind*. Cambridge: Cambridge University Press.

McDougall, W. (1932) *The Energies of Man*. London: Methuen.

Menzies, I. E. P. (1970) *The Functioning of Social Systems as a Defence Against Anxiety*. London: Tavistock Institute of Human Relations.

Menzies, I. E. P. (1977) *Staff Support Systems: Task and Anti-task in Adolescent Institutions*. London: Tavistock Institute of Human Relations.

Millham, S., Bullock, R., and Hosie, K. (1980) *Learning to Care*. Farnborough, Hants: Gower.

Moos, R. H. (1976) *The Human Context: Environmental Determinants of Behavior*. New York: John Wiley.

Newman, N. and Mackintosh, H. (1975) *A Roof Over Their Heads? Residential Provision for Children in S.E. Scotland*. Edinburgh: University of Edinburgh, Department of Social Administration.

Pfeffer, J. and Salancik, G. R. (1978) *The External Control of Organizations: A Resource Dependence Perspective*. New York: Harper & Row.

Pizzat, F. (1973) *Behavior Modification in Residential Treatment for Children*. New York: Behavioral Publications.

Reed, M. J. (1977) Stress in Live-in Child Care. *Child Care Quarterly* 6 (2): 114–20.

Russell, K. J. (1975) Variations in Orientation to Work and Job Satisfaction. *Sociology of Work and Occupations* 2 (4): 299–322.

Weber, G. H. (1961) Emotional and Defensive Reactions of Cottage Parents. In D. Cressey (ed.) *The Prison: Studies in Institutional Organization and Change*. New York: Holt, Rinehart & Winston.

Weick, K. E. (1969) *The Social Psychology of Organizing*. Reading, Massachusetts: Addison-Wesley.

Weihs, T. J. (1971) *Children in Need of Special Care*. London: Souvenir Press.

Weil, J. L. (1974) *A Neurophysiological Model of Emotional and Intentional Behavior*. Springfield, Illinois: Charles C. Thomas.

Whittaker, J. K. (1979) *Caring for Troubled Children*. San Francisco: Jossey-Bass.

Section III

Career development and training

8 Patterns of career development in group care

Karen D. VanderVen[1]

Introduction

The significance of group care of children as a mode of service provision is highlighted by Bronfenbrenner, who states, 'besides home, the only setting that serves as a comprehensive context for human development is the children's institution' (1979:172). On the premise that group care is not only a mainstay of children's services, particularly in its newer community context, but also that it will be subject to change under the impact of altering societal influences, it is then crucial to consider the preparation and maintenance of group care practitioners who will be able to respond to the demand for group care services in years to come. This chapter describes a conceptual formulation for defining a variety of skills and attributes required at various levels of group care work based on a consideration of particular trends in human services today.

Child ecology and other trends in the delivery of group care services

Perhaps the most significant theoretical advance in the field of child development in the last decade or so has been the recognition that to have a significant impact on children's development requires a comprehensive ecological approach that influences all of the environmental systems which impinge on children. Ecology's relevance to group care is illustrated by several examples. In the area of residential treatment, there has been the historical precedent set by the early child guidance movement in which individual therapy with identified children was considered the primary mode of treatment. Applied to the residential setting this meant providing a custodial or at best hygienic environment for children while they awaited their treatment sessions. In the last several decades, this orientation has changed, as is well documented by Davids (1975). Today, multiple influences such as increased professionalism in the child care field (Beker, 1976; 1979); and developments in the concept of the therapeutic milieu, contribute to the emergence of the group care worker as the key staff member with potential to affect the total milieu of children in care (Beker, 1979). This means that 'the other 23 hours' (Trieschman, Whittaker, and Brendtro, 1969) and not simply the 'clinical hour' now comprise the core of the child's treatment.

Another example is provided by group care programs for young children such as Head Start. These were designed as interventive services that would promote ongoing and positive development of cognitive, social, and other abilities which children needed for later school success. Evidence suggests that the effectiveness of these programs is related to the degree to which the services offered have been targeted not only on the children themselves, but also on such additional influences as living situation, health status, and economic factors. These examples, and there are others, all suggest that successful promotion of children's development and positive mental health must be aimed at *both* the child himself and at his total environment.

The ecological formulation indicates that the environment in which children grow and with which they interact is composed of a *hierarchy of settings ranging from immediate influences to the broadest context of society*. This view has been articulated by Bronfenbrenner (1977, 1979) who states 'that the person's development is profoundly affected by events occurring in settings in which the person is not even present' (1979:3), and by Brim (1975) who describes 'macroinfluences' on children as ways in which broad reaching societal factors affect the course of development.

Whittaker (1979) is among the increasing number who recognize the implications of the concept of ecology for designing and implementing children's services. This requires that group care practitioners embrace a concept of group care which transcends its direct delivery in an immediate setting, and also that they be educated in the prerequisite skills and attributes necessary to function at the various hierarchical levels in the ecological system. Because these qualifications are so varied, it is not possible to inculcate them solely in an initial training effort. Thus, education must be concerned not only with initial preparation, but in promoting ongoing personal and professional development which will help ensure that practitioners have the abilities to meet the particular demands of each level.

A full consideration of the needs for preparing group care practitioners requires that other recent trends in human services design and delivery be considered and related to the formulations proposed. These include developments in at least five areas. First, growing attention in work for children's mental health and positive development is being focused on the prevention of disorders, as well as on the cure of identified and well-established cases. Thus, the well-known mental and public health model of primary, secondary, and tertiary prevention has particular relevance for education of group care practitioners.

Traditionally, group care personnel have been provided through training with skills primarily oriented towards tertiary prevention. Such skills are aimed at the rehabilitation of disorders which are already present, with an attempt to reduce their severity and degree of disability (Bloom, undated). This function is analogous to that of the direct care worker in a residential context, involved with children who have already evidenced the need for therapeutic or rehabilitative approaches. Activity in secondary prevention, attempting to reduce the duration of impairment in cases already identified, and primary prevention, reducing the actual incidence of disabilities, has not come under direct purview of those directly involved in group care service delivery. This is particularly true of those who have entered this field of work as direct care workers in specific settings but who have left it early due to lack of education, stress, lack of career mobility, and other factors which have contributed to a 'short life' of group care workers. The result has been a weakening of their representation in more responsible and influential modes of practice, beyond the direct care level.

If the provision of group care services for children is to develop an orientation to primary prevention then at least *some* practitioners must be qualified to work with the broader social system. This development is important since the broader social system has a strong, although indirect, impact on the pattern of service response. Even those who have criticized the concept of primary prevention have cited how certain children's programs with a group focus have served an effective primary prevention function, such as carefully designed settings for homeless infants (Lamb and Zusman, 1979).

Closely allied with the concept of primary prevention is a second trend in service design and delivery, that of encouraging positive development, even in children with identified disabilities. This involves providing a constructive and educative environment, rather than solely directing efforts at rehabilitation of a psychiatrically diagnosed syndrome. As Bloom (undated) says, 'Much human misery appears to be the result of a lack of competence, that is, a lack of control over one's life, of effective coping strategies, and the lowered self-esteem that accompanies these deficiences'. This stress on development of self-esteem through encouraging a sense of competence and social skills for daily living is considered the crux of primary prevention (Bloom). It is also the basis for effective tertiary prevention (remediation), and has already been applied to group care of children. Hobbs' Re-Ed concept (Hobbs, 1974) which Whittaker (1979:72) describes as 'having the most direct and immediate bearing on the development of community based group care settings for troubled children', is an educative approach, emphasizing 'competence across the total spectrum of the child's development' (Whittaker, 1979:71). Hobbs is described as having named particular biases as characteristic of this approach: biases towards learning, towards growth and social systems intervention, and away from dynamic psychology' and formal psychiatric diagnosis.

The philosophic underpinnings of the Re-Ed approach and other similar approaches have great implications for group care delivery. They suggest a crucial teaching and development function which is highly appropriate for group care practitioners to fulfill. This is not to say that workers would not require understanding of children's psychodynamics, but that professional skills aimed at re-education for children in social and cognitive abilities will be particularly important for the new roles in which practitioners will be expected to work.

A third trend which has influenced service design and delivery has been the growing recognition that narrow perspectives on children and their needs, through views espoused by particular disciplines or by diagnostic labels, have prevented effective service design and delivery (Arthur and Birnbaum, 1968; Hobbs, 1974; Schopler and Reichler, 1976; Vinter, 1973). This trend has led to the development of generic perspectives. Hobbs documents the deleterious effects on children of specific diagnostic labels which do not actually 'fit' a child's characteristics and capabilities, which may stigmatize them, and which may result in an extremely poor balance between a child's needs and services actually received. Similarly, working with children through the sole perspective of one discipline can lead to a limited understanding which omits significant variables and influences in their lives. Because some factors may not fall within the scope of a particular discipline, insufficient account is taken of these in designing interventions, and this obviously results in an adequate service response.

Thus, effective work with children through any pattern of service must rely on educational preparation of practitioners which develops and maintains at least some workers with a broad knowledge base and a systems perspective so that the restrictions imposed by narrow visions can be ameliorated. Because such a 'mature' mode of functioning cannot be expected as characteristic of the beginning worker, it is necessary for career mobility in the field to be provided in such a way as to retain practitioners in the mainstream of group care work until they have developed professional maturity through further education and experience. If the group care worker increasingly functions as the coordinator and integrator for the child through his total life experience in the milieu (Barnes and Kelman, 1974) then this worker is the ideal professional in whom to encourage ongoing development of a broad, encompassing perspective.

The social upheavals of the 1960s helped to shape a fourth trend which has influenced the balance of decision making in the human services. Previously policy and treatment decisions were made solely by professionals, with clients as passive recipients. Presently, in line with the general consumer movement, clients are increasingly involved as participants in the decisions and resultant actions which affect their lives. This shift in service delivery has several important implications for group care.

The first concerns the role of parents. Prior to the advance of participatory models, parents were generally considered to be the sole 'cause' of their children's problems. There was therefore little professional empathy with the situation of being a parent of a child needing special help. As a result, parents were not involved as collaborators in the treatment process. More recently, however, parent involvement which has been a cornerstone of programs such as Head Start, is becoming a much more central part of other group care programs for older and/or exceptional populations (VanderVen and Griff, 1978). Such parent activities include participation in administrative planning and decision making, sharing in the design and delivery of specific services, and in the securing of resources for programs. Parents as actual partners in the implementation of treatment plans is another aspect of parent activity. Here, professional work with parents may include training them in specific skills (Conte, 1978) which extend those of the helping professional, relying less on ameliorating pathology alone.

Children, too, in line with the 'child advocacy' movement, are participating more in decisions concerning the services they receive and their quality. Indications of advances in this area are described by Goldsmith (1976). Modes include, for example, children joining in treatment planning conferences, commenting on behaviour records and participating in other activities which heretofore have been considered sacrosanct to professionals, particularly where child clients have been involved. The growing significance of this concept of client participation is articulated by Fischer and Brodsky (1978) as the Prometheus Principle. This refers to the informed participation which allies human service consumers along the course of treatment in reviewing and responding to information collected about them and the decisions and actions that are predicated on this information.

This movement towards increased client involvement again has great implications for professional development of group care practitioners in the future. 'Test scores, . . . diagnoses and traits . . .' are reduced in their importance, as daily life events become the central focus of activity and collaboration with clients (Fischer and Brodsky, 1978). The education and development of group care givers must prepare them to function in this new mode of collaboration. It should be pointed out that the skills group workers already have in milieu work makes them particularly suited to this approach.

No discussion of significant trends in group care is complete without consideration of the growing pressures for demonstrating 'accountability' or the degree to which programs are achieving the outcomes for which they have been provided support (Whittaker, 1979). Accountability factors bring group care practitioners, even at the *direct care* level, into new attitudes and skills. The related areas of cost-effectiveness and evaluation are not practices which are readily congruent with the general orientation of the human services worker. Attempts which have been initiated to demonstrate accountability in group care services involve the application of managerial concepts, such as goal and objective setting, planning, team organization, budgeting, and resource allocation to the conduct of the program. For the direct care worker, goal-directed activity, focused on helping children meet specific objectives, is increasingly the norm of practice. Such workers may or may not have participated in setting the objectives which now guide their activity.

The attitudes and skills involved in such activities as goal and objective setting, have not traditionally been taught or inculcated in group care workers. This is true in other human service professions, as well, such as social work (Patti and Austin, 1977) and psychiatry (Klerman and Levinson, 1969). One reason for the lack of attention to such material in human service training efforts is the clash which many clinically oriented or humanistically inclined members of these professions feel towards anything that smacks of 'business', management, and even financial matters. Thus, the ability to respond to requirements for accountability will require a tremendous shift in orientations to professional practice and in modes of functioning.

Attributes and skills required of group care practitioners

The preceding discussion of current trends in human service provision, with its prime focus on an ecological framework, has identified areas in which group care practitioners must have appropriate attributes and skills in order to have a far reaching and lasting impact on the lives of children for whom they work. The following section will utilize Bronfenbrenner's description of hierarchical levels in a total ecological system. This organizing schema designates associated levels of group care practice, on the premise that practitioners at *each* level must be available if truly effective care is to be given. The requirement is for persons with prerequisite skills and attributes who can operate within the various ecological levels, recognizing that differences do exist from level to level.

Level 1: the microsystem – direct work with children

The microsystem refers to the structure of the immediate environment containing a child 'and the complex of relations between the developing person' (Bronfenbrenner, 1977:517). Its elements include physical features of the setting, role relationships among persons immediately involved in the setting, and the activities conducted in the setting. Examples of the microsystem would include home and school (Bronfenbrenner, 1977; 1979), while in an extended group care context they would include settings such as the day care centre, the residential treatment centre, and the hospital.

The microsystem concept suggests that effective practitioners at this level will be highly prepared in *direct care giving skills* which are designed to make children feel special and nurtured. Some components of this *primary care* given to children in their immediate settings is best described by Maier (1979). These include the providing of bodily comfort; handling based on the child's unique individuality; ensuring predictability and dependability; and giving personalized behaviour training, i.e. socializing the child. In addition, such practitioners will have skills in the area of *environmental design* and *activity programming*, so that they can use physical arrangements of equipment, playthings, developmental media, and other elements in their settings in helping children develop a sense of competence and social skills. Also required is a knowledge of their own *professional identity* as group care workers as well as a knowledge of the roles and functions of other adults with whom they work collaboratively in the children's settings. Knowledge of the structure and dynamics of *teamwork* is also appropriate for the microsystem worker, in view of the significance which all relationships have within the microsystem.

These areas of skill are related to many of the current trends in human services. Workers employing these skills in settings such as infant and preschool group day care, will be serving a *primary prevention* function for these children through the positive nurturing they offer in a facilitating physical environment. Workers in settings dealing with children with special needs such as residential treatment centres, will be employing primarily a *rehabilitative* (tertiary prevention) role. In all modes of group practice in the microsystem, the group care worker will be closely involved in encouraging *positive development*, as the ideal person whose skills and resources can facilitate children's developing social competence. Because these workers may be unfamiliar with practices which encourage client participation, *client participation* skills will have to be developed by microsystem group care workers. They may include working conjointly with parents and allowing children to participate actively in making decisions which influence their lives in the setting. Planning skills, such as the ability to set and work for specific goals and objectives with children, will also be needed. These skills should be in keeping with the trend towards identity amongst group care workers in the microsystem which will strengthen their roles as *coordinators and integrators* of a child's total life experience in care. It will help to provide the practitioner with means at that level to encourage a *generic perspective* to the work. Such a perspective is important if he is to gather and synthesize information from various others in the child's life space, and to use this constructively in the group care environment.

Level 2: the mesosystem – indirect work with children and work with adults

The mesosystem 'is comprised of *interrelations* among major settings which contain the developing person at a particular point in his or her life . . . (or) a system of microsystems' (Bronfenbrenner, 1977:515). Such interrelations, or linkages, exist for children between their homes, schools, recreational facilities, service agencies, and similar institutions. The mesosystem still contains the developing child within its linkage system. In the Level 1 schema the interrelations *within* a setting with a hierarchy of role functions were not included. For purposes of this Level 2 formulation, these interrelations, involving the pattern of interaction among the serving adults in the settings, because they do involve hierarchical aspects, will be considered as characteristic of the mesosystem. Skills required for practice in various relationships within the mesosystem are radically different from those of the microsystem. Tasks required take the worker from providing *direct* care to *indirect* care or working through intermediaries as Dockar-Drysdale suggests (1975). It is indirect since the mesosystem worker is primarily involved with facilitating the quality of care delivered by others. He may serve as their supervisor or teacher, or he may have administrative responsibility for services. Care and attention is directed towards the organizational structure and climate he creates, knowing how this indirect care exerts an influence on the effectiveness of primary care givers and their work in the setting. His responsibilities in staff development and supervision, and his attention to program design and coordination, relate closely to the requirement of accountability. In other words, the mesosystem worker is basically concerned about working with the *other adults* who operate within the child's microsystem. In many ways the modes of work are very similar to those characteristic of the microsystem. The major difference is that these patterns of work activity are directed at other adults and thus only indirectly to children.

The mesosystem worker must have an *initial* level of organizational skills. These skills include the ability to gather and synthesize information in the activity of *coordination*, since this is one of the major ways of forging links within and between specific settings. *Communication* skills are also required, so that the mesosystem worker knows the greatest number of ways of making contact with others and conveying information which can be utilized to the best advantages for children being served. *Knowledge of organizational structure* is required as is knowledge of the relationships between specific aspects of organizational structure and the kind and quality of care being delivered. Included here would be skills in the various aspects of *team building* (VanderVen, 1979c). These skills are vital since group care delivery at the indirect level today involves collaboration of members from various disciplines and backgrounds. Team building with other adults is an upward extension of the first indirect level where the microsystem group care worker served as an *integrator* for the child of services offered him by various disciplines. To the extent that teams involve all appropriate workers in the setting, this may be considered an extension of the client participation principle. Similarly, an understanding of adult group dynamics is necessary for the mesosystem practitioner.

Knowledge and skill in *education* of adults is essential for the mesosystem worker, paralleling those required of the microsystem worker working with children. This includes the ability to assess learner characteristics, and to design, effectively deliver, and evaluate instruction. The mesosystem worker, too, is concerned with the building up of competence and mastery among those with whom they serve as immediate supervisors or teachers.

The mesosystem worker must have skills in *working with parents*, who are an essential linkage for the group care setting which serves children. This extends the principle of primary work with other adults. All of these functions require that group care practitioners at this stage have the ability to identify and empathize with adults and their concerns, just as the microsystem worker must do with children. As group care workers affect relationships and linkage in the mesosystem through working with other adults, they will be moving towards a general *primary prevention* function. Through encouraging a number of others in their ability to provide quality services, their sphere of influence is extended, consequently coming to bear on the wider systems which affect the child.

Level 3: the exosystem – work with the human service system

The exosystem is

> 'an extension of the mesosystem embracing other specific social structures, both formal and informal that do not themselves contain the developing person but impinge upon or encompass the immediate settings in which that person is found, and thereby influence, delimit, or even determine what goes on there.'   (Bronfenbrenner, 1977 : 515)

The skills required for practice in the exosystem are logical extensions of those utilized in the mesosystem. Because the area of concern is – like the earlier – a system, the transition process for a practitioner moving from one level of practice to another is not as radical, although the complexity of the systems vary. Exosystem workers must have skills in *organizational* matters, although now this is at a managerial level, in terms of carrying out major planning and problem solving functions. Here, involvement of the practitioner is in activities which influence the design of entire caring systems, such as a network of day care centres or group homes. This contrasts with the mesosystem worker who functions within the organizational structure of one setting and a specific program. Skills which are required include those of *coordination* and *communication*, but are applied across a service network. Additional skills in *financial planning and budgeting,* fiscal administration, and perhaps fund raising are required at the exosystem level.

Another arena of central activity comes into the scope of the *exosystem* worker: the political setting. For practitioners to influence the exosystem, political skills in negotiation, policy design, lobbying, and debate are crucial. While group care has always been subject to political activities, it has become increasingly politicized in recent years, with the formation of social policy and enactment of legislation which has exerted important influences on child and family life. Defining the exosystem for group care practitioners includes the naming of government agencies as exosystem structures. Thus, workers in this sphere exert an influence over the pattern of group care services at earlier levels through assuming instrumental roles in agencies which control and shape the nature of child and family life in the country. This orientation has not been a traditional one for group care practitioners. Major examples of positions in the exosystem include local and regional politicians, governmental officers involved with health and welfare planning, and perhaps researchers or writers on group care practices whose work is widely disseminated. *Communication* and *organizational skills* acquired in earlier work are therefore re-applied in new, more embracing contexts. The relationship of *client participation* skills to political action is obvious, as any successful worker in a political context will know ways of involving his constituents. *Accountability* for practitioners in the exosystem involves the ability to evaluate success of various broad-reaching programs, information which is then used as a basis for policy-making and legislative design. The need for *generic perspectives* in such complex activity is obvious.

Those who attain the level of working within the exosystem have the opportunity to achieve a role in *primary prevention*. It is at this level that far-reaching decisions on social and economic policy are made and these reach incisively into the very quality of child and family life.

Level 4: the macrosystem – work within the culture

The macrosystem

'refers to the overarching institutional patterns of the culture or sub-culture, such as the economic, social, educational, legal and political systems, of which micro- meso- and exo-systems are the concrete manifestations. Macrosystems are conceived and examined not only in structural terms, but as carriers of information and ideology that, both explicitly and implicitly, endow meaning and motivation to particular agencies, social networks, roles, activities and their inter-relations'.   (Bronfenbrenner, 1977:515)

To be able to influence the global attitudes and viewpoints of a culture or subculture is, of course, an achievement that will be made by very few individuals. Those in society who do ultimately have such an effect are usually not those who have followed a career in group care with children. Rather, such people may be entertainers, political figures, writers, industrial leaders, and others who have achieved a national prominence. Dr Benjamin Spock, author of the book *Baby and Child Care* which has sold millions of copies over the years has been cited as a major influence on child care practices and attitudes towards child rearing. As such, Spock might be considered as someone in the field of child care who has had an impact on the macrosystem. It is not beyond the realm of possibility that others might emerge within the broad field of group care practice whose work will ultimately have this range of impact. It is through the emergence of such persons, albeit few at this level, that impact will be made on 'the place or priority (which) children and those responsible for their care (receive) in such macrosystems'. Impact in the macrosystem can also influence 'how a child and his or her caretakers are treated and interact with each other in different kinds of settings' (Bronfenbrenner, 1977:515).

Encouraging personal and professional development

It is obviously impossible to inculcate in one group care practitioner all of the skills and attributes necessary for practice at the various ecological levels in an initial educational effort. Furthermore, many of the requirements for practice at upper levels require a certain perspective and maturity which can be achieved only by special preparation and experience, gained over an extended period of time. Implications are apparent, therefore, for any concerned with extending the professional impact of group care practitioners, to be able to ensure longevity in the field for a substantial cadre of its initial (microsystem) practitioners. This may be done through providing activities which facilitate an extended process of personal and professional development into new modes and levels of practice.

Recent advances in developmental theory can be applied to the tasks of promoting personal and professional development of group care practitioners.

One of these is the increasing recognition that children, with their particular temperamental and behavioural characteristics, can have an impact on their caregivers (Thomas, Chess, and Birch, 1968; Bell and Harper, 1977) in the same way that the caregivers and their practices have an impact on children. 'Actual behavior is a function of a continuous process of multidirectional interaction or feedback between the individual and situations he or she encounters' (Magnussen and Endler, 1977:4). Such an interactive process suggests that any *ongoing* professional development of workers with children should take account of how involvement with child care work is likely to have a transforming impact on their own development as persons and as practitioners.

The other recent advance in developmental theory which is relevant to group care practitioners concerns the extension of the concepts in child development into adult development. In this way, the adult, like the child, is involved in an ongoing process of growth and change throughout the life cycle. The life cycle itself, even in adult life can be conceptualized in stages, as has been proposed in the two well-known formulations of adult development of Erikson (1950) and Levinson *et al.* (1978).

In the field of adult development, it is recognized that the relationship between personal growth and change is integrally linked with professional development. A change in one area will have an impact on the other, and the educational process itself is considered to be an influence on personal development. Specific changes related to practice ability take place in students during their initial period of professional preparation. Such changes are documented by studies in various professions, such as medicine (Zabarenko and Zabarenko, 1978); occupational therapy (Butler, 1972); and nursing (Olesen and Whittaker, 1968).

Entry into professional practice itself constitutes a stage of development as described by Babcock (1964). Further, it seems that ongoing professional activity is marked by transitional periods when practitioners move from one mode of practice to another. This pattern is indicated in such articles as 'Becoming the Director: Promotion as a Phase in Personal-professional Development' (Klerman and Levinson, 1969) where changing from a primarily clinical to administrative approach in psychiatrists' careers is considered. In the field of child care, several recent discussions articulate the developmental characteristics of child care practitioners in relation to educational preparation and modes of practice (VanderVen, 1979a; Sobesky, 1976; Bayduss and Toscano, 1979). Similarly, Katz (1977) describes developmental stages of preschool teachers. That adult workers with children can be influenced in their own development by the very fact of having contact with children, and also that workers proceed through stages of personal and professional development as the result of educational preparation and experience, both combine to form a core issue for the group care field.

Given the above, it is possible to formulate a set of developmental characteristics for group care practitioners at various stages in their personal and professional development. These relate to acquiring and utilizing attributes and skills which are required for practice at the various levels set out earlier. Implications for the structure of supportive education and professional development can also be described.

Major life issues for workers at Level 1   Many group care practitioners who are involved in either preparation for microsystem work or who have entered the field as direct group workers without initial preparation are usually young people. In line with Erikson's (1950) formulations concerning life stage development, they may still be in the process of consolidating their own sense of personal identity and may also be involved in resolving issues of authority and individualism from their own parents. These dynamics of personal development are often characteristic of the microsystem group care worker, particularly in the beginning while actually participating in the setting.

At Stage 1, the worker usually has limited aspirations for professional development and expanded role function. Attention is more singularly focused on the clinical demands of specific children with whom he is working. This strong identification with *childhood as a life stage* (VanderVen, 1978a) is a normal characteristic of such practitioners. They see and approach situations from children's perspectives. Occasionally they may 'overidentify' with children, acting as a peer rather than an adult counterpart, and possibly colluding with children against other adults – rather than differentiating their role. Related to this characteristic is a *counteridentification with adults and the system,* congruent with still unresolved ties with parents and authority figures. It may be reflected in the general tendency to view other adults as rigid and possibly even bad for the children. Parents are seen as being at fault for causing their children's problems, and supervisors and administrators may be seen as arms of a repressive bureaucracy. Interestingly, such disdain seems to give these new workers the special energy which brings singular dedication and vitality to their direct work practice. It almost seems to give them strength to withstand numerous realistic frustrations in the work. With peers, the worker may form collusive relationships which are counter to the policies and mores of the agency, especially when the worker is treated as a low-status person. In more democratically run programs, the line worker finds peers a strong source of support.

Eschewment of adult functions often means that the level of aspiration of workers at this level usually does not extend beyond direct care work. The traditional reward system in group care practice has not included opportunities for career mobility. These factors, combined with others, make direct care work highly stressful (Mattingly, 1977), and many have left the field before their development might have encouraged assumption of role functions at the next level. This has contributed to the contemporary situation where practitioners assigned to indirect roles, with potential to influence the broad group care system, do not come from the area of group care work. Thus, the educational and employment system has a responsibility for encouraging the ongoing continuation of microsystem workers in the field.

Beginning microsystem workers may hold a strong *rescue fantasy* – their conviction being that they, with their tremendous warmth and dedication, can make up to the children what their deprived pasts have failed to give. These workers may feel that agencies and others are depriving. Policies 'equalizing' treatment for all children or guidelines for 'professional' relationships are viewed as unreasonable, for they fly in the face of their wish to give. Once again, a moderate rescue fantasy should not be seen as negative. It might even be conceived as an essential ingredient for successful performance of a worker's major nurturing role, in line with the characteristics of primary care outlined by Maier (1979).

An 'unproductive humility' (VanderVen, 1978a) is characteristic of many direct group care practitioners. In their dedication to a specific group of children, direct care workers may hold the conviction that advancement, pursuit of additional resources or participation in political activity is self-seeking. Workers often fail to take advantage of real opportunities for professional advancement which might be available. They are saying, in effect, 'What, little me? I can't do that!' An example might be the practitioner who is invited to participate in a workshop in an area of his experience, but refuses for no justifiable reason and hence limits his potential for advancement.

The microsystem practitioner has a primarily *affective* orientation to the work (VanderVen, 1978a; 1979a) which involves responsiveness to feelings, interpersonal relationships, and group process. Educationally, clinical material and experiential teaching strategies appeal to the Level 1 worker in his *affective* stance. Cognitive activity – theory, research, writing – may be seen by this worker as irrelevant to genuine practice in the field and thus rejected. Similarly, the microsystem practitioner reflects an *expressive*, as contrasted to an instrumental, approach to his activities.

A beginning worker in the microsystem usually espouses a *singular approach* to group care practice, seeing others' ways of viewing and caring for children as negative. For example, he might strongly embrace the 'behavior modification' approach. This may be associated, of course, with his limited exposure to other approaches. Even so, his ardent acceptance is probably related to his developmental stage. It may also contribute to his sense of identity as he can at least align with others who share his views against those who do not. Related to this is the characteristic of being *non-synergistic*, based on King's (1975) formulation of synergy – the ability to see things from a variety of perspectives. The initial practitioner therefore tends to see things in a one-or-the-other perspective; parents are bad, organizations stifle, commitment is good, rather than taking a comprehensive stance and seeing both the strengths and weaknesses of different approaches.

Advances in the fields of adult development and education have contributed to considerations of learning styles characteristic of adults at various stages in their own development. An attempt can be made to relate these to group care practitioners. At the microsystem level, workers' learning styles probably relate most closely to Kolb's (1976) concept of *accommodator*. Here the greatest interest lies in doing things and being involved in new experiences which can then be adapted to new circumstances. The accommodator solves problems utilizing intuitive rather than analytic ability. The perception of the *field-dependent* learner (Witkin *et al.*, 1977) is highly determined by what is around the worker or by the organization of the surrounding field. Because 'field dependent' learners are sensitive to social cues and interested in others, one can hypothesize that most group care practitioners are field-dependent learners. This is not inconsistent with Witkins *et al.* who describe field-dependent learners as having a 'with people' (1977:12) orientation.

The learning styles of group care practitioners have implications for the design of their educational experiences. These learning styles may also be subject to change under the impact of growth and experience. This would mean that different instructional modes may be more effective for workers at different levels.

Major life issues for workers at Level 2 Workers in the mesosystem in general may be dealing with different life issues than those in the microsystem. It might be hypothesized that they may have mastered the developmental tasks of Level 1 in passing on to Level 2. In this level, the major life issues concern establishment and maintenance of a completely adult mode of living: finding a home which is at least semi-permanent, possibly getting married and becoming a parent, in line with Erikson's stage of *intimacy*. Some time during this period the practitioner is capable of broadening some perspectives from the initial level. Professional requirements for Level 2 work, with its focus on working with the other adults who are providing direct care of children, means that the practitioner needs to assume a different viewpoint towards both parents and those with administrative and supervisory responsibilities.

Effective mesosystem workers will now be developing a more expanded concept of their professional development and role function. There is concern with the care required for various groups of children, but this concern is focused through a specific investment and encouragement towards the effectiveness of adults who have primary caregiving responsibilities. Thus, developing mesosystem workers shift from identification with childhood as a life stage to *identification with adulthood as a life stage*. Here, workers see and approach situations from both children's and adults' perspectives, being able to empathize with the position of other adults *vis-à-vis* children, as well as that of the child *vis-à-vis* the adult. The mesosystem worker, in contrast with the microsystem worker, is less likely to be involved in collusion with children against other adults. This may result through partial resolution of earlier developmental issues around authority and separation from his own parents. The practitioner is more able to empathize with parents, seeing the many stresses and difficulties of the parental role, especially around parenting a difficult child or one with special needs. Similarly, mesosystem workers are more able to practise and identify with the role of the supervisor, administrator, or teacher in involvements with other adults. Effective mesosystem workers develop a more extended level of aspiration. If they have remained in the field of practice, they have already in this level surmounted the factors previously described which contributed to the 'short life' of direct care workers. Possibilities for a long term career commitment in the field have been seen.

Mesosystem workers like microsystem workers continue to hold a *rescue fantasy*, but now it has a different form and content. There may be a realization or feeling that both children and their parents are victims – possibly of society as a whole – and workers wish to alter the system that is not treating their clients properly. This provides emotional fuel for their investment in the development of other adults working with children. They want to have many elements working effectively to enact change. The 'unproductive humility' of Level 1 workers is rapidly disappearing in the mesosystem practitioner. The necessity for initiative-seeking and authoritative, *instrumental* behaviour is recognized and utilized in order to have a wider influence.

Effective mesosystem workers may be able to function this way because at this stage they are cognitively ready to assume a broader generic perspective. The assets of more than one approach may be appreciated and integrated into a personal philosophy. This may occur because the primarily affective orientation of Level 1 shifts towards a more *cognitive* one. Practitioners, without abandoning concern with feelings, relationships, and processes, at this point become more receptive to theory, research results, and the value of producing ideas in writing. This cognitive development contributes to an ability to think synergistically or from a variety of perspectives. Both the child's and adult's viewpoint can be seen. The strengths and weaknesses in a given developmental or treatment approach can be seen.

Kolb's work on adult learning styles suggests that learning styles amongst adults can actually change through the transformation of ongoing experience. Thus, it is possible to hypothesize that some mesosystem practitioners will begin to manifest *divergent* learning styles (Kolb, 1976). The divergent learner is one who is interested in people and can view concrete situations from many perspectives. Such a learner may still be field-dependent, however, since it is suggested that this general orientation is fairly stable (Witkin *et al.*, 1977). In that education for group care practitioners is assumed to be continuous no matter what the particular levels of operation, characteristic learning styles at this stage continue to have important implications.

Major life issues for workers at Level 3 By the time practitioners have advanced to working in the exosystem, effectiveness is quite likely to reflect differences in personal development and professional orientation from the microsystem and even mesosystem workers. Considerable growth and transformation have taken place by the time the person comfortably and adequately functions in exosystem activities. Exosystem workers may reflect characteristics of Erikson's (1950) *generativity* stage in which a genuine concern for the well-being of the next generation is held. A stable life style and ongoing professional advancement have contributed towards an even broader perspective than those characteristic of mesosystem workers. There is not only investment in the direct development of those who have primary responsibility for group care service delivery, but also concern with the adequacy of systems which influence the extent to which these adults can be effective.

Effective exosystem workers are likely to have consolidated a potent professional identity as group care practitioners, through being able to sustain involvement to practise at this level. Identifications have continued to shift from identification with children to identification with adults and now *identifying with systems*. This does *not* mean that there is failure to see flaws in the system that contain and affect children and families. Rather, these very systems become the area in which work is directed. Having developed greater ability to recognize relationships between caring systems and the quality of direct care provided, effective workers seek to exert an influence in the exosystem to encourage a positive change. Such activity requires many new personal skills and attributes.

Exosystem workers, like colleagues at the two less complex levels, continue to hold a *rescue fantasy*, which provides the emotional energy to work in a frustrating and challenging context. Concern is with children, families, *and* those who work within the system to provide positive care. It is reflected in a wish to work within an *organizational* context where no direct or 'clinical' contacts are the objects of work efforts.

Effective exosystem workers are likely to reflect a *strong instrumental* orientation, recognizing that only through exerting initiative, direction, and authority can they operate within the organizational context which is characteristic of the exosystem. It is acceptable to move from direct client interaction, and also to function in discordant relationships. Exosystem practice requires the exercise of power and control and this does not always lead to popularity. Thus, the practitioner evolves considerably in his progression from Level 1 to Level 3. In the initial level, concerns were with warm peer relationships and these may have been used as a vehicle for expressing disdain for those at higher levels. At Level 3, a practitioner may have to perform without such a support system, and function in ways which require considerable maturity and vision.

Cognitively, the exosystem worker is deliberately concerned with a wide variety of theoretical and empirical information. This is needed as a background for complex planning and decision making. The cognitive mode is likely to be well integrated into the practitioner's professional orientation. Like the Level 2 worker, those in the exosystem continue to manifest synergistic thinking. This thinking is even more encompassing however, for complexities in organizational structure and the interrelationships among clients must be perceived. Relationships between specific organizations serving a clientele and the networks which link various organizations together must also be perceived. Such synergeistic thinking is essential for complex financial planning, for effective work in the political sphere, and in giving direction to a central agency which coordinates the service delivery of a large number of subordinate agencies.

It can be hypothesized that effective exosystem practitioners have shifted in learning style to that which is characteristic of the *assimilator* (Kolb, 1976). There is now capacity, and frequently the requirement, to create theoretical models assimilating disparate observations, experiences, and empirical data into an integrated perspective. These in turn can be communicated effectively to a broad and complex constituency.

Major life issues for workers at Level 4 Because, as previously stated, there are apparently so few group care practitioners working in the macrosystem, and actually affecting this sphere, it is difficult to articulate developmental characteristics in detail. Some general projections are in order, however. In terms of personal development, it can be proposed that the individual has mastered tasks in Erikson's stage of generativity and may still be in that stage. Others may have passed on to the final life stage encompassing a sense of *integrity* and completion.

Professional activity for the successful macrosystem worker is likely to extend to a variety of activities with children, families and with other adults serving in various capacities, throughout different organizations, and their broader networks. There is experience in the complete range of modes of professional practice, direct and indirect. All of these factors contribute to a firm sense of professional consolidation. Interestingly, a worker at this level is probably not subject to some of the isolation and hostility experienced by exosystem workers. They are now eminent in professional circles and shown respect.

Traces of orientation to initial microsystem work have long since been transformed in the macrosystem practitioner. Unproductive humility has given way to a *sense of entitlement*. Such persons may recognize that they have made important contributions and there is an expectation of respect by others. The macrosystem practitioners maintain an identity which has moved from the initial identification with childhood to a total *identification with the human condition*. They are able to stand back and reflect, with empathy, on a wide variety of experiences. An *instrumental* mode continues, in wishing to utilize ideas by communicating thoughts which have been generated. For some, this might be manifested through publication. For others, extensive contact is maintained with a wide audience of practitioners and with the general public, through lectures, public appearances, and such like.

Summary and conclusion

To be able to significantly affect the quality of human services delivered to children requires a comprehensive ecological approach that can influence all of the environmental systems that are now recognized as impinging on children and affecting their lives. This effort will be even more effective if it accommodates current trends in developmental theory and human service delivery. Because group care is a crucial and established aspect of the service delivery system for children, it is essential that group care practitioners hold the skills and attributes necessary for effective work not only with children directly, but also with the environment which exerts an indirect but highly potent influence. Provision of these persons requires their engagement in an *ongoing* process of personal and professional development, since the needs for ecological intervention at successively encompassing environmental levels cannot be met by those prepared for, and engaging in beginning practice.

Because the group care field has not developed ongoing educational and staff development efforts to the same extent that other more established human service disciplines have, it is important that those concerned with advancing the field mount efforts to do so. Special attention should be given to career development activities, such as the development of appropriate levels and content of education, job structuring and enrichment, and facilitation of relevant personal skills and interpersonal relationships. While some progress has already been made in increasing educational opportunities and developing professional associations, much more needs to be done. Hopefully these activities will strengthen manpower in group care services through achieving increased professionalism.

Group care practice with children is rapidly becoming a 'semi-profession' (Etzioni, 1969) where, in terms of responsibility, status, and impact, advancement in the field requires moving successively away from clients as embodied in the various levels of the ecological hierarchy. This is the model proposed in this chapter, for presently it is in these areas of indirect practice that more strength and representation is needed. Thus, the current effort needs to be focused on encouraging the development of indirect practice skills and attributes. Eventually, effective practitioners will be found at all levels. As this occurs, it can be anticipated that quality of care will be further enhanced by the development of a career progression for clinical practitioners throughout the field. This would be in line with Etzioni's criteria for a full profession, in which skilled and highly experienced clinicians achieve the highest professional regard and respect for their work.

Note

(1) Associate Professor of Child Development and Child Care, School of Health Related Professions, University of Pittsburgh, Pittsburgh, USA.

References

Adams, M. (1971) The Compassion Trap. In V. Gornick and B. Moran (eds) *Women in Sexist Society*. New York: Basic Books.

Ainsworth, F. (1980) The Training of Group Care Personnel in the Personal Social Services. In R. G. Walton and D. Elliott (eds) *Residential Care*. Oxford: Pergamon Press.

American Association for Children's Residential Centers (1972) *From Chaos to Order: A Collective View of the Residential Treatment of Children*. New York: Child Welfare League of America.

Arthur, B. and Birnbaum, J. (1968) Professional Identity as a Determinant of the Response to Emotionally Disturbed Children. *Psychiatry* 31: 138–49.

Babcock, C. G. (1964) Having Chosen to Work with Children . . . the Common Problems that Face the Professional Person. Paper read for the Extension Division of the Child Therapy Program. Chicago: The Institute of Psychoanalysis.

Barnes, F. H. and Kelman, S. M. (1974) From Slogans to Concepts: A Basis for Change in Child Care Work. *Child Care Quarterly* 3 (1): 7–24.

Bayduss, G. and Toscano, J. A. (1979) The Development of Child Care Workers: Correlates between Occupational and Social-emotional Growth. *Child Care Quarterly* 8: 85–93.

Beker, J. (1976) Towards the Unification of the Child Care Field as a Profession. *Journal of the Association for the Care of Children in Hospitals* 5 (1).

Beker, J. (1979) Training and Professional Development in Child Care. In J. Whittaker *Caring for Troubled Children*. San Francisco: Jossey-Bass.

Bell, R. and Harper, L. (1977) *Child Effects on Adults*. Hillsdale, New Jersey: Lawrence Erlbaum.

Bloom, B. (undated) Prevention of Mental Disorders: Recent Advances in Theory and Practice. Unpublished paper.

Brim, O. (1975) Macro-structural Influences on Development: Need for Childhood Social Indicators. *American Journal of Orthopsychiatry* 45: 516–24.

Bronfenbrenner, U. (1977) Toward an Experimental Ecology of Human Development. *American Psychologist* 32: 513–30.

Bronfenbrenner, U. (1979) *The Ecology of Human Development: Experiments by Nature and Design*. Cambridge, Massachussetts: Harvard University Press.

Butler, H. F. (1972) Student Role Stress. *American Journal of Occupational Therapy* 26: 399–405.

Committee on Child Psychiatry (1973) From Diagnosis to Treatment: An Approach to Treatment Planning for the Emotionally Disturbed Child. Unpublished report, Group for the Advancement of Psychiatry, New York.

Conte, J. R. (1978) Helping Groups of Parents Change Their Children's Behavior. *Child and Youth Services* 2: 1–9.

Davids, A. (1975) Therapeutic Approaches to Children in Residential Treatment. *American Psychologist* 32: 809–14.

Dockar-Drysdale, B. (1975) Staff Consultation in an Evolving Care System. In J. Hunter and F. Ainsworth (eds) *Residential Establishments*. Dundee, Scotland: Dundee University, Department of Social Administration.

Erikson, E. H. (1950) *Childhood and Society*. New York: Norton.

Estes, R. J. (1975) Learning Style Preferences of Community Mental Health Professionals. *Community Mental Health Journal* 11: 450–61.

Etzioni, A. (1969) *The Semi-professions and Their Organization*. New York: Free Press.

Fischer, C. and Brodsky, S. (eds) (1978) *Client Participation in Human Services: The Prometheus Principle*. New Brunswick: Transaction Books.

Goldsmith, J. (1976) Residential Treatment Today: The Paradox of New Premises. *American Journal of Orthopsychiatry* 46: 425–33.

Goode, R. (1969) The Theoretical Limits of Professionalization. In A. Etzioni *The Semi-professions and Their Organization*. New York: Free Press.

Henderson, P. (1978) A Developmental-adaptive Model for Use in Service-matrix Planning for Youth. *Child Psychiatry and Human Development* 8: 162–74.

Henry, W., Sims, J., and Spray, S. (1973) *Public and Private Lives of Psychotherapists*. San Francisco: Jossey-Bass.

Herstein, N. (1977) Reflections on the Primacy of the One-to-One Model on Residential Treatment. *Child Welfare* 56: 311–20.

Hobbs, N. (1974) Helping Disturbed Children: Psychological and Ecological Strategies. In M. Wolins *Successful Group Care*. Chicago: Aldine.

Kanter, R. (1976) The Impact of Hierarchical Structure on the Work Behavior of Women and Men. *Social Problems* 23: 415–30.

Katz, L. (1977) *Talks with Teachers*. Washington, DC: National Association for the Education of Young Children.

Katz, L. (1979) Principles of Staff Development in Programs for Younger Children. *Children in Contemporary Society* 12: 2.

King, M. (1975) *For We Are: Towards Understanding Your Personal Potential*. Reading, Massachusetts: Addison-Wesley.

King, M. and VanderVen, K. (1980) Creative Behavior is involved in Personal Growth, Development and Values of Child Care Practitioners. *The Creative Child and Adult Quarterly* 5 (2): 86–93.

Klerman, G. and Levinson, D. (1969) Becoming the Director: Promotion as a Phase in Personal-professional Development. *Psychiatry* 32: 411–27.

Kolb, D. (1976) *Learning Style Inventory*. Boston, Massachusetts: McBerard.

Lamb, H. R. and Zusman, J. (1979) Primary Prevention in Perspective. *American Journal of Psychiatry* 136: 12–17.

Lanier, D., Moriwaki, S., and Wolkon, G. (1971) Organization Functioning and Care in a Children's Treatment Center. *Journal of Health and Social Behavior* 12: 248–54.

Levinson, D. J., Darrow, C. N., Klein, E. B., Levinson, M. H., and McKee, B. (1978) *The Seasons of a Man's Life*. New York: Alfred Knopf.

Magnussen, D. and Endler, N. (1977) Interactional Psychology: Present Status and Future Prospects. In D. Magnussen and N. Endler (eds) *Personality at the Crossroads: Current Issues in Interactional Psychology*. Hillsdale, New York: Lawrence Erlbaum.

Maier, H. W. (1977) The Child Care Worker. In John Turner (ed.) *Encyclopedia of Social Work*. New York: National Association of Social Workers.

Maier, H. W. (1978) Piagetian Principles applied to the Beginning Phase in Professional Helping. In J. F. Magary, M. K. Poulsen, P. J. Levinson and P. A. Taylor (eds) *Piagetian Theory and the Helping Professions*. Los Angeles: University of Southern California Press.

Maier, H. W. (1979) The Core of Care: Essential Ingredients for the Development of Children at Home and Away from Home. *Child Care Quarterly* 8: 161–73.

Mattingly, M. (1977) Sources of Stress and Burn-out in Professional Child Care Work. *Child Care Quarterly* 6: 127–37.

Mayer, M., Richman, L., and Balcerzak, E. (1977) *Group Care of Children: Crossroads and Transitions*. New York: Child Welfare League of America.

Mearig, J. S. (1978) *Working for Children: Ethical Issues beyond Professional Guidelines*. San Francisco: Jossey-Bass.

Mendelsohn, R. (1978) Rights and Rites of Professionalism. In J. Mearig *Working for Children: Ethical Issues beyond Professional Guidelines*. San Francisco: Jossey-Bass.

Moos, R. H. (1976) *The Human Context: Environmental Determinants of Behavior*. New York: John Wiley.

Olesen, V. and Whittaker, E. (1968) *The Silent Dialogue*. San Francisco: Jossey-Bass.

Patti, R. and Austin, M. (1977) Socializing the Direct Service Practitioner in the Ways of Supervisory Management. *Administration in Social Work* 1: 267–80.

Rowbottom, R. and Billis, D. (1977) The Stratification of Work and Organizational Design. *Human Relations* 30: 53–76.

Rozentals, V., Piper, A., and Whipple, H. (1974) Professionalizing the Child Care Worker. *Child Welfare* 53: 9.

Sandler, B. (1974) Eclecticism at Work: Approaches to Job Design. *American Psychologist* 30: 767–73.

Schopler, E. and Reichler, R. (eds) (1976) *Psychopathology and Child Development: Research and Treatment*. Especially, Developmental Therapy: A Program Model for providing Individual Services in the Community. New York: Plenum Press.

Sobesky, W. (1976) Youth as Child Care Workers: The Impact of Stage of Life on Clinical Effectiveness. *Child Care Quarterly* 5: 4.

Thomas, A., Chess, S., and Birch, H. (1968) *Temperament and Behavior Disorders in Children*. New York: New York University Press.

Trieschman, A. E., Whittaker, J. K., and Brendtro, L. K. (1969) *The Other 23 Hours*. Chicago: Aldine.

VanderVen, K. (1976) Agency Administration, Effective Child Treatment, and Professionalization of Child Care Workers: Some Relationships and Suggestions. Unpublished rough draft of a paper delivered at Child Care Sessions, American Orthopsychiatric Association Meetings, Atlanta, Georgia.

VanderVen, K. (1978a) A Paradigm describing Stages of Personal and Professional Development of Child Care Practitioners with Characteristics associated with Each Stage. Paper delivered at Ninth International Congress of the International Association of Workers with Maladjusted Children, Montreal.

VanderVen, K. (1978b) Child Ecology: The Changing Concept of Human Development. *Children in Contemporary Society* 11: 4.

VanderVen, K. (1979a) Developmental Characteristics of Child Care Workers and Design of Training Programs. *Child Care Quarterly* 8 (2).

VanderVen, K. (1979b) Encouraging Personal and Professional Development of Child Care Practitioners. *Children in Contemporary Society* 12 (2).

VanderVen, K. (1979c) Towards Maximum Effectiveness of the Unit Team Approach in Residential Care: An Agenda for Team Development. *Residential and Community Child Care Administration* 1: 287–98.

VanderVen, K. and Griff, M. (1978) Expanded Roles for Child Care Workers: Work with Families. Unpublished paper.

Vinter, R. (1973) Analysis of Treatment Organizations. *Social Work,* 3–15.

Whittaker, J. K. (1979) *Caring for Troubled Children.* San Francisco: Jossey-Bass.

Witkin, H. A., Moore, C. A., Goodenough, D. R., and Cox, P. W. (1977) Field-dependent and Field-independent Cognitive Styles and Their Educational Implications. *Review of Educational Research* 47: 1–64.

Wolins, M. (1974) *Successful Group Care: Explorations in the Powerful Environment.* Chicago: Aldine.

Zabarenko, R. and Zabarenko, L. (1978) *The Doctor Tree: Developmental Stages in the Growth of Physicians.* Pittsburgh, Pennsylvania: University of Pittsburgh Press.

9 The training of personnel for group care with children

Frank Ainsworth

Introduction

In Britain, North America, and other countries, concern exists as to the quality of the living, learning, and treatment opportunities that are provided for children who enter institutional, residential, day, and other group focused programmes which constitute the group care field. Because of the manner in which this field spans the major societal resource systems of health care, education, justice, and social welfare it carries responsibility for services to many normal as well as the most needy and troubled sections of the child population in each country.

This concern is manifested in each situation in various efforts to reform existing service provision, and to maximize the relevance of training for personnel engaged in group care practice (Ainsworth, 1980; Beker, 1979; Cox, 1979). The purpose of this paper is to examine the training issues in regard to group care for children in Britain and North America. This will involve comment about the influence on training of differences in patterns of higher education, service organization, and social policy as well as the manner in which existing occupational interests restrict or enhance opportunities for the emergence of new training initiatives for the group care field. A substantial section of the paper will be devoted to a discussion of materials that warrant attention in training programmes for personnel entering group care. The intention is to present this later material in a form that transcends national differences and is consumable by audiences in many different situations.

Background to training efforts

Any new training initiatives that attempt to meet the needs of group care personnel are mounted against an historical background of neglect, limited success in earlier training efforts, and – in some instances – a positive aversion to any artificial form of group living displayed by some other personnel engaged in providing services to children. This situation is reflected in a host of studies that have reported on the restrictive features of life for exceptional populations in institutions (Goffman, 1961; Polsky, 1962; Stanton and Schwartz, 1954). The negative impact on child development of some aspects of institutional life also receives much attention. Finally, a number of evaluative studies are reviewed elsewhere in this volume that claim to demonstrate the ineffectiveness of group care for children (see chapter 10).

These studies, many from an earlier era of institutional care, and often from the health care (mental health and retardation) and justice systems are however liable to distort the view of the group care field, as presently constituted. They focus on a single component of the field (problem populations) and fail to do justice to the diversity of programmes – residential, day, and other forms of intermediate care and treatment that make up group care for children. Nor do they necessarily acknowledge sufficiently the extent to which the main strength of group care programmes are and always have been in the social welfare or educational systems where programmes also relate to non-exceptional populations and tend to be smaller in size and less institutional in flavour. Thus these programmes provide more opportunity for focusing on the developmental needs of children, rather than the needs of staff and the maintenance of institutional structures.

Group care has therefore to be released, for purposes of contemporary understanding, from some of the negative images, sometimes promoted properly, but often unselectively by the readers – if not the authors – of institutional studies. An approach to the group care field which supports indiscriminate de-institutionalization (Mayer, Richman, and Balcerzak, 1978) because of some of these findings, or opposes the use of any form of group living for children, is less than helpful. It is as harmful as earlier indiscriminate institutionalization because it limits attempts to create a broad spectrum of services for children. The need articulated elsewhere in this volume (see chapter 5) is rather to locate institutional programmes within an overall service structure, and for these and other group care programmes to be seen as family support services rather than isolated forms of substitute care. Hard gained experience with troubled children indicates that socially engineered group living situations remain a necessary treatment provision for some children, albeit a provision which has to be wisely and sparingly used. Such group living situations may be used providing of course that these programmes offer nurturing care, socialization, and specific therapeutic interventions in a planned and purposeful way for children needing new opportunities for growth and development (Maier, 1979). To date, attempts in Britain and North America to provide training for practitioners capable of working in this manner have not met with noticeable success. This then is the situation that faces those concerned with developing new training efforts.

The comparative position

North America

In North America attempts to create a new discipline of group care practitioner, or as they are more usually called 'child care worker', are now clearly visible. These attempts are manifested in the emergence of both new training opportunities (Beker, 1979) and in efforts to organize bodies at local, state, and national level that represent the interests of those who seek to work and develop career patterns in this area of practice (VanderVen, 1980). Academicians from different disciplines, schools, especially of education, social work, and psychology as well as some centres of child development and child care within a range of higher educational institutions from community colleges to universities, are now beginning to offer limited forms of training. These vary from initial certification programmes to higher degree studies that seek to equip individuals to work at different levels in some aspect of the group child care field. The conference-research sequence on child care education funded by The National Institute for Mental Health (1979–82) and sponsored by the University of Pittsburgh, School of Health Related Professions, represents the latest attempt to focus these efforts and advance the process of professionalization.

All these developments need to be seen in the context of other attempts at professionalization and the routes traditionally taken in North America by occupational groups seeking this form of recognition. They also need to be linked to current attempts to re-define the institutional and residential component of the group care field as family support services and to locate these services more centrally within a child welfare service. These efforts result in group care practitioners expecting equal participation with other professionals like psychologists, social workers, educationalists, or doctors in decision-making processes as they affect programme functioning and a child's well being. An outcome of this has been the urge for similar academic validation for group care practitioners as is available to these other groups. Many more events slowly follow these thrusts towards professionalization and include upgrading of practice standards, specification of educational qualifications required on entry to the field and – for advanced practice positions – definition of professional boundaries and areas of competence as well as a state or professionally controlled credentialling system. In North America work has clearly begun on all these matters in regard to the group care field for children.

It is therefore possible to conceive in North America of group care services of the not too distant future, that are staffed by personnel qualified at various academic levels in training programmes specifically geared to child care practice. This will of course be the culmination of a long sought after development. For far too long group care programmes have depended on the personal attributes of staff rather than on developed skill, knowledge, and understanding that trained practitioners ought to possess. This dependence only adds to the inappropriateness and ineffectiveness of some group care programmes, especially those in institutional and residential units for troubled children which constitute part of the group care field. However, given the impact of new economic circumstances in North America and changing social policy that these will promote, new patterns of service are almost certain to emerge in the 1980s. These are likely to contain levels of accountability hitherto unknown. They will almost certainly call for new commitments and levels of ingenuity, skills, and techniques that can only be built on the kind of appreciation of child development and child care that comes from achievement in academic studies and through professionally supervised practice. In this respect professionalization of group care practice in North America now seems both inevitable and essential.

The present decline in student enrolments in many areas of higher education in North America, whilst economically problematic for that system, can also be seen as favourable to advances in professionalization in group care. This is because the process of professionalization requires that existing and new members of the group care field gain increasing access to graduate and postgraduate educational programmes. Additionally it requires the urgent creation of new specialist training programmes that specifically address this practice area. The excess capacity that clearly now exists within the higher educational system in North America could therefore be utilized for programmes that prepare entrants for the emerging profession of group care.

It is also worth noting that this field, especially those aspects of it which relate to the social welfare, and to a lesser extent educational, systems, contains one of the largest groups of untrained or partially trained personnel still remaining in the human services arena. The attraction of this group of personnel into training programmes may well be seen by educational planners as an interesting possibility. The ability of the educational system to respond positively to this new educational need through modification of existing programmes in professional schools in allied practice disciplines has therefore to be reckoned with. No doubt the market forces identified above will advance these modifications and over time create completely new educational programmes or schools for group care practitioners.

Within the service delivery system pressure from accountability studies and the new economic situation already referred to are already impacting the group care field, irrespective of its location in the health care, education, justice, or social welfare system. Indeed these studies cause revision of programme design and influence the recruitment of practice personnel. These pressures in turn also provide opportunity for newly qualified group care personnel to acquire positions, demonstrate understanding of, and establish competence in the delivery of service to children in group care that is superior to that of other contenders for appointment from other training backgrounds.

Britain

The major systems of health care, education, justice, and social welfare in Britain each carry responsibility for the training of personnel who work within these systems through nationally sponsored training councils, central government departments, and a range of professional organizations. Within each of these service areas group care programmes are therefore generally staffed by personnel whose principal qualification (if any) and career avenues are closely tied to a specific service system; examples of this are teachers in education, nurses in health care, social workers in social welfare.[1] Yet it seems that little attention is paid during nursing or teacher training to the particular requirements of group care practice. Such training about group care that is offered to these occupational groups is sparse and invariably located at a post qualification level rather than in basic training and is only available after a substantial period of direct practice. This is in spite of the involvement of both the health care and education systems in providing group care services for children with learning difficulties as well as normal populations.

The largest concentration of group care services for troubled children is however to be found in the local authority social services sector. These services are often concerned with delinquent children and may therefore have a common boundary with the justice system, although this is not true for all local authority group care units. It is, however, in this sector that the debate about and criticism of current training provision for those who enter group care practice usually referred to as 'residential social work' is mostly heard. This criticism highlights a continuing, if diminished, division in British social work and social services training between residential and community or field services personnel, that has its origin in earlier specialist forms of training for child care and residential care practitioners. Further, this is not resolved by the superficial conceptualization of the 'residential social work' task which is offered by the largest association of social workers in Britain (British Association of Social Workers, 1977). Curiously, training for other aspects of the group care field, namely day services or intermediate forms of group care, seem less prone to comment.

Interestingly, these earlier separate specialist training programmes out of which might have emerged a separate group child care profession either ceased to exist or were merged during the 1970s with the larger and more numerous training programmes for social workers with community or field service interests. This development was advanced by the creation of a Central Council for Training and Education in Social Work (CCETSW) in 1973 which has responsibility for training personnel for work in all aspects of the social services – community, field, residential, and day provision – and for the validation of social work and social services training programmes. The Council promoted a policy whereby training for residential practice or group care practice became incorporated into mainstream social work training programmes. Incidentally this trend had begun before the Council's creation but had lacked until that time formal recognition.

This merging of interests between group care practitioners and social workers resulted in a situation where both groups have a degree of identification as a result of shared studies and the achievement of common qualifications. This can be either the Certificate of Qualification in Social Work (CQSW) or the Certificate in Social Service (CSS), an alternative and newer form of training that has been developed on a joint service agency-educational institution basis in response to the needs of several staff groups other than social workers who are employed in the social services.

This training development reflects the re-organization of the social services at the onset of the 1970s and also follows some logic, especially when it is recognized that most group care units (with the exception of those with a specific educational or health care focus) and the general legislative responsibility for services for troubled children reside within the social services sector. This sector is mainly controlled by social workers who occupy the major service management and planning positions. It has also led to an increase in the status of the group care practitioners who are employed in this sector and to enhanced remuneration, as well as better conditions of work and career opportunities that might otherwise not have been achieved. However, some unease about these training developments exists for it is argued by some commentators that this merger of interests, whilst sensible from a social services manpower planning point of view has resulted in the submerging of group care practice in a larger more generalist field dominated by a social service perspective. This has resulted in the loss of specialist teaching that specifically refers to the health care, educational, recreation, counselling, and caring needs of children in training programmes. Because of their wider concerns these programmes only place minor emphasis on the needs of group care practitioners who are invariably a minority group within the more general training provision. However, it is worth noting that the strategy adopted also appears to have raised the educational standard of personnel who are now entering the group care field (Millham, Bullock, and Hosie, 1980) and this is no mean achievement as it is an important step in any professionalization process.

A problem with this approach is, however, that the qualification obtained in the social work or social service training system by group care practitioners is unlikely to be recognized within the other resource systems which provide group care services – namely health care, justice (with the exception of the probation and after care services), or education. This follows, as was stated earlier, because training programmes in Britain tend to be closely tied into a single service delivery system with each favouring their own basic training patterns which emphasize the particular system and special skills used in that system. Thus, the status quo emphasizes different professional approaches rather than the special client populations or practice contexts, like group care for children, that cross the various service systems. Transfer opportunities between major systems for personnel are therefore minimal and the cross fertilization of ideas and innovations in group care practice in the various systems is problematic. The major exceptions to this position are some minimal formal training programmes which pre-date the social services re-organization of the 1970s and attempt to provide advanced training at a post qualification level for both teachers and social workers in group care practice.

Only in the retardation field is there any visible sign of change and this is largely the result of pressures for the deinstitutionalization of services for children in favour of group homes based in the community. This pressure stems from research reports, parent advocacy, and economic factors as much as from professional initiatives. A recent proposal (Jay, 1979) that responsibility for staff training for this field should be moved into the social services sector and that the accepted qualification should be the Certificate in Social Services (CSS) rather than the present nursing (Registered Mental Nurse, RMN) studies has however caused great argument. It is therefore doubtful if this shift of training responsibility for personnel in the retardation field from health care to social services will be implemented. The proposal does, however, suggest a directional thrust that may have long term significance.

Comment

From this broad overview, which attempts to outline two national positions and identify current trends, some conclusions can be drawn. It can, for example, be seen that group care practice in each country is in a different organizational, developmental, and professional position. These facts are worth considering by way of a brief reference to the position in many European countries, especially those which, since the 1940s at least, have had an established group care profession for children more commonly referred to as *éducateurs* or 'social pedagogues' (Linton, 1971; Ginger, 1971). This is because it is possible to see that these professions grew out of a national need captured at a particular moment in time and that their professional basis and their strong alliance with education reflect the political, social, and cultural climate of these countries during the period of the inception of those professions.

If this is correct, then it is equally possible to see why in Britain training for group care practice is so closely aligned with social service organizations and social work. This reflects the growth of social services in the 1960s and 1970s and the powerfully felt need at that time to improve the quality of group care practice within the re-organized social services. An alliance between group care and social work training thus became an inevitable outcome of climatic forces similar to those which in an earlier era in Europe had created the link for group care practice with education. However, for Britain this alliance may limit the opportunity for group care practitioners to work with normal children because of the emphasis in the social services on work with problem populations. This limitation is less in evidence when group care is linked to education rather than social work or social services.

This line of reasoning indicates that the thrust towards the creation of a profession of child care work or group care practice with the necessary supportive training arrangements as in North America, may also be a response to time and climatic factors. The limited awareness among established professional schools which teach social work, education, or health care personnel about the special needs of group care practitioners is no doubt one reason for efforts to build this new professional identity and develop concomitant training programmes. The way market forces are also opening up space within the North American higher education system for alternative developments is also offered as another timely influence on this process.

Of comparable importance is the absence in North America of a co-ordinated child welfare policy or service delivery system, the creation of which still awaits the arrival of an effective lobby. The absence of such a lobby exists, in spite of a national preoccupation with the health of family life, and moves towards improved parenting and child care practices. All this suggests that a new profession concerned with group care practice may now find a place in the highly diversified and entrepreneurial service delivery system that addresses the needs of children in North America. It certainly stands to capitalize on the social and political mood of the country at this time which is manifested in the trends that have been described above.

This historical and contemporary view of professional development in regard to group care practice in more than one country also offers some explanation as to why earlier attempts to transplant models of professional training from other countries into North America have met with only limited success. Efforts have included *éducateur* training programmes (Guindon, 1970; Hobbs, 1964) and developments within a single service system (Reiger, 1977). It also suggests that the latest attempts that reflect a more natural evolution and coalescence of interests may be more successful in professionalizing this area of practice.

However, it is possible, when discussion training matters, to transcend these national issues. Whilst the organizational location of the personnel concerned with group care practice may vary – as indeed may their title from country to country – the training needs seem to remain the same. Issues about what group care practitioners need to know and be able to do and how this can best be taught are in the end common to all concerned with group care practice with children regardless of national boundaries. The remainder of this paper will therefore be devoted to a discussion of these matters, in the belief that they bind all group care personnel together and create an international community that is of greater importance than the differences in title used or the system within which practitioners work.

The practitioners' function

Group care practitioners are concerned to provide developmentally enhancing services to children in a range of environments whether ordinary living, learning or special treatment. Practitioners may therefore be engaged in indirect service as service planners, or in monitoring or supervisory positions as well as in direct care posts. When engaged in all these ways – but especially in direct care – practitioners occupy immensely powerful positions in relation to children because of their ability to control resources, their involvement in extended contact (up to but not necessarily including twenty-four hours duration) and the close sharing of life events.

Unlike other personnel (e.g. nurses in health care, teachers in education, most social workers in social welfare, and personnel in the justice system) group child care practitioners take as the theatre for their work the actual living situations as shared with and experienced by the child. This is because of the view that it is through events that occur and experiences that are acquired in this life space that developmental opportunities are either reduced or enlarged for a child (Redl, 1959). The group care practitioner therefore seeks to use the natural opportunities provided by daily life events within a group care programme (such as the provision of food, clothing and play opportunities) as foci for interventive acts that raise a child's level of personal functioning. Planned interventions are also arranged which exploit the total environment of a programme in order to provide experiences that promote growth and development in children. Such interventions involve making disciplined use of time, space, objects, events, activities, and exchanges between children and significant others be they staff or children in the programme. Thus, it is in the midst of life rather than in artificially defined professional territory that the group care practitioner works to offer learning opportunities and influence development in such a way that a child is encouraged to reach a level of functioning that is satisfactory to the individual and to those with whom he or she is engaged.

The functions of group care practitioners may in this respect be described as equal to but unlike those of parents (Maier, 1978). Unfortunately, the similarity of function has encouraged this parenting analogy and has also made it difficult to define in any universal way the role of group care practitioners. The analogy fails, however, because of the absence of familial bonds between practitioner and child and because of the understanding of child development and child care that is explicitly required of group care practitioners, but not of parents. Terms like 'surrogate parent' or titles like 'house parent' that have been popular also fail to acknowledge the diverse range of positions that practitioners now occupy in all forms of group care work.

Variations in the way the role of group care practitioner is seen may also be associated with the theoretical framework that underlies a particular programme. For example, in behaviourally oriented programmes at the University of Kansas/Achievement Place the group child care practitioners is regarded as a teaching-parent (Elery, *et al.*, 1974). In the Peabody College/RE-ED program, the approach is more as an *éducateur*, similar to European lines (Hobbs, 1964). In other programmes with a psycho-analytic orientation such as the Mulberry Bush (Dockar-Drysdale, 1968) or Orthogenic School (Bettelheim, 1974), the role of the group care practitioner as therapist is emphasized.

Understanding of the function of group care practitioner may, however, be furthered by reference to recent writing in the adult development field about the mentoring relationship (Levinson *et al.*, 1978). Mentor is a term that means teacher, sponsor, or adviser but in the context of adult development is used to specify the character of the relationship and the function it serves, rather than to define formal roles. Adapted for the group care arena the functions can be listed as:

(1) to act as a teacher to enhance a child's skills and intellectual development;
(2) to serve as a sponsor and use influence to facilitate the child's advancement;
(3) to be host and guide welcoming the child into new situations and the social world and acquainting the child with its values, customs, resources and cast of characters;
(4) to act as an ideal model through demonstrating virtues, achievement and ways of living that the child can admire and seek to emulate;
(5) to provide counsel and moral support in times of stress;
(6) to support and facilitate the child's development and realization of personal goals.

This list of functions provides an interesting construct against which group care practitioners can evaluate the usefulness of practice and the best use of everyday life events. A clearer conception of the role of group care practitioners who are concerned with providing developmentally enhancing services to children also seems to stem from consideration of these factors.

Curricula outline

During the course of training, group care practitioners are engaged in important socialization processes which encourage identification with the chosen field. Studies also have to ensure clarity about the function of group care and encourage the development of a professional and personal style of practice that is relevant to programme settings. These achievements need to take place within training programmes which contain courses that address four core areas. These are child development, policy studies, research in child development and child care, and child care methods and practice.

Child development

A unique feature of group care practitioners, as referred to in this volume, is their focus on providing services to a single client population. Other occupational personnel who work with children invariably prepare for practice with other age or client groups as well, with the consequential emphasis in their training on abstract professional skills or areas of expertise and only later specialization in work with child populations. Group care practitioners have as a result to concentrate from the onset of training on learning about child development. It is from this knowledge that skills specific to work with this client population evolve. This area of the curriculum is therefore worthy of favourable time allocation, coupled with rigorous course requirements and extensive attention to the process of academic assessment.

Teaching about child development has of course to incorporate a diversity of theoretical perspectives and give recognition to important variations in cultural patterns of child rearing. It is therefore necessary for programme participants to be alerted to those psycho-dynamic, behavioural, and cognitive perspectives that usually provide the theoretical underpinnings for group care services. Attention also needs to be given to the establishment of understanding of the maturational factors inherent in social, emotional, intellectual, and psychological development. Also of importance is an appreciation of variations in patterns of child development as this relates to both normal and exceptional populations.

Alongside this teaching there is also a need for consideration of material about family functioning. Group care services are increasingly being defined as family support services with this leading to a recognition that group care practitioners of the future may have to provide significant services to actual parents (Whittaker, 1979; Keith-Lucas and Sanford, 1977; Ainsworth, 1980). Teaching sequences that reference the family in all its cultural manifestations as a major socialization influence and foundation of individual identity are therefore important. These also need to reflect adaptive and maladaptive forms of family functioning and potential interventive formats. This is so that future group care practitioners, in addition to offering services directly to children and if appropriate to parents, may also work compatibly with other professionals who are engaged in family services, acting as co-partners in these efforts.

The teaching of these sequences on child development and family functioning are important matters. Training programmes for group care practitioners that do not include applied teaching of this type are likely to be of limited long term benefit to practitioners. Group care practitioners need to demonstrate in practical ways superior understanding of child development and a greater ability to use this knowledge in action, than personnel with other training backgrounds. Only in this way will group care practitioners be seen as worthy of special attention and employment. Otherwise, they will simply be seen as interchangeable with a diverse range of personnel and will not be allowed to occupy positions of major influence in group care programmes.

Policy studies

The purpose of these studies is to allow group care practitioners to see themselves as part of the total provision that constitutes the field of human services. To achieve this the legislative constraints and social policy frameworks that surround the health care, education, social welfare, and justice systems need both explanation and analysis. Like so many other matters, social policy and legislation also have national, regional, and local aspects. These reflect values which vary according to the level of government under consideration, characteristics of the different service systems and geographic locality. As these invariably impact the way in which group care services operate, it is important during training to create understanding of these dimensions.

In teaching about these matters it is also important to reference not only statutes but how legislation and social policy are moulded by broader philosophical and political ideas. The inculcation of an historical perspective on policy development and the legislative process is useful to practitioners in that it adds to their opportunity to identify with the long standing traditions of professional service to children. To be able to place oneself within an ongoing tradition and alongside prestige figures from the past is also important for practitioners who may be struggling to provide services in difficult situations. Importantly it shows how in spite of immense odds, movements are made over the course of time and that small changes which may seem unimportant often have an incremental impact that ultimately add up to professional advances.

Studies can also show how changes in legislation, policy, and service organization (whether at a national, regional, or local level) have been achieved by practitioners who have an understanding of political and organizational processes (Weissman, 1973; Brager and Holloway, 1978; Patti and Resnick, 1972; Fulcher, 1979). Materials from the area of organizational studies, therefore, merit inclusion not simply in order to create understanding of the organizational characteristics of the system within which group care practitioners find employment but also to encourage a capacity for action. This is because group care practitioners are almost certain to be engaged in practice in large organizational contexts, rather than as independent private practitioners. Therefore the capacity to work within these situations and to ensure that the services offered remain responsive to the needs of children and do not merely reflect organizational demands is a significant professional requirement.

Research

It has been pointed out elsewhere (Mayer, Richman, and Balcerzak, 1977; Ainsworth, 1980) that many studies which are critical of group care have been undertaken by academicians from a variety of displines, but that studies of this field by group care practitioners themselves are less plentiful. Additionally, the way in which child development and child care interests are often pursued in separate research and teaching departments of higher education institutions, has also been commented on (Maier, 1979). It is also apparent that occupational personnel who are seeking higher status (as are group care practitioners) try to demonstrate by way of growth in research studies the commitment of those concerned with the area to building theoretical knowledge and improving practice techniques.

Elsewhere in this volume a paper reviews research into group care for children (see chapter 10). The potential use of institutional settings or residential units in the group care field as centres for advanced practice and research is also discussed (see chapter 5). This inclusion of these two papers in this volume demonstrates that group care practitioners are now seeking to satisfy the research commitment expected of a professional discipline. It also points to the way in which training programmes for group care practitioners have to equip aspiring practitioners to undertake research tasks and how these tasks can no longer be preserved for the pretentious few but are an integral responsibility for all qualified personnel. Group care practitioners therefore need to be aware of current research, able to evaluate critically reports and use the findings as guides to improve practice. They also need to master research skills for use in their own situation. In addition, they need to take account of issues associated with the formulation of research problems, the construction of instruments for measurement purposes, data collection and ultimately the analysis and interpretation of findings. These issues operate on at least two levels of consideration that are associated with overall programme evaluation and individual child development.

Teaching in the research area is therefore no longer an optional extra only to be provided in training programmes if time allows or at extra cost. It is now an integral requirement for all group care training programmes. It is, however, worth noting that materials acquired through research and evaluation studies may provide the practitioner with invaluable supports in the search for and justification of resource allocation to this field of service. Such an allocation is central to service development and provision of a professional level of care and treatment for children in group care.

Child care methods and practice

In considering group care practice and the area of skills teaching, it is useful to adopt a direct and indirect categorization of the methods that are available. This division allows for greater clarity about the function of different practitioners and also about the various types of work that have to be undertaken in group care programmes. The space available here prevents extensive treatment of this subject. However, a selective outline of the areas that need to be covered in methods and skills sequences in training programmes will be offered. A diagrammatic presentation of this material *(Table 9(1))* is also made available.

Direct care

Direct care personnel are those engaged in continuous daily contact with children. Their purpose is to provide through everyday events in a planned environment a blend of care, counsel, education, and recreation that respects and responds to the needs of children. They promote by way of these activities the growth and development of those with whom they engage. The many different facets which make up these seemingly abstract activities, but which have a strong practical component, have been identified as:

> 'physical care (providing food, clothes, rest), habit training (personal and inter-personal hygiene), first aid (health care maintenance and restoration), self-management in inter-personal contacts (peer and adult relationships) and the introduction of new stimulations and variations in daily life experience (planning new social contacts in the world of play, work and routine).'   (Maier, 1978)

The manner in which direct care practitioners engage with children and personalize these matters through various caring, counselling, teaching, and recreational formats is of course a key variable. Training which supports practitioners while they acquire some comfort in the role of group care worker and competence in the execution of these duties as well as a style of practice which acknowledges their own personal attributes is therefore of vital importance. Valuable assistance is obtained by practitioners through the provision during training of opportunities to use those methods and skills that are well established. These areas are:

Table 9(1)   *Group child care methods and skills in direct and indirect care*

Direct care (work with children)	Indirect care (work for and on behalf of children
Provision of everyday personal care (food, clothes, warmth)	Environmental planning (fabric maintenance, improvement, modification, or extension and purchase of personal care essentials and equipment)
Formulation of individual care and treatment plans	Design implementation and evaluation of unit programme
Developmental scheduling (individual and group) play and activity based	Administration and management of programme budgets, data collection, and resource acquisition exercises
Activity programming (individual and group) play, recreation, and informal education	External relations with media, local community, kindred systems, and significant others
Group work (educational, activity, and therapeutic formats)	Programme leadership and team development
Life-space counselling (individual and group)	Selection, training, and assessment of performance of practitioners
Programme planning-unit level	Supervision and monitoring of practitioners' work and programme achievement

provision of personal care, formulation of individual care and treatment plans, developmental scheduling, activity programmes, group work, life space counselling, and programme planning (VanderVen, 1972; Whittaker, 1979; Vinter, 1974; Konopka, 1954; Maier, 1965; Redl, 1959). Teaching sequences that are supportive of these methods and skills are therefore worthy of, if not essential for, inclusion in training programmes. This selection tries to take account of the actual work schedule of a direct care practitioner and recognize their need to be able to perform the duties outlined in relation to both an individual child and a group of children. It specifically acknowledges that the practitioner has to be able to manage group interaction and organize group activity

constructively in order to meet individual and overall programme aims.
Direct care personnel also need to have some preliminary skills in programme planning. Elsewhere in this volume the notion of programme is
explored in detail (see chapter 3). Below, there is an attempt to identify
programme planning as an indirect method of intervention. Programme
planning can, however, be considered at many different levels but
within the context of this discussion of training for direct care practitioners it is intended to refer to the unit programme only. The
systematic use of the direct care methods and skills identified earlier
implies the existence of an overall programme design and structure
within which to apply these approaches. An appreciation of this fact and
an understanding of some of the indirect service approaches that support overall programme planning is important for direct service practitioners. Within all programmes the direct and indirect service
methodologies have to interact in a dynamic yet ordered manner in order
to ensure that group care programmes provide nurturing and socialization experiences and (if necessary) specific therapeutic opportunities
that aid children in their search for growth and development.

Indirect care

This refers to those aspects of group care practice which, while occurring
away from the direct interaction between group care worker and child,
nevertheless have a bearing on the context in which this takes place and
the conditions under which it occurs. Practitioners in indirect care
positions are engaged in carrying out executive, advisory, and consulta-
tive duties in regard to overall programme matters. This includes
managerial and administrative tasks that incorporate external programme relations but which more often focus on internal affairs such as
environmental planning, the design and implementation of the programme, and the evaluation of achievements *(see Table 9(1))*. Also
included are financial budgeting, data collection, and resource acquisition as well as the important task of team leadership and development
plus selection, training, and supervision of personnel.

This work is obviously different from that of the direct care practitioner
and reflects concerns about the effectiveness and efficiency of the total
programme. Different practice methods and skills are required for this
type of work. Training programmes for group care practitioners therefore need to provide teaching that supports acquisition of competency in
these matters. For the execution of these tasks in a skilled and
methodologically sound manner that is compatible with the practice of
direct care requires both substantial technical knowledge and an inti-

mate understanding of that practice. In fact, all the efforts of indirect care practitioners have to be geared towards making the direct care practitioner more effective in work with children. This is because the direct care practitioner personifies the programme aims and, because of the length of time he or she spends in contact with the child, has the potential to be the principal agent for achieving from the programme the hoped for growth and development of the child. Paradoxically, however, some studies of human service organizations have shown that the ability of direct care practitioners to assist children is materially influenced by administrative procedures that are devised well away from the actual interface between practitioner and child (Raynes, Pratt, and Roses, 1979). This draws attention to the way indirect care personnel, whilst borrowing specialist knowledge and skills from outside the human services field, have to ensure that their application is in sympathy with the aims of group care practice.

The commitment and attitudinal position that encourage this adaptation and application of knowledge and skills from other sources in this way most usually comes from those who identify themselves as group care practitioners. Common studies with those who intend to act as direct care practitioners and even the provision of experience of direct care practice is an obvious way in which training programmes can contribute to this process for those individuals interested in indirect modes of care and treatment. There is, however, a tendency to diminish the importance of indirect modes of practice and this stems from the wish of many persons who enter group care practice to assist children directly. There is a further tendency for the view to be adopted that these competencies can be acquired later or that this work can be left to personnel with training only in business, management, administration, or organizational matters. This, it is suggested, is an error that results in useful methods and techniques from other disciplines often being inadequately modified for use in group care practice.

Training for group care practice self-evidently cannot be totally contained in a college situation. All who seek to equip themselves as practitioners require opportunity during training to apply learning in actual service with children. Indeed in any credible pattern of professional training there has to be an insistence that potential practitioners demonstrate, in order to qualify, an ability to use in practice knowledge gained in academic studies. This is certainly true for group care practitioners and clearly refers to the use of both direct and indirect care methods and skills. Controlled involvement in practice situations during training is therefore necessary for students consuming these course sequences. This then turns a training programme into a dynamic enterprise rather than being a static or arid academic exercise.

Summary

Hopefully this discussion of the current situation and of influences on training for group care practice in more than one country will allow a greater sense of common interests to emerge amongst those engaged in this field. The attempted clarification of the training needs of group care practitioners regardless of national situations also assists in this process.

Those concerned with group care practice, regardless of country, will no doubt continue to press for recognition, although in different ways. This recognition is not only concerned with personal status, but arises from the importance of group care for children as an area of professional concern. For only with this recognition are present and future generations of children from both normal and special populations likely to find themselves in receipt of the group care services they deserve – services which will provide them with the best opportunities that we can devise for growth and development.

Note

(1) Reference to key personnel in the justice system in a similar manner is less easy. Persons employed as group care workers in this system are variously called warden, warder, officer, guard, or corrections counselor.

References

Ainsworth, F. (1980) The Training of Group Care Personnel in the Personal Social Services. In R. Walton and D. Elliott (eds) *Residential Care: A Reader in Current Theory and Practice.* Oxford: Pergamon.

Beker, J. (1979) Training and Professional Development in Child Care. In J. K. Whittaker *Caring for Troubled Children.* San Francisco: Jossey-Bass.

Bettelheim, B. (1974) *A Home for the Heart.* London: Thames & Hudson.

Brager, G. and Holloway, S. (1978) *Changing Human Service Organizations: Politics and Practice.* San Francisco: Free Press.

British Association of Social Workers (1977) *The Social Work Task.* Birmingham: BASW.

Cox, L. (1979) Co-operative Training for Residential Child Care Staff – Curriculum, Delivery and Background Study (mimeographed report). Victoria, Australia.

Dockar-Drysdale, B. (1968) *Therapy in Child Care.* London: Longman.

Elery, L., Phillips, L., Phillips, E. A., Fixsen, D. L., and Wolf, M. M. (1974) *The Teaching-Parent Family Handbook.* Lawrence, Kansas: University of Kansas.

Fulcher, L. C. (1979) Keeping Staff Sane to Accomplish Treatment. *Residential and Community Child Care Administration* 1 (1): 69–85.

Ginger, S. (1971) The Problem-Éducateur. *International Child Welfare Review* 9: 16–23.

Goffman, E. (1961) *Asylums.* New York: Anchor Books.

Guindon, J. (1970) *Les Étapes de la Re-Éducation.* Paris: Editions Fleurus.

Hobbs, N. (1964) *The Process of Re-Education.* Nashville, Tennessee: George Peabody College.

Jay Report (1979) *Report of the Committee of Enquiry into Mental Handicap, Nursing, and Care.* London: Her Majesty's Stationery Office.

Konopka, G. (1954) *Group Work in the Institution.* New York: Association Press.

Keith-Lucas, A. and Sanford, C. W. (1977) *Group Child Care as a Family Service.* Chapel Hill: University of North Carolina Press.

Levinson, D. J., Darrow, C. N., Klein, E. B., Levinson, M. H., and McKee, B. (1978) *The Seasons of a Man's Life.* New York: Alfred Knopf.

Linton, T. E. (1971) The Educateur Model: A Theoretical Monograph. *Journal of Special Education* 5: 155–90.

Maier, H. W. (1965) *Group Work as Part of Residential Treatment.* Washington: National Association of Social Workers.

Maier, H. W. (1978) Child Welfare: Child Care Workers. In *Encyclopaedia of Social Work.* New York: National Association of Social Workers.

Maier, H. W. (1979) The Core of Care: Essential Ingredients for the Development of Children at Home or Away from Home. *Child Care Quarterly* 8 (3): 161–73.

Mayer, M. F., Richman, L. H., and Balcerzak, E. A. (1977) *Group Care for Children, Crossroads and Transitions.* New York: Child Welfare League of America.

Millham, S., Bullock, R., and Hosie, K. (1980) *Learning to Care.* Farnborough, Hants: Gower.

Patti, R. and Resnick, H. (1972) Changing the Agency from Within. *Social Work* 17 (1): 48–57.

Polsky, H. (1962) *Cottage Six: The Social System of Delinquent Boys in Residential Treatment.* New York: Russell Sage Foundation.

Raynes, N. V., Pratt , M. W., and Roses, S. (1979) *Organisational Structure and the Care of the Mentally Retarded.* London: Croom Helm.

Redl, F. (1959) Strategy and Technique of the Life Space Interview. *American Journal of Ortho-Psychiatry* 29 (1): 1–18.

Reiger, N. (1977) *The Child Mental Health Specialist.* Report to the National Institute of Mental Health. Camarillo, California: Children's Treatment Centre.

Stanton, A. H. and Schwartz, M. S. (1954) *The Mental Hospital: A Study of Institutional Participation in Psychiatric Illness and Treatment.* New York: Basic Books.

VanderVen, K. D. (1972) Developmental Scheduling. In G. W. Foster (ed.) *Child Care Work with Emotionally Disturbed Children.* Pittsburgh: University of Pittsburgh Press.

VanderVen, K. D. (1980) News from the Field *Child Care Quarterly* 9 (1): 62–5.

Vinter, R. D. (1974) Program Activities: An Analysis of Their Effect on Participant Behaviour. In P. Glasser, R. C. Sarri, and R. D. Vinter (eds) *Individual Change through Small Groups.* New York: Free Press.

Weissman, H. H. (1973) *Overcoming Mismanagement in the Human Services.* San Francisco: Jossey-Bass.

Whittaker, J. K. (1979) *Caring for Troubled Children.* San Francisco: Jossey-Bass.

Section IV

Research and evaluation

10 Research and evaluation in group care

Chris Payne[1]

Introduction

The literature on programme evaluation reveals many unresolved problems of a conceptual, methodological, political, and ethical nature (Weiss, 1972). Given such problems, how do we set about evaluating group care? What role does evaluation play in programme development? These are the issues with which this paper is concerned. My approach is to ask some simple, but far-reaching questions. What has been accomplished by way of evaluation work to date, particularly in Great Britain? Then, what are the purposes of evaluation? What are its main concerns? What kinds of evaluation are we seeking to make? How are they made and who should be involved? Running through the discussion is a central question: How can evaluation influence the management and practice of group care?

To begin, I need to sketch the background against which the discussion takes place.

Research and evaluation in Great Britain

Although the grass is always greener on the other side, it is evident that programme evaluation in the United States and Canada has reached a different 'state of the art' compared to Great Britain. In North America, to judge by the burgeoning literature and the armament of methods and techniques which are described there, an evaluation industry has developed over the last two decades. In a comprehensive review, Durkin and Durkin (1975) discuss evaluation designs which have rarely, if at all, been used to evaluate group care in Britain (including goal attainment models, systems approaches, and process evaluations). In addition they discuss descriptive studies, outcome, and follow-up research, some examples of which can be found in the British literature. In a selective but more recent review, Whittaker (1979 : chapter 8) discussed goal attainment scales (see also Kiresuk and Sherman, 1968) and several experimental single subject designs (see also Hersen and Barlow, 1976). Also a study by Reichertz, Kislowicz, and Stalinski (1978) in Canada uses instruments first developed by Thomas (1975) in Georgia to measure the 'community orientedness' of group care programmes. Few British practitioners are likely to be familiar with these approaches.

In a valuable contribution to the literature on group care, Whittaker (1979 : 58–65) discusses the behaviour modification programmes developed at 'Achievement Place', a community based residential programme for young offenders (see also Phillips, Fixsen, and Wolf, 1979). Built into the behavioural methodology is the need for regular evaluation of treatment effectiveness. However, behavioural approaches have not had the same impact in Great Britain as in North America, being practised in only a few settings, primarily where treatment is being given under conditions of security (Brown, 1977; Hoghugi *et al.*, 1977; Barlow, 1979). British exponents of behaviour modification are not often employed in mainstream child care work and few resources have been devoted to the dissemination of behavioural approaches in group care settings (Brown, 1978). The exception, perhaps, is the field of mental handicap, where behaviour modification programmes are developing under the supervision of clinical and educational psychologists.

In the British context most of the important research studies of recent times have concerned institutions for young offenders which is perhaps indicative of where societal and official interest lies (Cawson, 1978; Cawson and Martell, 1979; Clarke and Cornish, 1972, 1975; Dunlop, 1975; Gill, 1974; Hoghugi, 1978; Millham, Bullock, and Cherrett, 1975; Millham, Bullock, and Hosie, 1978). There have been fewer major studies in other fields of group care though services for mentally handicapped children have been the focus of important studies by King, Raynes, and Tizard (1971), Kushlick (1972, 1974) and Oswin (1971, 1978). From her review of residential child care research in the period from 1966 to 1974 Prosser (1976) concluded that our knowledge of child care had advanced only slightly, if at all, in the decade since a similar review by Dinnage and Pringle (1967) and that there is still a 'dearth of evidence concerning different types of residential care and the effects of different types of care on different types of children' (1967 : 16). Prosser points out that comparative research has been largely ignored. The need for more comparative studies has also been expressed by the late Professor Tizard: to identify general factors influencing the quality of care; and knowledge which could then be applied throughout the spectrum of residential care

(Tizard, Sinclair, and Clarke, 1975). Many of the research studies cited above are psychological and sociological; if they are 'evaluative' it is in effect and interpretation rather than by design. Only the 'Kingswood' study of Clarke and Cornish, which is discussed later (see pages 258–59), and Kushlick's 'Wessex' experiment, are explicitly evaluative research projects. The Wessex project is an ambitious programme to evaluate services for mentally handicapped children and their families, based on an epidemiological assessment of need followed by controlled trials to determine the relative effectiveness and efficiency of different forms of service delivery including different residential care practices (Kushlick, 1972; 1974). A comparative study that is more evidently evaluative is by Berry (1976) of forty-four residential child care settings, which included independent boarding schools for 'ordinary' pupils, schools for mal-adjusted children, children's homes, and community homes catering for young offenders. Berry identified institutions providing 'good enough' care from those providing 'not good enough' care, of which there was a large proportion. Although aspects of the methodology are question-able, her main conclusion is an important one, namely that it is the quality of support offered to primary care givers, which makes the crucial difference in being able to offer 'good enough' care.

These studies apart, evaluation either in terms of individual pro-grammes or comparative studies to identify the relative effectiveness of care, is remarkably jejune. Much evaluation work appears to have taken the form of descriptive and impressionistic studies conducted by work-ing parties and committees. Only a few local authorities are currently attempting to evaluate their residential programmes (see University of Birmingham, 1979). As an indication of the lack of evaluation, a serious deficiency considering the 'new' forms of care developed as a result of the 1969 Children and Young Person's Act; Reinach and Roberts (1979) can claim with some justification that their follow-up study of children admitted to a new observation and assessment centre to be 'unique'. It is significant that the Social Science Research Council (SSRC) – the main research funding body in Britain – has recently announced that it is establishing a comprehensive research programme into children in need of care and has identified evaluation of alternative forms of care as one of the priority areas (SSRC, 1980).

The need for more programme evaluation is not confined to the resi-dential services. Brown (1978:325) complains that 'intermediate treat-ment' programmes (community care schemes for young offenders and other children 'at risk') have been 'adopted largely willy-nilly without any emphasis on careful evaluation, research into technical develop-ment and funding of specific training courses'. There are currently more attempts to evaluate intermediate treatment projects than is implied by this statement, although it is difficult to assess the scientific merits of some of the approaches (see University of Birmingham, 1979; Thomes, 1977).

This then is the state of the art, but what of the future? Before responding to the clarion call for more evaluation, we perhaps need to consider in more depth its meaning and purpose. The rest of this paper therefore focuses on some of the issues that have to be tackled in the development of evaluation strategies. First, we look at the meaning of evaluation.

The concept of evaluation

There can be no doubt that evaluation is an ambiguous concept. Evaluations are essentially judgments of worth or value – of people, activities, objects, and events. But here we need to distinguish those value judgments which are made informally and often unconsciously about daily life and practice, and formal evaluations that imply some organizing principles for collecting and appraising data systematically and identifying evaluative criteria. But note that these so-called 'informal' evaluations, as we will see later, are sometimes powerful influences on policy formulation and decision taking.

When considering formal evaluation, an important distinction can be made between two types of evaluation each containing different processes. Scriven (1972) uses the term 'formative' evaluation to convey the idea of *continuous* review and evaluation. Every group care programme possesses the vehicles to make this kind of evaluation by way of case-planning, recording and reviewing procedures, staff supervision and appraisal systems and so on. These yield a steady stream of data which can indicate to the practitioners, programme managers, and other interested parties how well or badly the programme is doing. Scriven also discusses the concept of summative evaluation, which can be interpreted in the group care context, in terms of regular, systematic reviews of all programme functions, which can lead to revisions of objectives, priorities, and methods. Different methods for conducting this kind of evaluation are discussed later.

The purpose of evaluation

Social work has come under considerable criticism both within and without the profession for failing to take evaluation seriously, there being only a few evaluative studies of field social work (for example Goldberg, 1979). Nevertheless, there is still no universal agreement about the desirability of formal evaluation in group care. Some eschew evaluation as being too mechanistic, complaining that the instruments are insufficiently sensitive to reflect the underlying realities of residential living, with its complex interplay of personal and social forces. For example, in his description of a children's home with deeply rooted religious traditions, White (1979:96) states 'if the home is alive, then a context for evaluation and assessment is provided; if not, analysis and treatment become part of the end of the home, as well as the means to that end'. Also Righton (1979:15) argues that a 'therapeutic community' is *primarily* the expression of a *moral commitment* and only *secondarily* a treatment milieu. Its major justification lies not so much in techniques and results as in the quality of life experience generated by the interactions of staff and residents. He goes on to make the point that the code of values on which the community is founded – egalitarianism, shared responsibility, the idea that children should be treated as 'normal' rather than as 'sick patients', and the power of loving relationships – is *self-validating* and therefore not subject to negotiation or analysis.

The concept of personal commitment underpins a great many residential programmes, particularly those run by voluntary or independent organizations. Evaluations of these programmes raise considerable difficulties for they have to take into account the *a priori* moral, religious, and political principles that permeate any discussion of ends and means. The members themselves might argue that evaluations can be made only of the means and processes, which help or hinder the programme to conform to its ideals. To their way of thinking, evaluations can only be made from what Rein (1976) describes as a 'value committed' perspective, that is, acceptance of the assumptions on which the programme is based. In other words, evaluation takes the form of a political or ideological rather than a scientific debate.

What purposes then can be served by evaluation? We need to consider evaluations as no more or no less than as organizational and professional tools that have instrumental value on different levels of policy development and decision taking. For our purposes, four such levels can be identified:

(1) At the level of *strategy*, evaluations help to determine what provisions should be made in terms of kind and quantity for the child care population needing services. How much residential provision is needed? Should there be more emphasis on finding alternatives to residential care?

(2) At the level of *executive decision making* they assist with the planning and development of service delivery. Should this patently ineffective programme continue? Which one should be closed in order to reduce public expenditure?

(3) At an *operational* level evaluations are made to shape the nature and

direction of the treatment programme. Which methods apear to be most effective for an individual child or group of children?

(4) Finally, at an *individual* level they help to assess progress and whether changes in *children's* behaviour, attitudes, or personality are consistent with treatment aims and expectations. Also for child care *staff*, evaluations of their performance and development are needed to identify strengths and weaknesses and to indicate their supervision and training needs.

Objectives of evaluation

From the range of evaluation functions, two primary objectives can be identified. One is to increase the accountability of programme or services provision to the resource controllers, and ultimately the community at large; the other is to bring about changes and improvements in service delivery.

Accountability, however, is one of those ambiguous concepts that can all too easily be interpreted in terms of establishing bureaucratic control over activities, when it often needs to be seen in a wider context of ensuring public or democratic control. In making evaluations, therefore, a broad spectrum of views may need to be sought about a given programme's objectives and what constitutes their success or failure. This broader concept is reflected in some evaluation approaches which actively seek the views of the consumer, as in the 'Who Cares!' project (Paige and Clarke, 1977) or the views of people who give the programme credibility. A good example here is 'Achievement Place' which seeks the judgment of schoolteachers, police, parents, and others on the progress made by the young people admitted to the programme (Phillips *et al.*, 1974).

The emphasis on accountability can nevertheless obscure or reduce the importance of the second major objective which reflects vital *educative* functions. Indeed my own interest in evaluation goes back to when, as director of a programme which provided diagnostic and treatment services to children in care, I became acutely and painfully aware of the lack of any systematic evaluation which I felt was needed to assess how far our services and methods were meeting, in form and quality, the children's needs and those of the wider agency (a local authority social services department) (Payne, 1979). It was evident to me then, and remains the case now, that all practitioners need feedback to help them and the agency's decision making and forward planning, to identify their strengths and weaknesses, to re-establish goals and priorities, and to find fresh impetus to their problem solving efforts. In other words, practitioners need some tools so that they can learn from their experience. Children learn how to modulate the pitch and tone of their voices by acting on feedback from their own and others' speech; and without feedback, group care managers and practitioners often fail to meet changing needs and circumstances.

The focus of evaluation

With these objectives in mind what then are the major concerns of evaluation? To answer this three further questions stand out. First are the questions asked to establish the *ethicality* of the programme. Is what is being done morally right? Secondly, are questions about the programme's *effectiveness*. Is it achieving its purpose? Third, are *economic* questions. Is value for money being given?

Ethicality The authors of a recent study of the child care system argue that principles of natural justice are often circumvented or denied when children are taken into care. They claim that decisions taken by social workers and magistrates are often not in the children's best interests; so the principles on which the system is based are invalidated. They also argue that the treatment methods used in institutions for deprived and disturbed young people are in many cases morally questionable (Taylor, Lacey, and Bracken, 1980). These arguments suggest that the single most important justification for programme evaluation is to ensure that human rights are upheld, to check against possible abuses and to insure that care and treatment are morally, professionally, and socially acceptable.

Effectiveness However, the more familiar arguments for evaluation are in economic rather than moral terms. It is argued that programmes need to demonstrate their effectiveness to justify the heavy investment of resources – financial, material, and human. This argument is most prominent in periods of financial stringency, when competition for scarce resources is at its fiercest and priority issues feature uppermost in the minds of the resource-controllers. This leads to the question, what is effective care? A programme is said to be 'effective' when its objectives are achieved, but this begs more questions than it answers. What are the objectives of group care? There is still considerable confusion and uncertainty about objectives, without which evaluative criteria or standards and measures of effectiveness must also remain ill-defined.

Another question is, who decides what the objectives should be? Objectives are essentially value judgments, which refer to the ends being sought by taking particular courses of action. What values are being referred to? And, of equal importance, whose values? As Algie (1972a) has stated, evaluations are made to determine a programme's relevance, but who decides what is to be relevant? Views about what are relevant objectives vary considerably amongst people occupying different positions in the organizational hierachy. For example, programme managers and administrators will often hold different and conflicting views to practitioners. The Harlesden Community Project, which set out to integrate community work and a residential care service for adolescents of mainly West Indian origins is a good case in point. The story of this project is one of conflicting objectives between the project workers and their management, a local authority social services department, which resulted in the premature closure of the residential programme. In a penetrating, albeit subjective evaluation, the project workers have suggested that the social services management were under constant pressure 'to keep children's homes as clean and tidy places where the primary requirement is "good" behaviour', whereas they felt that to provide effective help to some very troubled young people they had 'to face up to and cope with many kinds of difficult untidy behaviour, some of which inevitably spilled into the community' (Harlesden Community Project, 1979:340–41). Unfortunately, we do not have the management views of the project, but from the workers' account it is evident that a fundamental problem here was the failure to reach any agreement on objectives and methods. In the final analysis, therefore, the decision to close the programme was taken as a political decision. It was not taken on the basis of any objective view of ineffectiveness.

The next question is, how do we assess effectiveness? For example, is effectiveness determined by outcomes, that is, what happens to children after they leave the programme as indicated by their subsequent social adjustment, employment record, recidivism, etc. If so, in the case of children who have experienced long term care, White (1979) argues that a generation or so must pass before the effectiveness of their upbringing can be determined, when they are themselves parents. Alternatively, is effectiveness determined by what happens to children as they pass through the programme, in terms of any changes and improvements in their behaviour, attitudes, educational attainments, personality dimensions, and so on?

'Outcome' evaluation   We examine 'outcome' evaluation first. From the literature it would appear that outcome evaluation has yet to resolve two essential issues. The first is to define criteria that indicate successful outcomes, and this implies that programme objectives must also be clearly defined. The second is to find some way of distinguishing between outcomes that are a consequence of the programme and those that are a consequence of something else (Paley, 1977). Whittaker (1979) has criticized

the narrowness and the simplistic nature of the criteria often used as measures in outcome research and he cites studies that suggest the biggest single factor determining a successful or unsuccessful outcome is the quality and supportiveness of the post-care environment (Allerhand, Weber, and Haug, 1966; Taylor and Alpert, 1973). If this is the case, it is nonsense to use outcome as the sole criterion of treatment effectiveness.

Process evaluation   The problems associated with outcome studies have accordingly resulted in a shift of emphasis resulting in more efforts to discover changes taking place while children are in the programme. Process studies set out to measure changes which occur in individual or groups over time from an identified baseline. Although in Great Britain process evaluation is still rudimentary, it is the focus of recent research of some intermediate treatment programmes (Warburton, 1979; Paley and Thorpe, 1974). Whittaker (1979) also describes a number of single subject designs, that may well provide the basis for further work in the area.

Process evaluations are potentially of considerable practical value in two important respects. First, as part of a formative evaluation strategy, they may give some direct feedback to practitioners about the effectiveness of their methods, thus indicating where their intervention plans need to be modified. Secondly, as Millham, Bullock, and Cherrett (1975) study of the former approved schools has indicated, children's behaviour, attitudes, self-concepts, etc. often do change during their period in the programme which contrasts with the rather bleak results of most outcome research. The problem then is how to help the child maintain progress after his or her discharge from the programme. However, many methodological issues remain. One is to demonstrate which variables actually account for any changes; another is to identify baselines. One study (though admittedly not a process evaluation – Dunlop, 1975) identified selection as a key factor distinguishing the more successful from the less successful approved schools, i.e. the 'better' schools were admitting less delinquent children, thus their 'success' was to a large extent self-fulfilling.

Irrespective of the criteria finally used, it is probably well to remember that judgments of success, failure, and any other attributes of care are always open to interpretation. At best, even with sophisticated designs, evaluations are approximate indications of whether individual children in the programme as a whole are moving in positive or negative directions, and whether particular objectives are being achieved more or less as expected.

Effective or efficient programmes?   The question, is there value for money, is generally answered by carrying out cost-effectiveness and cost-benefit studies. But, in practice, sometimes the criterion of effectiveness is confused with 'efficiency'. Few argue about the need for 'good housekeeping', that is to make efficient use of material, financial, and human resources. But it is apparent that insensitive administrative practices can often impair the quality of care. For example, many long stay residential homes are expected to make bulk purchases of food and clothing, which may be cost-effective. However, these purchasing methods often deprive children of invaluable social learning experiences. Thus ineffective care may result when administrative objectives dominate primary care objectives. As Algie (1972a : 2523) succinctly states 'efficiency' is 'getting more out of less *without* lowering professional standards'.

In the human service context 'efficiency' is difficult to define and to measure. It may be easier to obtain efficiency measures of the material and financial resources; but, *cliché* though it may be, it is the human resources that are the most important resources in group care practice. How do we determine how well human resources, in terms of application of knowledge and skills, time, energy, etc. are being employed? What tools can be used to determine: the efficient use of time, space and equipment; how well staff are relating to one another; whether communications – formal and informal – are good or bad; the adequacy of the recording system. How well are records used; and are records used to keep the administration happy or as an important staff supervision and development tool? Are staff support systems working well? Is staff development given sufficient priority? Note the value assumptions implicit in these questions, then consider the thorny methodological problems that they create. Although Whittaker (1979) considers that they may be too complex for practical purposes, systems approaches, as described by Durkin and Durkin (1975), at least provide some interesting possibilities. Systems analysis assumes a variety of interrelationships within the group care environment and sets out to assess the contribution of different inputs to programme objectives.

One criterion that receives considerable attention from practitioners and others concerned about quality of care, though it receives rather less attention in the evaluation literature, is *adequacy* of resources. For example, it is an established fact that a large proportion of group care staff are unqualified and untrained, yet there are still expectations that they can manage and treat the very damaged children in their care. Some can and do, but the fact remains that programmes often appear to be failing because expectations are too high. With clearer and more modest objectives a higher degree of success might well be demonstrated. The answer to the problem of inadequate resources does not of course necessarily lie with 'more' resources. Improved staffing levels and a bigger budget do not make for more effective practice. Some programmes require minimal staffing resources in terms of numbers, but those appointed need to be of the highest calibre.

Models of evaluation

To this point it is evident that evaluations involve some highly value laden processes (if the tautology can be permitted). How then do we develop evaluation approaches that grapple with these issues of ethicality, effectiveness, efficiency, adequacy, and other criteria? In this section we examine evaluation approaches from two contrasting perspectives.

A *The research model*

This is the dominant perspective in the evaluation literature. One of the chief exponents is Suchman (1967) who makes a distinction between 'evaluation' which may imply some logical or rational basis for making a value judgment but does not require systematic procedures and evaluative research. By 'evaluative research' is meant a type of research that involves systematic procedures for marshalling and presenting objective evidence, to increase the probability of proving instead of merely asserting the value of a given social activity. This like any other research is conducted as a 'neutral' enquiry, as if the researchers had no vested interest in the outcome of their work. Rein (1976) uses the term 'value-neutral' to describe this perspective. We might also call it the 'Grabgrind' model, after the Dickens character in *Hard Times* 'who with a rule and a pair of scales and a multiplication table in his pocket could weigh and measure any panel of human nature and tell you exactly what it came to'.

This model functions as a superior technical service, with the evaluators feeding back information into the operational system, where it is 'picked-up' and utilized in various ways by the practitioners, managers, politicians, etc. They then interpret and use the information according to their vested interests and from particular role perspectives. Inevitably, this knowledge is used selectively and, as Rein (1976) suggests, often to justify actions taken on other grounds.

Time and costs An important feature of the research model is time needed to go through the various stages of data collection and analysis before feedback can be given. The use of controlled observation, logical analysis, development of objective indicators, and other attempts to resolve problems of 'subjectivity', all take time – and money. From the point of view of costs alone, it is doubtful whether there can be many of the more ambitious projects, like the Wessex experiment, undertaken at any one time.

Relevance   Several writers have also commented on the problems of utilizing research results. For example, Nelson, Singer, and Johnson (1978) writing in the American context comments that child care workers may reject and ignore even positive evaluations because the results come to them as 'old hat' reinforcing what they intuitively know already. It is evident that the impact of research on policy and practice is always unpredictable. As Ward and Kassebaum (1972) ruefully conclude from personal experience in America, even a highly sophisticated and technically correct piece of research can, by implication, be declared redundant because of lack of 'take up' on completion. In Britain two recent studies have questioned the validity of treating children under conditions of security (Millham, Bullock, and Hosie, 1978; Cawson and Martell, 1979). However, they do not appear to be having much influence over social policies that are geared towards the extension rather than reduction of such facilities. Writing in another context Millham (1977) puts the issue in a nutshell when he says that even if 'dazzling' success could be demonstrated for intermediate treatment, the fact would be unlikely to have much influence on the practice of the courts. In other words, research findings, as any formal evaluation, are only ever one of many factors that are taken into account in policy formulation and the taking of decisions.

The Kingswood study   Sometimes, however, research may be accredited more status than it really deserves. Whittaker (1979:203) has commented that 'many attempts at programme evaluation have failed because they are too cumbersome, unwieldy, or ambitious'. His point is well illustrated by the 'Kingswood' study, an interesting case example of some of the problems of research design. It also raises many issues relating to cost effectiveness and practical relevance of research. This study actually began in 1964 although the final report was not published until eleven years later in 1975! Its purpose was to investigate whether a 'therapeutic community' was more or less effective in treating the delinquent boys passing through it than a 'traditional' approved school approach. The research used a classical experimental design – the controlled trial – with intake into the experimental and control groups determined by random allocation. It is interesting that the first published report of this research was confined to a discussion of the ethical, conceptual, and technical problems of the research design, said to be unsatisfactory on a number of counts. The researchers point out that these difficulties had contributed to the premature closure of the research project, but even if it could have been completed as planned they felt it would have been of doubtful scientific value and few generalizations about effective treatment methods could have been made (Clarke and Cornish, 1972). These conclusions were made long before the final report which when published came to the staggering conclusion that there was a 'seeming failure of residential methods to have any lasting effect on the rehabilitation of delinquents!' (Clarke and Cornish, 1975). Subsequently the principal of the school where the experiment had been conducted wrote a very interesting article. Not only did he criticize the report for devoting only *three and one half* out of *seventy-four* pages to a discussion of the actual results of the experiment but he states (the emphases are mine):

> 'A research project set up to discover for *residential child care* workers the relative merits of two different methodologies led in fact to a report which gave scant coverage to the data uncovered by the fieldwork, used only *one criterion* (in an unmodified fashion) of "success" and which was given over to suggestions as to how to set about *preventing* delinquency. Far from helping *residential child care workers* the research report has been cited repeatedly as *proof* that "residential treatment" does not cure delinquency!' (Burns, 1976:416)

It is apparent that a major problem of the Kingswood study was that it considered a whole approach (a therapeutic community) as a single variable. As Manning (1979) suggests, comparing whole institutions is unhelpful because they are multi-dimensional whereas experimental designs require single-dimensions to be isolated and systematically manipulated. Clarke and Sinclair (1973) have suggested that some of the problems associated with 'spot the winner' research can be overcome by more comparative studies.

One of the lessons of the Kingswood study is that less cumbersome though no less technically competent designs are needed if it is going to be possible to identify scientifically the relative effectiveness of different treatment variables. A compromise solution is suggested by Brown (1978) who is interested in the development of behaviour modification programmes. He advocates that research resources should be devoted to small scale demonstration projects, to increase understanding of the different contexts in which such methods might develop and to assist the controlled dissemination of new ideas.

B Evaluation as critical appraisal

In a very useful summary of the concepts and methods of programme evaluation for use in community work, Key, Hudson, and Armstrong (1976) use the concept of 'critical appraisal' to describe an approach which aims to achieve a 'controlled subjectivity' in the making of an evaluation. This, as Rein (1976) suggests, allows for subjective preferences to be guided by rational and intelligible criteria and can develop from the judicious use of both 'hard-line' and 'soft-line' methods of data collection and appraisal.

By hard-line is meant an exact definition of evaluation and a set of specific procedures of a rational and objective kind, i.e. scientific methods. Soft-line approaches are characterized by a general and vague definition of evaluation, with few specific procedures, which where they exist tend to be subjective and open to interpretation. However, Key, Hudson, and Armstrong (1976) argue that one approach is not inherently superior to the other, different approaches being needed for different purposes. This argument can be taken further. So-called 'soft-line' approaches can represent radically different ways of 'interpreting the world' and are only soft in the context of the scientific paradigm. From a phenomenological perspective, for example, 'soft-line' methods can be developed as systematized ways of analysing human experience and are particularly useful for evaluating particular aspects of group care practice.

In his critique of the 'Kingswood' study Burns (1976) raises a central issue, that is, who are evaluations for? Now, we have already indicated that evaluation should lead to changes being made in day-to-day practice if they are to have any practical meaning. Algie (1972b) states evaluation is a dynamic process that strives to find better solutions to daily work problems and issues. One of the problems practitioners experience is that they cannot obtain, process, or interpret data with the same degree of systematization and 'objectivity' as independent researchers. At best, they can only evaluate their work by giving themselves enough 'space' from the daily bombardment of work activities to make a critical appraisal of the ends they are seeking and the employment of appropriate means. In their context evaluation is analogous to Freire's concept of 'critical reflexion' (Freire, 1972). Freire's model of dialogical education is a useful one for understanding evaluation in the practice context, in several ways. First, it is a theory of *action* – critical reflection helps to understand one's social situation in order to *change* it. Secondly, it emphasizes the importance of engaging people actively in their own evaluation, i.e. learning and change processes. Thus evaluation becomes a form of *'self-evaluation'* and 'self-learning' as part of a broader movement of change and social action. Thirdly, it identifies the role of an 'external' evaluator not as a 'neutral fact finder' as in the empirical model, but as an enabler or facilitator who uses his or her expertise to help people analyse and solve their own problems. Thus the external agent functions to provide the structures and frameworks (analogous to Freire's ideas about 'generative themes') so that participants can enter into an exchange of views (dialogue), start working together to comprehend their situation and negotiate with each other about changing and improving it. Are there any recognized approaches that follow this 'critical appraisal' model? In the following sections I discuss a number of possibilities.

'Self-evaluation'   By 'self-evaluation' I am referring to those approaches that involve practitioners and where appropriate consumers in evaluating the effectiveness of the work on two levels: at programme level and at individual case level. Durkin and Durkin (1975) concluded that more attention should be paid to the idea of programmes developing their own evaluative designs. Unfortunately they are able to devote only one page out of fifty to indicate how this might be accomplished. Whittaker (1979) also argues that it is important for practitioners to be involved in all aspects of the evaluation process – in problem formulation, instrument development, data collection, and analysis. He cites the 'goal attainment' methods of Kiresuk and Sherman (1968) as a method of evaluation that encourages the involvement of clients and practitioners.

It is interesting that goal attainment methods are usually described as 'hard-line' but from their admittedly limited application in Great Britain they can fit neatly into the model of 'critical appraisal'. For example, Algie (1972b) describes a project to evaluate a residential home for the elderly, using goal attainment methods. He admits that his approach generates much greater uncertainty than is normally tolerated by academic researchers, because it makes explicit use of 'soft' data. He argues nevertheless it is still a systematic approach falling some way between being purely subjective and objective.

The procedures used in this type of evaluation are as follows. First, a project group which may be composed of different grades of staff, their line managers and possibly residents, is assembled usually under the supervision of an outside consultant. Their task is to examine programme objectives and evaluate its effectiveness and efficient use of resources. Some initial work to identify programme objectives may have to be completed. This, however, provides an opportunity for an exchange of views about the objectives different people seek or assume they are following, which also means there is some debate about the values contained in their work. Thus the formation of the project group consisting of people in different positions to discuss issues within a reasonably 'safe' structure has an important expressive as well as instrumental value.

The job of the outside consultant is to provide the frameworks and materials so that the group can complete its work, for example, by issuing checklists of key questions related to important themes in the development of the programme. An example may be questions related to the quality of staff-child interactions. After each set of questions come the riders: 'What is your evidence?' 'What do you need to improve matters?' The checklists help the group to identify key objectives which they can then begin to evaluate. For each objective identified, a scale is devised to evaluate current levels of success in its achievement. These scales are classed as 'surrogate' or 'proxy' measures used to assess the qualitative aspects of the programme. They are called 'surrogates' because they represent qualities that cannot be observed directly. Consider for example the objective: 'to provide opportunities for children to have some choice in their daily lives'. This objective may be seen as one that has some value in its own right, i.e. because we think it desirable that children should be able to exercise choice, but also we might relate it to other social learning objectives. There is, of course, no one way of meeting this objective, and a variety of experiences may have to be provided, for example, by encouraging children to go out and buy their own clothes, to decorate their bed-space according to their own wishes, to be given some choice in what they eat at mealtimes and when they eat. Now direct observations cannot be made of whether children are exercising 'choice', which is an abstract concept, but observations can be made of:

(a)   whether the conditions of the programme enable children to learn how to make choices, and
(b)   the extent to which the children individually or collectively actually learn how to do so.

The scales, therefore, can be used to indicate, for example, whether all children decorate their bed-space (which might reflect lack of choice); whether most do or only a few. But they provide a qualitative rather than quantitative assessment which then stimulates discussion about the desirability and shortcomings of practices within the programme so that appropriate changes and improvements can be made. All aspects of the programme can be critically examined in similar ways.

At individual case level   Objective setting methods can also be used to help the development of and evaluation of individual treatment programmes as exemplified by the task-centred approaches of Reid and Epstein (1972), the behaviour modification techniques used at 'Achievement Place', which have already been mentioned and the 'goal attainment scales' developed by Kiresuk and Sherman (1968). In Great Britain Reith (1979) describes a useful case-planning tool based on a unitary model which can be adapted for group care purposes and in a short but useful article Gregory and Tweddle (1979) discuss how behavioural objectives can be developed and applied in child care settings. The technology which would enable a more proactive approach to case-planning and evaluation is certainly available but needs to be implemented on a wider scale. One of the major advantages of these planning tools is that the children can be involved in the setting of their objectives and targets, which means that they can learn how to participate more fully in decision-making and be more involved in evaluating their own progress.

Peer evaluation A second approach consistent with a model of 'critical appraisal' comes from thinking about the projects undertaken by the Development Group of the Department of Health and Social Security (DHSS). Several of these projects are described in reports issued by the DHSS including one undertaken in a group care setting where major changes in organization and practices were under consideration (DHSS, 1976). The Development Group members act as consultants and their projects are often developed in two or more stages. The first stage often takes the form of a conference or workshop attended by people who are invited for their ability to contribute from a variety of perspectives. Consumers may also be included in the membership. Workshop members are given a number of tasks, aided by any relevant research data and 'keynote' papers. From its subsequent analysis the conference comes up with a number of recommendations for changes and improvements. The management of the programme then have to decide which recommendations to accept and implement. Usually a follow-up conference is arranged to review any changes that have been made.

The concept of the 'development exercise' is an interesting one, although it is difficult to assess just how effective it really is in bringing about change. The principles could certainly be followed on a smaller scale, for example, by a local authority bringing groups of staff together to help each other evaluate their respective programmes using outside consultants if necessary and possibly some of the goal attainment methods discussed in the previous section.

Evaluation by 'informed observers' A third approach comes from considering the functions of the monitoring and review services that were formerly performed by the Home Office Children's Department and which have been taken over by the Social Work Services of the DHSS. Formal inspections are now considered to be old-fashioned – inspectors are 'advisors'. Although few would wish to return to the old style of inspection, the gap left by the Inspectorate's change of role has never been adequately filled. Some might consider it regrettable that the recommendations of the Personal Social Services Council (1977) for a 'local inspectorate' to provide a monitoring and review service have never been implemented.

'Inspections' belong to the 'outsider-looking-in' type of evaluation of which several examples can be found in the literature. Durkin and Durkin (1975) describe an evaluation programme undertaken by Bower *et al.* (1969) involving four competent and professional observers, all knowledgeable in the field of residential child care, who evaluated a residential programme at intervals over a period of two years and in the process shared and discussed their findings with the staff. A similar study in Britain was made at a Youth Treatment Centre for highly disturbed young people in need of care and treatment. This study which examined the appropriateness of methods of care and treatment developed at the Centre was undertaken by a committee representing the different disciplines employed there. The methods used included interviews, group discussion, participant observation, and analysis of documents and records, and the findings were written up in a report which was submitted to the management and staff (DHSS, 1979).

Another example but from a different perspective is provided by Douglas (1980) from his experience as a Placement Officer employed by a local authority social services department. The components of this job included monitoring and reviewing the residential resources currently used by the local authority and visiting and evaluating other resources that might be used in the future. An important aspect of the work here was the contact made with residential staff to encourage them to evaluate their own work and thus participate more in organizational decision-making.

There appear to be advantages and disadvantages to evaluation by 'informed observers'. In terms of simplicity, flexibility, and inexpensiveness compared to a long-term research project there are obvious advantages. More importantly the feedback given to direct service staff and their managers, who easily become very inward looking, provides fresh perspectives; enabling the reconsideration of tasks which may be receiving lower priority than they ought to be receiving. The feedback may also give clues as to why certain difficulties are being experienced and suggest lines of action to resolve them. Also it is not always necessary to employ the services of so-called 'experts' to make this kind of evaluation. For example, some of the most useful evaluative feedback I received as a practitioner came from students on practice placements at the centre. One study by a postgraduate student from a social work course has been published elsewhere (de Barros and Payne, 1978).

The main weakness of the approach, as I see it, comes about when trying to fulfil the rigorous conditions of the scientific paradigm, without having the necessary resources of time, instrumentation, and expertise; in consequence a second or third rate piece of research, which is of little use to anyone, tends to be produced. I suggest this type of evaluation is more effective when interpreted as critical appraisal, with the evaluator speaking from but also articulating his own values and assumptions, laying out his criteria so that they too can be subject to critical analysis and debate. This does not imply that 'hard' data should be ignored, but judgments based on different kinds of evidence need to be carefully sorted out.

From experience as an evaluator and of being evaluated it is also evident that a number of conditions need to be met. First, the role of the evaluator needs to be clearly defined and his position must be made clear to all staff, who can be easily threatened and confused by the presence of the evaluator(s). Secondly, contractual relationships must be established between all parties involved about the purposes and methods to be used in making the evaluation, and issues of confidentiality, etc., thoroughly discussed. Thirdly, particular attention must be paid to the arrangements needed for giving feedback, in terms of the *type* of feedback to be given: verbal, written or both; also *when* it should be given and to *whom*.

Conclusions

In this discussion I have pointed to some of the issues involved in evaluating group care and considered how programme evaluation might develop in Great Britain where work to date has been piecemeal. The more substantive literature on the subject is based on North American experience and because of this I have throughout attempted to cite British work. From my assessment of the 'state of the art' in Britain more evaluation is clearly needed, not least of the 'new' forms of care that have emerged in recent years.

However, more evaluation is not just a question of more research. As my brief survey shows this too is badly needed, particularly to examine the relative effectiveness and benefits of different programmes and methods. Overall, however, a differential approach to evaluation work is required; different approaches for different purposes.

It is also evident that more attention is needed on training programmes to teaching practitioners to evaluate their practice and develop a more proactive orientation. Group care workers receive little or no training in planned intervention so that they do not learn how to set goals and priorities, which can be evaluated over time, using explicit criteria and measures to assess degrees of success achieved. Training programmes give much higher priority to developing knowledge and skills for direct practice, and practitioners appointed to senior positions often possess few skills in programme management.

Every setting has the mechanisms for monitoring and continuous evaluation but these mechanisms have to be used effectively and as part of a co-ordinated evaluation strategy. Regular evaluations need to be able to examine programme effectiveness and efficiency, taking into account the views of the many groups of people with some interest in its course and outcome, not least staff and the consumers. These evaluations should make judicious use of 'hard' and 'soft' line methods.

Finally, it should be remembered that criteria of relevance and utility should always be to the fore; evaluations are of little consequence unless they contribute to service-development and decision-making. Costs also need to be considered. Evaluations are by no means self-justifying and the question 'Is it worthwhile?' is one that always needs to be asked.

Notes

(1) Lecturer in Residential Social Work at the National Institute for Social Work, London, England.

(2) I would like to make some acknowledgement of my colleagues, Robin Douglas, Clive Miller, and Tony Scott, all Lecturers in Management Studies at the National Institute for Social Work, London, whose ideas on evaluation have certainly influenced the writing of this paper.

References

Algie, J. (1972a) Evaluating the Social Services – 1. *British Hospital Journal and Social Services Review* 11 November: 2523–524.

Algie, J. (1972b) Evaluating the Social Services – 2. *British Hospital Journal and Social Services Review* 18 November: 2586–588.

Allerhand, M. E., Weber, R., and Haug, M. (1966) *Adaptation and Adaptability: The Bellefaire Follow-Up Study.* New York: Child Welfare League of America.

Barlow, G. (1979) Glenthorne Youth Treatment Centre. In C. Payne and K. J. White (eds) *Caring for Deprived Children International Case Studies of Residential Settings.* London: Croom Helm.

Berry, J. (1976) *Daily Experience in Residential Life. A Study of Children and Their Care Givers.* London: Routledge & Kegan Paul.

Bower, E., Laurie, R., Strutter, C., and Fetherland, R. (1969) *Project Re-ed: New Concepts for Helping Emotionally Disturbed Children: Evaluation by a Panel of Visitors.* Nashville, Tennessee: John F. Kennedy Centre for Research on Education and Human Development, George Peabody College of Teachers.

Brown, B. J. (1977) Gilbey House: A Token Economy Management Scheme in a Residential School for Adolescent Boys in Trouble. *British Association for Behavioural Psychotherapy Bulletin* 5 (3): 79–89.

Brown, B. J. (1978) Behavioural Approaches to Child Care. *British Journal of Social Work* 8 (1): 313–26.

Burns, J. L. (1976) The Evaluation of Research Data and the Orientation of Results Papers; A Commentary on 'Residential Treatment and its Effects on Delinquency'. *Community Homes Schools Gazette* December: 411–16.

Cawson, P. (1978) *Community Homes: A Study of Residential Staff.* Department of

Health and Social Security, Statistics and Research Division, Report No. 2. London: Her Majesty's Stationery Office.

Cawson, P. and Martell, M. (1979) *Children referred to Closed Units.* Department of Health and Social Services, Report No. 5. London: Her Majesty's Stationery Office.

Clarke, R. V. G. and Cornish, D. B. (1972) *The Controlled Trial in Institutional Research – Paradigm or Pitfall for Penal Evaluations.* Home Office Research Studies, 15. London: Her Majesty's Stationery Office.

Clarke, R. V. G. and Cornish, D. B. (1975) *Residential Treatment and its Effects on Delinquency.* Home Office Research Studies, 32. London: Her Majesty's Stationery Office.

Clarke, R. V. G. and Sinclair, I. (1973) *Towards More Effective Treatment Evaluation.* Strasbourg: Council of Europe.

de Barros, J. and Payne, C. (1978) Teamwork: A Study of Roles and Relationships. *Community Homes Schools Gazette* Part 1, February; Part 2, March.

Department of Health and Social Security (1979) *Report of St Charles Youth Treatment Centre Evaluation Team.* London: DHSS Children's Division.

Dinnage, R. and Pringle, K. (1967) *Residential Child Care: Facts and Fallacies.* London: Longman.

Douglas, R. (1980) Evaluating the Effectiveness of Different Establishments. In *Why Care?* Residential Care Association Annual Review. London: Residential Care Association Publications.

Dunlop, A. (1975) *The Approved School Experience.* London: Her Majesty's Stationery Office.

Durkin, R. P. and Durkin, A. B. (1975) Evaluating Residential Treatment Programmes for Disturbed Children. In M. Guttentag and E. L. Struening (eds) *Handbook of Evaluation Research,* Vol. 2. Beverly Hills, California: Sage Publications.

Elery, L., Phillips, L., Phillips, E. A., Fixsen, D. L., and Wolf, M. M. (1974) *The Teaching-Parent Family Handbook.* Lawrence, Kansas: University of Kansas.

Freire, P. (1972) *The Pedagogy of the Oppressed.* Harmondsworth, Middlesex: Penguin Books.

Gill, O. (1974) *Whitegate: An Approved School in Transition.* Liverpool: Social Research Series, Liverpool University Press.

Goldberg, E. M. (1979) *Ends and Means in Social Work: Development and Outcome of a Case-Review System for Social Workers.* National Institute Social Services Library No. 35. London: Allen & Unwin.

Gregory, P. and Tweddle, D. (1979) Teaching Independence in Community Homes. *Social Work Service* 19 March: 48–52. London: Department of Health and Social Security.

Harlesden Community Project (1979) *A Community Project in an Inner City Local Authority by a Group of Workers from the Harlesden Community Project 1971–76.* Ilkley, England: Owen Wells.

Hersen, M. and Barlow, D. H. (1976) *Single Case Experiment Designs.* Elmsford, New York: Pergamon Press.

Hoghugi, M. S., Cumiskey, P. D., McAffrey, A., and Muckley, A. (1977) *The Franklin Token Economy.* Aycliffe, England: Aycliffe Studies of Problem Children.

Hoghugi, M. A. (1978) *Troubled and Troublesome – Coping with Severely Disruptive Children*. London: Burnett Books in association with André Deutsch.

Kahan, B. (ed.) (1976) *Approved School to Community Home*. Department of Health and Social Security Development Group. Social Work Service. London: Her Majesty's Stationery Office.

Key, M., Hudson, P., and Armstrong, J. (1976) *Evaluation Theory and Community Work*. London: Young Volunteer Force.

King, R. P., Raynes, R. D., and Tizard, J. (1971) *Patterns of Residential Care*. London: Routledge & Kegan Paul.

Kiresuk, T. J. and Sherman, R. E. (1968) Goal Attainment Scaling: A General Method for Evaluating Comprehensive Community Health Programs. *Community Mental Health Journal* 4 (6): 443–53.

Kushlick, A. (1972) Evaluating Residential Services for the Mentally Handicapped. In G. McLachlan (ed.) *Approaches to Action – A Symposium on Services for the Mentally Ill and Handicapped*. Oxford: Oxford University Press for Nuffield Provincial Hospitals Trust.

Kushlick, A. (1974) Evaluating Residential Services for Mentally Handicapped Children. In J. K. Wing and H. Hafner (eds) *Roots of Evaluation. The Epidemiological Basis for Planning Psychiatric Services. An International Symposium*. Oxford: Oxford University Press.

Manning, N. (1979) Evaluating the Therapeutic Community. In R. D. Hinshelwood and N. Manning (eds) *Therapeutic Communities: Reflections and Progress*. London: Routledge & Kegan Paul.

Millham, S., Bullock, R., and Cherrett, P. (1975) *After Grace – Teeth: A Comparative Study of the Residential Experience of Boys in Approved Schools*. London: Human Context Books.

Millham, S. (1977) Intermediate Treatment: Symbol or Solution. *Youth in Society* 26 December: 22–4; 27 February 1978: 14–16.

Millham, S., Bullock, R., and Hosie, K. (1978) *Locking Up Children: Secure Provision within the Child-Care System*. Farnborough, Hants: Saxon House.

Nelson, R. H., Singer, M. J., and Johnson, L. O. (1978) The Application of a Residential Treatment Evaluation Model. *Child Care Quarterly* 7 (2): 164–73.

Oswin, M. (1971) *The Empty Hours: A Study of the Weekend Life of Handicapped Children in Institutions*. Harmondsworth: Penguin Books.

Oswin, M. (1978) *Children Living in Long-Stay Hospitals*. Spastics International Medical Publications. Research Monograph No. 5. London: Heinemann Medical.

Paige, R. and Clark, E. A. (1977) *Who Cares? Young People in Care Speak Out*. London: National Children's Bureau.

Paley, J. (1977) Intermediate Treatment Research Project. Lancaster University, Department of Social Administration. In J. Thomes (1977) *Profile: Research and Evaluation in Intermediate Treatment*. Leicester: National Youth Bureau.

Paley, J. and Thorpe, D. (1974) *Children: Handle with Care*. Leicester: National Youth Bureau.

Payne, C. (1979) A Children's Centre. In C. Payne and K. White (eds) *Caring for Deprived Children, International Case Studies of Residential Settings*. London: Croom Helm.

Personal Social Services Council (1977) *Residential Care Reviewed. The Report of the Residential Care Working Group incorporating Daily Living Questions for Staff.* London: Personal Social Services Council.

Phillips, E., Fixsen, D., and Wolf, M. (1979) Residential Adolescent Treatment. In C. Payne and K. White (eds) *Caring for Deprived Children, International Case Studies of Residential Settings.* London: Croom Helm.

Phillips, E. L., Phillips, E. A., Fixen, D., and Wolf, M. (1974) *The Teaching-Family Handbook.* Lawrence, Kansas: University Printing Service.

Prosser, H. (1976) *Perspectives on Residential Child Care. An Annotated Bibliography. Research and Other Literature in the United States, Canada and Great Britain 1966–1974.* A National Children's Bureau Report. Windsor, Berkshire: National Foundation for Education Research.

Reichertz, D. in collaboration with Kislowicz, L. and Stalinski, J. (1978) *Residential Care: The Impact of Institutional Policies, Structures and Staff on Residential Children.* Montreal: McGill University, School of Social Work.

Reid, W. J. and Epstein, L. (1972) *Task Centred Casework.* New York: Columbia University Press.

Rein, M. (1976) *Social Science and Public Policy.* Harmondsworth: Penguin Books.

Reinach, E. and Roberts, G. (1979) *Consequences – The Progress of 65 Children after a period of Observation and Assessment.* Portsmouth: Portsmouth Polytechnic/ Hants Social Services Department, Social Services and Research and Intelligence Unit.

Reith, D. (1979) A Family Assessment Guide. *Social Work Today* 10 (1): 18–19.

Righton, P. (1979) Ideals in Jeopardy. *Social Work Today* 11 (2): 15.

Scriven, N. (1972) The Methodology of Evaluation. In C. H. Weiss (ed.) *Evaluating Action Programs.* Boston, Massachusetts: Allyn & Bacon.

Social Sciences Research Council (1980) *Children in Need of Care – A Report to the Research Initiative Board.* London: SSRC.

Suchman, E. L. (1967) *Evaluative Research.* New York: Russell Sage.

Taylor, D. A. and Alpert, S. W. (1973) *Continuity and Support Following Residential Treatment.* New York: Child Welfare League of America.

Taylor, L., Lacey, R., and Bracken, D. (1980) *In Whose Best Interests? The Unjust Treatment of Children in Courts and Institutions.* London: Cobden Trust/MIND.

Thomas, G. (1975) *A Community-Oriented Evaluation of the Effectiveness of Child-Caring Institutions.* Athens, Georgia: Regional Institute of Social Welfare Research.

Thomes, J. (1977) *Profile: Research and Evaluation in Intermediate Treatment.* Leicester: National Youth Bureau.

Tizard, J., Sinclair, I., and Clarke, R. V. G. (1975) *Varieties of Residential Experience.* London: Routledge & Kegan Paul.

University of Birmingham (1979) *Clearing House for Local Authority Social Services Research* 5. Birmingham: University of Birmngham.

Warburton, W. (1979) Ends and Means in Intermediate Treatment. Cambridge Social Services Department. In University of Birmingham (1979) *Clearing House for Local Authority Social Services Research* 5. Birmingham: Univerity of Birmingham.

Ward, D. A. and Kassebaum, F. F. (1972) On Biting the Hand that Feeds: Some

Implications of Sociological Evaluations of Correctional Effectiveness. In C. H. Weiss (ed.) *Evaluating Action Programs*. Boston, Massachusetts: Allyn & Bacon.

Weiss, C. H. (1972) *Evaluating Action Programs*. Boston, Massachusetts: Allyn & Bacon.

White, K. (1979) Independent Long-Stay Children's Home. In C. Payne and K. White (eds) *Caring for Deprived Children, International Case Studies of Residential Settings*. London: Croom Helm.

Whittaker, J. K. (1979) *Caring for Troubled Children*. San Francisco and London: Jossey-Bass.

11 Cost factors in group care

Martin Knapp[1]

In recent years it has been rare indeed to find a change or development of child care policy or practice that has not had to run the gauntlet of a long line of 'But what does it cost?' questions. The economic problems that beset Western economies in the mid-1970s, precipitated by the so-called oil crisis, forced upon public, private, and voluntary providers of care a degree of cost consciousness hitherto unknown in the post-war period. It is true that for years each new policy initiative and each new extension of existing policies had to be viewed within a cost constraint, but that constraint was never as tight as the constraint faced today. Many an eminently reasonable policy change has been postponed, rejected, and at times abused because it has been felt to be 'too expensive'. As a consequence, the cost constraint has been the subject of considerable criticism, and the penny-pinching politician, the short-sighted accountant, and the hard-headed economist have come to be viewed as the chief villains of the piece. Social care services, it has long been felt, are the preserve of the social worker or the student of social policy. These services, it is argued, should not be the testing ground for economic theories or cannon fodder for central government fiscal policies. Costs, in short, are anathema to social care.

The move towards cost-consciousness has, to the economist at least, three saddening features: unwarranted denigration, unfortunate belatedness, and unselective over-reaction. The denigration, rather than applause, which greets each new attempt to impose a degree of 'cost effectiveness' or 'economic rationality' upon child care policies is the most immediately recognizable feature of current trends. Criticism of the introduction of the economic element into policy-making stems in part from a feeling that services as indubitably and inherently 'desirable' as child care should be above the vicissitudes of national economic welfare, and that public expenditure cuts should fall elsewhere. Similarly, private and voluntary caring agencies should be compensated for their unavoid-able difficulties. Such arguments unfortunately confuse ideology and rationality. Nobody would deny the need for child care or other personal social services, but it would be dangerous and foolish to argue that certain activities are beyond economic analysis. Very few activities in modern society are costless. Resources, including child care services, are scarce and therefore have a positive value or cost to society. Allocating resources in one way immediately implies the rejection of an alternative allocation. The current recession has heightened our awareness of scarcity, and it is scarcity which signals the arrival of the economist. If we want to make the best use of our scarce resources, if we want to deploy our available group care services in such a way as to maximize their effectiveness or their success, then we must ensure that we are getting value for money; in other words, we must take a long and careful look at the cost implications of a policy decision.

The second and related saddening feature of recent experience has been the fact that child care administrators – just like the administrators of other welfare services – have only turned to a careful examination of the costs of their services at a time of economic adversity. Most children in care in Britain are the responsibility of local authorities and these authorities sailed through the halcyon days of growth of expenditure and expansion of services with barely a fleeting backward glance at the cost trail left behind. When recession bit, and bit deep, it was these public providers of care who were shown to be least prepared for the challenge. Recession revealed an embarrassing ignorance of the basic principles of economic management and a distinct lack of both the necessary data and information for sensible policy making, and the requisite expertise for gathering and applying it.

We can do nothing about the second of these features, and we can only hope that the gradual acquisition of information and expertise, and the gradual realization of the need for careful cost planning, will help to remove the first feature. It is the third feature which is the subject of this paper. Faced with a shrinking budget and a growing potential clientele, politicians, administrators, and lower-level managers have grasped unselectively the nettles of cost information readily available or readily collected. There has been little discrimination among available information sets and even less apparent understanding of the problems of applying them in practice. Residential care has been given the 'Too Expensive' label, higher staffing ratios have been criticized for wasting valuable skilled resources, maintenance expenditure has been halved in the name of efficiency, and new capital projects – of which there have been precious few – have been pruned and delayed in the name of cost reduction. The sad fact about all this generally well-meant, frenetic activity is that it is largely misplaced and misdirected. Not only are administrators making either improper or inadequate use of the cost information that is currently available, but also this information is really not the kind of cost information that we should be using. If we *really* want to get value for money – and that means, if we *really* want to ensure that our available care resources are used in the best possible way – then we should be making specific collections of information which allow the proper and reliable computation and comparison of group care costs.

In the remainder of this paper, it is my intention to set out an 'ideal' cost measure for use in child care planning. It will be seen that the collection of the information necessary to obtain such an 'ideal' measure is itself costly and that therefore the administrator may, initially at least, prefer to make use of information currently available to him in the annual accounts drawn up by his treasurer. We therefore move on to a consideration of the uses of routinely available cost data, and at this point say a word or two about the types of routine information of *most* use for rational planning purposes. Our major concern here, however, will be how to use *sensibly* the available information, and this sensible use revolves around three issues: variability, comparability, and predictability. This leads us to the description of three popular techniques of cost analysis, techniques that have long been employed in more conventional areas of economists' concern but which have just as much validity in studying the 'production of care services' or the 'production of wellbeing' (Knapp, 1979a).

The economist's definition of cost

'What does it cost to provide residential care for a mentally handicapped child?' This apparently straightforward and unambiguous question might be answered with an apparently straightforward and unambiguous answer, like 'one hundred pounds per week'. But this and other similar questions deceive by their simplicity, for they really hide a multitude of other questions. 'One hundred pounds per week' is similarly a screen, a smoke screen of little intrinsic value in itself which hides the answer, the *real cost* of care.

To illustrate what we mean by the real cost of care, let us take up an example familiar to students of economics and of English literature – the tale of Robinson Crusoe. Suppose that Crusoe, on that eventful Friday when he first saw the footprints in the sand, had found not a fit, athletic man but instead a severely mentally handicapped child. Would Crusoe have thanked us for giving him 'one hundred pounds per week' to care for the unfortunate child? Not at all, for money was of no use to him on his desert island. Much more useful would have been a gourd of goat's milk or a net of fish, for in caring for the mentally handicapped child, Crusoe would have to give up the time he would otherwise have spent milking or fishing. The *cost* to Crusoe of caring for the mentally handicapped child could not be reckoned in pounds or dollars but only in terms of what he had lost (the milk and fish) by not using his time and energy in an alternative pursuit (milking and fishing). Of course, Daniel Defoe's hero did not find a mentally handicapped child but this distortion of a familiar story well illustrates the economist's meaning of cost. The cost of an article, a resource, or a service cannot, in general, be reckoned merely by reference to its price but must be gauged in terms of what is given up in order to have the article, resource, or service. Sometimes the price paid will be a good approximation to the value of what has been given up, but this is by no means always the case. Many resources and services are not bought and sold on the open market, and those that are have prices that are frequently and largely influenced by market distortions. This definition of cost – what the economist sometimes calls the *opportunity cost* – will be seen to be intuitively appealing, to have considerable validity in the context of social care, and to possess a certain indispensability when we try to assess 'efficiency', or at least when we attempt to get 'value for money'.

Crusoe, when faced with a mentally handicapped child, had given up his milking and fishing, in order to provide care: the giving of care had cost Crusoe the milk and fish he had not been able to collect. A little nearer home we can imagine a child care agency having to decide whether to build a new secure unit for disruptive children or to use the available financial resources to open three new day care units. In this sense, the cost of the secure unit is equal to the three day units foregone, and the cost of a day unit is equal to one-third of a secure unit. Alternatively, consider the case of the qualified social worker waiting in court to attend a five minute hearing for one of his juvenile clients charged with shop-lifting. The time spent in court might alternatively have been spent visiting the mother of another child on his caseload or perhaps attending an afternoon seminar on intermediate treatment work with juvenile delinquents. The cost of the court attendance is thus to be reckoned in terms of the opportunities missed by not visiting the other client or not attending the seminar. In each of these cases we are expressing the cost of supplying a service or employing a resource in terms of the value of opportunities that have been missed. For this reason the economist's conceptualization of cost is called the *opportunity cost*:

> 'The cost of using a resource in a particular service or mode of care is not (in general) the money cost or price of the resource, but is the benefit foregone, or opportunity lost, by not using the resource in its best alternative use.'

The value of this cost definition is that it emphasizes the fact that our need for cost information stems from our need to choose between alternative claims, wants, or needs. Scarcity implies choice, and the act of choice gives us our definition of cost. From this chain of logical statements we can pick out a number of implications and characteristics of our opportunity cost definition. Opportunity costs are context specific, they are inherently subjective, they require knowledge of the alternatives open to us, and they are rejected benefits and thus measurable in benefit terms. In practice these are not problematic, for the context specificity of opportunities makes the computations relatively easy. Generally, we shall use the going currency to measure them – pounds sterling or dollars – either because market prices are reasonably accurate enough to allow such a measure to be used, or because money is a convenient common *numeraire* in which to express these various costs. One characteristic of opportunity cost is very important – they are subjective – and it is this characteristic which leads us irrevocably to a consideration of the difference between private and social costs.

The distinction between private cost and social cost can be viewed from two perspectives, depending on whether we are talking about bare expenditures, that is, accounting costs, or about opportunity costs. For example, we might ask the head of a children's home to tell us the annual cost of running the home. Consulting the financial accounts, she would be able to list expenditures on staff, provisions, laundering, electricity and gas, and so on. The same question posed to the director of social services or the director of the child care agency might elicit a slightly different answer, for he would probably add expenditure on peripatetic teachers and social workers and the costs of central administration to the head's list. These two services are financed by the social services department or care agency but do not appear in the financial accounts of the home. We could then go on to ask the Secretary of State or Governor the same question and he would probably add to this list the cost of doctors' visits to the home. It is clear that in Britain the Secretary of State's list of expenditures covers all, or at least most, of the services received by children in the home. His list of expenditures is thus much closer to the *social* cost of care than either of the other two lists. Clearly, when reckoning the cost of a service we should include *all* costs or items of expenditure.

Of course, as we have argued in this chapter, we should really look beyond the monetary 'veil' of expenditure figures and instead calculate opportunity costs. The distinction between private and social costs then becomes rather more marked. The *private opportunity cost* of employing a resource in a given use is the value of that resource in the next best alternative use available to the employer. For example, the private opportunity cost to a social services department of using a minibus to ferry handicapped children to and from day centres might be the value of using the minibus to deliver meals to elderly people in their own homes. In contrast, the *social opportunity cost* of employing a resource in a given use is the value of that resource in the next best alternative use available to the *whole society*. It may be, for example, that if the minibus were not used to transport day centre clients then it would be employed to take school children to and from a local swimming pool.

Which costs should we be looking at in our analysis of child care services? Firstly, as we argued above, we should be concerned with *opportunity* costs and not accounting costs or expenditures if we are to use costs as a true reflection of the value of the resources. Secondly, we should be looking at *social* opportunity costs – the value of alternative uses of resources available to the whole society. By their very nature, most child care services are *social* services and so to concentrate only on opportunity costs to the child care agency or the group care unit would be illogical indeed. We should look at *all* the resources used in providing a given service, whether or not they are financed out of the agency's budget, and consider their alternative uses to society as a *whole*.

A word of warning would not go amiss at this point. It is quite likely that the efforts expended in calculating opportunity, rather than accounting, costs will not be appreciated by the holders of the purse strings. Much of the research conducted by child care agencies, whether public, voluntary, or private, is interested only in expenditure, or accounting costs will not be appreciated by the holders of the purse spective may not be greeted with open arms. Research emphasis of this kind is usually explained or excused by reference to the constrained budget, but it should be recognized as somewhat myopic and socially inefficient, and it can lead to the misallocation of scarce resources.

Expenditures and accounting costs

Opportunity costs are not, unfortunately, readily observable or measurable. For some resources or services there may be a market price which is sufficiently free of distortions to be a useful and reliable indicator of opportunity cost, but many resources used in the provision of child care services simply are not bought and sold on the open market, and even those that are may have prices so distorted by market imperfections that they are far from reflecting the social opportunity cost of employment. However, because opportunity cost collection itself imposes an opportunity cost on the administrator we shall frequently feel that annually collected and published expenditure figures will suffice. These expenditure figures, typically appearing in the annual accounts of each child care agency, and probably each separate group care unit, we shall refer to as the *accounting costs*. It is these accounting costs that are being quoted when an answer of 'one hundred pounds per week' is given to the question about residential care costs.

Accounting costs clearly have a number of potential uses for the child care administrator and planner, but it is rare to find them quoted sensibly or employed properly to their full advantage. Capital costs are often omitted or misquoted, current costs are frequently incomplete, and most cost figures tend not to be qualified by reference to the myriad of factors which influence them and which therefore make bare comparisons a hazardous practice. Capital figures quoted in annual accounts are generally listed as debt charges and revenue contributions to capital outlay. These items of expenditure, notional or otherwise, are principally determined by the age or vintage of the capital resources and the discounting procedures adopted by the accountant. A common form of depreciation accounting is straight-line charging, capital resources being assumed to depreciate steadily and linearly over time. This method therefore assumes that all depreciation is physical deterioration that accompanies the mere passage of time and the value losses occasioned by technological progress (obsolescence). Use-depreciation, the deterioration attributable to actually operating or using the capital, is not separately recorded. If we are to make sensible and valuable use of costs data we must be sure that our capital cost information is accurate and valid. As well as these problems of interpretation of published capital figures, the conventional form of accounts will ignore various current overhead and incidental costs. The costs of group care should ideally include administrative costs and the costs incurred in the employment of peripatetic skilled social workers, teachers, child psychiatrists, paediatricians, and so on. Excluding these cost elements will partially invalidate comparisons between, for example, residential and day care services, where the incidence of these peripatetic and overhead services will probably be very different. The major problem on this count is to decide where to stop the process of counting. Do we, for example, need to include the costs of collecting taxes when assessing the overall cost of a publicly provided child care service? The answer, of course, is both 'yes' and 'no', for we *should* be including these costs if we are making a comparison between private and public services and we can clearly omit them for the reason that they do not vary if we are comparing *between* public care services. A third difficulty encountered in the use of accounting costs arises because there is a myriad of factors which exert an influence upon the costs and expenditures of a child care agency or a group care unit and it would be folly indeed to make a comparison between service types without taking these into account. It is to these variations and the factors that account for them that we now turn.

Factors influencing the costs of group care

It is a source of considerable dismay to note the number of times bare comparisons are drawn between current expenditures on different child care services without qualification for the many influential factors liable to render any such comparisons irrelevant. It does not take a great deal of research to find evidence of great variations in cost for any one service, variations both between and within administrative boundaries. Consider, for example, the figures presented in *Table 11(1)*, taken from an annual publication of personal social services expenditure in England and Wales.

Table 11(1)   *Variations in expenditure per child week between English and Welsh local authorities, 1977–78*

	Expenditure per child week[a]		
Service[b]	*Mean*	*Minimum*	*Maximum*
Hostels and other community homes	72.54	39.96	167.14
Observation and assessment centres	120.58	57.08	267.73
Residential nurseries	109.41	54.88	230.63
Community schools	107.26	40.49	277.70
Homes for mentally handicapped	101.28	55.01	237.86
Day nurseries[c]	30.70	11.35	52.35

Notes:
[a] Net cost per child week excluding capital charges, in pounds sterling, 1977–78, averaged over all relevant care units in a local authority.
[b] Services provided by local authority only.
[c] Net cost per child day multiplied by 5.
Source: Chartered Institute of Public Finance and Accountancy, 1979.

Table 11(1) shows the net cost per child week for six different group care services provided by English and Welsh local authorities. Average, minimum, and maximum expenditures are tabulated. The extent of the variation between local authorities is very marked indeed. Part of this variation is almost certainly due to differences in the classification of services between authorities. For example, an 'ordinary' community home may provide extensive observation and assessment services but not be classified as such. This would push up the expenditure of what is apparently a non-specialist residential home and thus distort the figures. This problem of classification highlights the real and major problem of making cost comparisons – we can only draw meaningful conclusions from comparisons if we are comparing like with like!

There are clearly a large number of factors which must be taken into account before we can claim to be comparing 'like with like', and in an attempt to impose some order on these factors we adopt a simple theoretical framework previously described by the author (Knapp, 1979a; and see Davies and Knapp, 1980). The theoretical framework assumes that child care services are directed at a number of objectives. These objectives might include improvements in physical, psychological, emotional, and social well-being, in educational progress, in behaviour and maturity, and so on. The 'success' of a child care service can thus be couched in terms of the extent to which such objectives are attained. Of course, the degree of 'success' attained by the child care agency will be dependent upon a number of factors, which we can arrange in three broad groups – the personal characteristics of the children (age, sex, reasons for being in care, background experiences, personality traits, and so on), the various dimensions of social environment or caring milieu (regime, social control and independence, privacy, stimulation and participation, interaction and communication, flexibility, homogeneity), and thirdly the characteristics of the physical or resource environment (including staff characteristics, attitudes, and experiences not covered by social environmental features). The boon of such a theoretical framework is its isomorphic correspondence with the economist's theory of production. Where the economist would talk of inputs combining together in various proportions to produce outputs, we can conceive of the various personal, social, and resource characteristics combining and interacting with each other in order to determine the degree of success achieved by the child care agency or group care unit. By reference to the economist's discussion of cost variations, of which there are many, this correspondence between our simple theoretical model of child care and the economic theory of production allows us to disentangle the many cost-influencing factors in order to draw meaningful comparisons of relevance for policy making in this difficult area.[2]

I now turn to a brief discussion of the major influences upon the costs of child care taking advantage of the insights afforded by the correspondence between explaining child care 'success' and explaining variations in output in more conventional production processes. In this discussion I shall confine my attention to the average cost per child week in a 'short-run' model of cost determination. In other words, it is assumed that there are certain capital resources necessary for the provision of child care services which cannot be increased in the immediate future. It takes time to design, construct, and open a new children's home or day unit and the assumption here is that the child care administrator must accept his currently available stock of homes or units as fixed. This assumption allows us to ignore the capital cost implications of alternative designs of building while including the *current* resource implications of capital outlay. The former are more appropriately the concern of the architect than the economist. In this 'short-run' world we can distinguish seven groups of cost-influencing factors: some of them are causally influential, and most are closely inter-related.

(a)   *Resource prices*

In *Table 11(1)* we set out the range of variation in average cost per child week for six publicly provided services in England and Wales. What is not recorded is the fact that for four of the five residential services tabulated the maximum expenditures per child week were incurred by London Boroughs and the minimum expenditures by local authorities in the very north of England.[3] It is well known that employers of care staff in all the personal social services must pay much higher rates in the south-east of England than elsewhere. Thus, much of the nationwide cost variation is attributable to differences in area wage rates. The first thing we should do when comparing service costs, therefore, is to standardize all cost figures for geographical (and other exogenous) resource price differences. Of course, the child care agency may itself be partly responsible for pushing wage rates higher in its own area than in other areas of the country or region. Labour markets for even the most skilled care staff tend to be localized and a heavy demand for skilled staff may well force wages up.[4] Geographical variations in cost attributable to differences in price levels were identified and modelled in a recent national study of observation and assessment centres (Knapp, Curtis, and Giziakis, 1979). When drawing comparisons between the costs of services within a local authority area, price variations may be much less important although the non-pecuniary ramifications of a standard pay structure, for example, should be examined.

(b)   *Charges*

Again referring to *Table 11(1)*, we notice that the statistics published annually for all English and Welsh local authority child care services do not distinguish between gross and net expenditures per child week. Ideally, we should be concerning ourselves with *gross* costs, for these give a better indication than net costs of the resources employed in the care process. If we are also interested in the respective shares of total expenditure incurred by the care agency and the child's family then at a *second* stage we could examine costs net of charges. It is important, however, to keep these two stages independent and to examine them separately. Charging policies tend to vary quite markedly between different public providers, between public, voluntary, and private agencies, and over time. Different charging structures may be a consequence of a whole host of factors, including the ability of the child's family to contribute to the costs of care and the provider's ability to attract gifts and charitable funds, and there is no reason for these to be systematically or consistently related to gross costs or the effectiveness of the child care agency. If therefore we wish to use cost figures as indicators of the resources employed in the care process, and this is really the only major justification for using them, then it is gross and not net costs that we should be examining. Criticisms of the rising costs of care in the last few years lose much of their weight if we take notice of the fact that revenue from charges has risen less fast than gross cost. The oft-quoted rate of inflation of net costs thus exaggerates the changing true resource consequences of care over a period of time.

Thus far our discussion of cost-influencing factors has been concerned with the *definition* of cost and not its determination through the processes, characteristics, and effectiveness of care. The two factors distinguished above serve to illustrate the need to start off with a definition of cost which is consistent between care agencies, areas, and time periods. Unfortunately, even this most basic of requirements is violated in many commentaries on social service costs and the usefulness of such figures as those presented in *Table 11(1)* is thus called into question. Assuming that we are now in a position to draw up consistently defined costs, what other factors are liable to cause costs to vary?

(c) *Outputs*

The word 'output' is used as a convenient shorthand term for the degree of success achieved by a care unit in reaching its explicit or implicit policy objectives. Two types of output may be distinguished. *Final outputs* measure the changes in individual well-being, adjustment, behaviour, and so on, as compared with the levels of well-being (etc.) in the absence of a caring intervention. They thus related success to the ultimate and individual-level goals of care. The second type of output is the *intermediate output* which is an indicator of the care services themselves, of workload, rather than the effects of these services on the children. Intermediate outputs are thus concerned with lower-level, service delivery objectives. Obviously, if our aim is to furnish the policy maker with information and recommendations for improving the delivery of child care services then we should be trying to measure final and not just intermediate outputs. We can, for example, picture two identical children's homes facing identical prices, and receiving identical children into care. One home, however, may have an annual expenditure figure vastly in excess of the other simply because the head of the home feels that staff should have more time to spend with the children and therefore the home needs more staff. A bare comparison of intermediate outputs – the number of children in care, weighted perhaps by their ages, sex, and dependency – will not shed any light on the reasons for the difference in cost. On the other hand, if the subsequent development of the children is taken into account, if their abilities to behave and interact in some 'normal' manner is reckoned, then the home with more staff and thus higher expenditure will probably also be the home with the higher final outputs; that is, greater success in achieving ultimate child care objectives. There are of course a number of fundamental problems that have been ridden roughshod over in this preliminary discussion of the output concepts – the identification and agreement, if that is possible, of service objectives and the measurement of success being principal among them, but the general thrust of the argument should be clear and, hopefully, widely accepted.

How then does the cost of care vary with the level of output? Firstly the two will generally be positively related, higher costs being associated with higher final and intermediate outputs. Secondly, we can expect the cost of each marginal or additional unit of output to differ from the cost of the previous unit. Consider for simplicity a very simple intermediate output indicator – the number of children in a home. We would reasonably expect to observe 'economies of scale' in child care, cost per child falling gradually as more children are accommodated in the home. These economies result from the more extensive use of fixed capital resources (with a fixed cost), from the fact that variable resource inputs increase less than proportionately with outputs, from the specialization of staff and other resources in areas of greatest competence made possible by larger scale[5] and from the bulk buying of some consumables.[6] Remaining in this intermediate output world we can also distinguish one or two reasons why the average cost per child may tend to rise beyond a certain scale of home – the burden of management and administration may increase to such an extent that inefficiencies creep in, the supply prices of scarce resources will be forced up by excess demand, and general inefficiencies will arise with resource implications. These are the conventional arguments used by economists to explain the observed curvilinear relationship between average cost and scale (Silbertson, 1972) and these would seem to be the factors accounting for similar observations in previous work on public child care costs (Knapp, 1977; Knapp, Curtis, and Giziakis, 1979). If we now move from intermediate to final outputs, the arguments about scale economies become more complicated and more interesting. If output is conceptualized in terms of child development then we must concern ourselves with the organizational and personal ramifications of large scale. In their classic study of residential care for the mentally handicapped, King, Raynes, and Tizard (1971) found no association between home size or living unit size and a child management practices scale, and Sinclair and Heal (1976) reached a similar conclusion from research on community homes. However, Grygier (1975) found that size was associated with low participation rates in activities, low co-operation with educators, and disciplinarian attitudes in his work on Canadian Training Schools. Furthermore, the Curtis Committee Report (1946), which provided the blueprint for the Children Act of 1948 and thus the first major statement of the British government's philosophy of child care, proposed that large institutions be abandoned in favour of small 'family' group homes with no more than twelve children under the charge of a married couple. A more recent central government study of British observation and assessment centres argued that:

> 'an assessment centre should not be so large that it is in danger of becoming institutionalised, nor so small that it would be uneconomic to provide the staff and specialist facilities necessary for thorough observation, diagnosis and assessment. For these reasons, we suggest that for an assessment centre an upper limit of about sixty places is appropriate. We realise that the size of any one centre will be determined to some extent by its geographical situation and by the area it serves, but we think that some children will need a range of facilities and expertise greater than that which could be provided in a small assessment centre. Within any centre there is likely to be some breakdown into smaller groups for various purposes.'
>
> (Department of Health and Social Security, 1971 : 69)

The introduction of final output considerations thus complicates the picture greatly, but it is this complication which holds the key to the successful marriage of the economic, sociological, and psychological approaches to the organization and planning of child care services.

(d) *Activity*

As well as the level of output, whether intermediate or final, it has been suggested that the costs of providing a service are also related to the *rate* of production of output. In a group care context, we should thus examine the influence of the rates of admission, turnover, or occupancy and the average length of stay. There are costs associated with receiving a child into care, particularly because more staff resources are required to help the child adjust to his or her new environment and because of administrative duties, and for this reason we might expect higher admission or turnover rates to push up average costs. The argument for examining the occupancy rate is that there are many costly resources, principally staff resources, which are geared to a particular level of operation and which cannot easily be adjusted to short term changes in occupancy rates. If a home is temporarily under-occupied, in so far as it has more spare places than usual, then other things being equal we would expect to see the average cost per child being slightly higher than usual. Finally we should also be looking at the association between cost and average length of stay, more especially in group care units with a specialist function. Thus, for example, the common problem of the 'silting up' of observation and assessment centres because of difficulties with delays in assessing children and placing them in suitable caring environments has the effect of 'wasting' the skilled resources available in these centres and pushing costs above the expected level (Brown, 1976; Harris, 1978; Knapp, Curtis, and Giziakis, 1979).

(e) *Aspects of care*

Probably the most important of all the influences upon the cost of child care, and certainly the influence of most relevance to the policy maker, is the level of final output discussed in (c) above. However, final outputs are also the most difficult to conceptualize and measure. Without the facilities afforded by a fairly expensive, longitudinal study of a large number of group care units, it will probably be impossible to include valid and reliable indicators of final output in, say, a costs study. However, the alternatives open to the researcher are capable of providing a number of valuable insights into the cost-output relationship. From previous research on child development, on the effects of interactions and attitudes in group care, of regime and independence, stimulation and privacy, it should be possible to draw up a list of factors and practices which have been found to be ameliorative in the developmental and caring processes. Drawing on longitudinal research of the type conducted by, among many others, Skeels and Tizard, provides insights of this kind (Skeels and Dye, 1939; Skeels, 1942; Tizard, 1970; Tizard, 1974; Tizard *et al.*, 1972; see also Rutter and Madge, 1976; Whittaker, 1978). The aim would be to identify care practices and other incidental factors associated with 'successful' child care and development, collect information on these practices and factors in the course of a relatively inexpensive cross-sectional research study, and examine their influence upon the costs incurred by the group care unit. This clearly takes us back to our discussion of the analogy between the economist's theory of production and the child care process, for basically one would be aiming to collect information on the non-resource correlates of successful care.[7] It should be emphasized that the availability of a reasonably comprehensive set of reliable final output indicators would obviate the need for such input and intermediate indicators.

(f) Child characteristics

One important set of factors which influence the success or otherwise of child care are the characteristics of the children themselves. Basic characteristics like age, sex, and handicapping conditions have obvious staffing implications, but aspects of personality and attitudes may also be important. Because of their impact on final output it would probably be unnecessary to include these factors as well as final output indicators but this is partly an empirical matter. In previous research on observation and assessment centres the sex ratio of children was significantly related to average cost, and work on old people's homes found resident dependency to be a very important influence (Davies and Knapp, 1978; Knapp, Curtis and Giziakis, 1979). Much of the observed variation in child characteristics between units and areas can be attributed to differences in policy. In England and Wales, local authorities adopt often quite different strategies for child care, some preferring to maintain a relatively large residential care sector, others favouring foster care or supervision at home. The relative size of assessment and other specialist facilities also varies between areas. These policy differences will be translated into differences in the characteristics of children found in any one type of care facility, because of the different roles that these facilities must therefore play (Davies, Barton and McMillan, 1972). In addition, differences in demand or, more correctly, need between areas will have important ramifications for child care policies and thereby costs (Bebbington, 1976; Bebbington and Giziakis, 1979; Curtis, 1979).

(g) Capital stock

Some aspects of the capital stock, particularly the design of the building and the durable resources used for care, will have implications for staffing, for energy resources, and thus for costs. Furthermore, these influences will probably not be picked up by the other cost-influencing factors mentioned above. Homes with oil-fired central heating will now appear to be rather more expensive relative to other homes than they were ten years ago. Of rather more importance in view of the labour-intensiveness of child care are the staffing implications of building design. The implications for child care costs are probably not dissimilar to those for the costs of care for old people, where the combination of a poorly designed building and a dependent clientele push up staffing requirement (Knapp, 1979b).

Using cost information for policy making

These seven groups of cost-influencing factors vary in a number of ways. Of immediate interest is the variation in the availability of information to the policy maker. As argued before, the most important group of factors is the set of final output indicators but these are notoriously hard to obtain, and even those child care agencies with comprehensive record systems may be hard pressed to accurately assess the development of the children in their care, and thus the success of the agency in pursuing its ultimate objectives. In contrast, most care agencies will have to hand reliable information on certain basic child characteristics (age, sex, reasons for care, background), on operating characteristics and activity indicators (admission and discharge rates, occupancy levels, lengths of stay), on charges and input prices, and on certain other aspects of care. Armed with this information it would then be possible so to standardize the available expenditure figures as to make comparisons between care units, agencies, and time periods very much more valuable for policy purposes. Until these basic factors are taken into account, many of them being outside the domain of control of the unit or agency itself, it is simply absurd to make recommendations on the basis of bare expenditure figures. Unfortunately, it is all too common to observe this method of policy making in practice.

For the purposes of policy making there are three major cost analytic techniques used by the economist: cost benefit analysis, cost effectiveness analysis, and cost function analysis. The basic principles and uses of these three methodologies have been set out and discussed in the context of child care on a previous occasion (Knapp, 1979a) and the arguments are not repeated here. It is sufficient to note here that cost benefit and cost effectiveness analyses are designed to answer questions about a small number of alternative projects or care services, such as: 'Is care service A worthwhile?', 'How much of A is worthwhile?' and 'Is A more worthwhile than B?' In each case the criterion 'worthwhile' is defined in terms of cost-benefit differences or cost-effectiveness ratios. Cost effectiveness analysis differs from cost benefit analysis in so far as the benefits or outputs of the project or care service are not valued in monetary terms. Cost effectiveness analysis cannot therefore answer questions of the first variety, for costs are not immediately comparable with outputs. The relative analytical and computational ease of the cost effectiveness method must thus be balanced against the greater power of the cost benefit method, and for this reason economists have sought far and wide for methods of valuing outputs in monetary terms. Pearce (1978) and Williams and Anderson (1975) give good accounts of the progress that has been made in this difficult area of benefit valuation.

The third method of analysis, cost function analysis, is rather more basic than the other two and provides a useful methodology both for standardizing bare cost figures for the variety of influential factors discussed above and for examining the cost-output relationship. The statistical technique used is multiple regression analysis. To describe the technique we may adapt Dean's (1976) argument by working through the eight stages of cost function analysis, illustrating each stage with a brief account of a study of English and Welsh community home costs currently being undertaken by the author.[8]

(1) *Select a care unit suitable for analysis* Ideally we should be looking at largely autonomous care units, such as separate residential homes or day units. Homes adopting 'family group' designs probably do not keep separate accounts for each group, so that cost information would not be available for a more disaggregated research design. In the community homes study, the individual home was chosen as the relevant unit of analysis. At this stage we should ensure that we have observations on enough care units to undertake multiple regression analyses.

(2) *Decide on the measurement of output* The researcher must decide whether he is going to seek information on final outputs or indicators of aspects of care which have previously been shown to be associated with final outputs. Only measures of intermediate output (child days), activity (occupancy rates), child characteristics (at a local authority level), and policies (again at a local authority level) are being used in our community homes work.

(3) *Determine the time unit of observation* Child care practices and policies vary almost daily within agencies and within units, but expenditure figures are rarely available for periods of less than one year. Only annual expenditure data were available for the present study. Much of the true variation in cost and thus the true cost-output relationship will be missed if the true unit of observation is too long.

(4) *Choose the period of analysis* In this case we are concerned with the choice between a cross-sectional or longitudinal design. While expenditure figures may be available for a number of years, it is rare indeed to find sufficient information on the major causal factors for each of a number of time periods to undertake a longitudinal study. The community homes research is being conducted on a sample of 1099 homes with data for 1977–78. The two alternative designs do allow slightly different policy questions to be answered.

(5) *Decide on the measure of cost* Ideally we would be using social opportunity cost figures, but the cost of collecting these figures will be considerable and we must generally rely on expenditure figures. Our

earlier discussion of expenditures and accounting costs described the major elements of cost to be included. In our study of community homes we are including all current expenditures, with the exception of debt charges and revenue contributions to capital outlay. Overhead administrative costs and capital costs have not been included although ideally these would not be omitted. The cost concept of interest should also be selected at this point, the choice being between average cost and total cost.

(6) *Deflate the cost data* At this stage we introduce the first two of the influential factors described above, correcting the expenditure figures for charges (to give us gross costs) and for resource prices. Deflation may be achieved directly by weighting the cost figures, or indirectly by including price data in the regression equation. In the present study by the author the latter course has been chosen, resource price information being available at a local authority level.

(7) *Match costs with outputs and other factors* Provided that there are no problems of associating an output observation with a cost observation (such as time lags in payments for resources), we may now proceed with the multiple regression analysis. The output variables and data for the other cost-influencing factors are now used as regressors to 'explain' variations in the standardized cost figures.

(8) *Select the form of the function* The researcher must now exercise considerable ingenuity and expertise in order to obtain that form of the multiple regression equation which best fits the available data and which accords most closely with reality. It is at this stage that the vast 'science' of econometrics comes into play, and this final stage can take a long time to complete particularly if, as in our present study, the number of influential factors is large and their influences various and highly intercorrelated.

Having completed these eight stages, the researcher will have a single equation linking the average or total expenditure by a child care agency or unit in a given time period to a number of influential factors. This *cost function* relationship can then be used to cast light on a number of policy issues.

Firstly, cost functions ensure that costs are viewed and compared within a proper theoretical context; that is, extraneous and exogenous influences upon the cost of care are taken into account before policy implications are examined. If the 'production of welfare' analogy is accepted as a valid representation of the child care process, then the cost function follows logically and immediately. The cost function approach co-ordinates and synthesizes the myriad of potential influences upon cost. An immediate corollary is that the estimated function allows us to assess and quantify the impact of the various causal factors upon cost. If the balance of care between residential, day, and foster care is to be altered, the cost function will tell us the cost or resource implications of the policy change. Similarly we are able to assess the cost implications of policies to use small rather than large homes, to locate regional assessment centres or secure units in rural rather than urban areas, to convert existing premises into day units rather than erect new purpose-built units, and so on. An important implication of this property is the fact that the cost function allows us to allocate joint costs. Within a residential home or a day unit, the children exhibit a great variety of needs and characteristics. The estimated cost function allows the researcher and policy maker to assess the resource implications of care for each child or each need characteristic. This property is especially valuable for comparing costs between modes of care where the varieties and balances of needs and characteristics probably differ to a considerable degree. In this way, child care policies can be examined from an economic perspective at an *individual* level.

There may be a number of alternative modes of care for a child with a given configuration of characteristics and needs. The policy maker should be concerned to allocate services to clients in order to achieve the best possible use of the available resources. This requires that the pattern of care services be as near as possible to achieving the ultimate objectives of the system whilst making efficient use of the scarce, and therefore costly, resources that are available. Only by taking account of the cost-influencing factors described earlier can we hope to achieve an efficient allocation of society's resources which has the desirable repercussions for the caring process. Child care agencies which impose charges can make use of an estimated cost function to set differential charging rates tailored to the characteristics of clients and services. This may be particularly useful for public authorities sharing regional assessment or other specialist facilities.

Until fairly recently the economic element in the planning of welfare service policies was relatively minor. Public expenditure cutbacks and the general economic recession have forced upon policy makers the need to examine economic and particularly cost factors rather more carefully. In this chapter some of the principles of cost analysis have been set out and illustrated with respect to child care services. The principal aim of economic analysis is the efficient allocation of scarce resources. Of course, efficiency is a very difficult concept to define and operationalize in a care context, but the economic approach, and thus the cost function approach, to planning child care services represents nothing more than an attempt to explicate and formalize a decision making process which has almost entirely been implicit and informal in the past, and which has been wasteful of available resources. Wasting resources in one location, which basically means using more resources than needed to attain a given set of objectives, leaves fewer resources for use in other locations. In other words, fewer services can be provided and fewer child needs met, through public, voluntary, or private care. By taking a closer and more careful look at child care costs we may be able to waste fewer resources and meet more needs.

Notes

(1) Lecturer in Economics and Research Fellow in the Personal Social Services Research Unit, University of Kent at Canterbury. The author would like to thank Sarah Curtis for comments on an earlier draft of this paper.

(2) The analogy we draw in particular is between the economist's production function and the child care researcher's attempt to 'explain' success in terms of care styles and milieux. In our discussion of cost variations we thus draw on the vast and various cost function literature to indicate the main influences on cost and their position in a logical framework of explanation and comparison. It should be emphasized that we should always be looking at the cost *function* and not the cost *equation* (cf. Hall, 1978), the latter being no more than an accounting identity which provides little or no information of value for policy making. A recent and very comprehensive account of cost function methodologies is provided by Dean (1976).

(3) The exception was residential care for mentally handicapped children.

(4) Even with nationally or regionally agreed wage scales, competition among employers will tend to push up the 'real' price of staff. This may come about by employers taking on slightly inferior staff, by regrading posts, or by offering non-pecuniary advantages such as accommodation, less disruptive hours, and so on. Non-pecuniary competition of this kind in the market for qualified social workers characterized the London authorities a few years ago.

(5) A small home may not keep a child psychiatrist fully occupied on tasks for which she is especially qualified and she may thus perform 'ordinary' care tasks more suitably undertaken by other care staff. In a larger home the child psychiatrist would be more fully and usefully employed (Harris, 1978).

(6) This is a contentious issue, as witnessed by the cornflakes served for breakfast in children's homes in Northern Ireland. Economies were sought through the bulk-buying of provisions and supplies for homes, but resulted in 'cornflakes which arrive in plain boxes marked "not for resale", catering managers imposing portion control on units, and government-issued soap and other toileteries'. These supplies were felt to 'work against . . . increasing some semblance of normal home life for the children in the home' (*Social Work Today*, **9** (30), 4 April 1978 : 5).

(7) The resource correlates of successful care are already included in the study for, by very definition, they are included in the cost figures. We should not therefore make the mistake of double-counting by including them as causal determinants of cost (cf. Hall, 1978).

(8) Further details available from the author upon request. The data were collected as part of the survey described by Knapp, Curtis, and Giziakis, (1979).

References

Bebbington, A. C. (1976) Policy Recommendations and the Needs Indicator for Social Service Provision for Children. Discussion Paper 34. University of Kent at Canterbury, Personal Social Services Research Unit.

Bebbington, A. C. and Giziakis, E. (1979) Social Services Expenditure in England and Wales: The Years 1974–75 and 1977–78. Discussion Paper 119. University of Kent at Canterbury, Personal Social Services Research Unit.

Brown, P. (1976) *Finding Children in Need*. London: Tavistock Institute of Human Relations.

Chartered Institute of Public Finance and Accountancy (1979) *Personal Social Service Statistics: 1977–78 Actuals*. London: CIPFA.

Culyer, A. J. (1976) *Need and the National Health Service*. London: Martin Robertson.

Curtis, S. E. (1979) The Needs Indicator Approach to the Study of Social Services for Children. Discussion Paper 140. University of Kent at Canterbury, Personal Social Services Research Unit.

Curtis Committee Report (1946) *Report of the Care of Children Committee*. London: Her Majesty's Stationery Office.

Davies, B. P., Barton, A., and McMillan, I. (1972) *Variations in Children's Services among British Urban Authorities*. London: Bell.

Davies, B. P. and Knapp, M. R. J. (1978) Hotel and Dependency Costs of Residents in Old People's Homes. *Journal of Social Policy* 7 (1): 1–22.

Davies, B. P. and Knapp, M. R. J. (1980) *Old People's Homes and the Production of Welfare*. London: Routledge & Kegan Paul.

Dean, J. (1976) *Statistical Cost Estimation*. Bloomington: Indiana University Press.

Department of Health and Social Security (1971) *Care and Treatment in a Planned Environment*. London: Her Majesty's Stationery Office.

Grygier, T. (1975) Measurement of Treatment Potential: Its Rationale Method and Some Results in Canada. In J. Tizard, I. Sinclair, and R. V. G. Clarke (eds) *Varieties of Residential Experience*. London: Routledge & Kegan Paul.

Hall, A. (1978) Estimating Cost Equations for Day Care. In P. K. Robins and S. Weiner (eds) *Child Care and Public Policy*. Lexington, Connecticut: Heath.

Harris, J. M. (1978) Child Observation and Assessment Centres: Psychiatrists' and Social Workers' Difficulties. *British Journal of Psychiatry* 132 (1): 195–99.

King, R. D., Raynes, N. V., and Tizard, J. (1971) *Patterns of Residential Care*. London: Routledge & Kegan Paul.

Knapp, M. R. J. (1977) A Cost Function for Children's Homes. Discussion Paper 81. University of Kent at Canterbury, Personal Social Services Research Unit.

Knapp, M. R. J. (1979a) Planning Child Care Services from an Economic Perspective. *Residential and Community Child Care Administration* 1 (3): 229–48.

Knapp, M. R. J. (1979b) On the Determination of the Manpower Requirements of Old People's Homes. *Social Policy and Administration* 13 (3): 219–36.

Knapp, M. R. J., Curtis, S. E., and Giziakis, E. (1979) Observation and Assessment Centres for Children: A National Study of the Costs of Care. *International Journal of Social Economics* 6 (3): 128–50.

Pearce, D. (1978) *The Valuation of Social Cost*. London: Allen & Unwin.

Rutter, M. and Madge, N. (1976) *Cycles of Disadvantage*. London: Heinemann.

Silbertson, A. (1972) Economies of Scale in Theory and Practice. *Economic Journal* 82 (1): 369–91.

Sinclair, I. and Heal, K. (1976) Diversity within the Total Institution: Some Evidence from Boys' Perceptions of Community Homes. *Policy and Politics* **4** (1): 5–13.

Skeels, H. M. (1942) A Study of the Effects of Differential Stimulation on Mentally Retarded Children: Follow-up Report. *American Journal of Mental Deficiency* **46**: 340–50.

Skeels, H. M. and Dye, H. B. (1939) A Study of the Effects of Differential Stimulation on Mentally Retarded Children. *Proceedings and Addresses of the American Association on Mental Deficiency* **44**: 114–36.

Tizard, B., Cooperman, O., Joseph, A., and Tizard, J. (1972) Environmental Effects on Language Development: A Study of Young Children in Long-stay Residential Nurseries. *Child Development* **43**: 337–58.

Tizard, J. (1970) The Role of Social Institutions in the Causation, Prevention and Alleviation of Mental Retardation. In H. C. Haywood (ed.) *Social-Cultural Aspects of Mental Retardation*. New York: Appleton-Century-Crofts.

Tizard, J. (1974) Longitudinal Studies: Problems and Findings. In A. M. Clarke and A. D. B. Clarke (eds) *Mental Deficiency: The Changing Outlook* (third edition). London: Methuen.

Whittaker, J. K. (1978) The Changing Character of Child Care: An Ecological Perspective. *Social Service Review* **52** (1): 21–36.

Williams, A. and Anderson, R. (1975) *Efficiency in the Social Services*. Oxford: Basil Blackwell; London: Martin Robertson.

Section V
Conclusion

12 Conclusion

Frank Ainsworth and Leon C. Fulcher

There is no easy way to draw neat conclusions from this series of papers. Indeed, to try to do so would be inconsistent with the developmental nature of the material presented. We think, however, that a final reference to the group care concept as outlined at the beginning of this volume is important. This is because of the way in which group care formulations may facilitate planning of services by helping to transcend traditional boundaries imposed by the four resource networks considered throughout – the health care, education, social welfare, and justice systems. We think that the group care formulation also helps to bind together the variety of children's services which these resource systems provide.

In the turbulent social and economic environment in which we live, continued survival and development of services require that we continue to consider new ways of viewing familiar situations. We have argued that group care is an adaptive concept that is not constrained by limitations imposed by existing professional and occupation interests or by traditional academic disciplines. In our view, neither the categorical and grossly fragmented service system in North America, nor the more closely-knit, state-sponsored service system in Britain offers much scope for advancing services for children.

It is of course worth recalling in the present climate that the institutional components of group care (which are now so readily criticized) are in fact the embodiment of care philosophies which evolved in an earlier era of harsh economic policy. Similar forces now abound but with paradoxical consequences. Suddenly, instead of large establishments, small units are beautiful and the resource-greedy institutions are out of favour. Once again new care philosophies and economic policies combine – albeit differently – to promote changes which may yet prove beneficial to new client populations. A group care formulation may assist this process by helping to highlight the varied ways in which interpersonal dynamics and organizational contexts are related, whether referring to institutional, residential group living or day care services.

We are, of course, aware that group care – defined as an occupational focus, a field of study and a practice domain – has a wider application than simply that associated with services for children. This is capable of extension to services for other client populations which range across the age span. We hope that this evolution will occur and look forward to making a contribution with others in advancing care services that enhance individual development and which are so essential in all Western societies.

Index

Name index

Adams, M. *221*
Adler, Alfred 30
Adler, J. *64*
Agassi, J. B. 184, *195*
Aichorn, August 94, *122*
Ainsworth, Frank 1–14, 71–86, 145, 185, *221*, *222*, 225–43, *243*, 295–96
Ainsworth, M. D. 31, *65*
Albee, G. W. 142, *146*
Algie, J. 253–54, 256, 260, *266*
Allen, K. E. 93, 101, *123*, *124*
Allerhand, M. E. 61, *65*, 106, *123*, 255, *266*
Alpert, S. W. 61, *69*, 93, 106, *126*, 255, *269*
Anderson, R. 286, *292*
Armstrong, J. 259, 260, *268*
Arthur, B. 204, *221*
Atkinson, Margaret 145
Atwater, J. 35, 49, *67*
Austin, M. 206, *223*
Ayres, P. R. 164, *167*

Babcock, C. G. 213, *221*
Baizerman, Mike 145
Bakker, C. B. 38, 42, 44, *65*
Bakker-Rabdau, M. K. 38, 42, 44, *65*
Balcerzak, E. A. 15, *69*, 78, *88*, *223*, *226*, 238, *244*
Bale, T. 53, *65*
Barker, K. C. *65*
Barker, R. L. 186, *195*
Barlow, D. H. 248, *267*
Barlow, G. 248, *266*

Barnes, F. H. 205, *221*
Barton, A. 285, *291*
Bayduss, G. 213, *221*
Bebbington, A. C. 285, *291*
Beedell, C. 72, *87*
Beit-Hallahmi, B. 84, *87*
Beker, Harold 145
Beker, Jerome 13, 58, 62, 64, *65*, 128–46, 202, *221*, 225, 227, *243*
Bell, R. 212, *221*
Bell, S. M. 31, *65*
Benson, J. 162, *167*
Berke, Monte 64
Berkman, W. A. 60, *65*
Berry, J. 62, *87*, 249, *266*
Bertscher, J. *65*
Bettelheim, B. 42, 43, 44, 63, 64, *65*, 91, 92–4, 108, *123*, 235, *243*
Billis, D. *223*
Birch, H. G. 26, 27, *69*, 212, *223*
Birnbaum, J. 204, *221*
Bixby, F. L. 111, *124*
Bloch, A. 152, *167*
Bloom, B. 203, 204, *221*
Blum, A. 91, *125*
Bordwell, Steve 195
Boswell, D. M. *87*
Bower, E. M. 113, 115, *123*, *124*, 264, *266*
Bowlby, J. *65*
Bracken, D. 253, *269*
Bradley, S. 59, *69*
Brager, G. 237, *243*
Braukman, C. J. 35, 49, *67*

Braukmann, C. T. 69
Brazelton, T. 28, 29, 35, 65
Brendtro, Larry K. 69, 80, 88, 110, 111, 119, 120, 122, 123, 126, 202, 223
Brieland, D. 186, 195
Briggs, T. L. 186, 195
Brim, O. 202, 221
Brodie, R. D. 100, 123
Brodsky, S. 205, 206, 222
Bronfenbrenner, Urie 32, 33, 39, 61, 65, 87, 87, 145, 146, 201, 202, 206–07, 208, 210, 211–12, 221
Brown, B. J. 248, 249, 259, 266
Brown, G. W. 185, 195
Brown, P. 284, 291
Browning, R. M. 34, 49, 65, 102, 106, 123
Brunner, J. S. 31, 65
Buell, J. S. 101, 123, 124
Bullock, R. 71, 78, 88, 185–86, 197, 231, 244, 248, 255, 258, 268
Burford, Gale 195
Burmeister, E. 49, 65, 91, 123
Burns, J. L. 259, 260, 266
Butler, H. F. 213, 221
Byers, P. 29, 65

Cameron, J. R. 27, 66
Cartwright, D. 178, 196
Cavior, E. C. 106, 123
Cawson, P. 185, 196, 248, 258, 266–67
Cherns, A. B. 195, 196
Cherrett, P. 78, 88, 248, 255, 268
Chess, S. 26, 27, 36, 66, 69, 212, 223
Churchill, Winston 40
Clark, E. A. 252, 268
Clark, F. W. 125–26
Clarke, R. V. G. 6, 15, 72, 88, 248–49, 258–59, 267, 269, 291
Claster, D. S. 68, 123, 125
Coffin, C. 67
Cohen, A. R. 165, 167
Cohen, H. L. 101, 102, 105, 123
Cohen, S. 65
Comoskey, T. J. 65
Condon, W. 29, 66
Conger, R. E. 97, 107, 125
Conte, Jon R. 64, 66, 205, 222
Cooperman, O. 284, 292
Cornish, D. B. 248, 249, 258–59, 267
Cox, L. A. 129, 147, 225, 243
Cox, P. W. 202, 204, 206, 215, 216, 217, 224

Cressey, D. 197
Culyer, A. J. 291
Cumiskey, P. D. 248, 267
Cummings, E. 92, 123
Cummings, J. 92, 123
Curtis, S. E. 280, 282, 284, 285, 291

Darrow, C. N. 184, 186, 196, 235, 244
Davies, B. P. 279, 285, 291
Davids, A. 202, 222
Davidson, P. O. 125–26
Davis, H. 178, 196
Davis, L. E. 195, 196
Dean, J. 287, 290, 291
de Barros, J. 264, 267
Defoe, Daniel 273–74
DeNoon, B. 57, 66
Dentler, R. A. 108, 123
Dickens, Charles 257
Dinnage, R. 248, 267
Dittman, A. T. 108, 125
Docker-Drysdale, B. 208, 222, 235, 243
Dohrenwend, B. P. 196
Dohrenwend, B. S. 196
Douglas, Robin 264, 266, 267
Dubin, R. 184, 196
Duff, D. F. 43, 64, 66
Dunham, J. 176, 196
Dunlop, A. 248, 255, 267
Dupont, H. 32, 35, 66
Durkin, A. B. 49, 61, 66, 90, 123, 137, 146, 247, 256, 261, 263–64, 267
Durkin, R. P. 49, 61, 66, 90, 123, 137, 146, 247, 256, 261, 263–64, 267
Dye, H. B. 284, 292

Ebner, M. J. 58, 66
Eisikovits, R. A. 139, 146
Eisikovits, Zvi C. 139, 145, 146
Elery, L. 234, 243, 267
Elias, A. 111, 124
Elliott, D. 88, 221, 243
Emerson, P. E. 27, 68
Emery, F. 186, 189–90, 191, 192, 193, 194, 196
Emery, M. 191, 196
Empey, L. T. 109, 110, 111, 123
Endler, N. 212, 223
Engelhard, C. 185, 196
Epstein, L. 262, 269
Erikson, E. H. 212, 213, 216, 218, 219, 222

Escalona, S. K. 26, 27, *66*
Ester, R. J. *222*
Etzioni, A. 220, *222*

Fanshel, D. 61, *66*
Faunce, W. A. 184, *196*
Fetherland, R. 113, 115, *123*, 264, *266*
Filipczak, J. 101, 102, 105, *123*
Fischer, C. 205, 206, *222*
Fixsen, D. L. 49, 50, *66, 68, 69*, 102, 103, 104, 120, *125*, 234, *243*, 248, 252, *267, 269*
Flackett, G. 109, *123*
Flackett, J. M. 109, *123*
Flood, Max 195
Foster, G. W. *244*
Freedman, J. L. 38, 43, *66*
Freire, P. 260, *267*
Freud, Anna 91
Freud, Sigmund 91, 94, 98
Freudenberger, H. J. 151, 157, 158, 160, 161, *167*, 176, *196*
Fulcher, Leon C. 1–14, 71–86, 170–95, 191, *196*, 237, *243*, 295–96

Gadon, H. 165, *167*
Gardner, E. R. 152, *168*
Garland, C. 80, *87*
Gill, O. 248, *267*
Ginger, S. 232, *243*
Ginsburg, E. 184, *196*
Giziakis, E. 280, 282, 284, 285, *291*
Glasser, H. H. *67*
Glasser, P. *88, 244*
Goffman, E. 6, *15*, 47, *66*, 108, *123*, 129, 138, *146*, 182, *196*, 226, *244*
Goldberg, C. 123, *125*
Goldberg, E. M. 250, *267*
Goldfarb, W. 92, *123*
Goldsmith, J. M. *66*, 205, *222*
Goocher, B. E. *66*, 107, *123*
Goode, R. *222*
Goodenough, D. R. 202, 204, 206, 215, 216, 217, *224*
Gorky, Maxim 122
Gottesmann, M. 78, *88*, 113, *127*
Gregory, P. 262, *267*
Griff, M. 205, *224*
Grossbard, H. 156, *167*
Grunewald, K. 75, *87*
Grygier, T. 283, *291*
Guindon, J. 113, *124*, 233, *244*
Gullion, M. 102, *125*
Guttentag, M. *123, 146, 267*

Hafner, H. *268*
Hall, A. 290, *291*
Hall, E. T. *66*
Hall, R. C. W. 152, *168*
Hammerlynch, L. A. *125–26*
Hammond, J. W. *66*
Harper, L. 212, *221*
Harrington, R. L. 185, *196*
Harris, F. R. 93, 101, *123, 124*
Harris, J. M. 284, 290, *291*
Harris, T. 185, *195*
Harstad, C. 112, *124*
Hart, B. M. 101, *123, 124*
Hassibi, M. 36, *66*
Haug, M. 61, *65*, 106, *123*, 255, *266*
Hazel, N. 9, *15*, 76, 78, *87*
Heal, K. 283, *292*
Heimler, E. 180, 188, 195, *196*
Henderson, P. *222*
Henry, Jules 108, *124*
Henry, W. *222*
Hersen, M. 248, *267*
Hersh, S. P. 29, *66*
Herstein, N. *222*
Herzberg, F. 187, 188, *196*
Hewitt, L. H. 137, *168*
Hill, J. P. *124*
Hinshelwood, R. D. *268*
Hirschbach, E. 137, *146*
Hobbs, Nicholas 113–18, *124*, 204, *222*, 233, 235, *244*
Hoghugi, M. S. 248, *267–68*
Hollister, W. G. *124*
Holloway, S. 237, *243*
Holms, T. H. 185, *196*
Holt, R. T. 78, *87, 88*
Horejsi, C. 52, *66*
Horowitz, M. J. 43, 64, *66*
Hosie, K. 71, 78, *88*, 185–86, *197*, 231, *244*, 248, 258, *268*
House, A. E. 97, *126*
Hubert, D. 152, *169*
Hudson, P. 259, 260, *268*
Hunter, J. *222*

Ittelson, W. H. 40, 41, *66, 68, 69*

Jackson, S. 152, *168*
Jacobs, A. *69*
Janes, R. R. 97, 107, *125*
Johnson, C. A. 107, *124*
Johnson, L. O. 258, *268*
Johnson, M. K. 101, *124*

Jones, H. 9, *15*, 71, *87*
Jones, Maxwell vii
Joseph, A. 284, *292*

Kafry, D. 152, *168*
Kagan, J. 33, 36, *67*
Kahan, B. *268*
Kanter, R. 222
Koracki, L. 106, *123*
Kassebaum, F. F. 258, 269–70
Katz, L. 213, *222*
Katz, R. C. 107, *124*
Kazdin, A. E. 49, *67*
Keith-Lucas, A. 236, *244*
Kelley, C. S. 101, *124*
Kelley, H. H. 180, *196*
Kelman, S. M. 205, *221*
Kessen, W. 39, *67*
Key, M. 259, 260, *268*
Kilpatrick, D. M. 98, *125*
King, M. 215, *222*
King, R. D. 6, *15*, 248, *268*, 283, *291*
Kiresuk, T. J. 248, 261, 262, *268*
Kirigin, K. A. 35, 49, *67*, *69*
Kislowicz, L. 248, *269*
Klein, E. B. 184, 186, *196*, 235, *244*
Klerman, G. 206, 213, *222*
Knapp, Martin R. J. 14, 84, 271–90, *291*
Kobak, D. 54, *67*
Kolb, D. 215, 217, 219, *222*
Konopka, G. 91, *124*, 240, *244*
Koreneff, C. 185, *196*
Koslowski, B. 29, 35, *65*
Kozloff, M. A. 107, *124*
Kroes, W. H. 162, 163, *168*
Kuhn, T. S. 51, *67*
Kushlick, A. 248, 249, *268*

Lacey, R. 253, *269*
LaFon, Robert 113
Lamb, H. R. 203, *222*
Lang, G. 154, *168*
Lanier, D. 222
LaPalombara, J. 78, *88*
Laurie, R. 113, 115, *123*, 264, *266*
Lee, D. *67*
Letulle, L. J. 59, *67*
Leuenberger, P. 186, *195*
Levin, K. 29, *66*
Levinson, D. J. 184, 186, *196*, 206, 212, 213, *222*, *223*, 235, *244*

Levinson, M. H. 184, 186, *196*, 235, *244*
Levinson, P. J. *67*, *196–97*, 223
Lewin, Roger *66*
Lewis, M. *65*, *67*
Lieberson, S. 180, *196*
Lindheim, R. *67*
Linton, T. E. 232, *244*
Long, N. J. 95, *124*
Loughmiller, Campbell 113
Lovaas, O. I. 101, 107, *124*
Lubeck, S. G. 109, 110, 111, *123*

McAffrey, A. 248, *267*
McCallum, Catherine 113
Maccoby, E. E. *67*
McCorkle, L. W. 111, *124*
McDougall, W. 176–78, *197*
Mack, J. E. 59, *69*
McKee, B. 184, 186, *196*, 235, *244*
Mackintosh, H. 185–86, *197*
Mackler, B. 108, *123*
McLachlan, G. *268*
McLean, A. 151, 166, *168*
McMillan, I. 285, *291*
McNeil, E. 117, *124*
Madge, N. 284, *291*
Magary, J. F. *67*, *196–97*, 223
Magnus, R. A. 59, *67*
Maier, Henry W. 13, 19–64, *66*, *67*, *68*, 79, 80, *88*, 173, 182, 183–84, 185, 186, *196*, 207, 214, 223, 227, 234, 239, 240, *244*
Main, M. 29, 35, *65*
Magnussen, D. 212, *223*
Makarenko, A. S. 113, 122, *124*
Manning, N. 259, *268*
Martell, M. 248, 258, *267*
Maslach, C. 151, 152, 157, 159, 160, 162, 165, *168*
Masters, J. C. *67*
Masuda, M. 185, *196*
Mattingly, Martha A. 13, 151–67, *168*, 176, *197*, 214, *223*
Mayer, Morris F. 6, 9, *15*, 64, *68*, 78, *88*, 91, *124*, *125*, 223, 226, 238, *244*
Mearing, J. S. 223
Mees, H. 101, *127*
Mehler, F. M. 31, *68*
Mehrabian, A. 42, *68*
Mendelsohn, R. 223
Menzies, I. E. P. 174, 176, 185, *197*
Mikes, G. *196*

Millham, S. 71, 78, *88*, 185–86, *197*,
   231, *244*, 248, 255, 258, *268*
Miller, Clive 266
Mintz, I. 92, *123*
Mooney, S. A. 59, *69*
Moore, C. A. 202, 204, 206, 215, 216,
   217, *224*
Moos, R. H. 82, *88*, 184, *197*, 223
Moriwaki, S. 222
Morris, R. 7, *15*
Morse, W. C. 95, *124*
Muckley, A. 248, *267*
Mordock, J. B. *68*
Murray, C. A. 129, *147*
Mussen, P. H. *67*
Myer, Geoff 195

Nasser, S. 185, *196*
Nelson, J. E. 159, 165, *168*
Nelson, R. H. 258, *268*
Newman, N. 185–86, *197*
Newman, R. G. 95, *124*
Nicholson, M. L. 57, *68*
Noshpitz, J. D. 91, 100, *125*

O'Connor, J. F. 180, *196*
Olden, C. 156, *168*
Olesen, V. 213, *223*
Oswin, M. 248, *268*
O'Toole, M. 79, *88*
Oxley, G. B. *68*

Paige, R. 252, *268*
Paley, J. 254, 255, *268*
Pappenfort, D. M. 98, *125*
Patterson, G. R. 97, 102, 107, *125*
Patti, R. 206, *223*, 237, *244*
Payne, Chris 10, 14, 189, 247–66, *266,
   267, 268, 269, 270*
Pearce, D. 286, *291*
Perl, M. 152, *168*
Pfeffer, J. 179, 180, 189, *197*
Pfefferbaum, B. 152, *168*
Phillips, E. A. 49, 50, 68, 102, 103, 104,
   120, *125*, 234, *243*, 252, *267, 269*
Phillips, E. L. 49, 50, *66, 68, 69*, 102,
   103, 104, 120, *125*, 234, *243*, 248,
   252, *267, 269*
Piaget, Jean 182
Piliavin, I. 108, *125*
Pines, A. 151, 152, 157, 159, *168*
Pinker, R. 73, *88*
Piper, A. *223*

Pizzat, F. J. 71, *88*, 187, *197*
Plank, E. 57, *68*
Pilnick, S. 109, *125*
Polsky, H. W. 57, *68*, 77, 81, *88*, 100,
   108, *123, 125*, 226, *244*
Poulsen, M. K. *67*, *196–97*, 223
Pratt, M. W. 242, *244*
Pringle, K. 248, *267*
Proshansky, H. M. 40, 41, *66, 68, 69*
Prosser, H. 248, *269*

Quay, Herbert C. 89, 90, 105, *125*

Rabin, A. I. 84, *87*
Raush, H. L. 108, *125*
Raynes, N. V. 6, *15*, 242, *244*, 283, *291*
Raynes, R. D. 248, *268*
Reed, M. J. 156, 158, *168*, 184, *197*
Redl, Fritz 2, *15*, 47, 57, *68*, 91, 94–7,
   100, 119, *125*, 234, 240, *244*
Regis, Steve 195
Reichertz, D. 248, *269*
Reichler, R. J. 93, 107, *126*, 204, 223
Reid, J. B. 97, 107, *125*
Reid, W. J. 262, *269*
Reiger, N. 233, *244*
Rein, M. 251, 257, 259, *269*
Reinach, E. 249, *269*
Repucci, N. D. 106, *125*
Resnick, H. 237, *244*
Rhodes, W. C. 122, *125*
Richard, M. P. 65
Richman, L. H. 6, 9, *15*, 78, *88*, 223,
   226, 238, *244*
Righton, P. 251, *269*
Risley, T. 101, *127*
Rivlin, L. G. 40, 41, *66, 68, 69*
Roberts, G. 249, *269*
Roberts, R. W. 98, *125*
Rose, S. D. 107, *125*
Rosenblum, L. A. 65, *67*
Roses, S. 242, *244*
Rowbottom, R. 223
Rozentals, V. 223
Rushforth, M. 78, 88
Russell, K. J. 187, 188, *197*
Rutter, M. 284, *291*

Sable, P. 36, *68*
Salancik, G. R. 179, 180, 187, *197*
Sandler, B. 223
Sarri, R. *88*, 111, *125, 244*
Saunders, J. T. 106, *124*

Scarpitti, F. R. 111, *126*
Schaefer, C. E. *68*
Schaffer, R. 25, 27, 29, 31, 35, 39, *68*
Schmidt, A. 106, *123*
Schopler, E. 93, 107, *126*, 204, 223
Schulze, S. 91, *126*
Schumaker, J. *69*
Schwartz, M. S. 6, *15*, 226, *244*
Schwartz, W. *68*
Scott, Tony 266
Scriven, N. 250, *269*
Scull, A. 4, *15*
Seed, P. 4, *15*
Segal, J. 27, 31, 35, 36, *68*
Seiderman, S. 152, *168*
Seidl, F. W. 49, *68*
Selo, E. 111, *125*
Shamsie, J. 154, *168*
Shaw, Bernard xiii
Sherman, R. E. 248, 261, 262, *268*
Shoman, L. 59, *69*
Shubin, S. 152, *168*
Silbertson, A. 282, *291*
Simon, Paula 145
Sims, J. 222
Sinclair, I. 6, *15*, 72, *88*, 248–49, 259, *267*, *269*, 283, *291*, *292*
Singer, M. J. 258, *268*
Sivadon, P. 43, *68*
Skeels, H. M. 284, *292*
Sobesky, W. 213, *223*
Somjen, L. 59, *69*
Sommer, R. 6, *15*, *69*
Spock, Dr Benjamin 211
Spradlin, W. W. *69*
Spray, W. 222
Sroufe, L. A. 31, 32, 33, *69*
Stalinski, J. 248, *269*
Stambaugh, E. E. 97, *126*
Standke, L. 163, *168*
Stanton, A. H. 6, *15*, 226, *244*
Stayne, D. J. 31, 65
Stea, D. 42, *69*
Steiner, Rudolph 187
Stephenson, R. M. 111, *126*
Stickney, S. K. 152, *168*
Stover, D. O. 34, 49, *65*, 102, 106, *123*
Stratton, L. O. 43, 64, *66*
Stroock, K. W. 92, *123*
Struening, E. L. *123*, *146*, *267*
Strutter, C. 113, 115, *123*, 264, *266*
Suchman, E. L. 257, *269*
Sylvester, E. 91, *123*

Taft, J. 99, *126*
Taylor, D. A. 61, *69*, 93, 106, *126*, 255, *269*
Taylor, J. J. 108, *125*
Taylor, L. 253, *269*
Taylor, P. A. *67*, *196–97*, 223
Teather, Ted 64
Teeter, Ruth 145
Thomas, A. 26, 27, *69*, 212, 223
Thomas, G. 248, *269*
Thomes, J. 250, *268*, *269*
Thorpe, D. 255, *268*
Tizard, J. 6, *15*, 72, *88*, 248–49, *268*, *269*, 283, 284, *291*, *292*
Toscano, J. A. 213, *221*
Tracy, M. L. 122, *125*
Trieschman, Albert E. *69*, 80, *88*, 119, 120, 122, *123*, *126*, 202, 223
Turner, Chris 195
Turner, John E. *67*, 78, 87, *88*
Tutt, Norman vii–ix
Tweddle, D. 262, *267*

VanderVen, Karen D. 14, 154, 166, *168*, 185, 201–21, 222, 223–24, 227, 240, *244*
Vinter, R. D. 71, 78, *88*, 204, 224, 240, *244*
Vorrath, H. H. 110, 111, 122, *126*

Wahler, R. G. 97, 107, *126*
Walton, R. G. *88*, *221*, 243
Warburton, W. 255, *269*
Ward, D. A. 258, *269–70*
Waters, E. 33, *69*
Watson, Decky 86
Wattenberg, M. W. 95, *125*
Wax, D. E. 40, 43, *69*
Weber, R. 61, *65*, 106, *123*, 255, 266
Weber, G. H. 185, *197*
Webster, C. D. 59, *69*
Weeks, H. A. 111, *126*
Weick, K. E. 182, 183, 184, *197*
Weihs, T. J. 187, *197*
Weil, J. L. 177, 195, *197*
Weinstein, L. 115, *126*
Weiss, C. H. 247, *269–70*
Weissman, H. H. 237, *244*
Werry, J. S. *125*
Whipple, H. 223
White, K. J. 251, 254, *266*, *268*, *269*, 270
White, M. S. 60, *69*
White, R. W. 119, *126*

White, S. 80, *87*
White, W. L. 152, 153, *168–69*
Whittaker, E. 213, *223*
Whittaker, James K. 13, *15*, 45, 49, 57,
  58, 61, *69*, 71, 80, 84, *88*, 89–122,
  123, *126*, 129, 140, *147*, 173–74, *197*,
  202, 221, *223*, *224*, 236, 240, *243*,
  244, 248, 254–55, 256, 258, 261, *270*,
  284, *292*
Wiher, A. G. 69
Williams, A. 286, *292*
Wilson, T. 56, 57, *69*
Wineman, D. 47, 57, 63, *68*, *69*, 91, 95,
  96, 97, 119, *125*
Wing, J. K. *268*
Wingrove, J. M. *87*
Winnicott, D. W. 39, *69*
Witkin, H. A. 202, 204, 206, 215, 216,

217, *224*
Wolins, M. 9, *15*, 78, *88*, 113, *127*, 129,
  147, *222*, *224*
Wolf, M. M. 35, 49, 50, *66*, *67*, *68*, 101,
  102, 103, 104, 120, *123*, *124*, *125*,
  127, 234, *243*, 248, 252, *267*, *269*
Wolkon, G. *222*
Wrenn, C. G. 25, 55, *70*
Wright, C. 185, *196*
Wylde, S. R. *70*

Yager, J. 152, *169*
Yahraes, H. 27, 31, 35, 36, *68*

Zabarenko, L. 213, *224*
Zabarenko, R. 213, *224*
Zander, A. 178, *196*
Zusman, J. 203, *222*

Subject index

abuses, institutional 90, 128, 253
acceptability of group care 74, 180, 253
accountability 206, 209, 211, 228, 229,
  252
Achievement Place 102–05, 109, 120,
  234, 248, 252, 262
activities, pattern of 80
adiagnostic approach 114, 116
administration *see* management
admission and discharge 81
affection *see* attachment
affective orientation 215
aggression 97, 183
America, North xiii–xvi, 71–5, 84, 90,
  91, 92, 129–30, 227–29, 247–48
American Association for Children's
  Residential Centers 221
American *v*. British terms xiii–xvi,
  71–2, 86–7
anger 19, 64n11
anorexia nervosa 92, 93
apathy 152, 160
approved schools 255
architecture 93
assessment centres 283, 284
attachment 23, 25, 30–4, 35, 39–40,
  54–5, 58, 59
attachment behaviour 32, 33–4, 36
attention 31–2, 35–6
attention-getting demands 35–6
attitudes 155–56, 158, 187–88, 191–92,
  211, 213–215, 242; *see also* values

authoritarianism 183
authority 213, 218–20
autism 91, 93, 101, 107
awakening 48
awareness, personal 157, 161

behaviour ix, 28, 33–4, 36, 39–43,
  53–4, 56, 74, 90, 95, 97, 99–103,
  105–08, 110, 116, 119–20, 122, 155,
  158, 176, 192, 254; *see also* behaviour
behaviour modification *see next entry*
behavioural approaches 34–5, 39–40,
  49–50, 52, 93–4, 101–08, 187, 234,
  248, 262
belongings 34–4, 51, 58, 64n11, 156
Birmingham University 249, 250, *269*
boarding school 88
boundaries, spatial 44–5, 46
Boys Town, Nebraska 103
Britain xiii–xvi, 71–5, 129–30, 229–32,
  247–50
British Association of Social Workers
  230, *243*
Bureau of Child Research, Kansas
  University 102–03
burn-out 151–52, 153, 156–60, 167

capital costs 277
capital stock 285
career mobility 204
caring for children 23–5, 32, 37, 50,
  54–5, 86, 207, 234, 239–40
Central Council for Training and

Education in Social Work 230
Centre for Youth Development and Research, Minnesota University 138, *146*
Centres for Advanced Practice and Research 131, 140–41, 142, 145
Certificate in Social Service 230, 231–32
Certificate of Qualification in Social Work 230
change, personal 25, 49–50, 53, 114, 116, 117, 255
charges 280–81
Chartered Institute of Public Finance and Accountancy *291*
checklists 261–62
Chicago University 86
child characteristics 285
child guidance movement 97–9, 201
child-care workers, problems of ix, 154–56, 170–71; *see also* frustration; job stress; personal problems
Children Act, 1948 283
Children and Young Person's Act, 1969 249
Children's Center, Madison 102, 106–07
Children's Village, Dobbs Ferry 98
choice 262
client participation 205–06, 208, 211; *see also* partnership with parents
closeness 24; *see also* attachment
cognitive orientation 217
colleagues 22, 157, 159–60, 164, 172, 214, 218, 263
collusion 160
combat neurosis 152, 167n2
comfort, physical 37–8, 47, 64n6
commitment 157, 158, 160, 173, 193, 194, 251
Committee on Child Psychiatry 222
communication ix, 32, 59, 209, 210–11
community 3, 62, 104, 129, 130, 137, 138, 139–40, 141–43, 145, 153, 231
community school movement 139–40
comparison of group care programmes 77–85
competence *see* social skills
compliance 50
concept of group care 1–3
conflict 24–5, 54, 57, 153, 154, 155
conformity 73, 81, 110
contemplation 42, 47

continuum of care 129–30, 131, 132, 134–35, 140, 146n5
control 100, 180–81, 252; *see also* social control
coordination of services 130–31, 133, 138
cost function analysis 287–90
costs 84, 89, 104–05, 128, 257, 271–90
counselling 20, 57, 63n2
creative thought 163
culture 52, 211, 236
Curtis Committee Report viii, 283, *291*

day care 9, 80, 274
decarceration viii, 7, 128, 138, 226, 231
decision-making 179, 186, 205, 218–19, 251
dedication 154, 214–15
deinstitutionalization *see* decarceration
delinquent subculture 109, 111–12
delinquents viii, 91, 94–7, 98, 100–06, 108–12, 122, 137, 144, 183, 229, 248, 255, 259
Department of Health and Social Security 263, 264, *267*, 283, *291*
dependency 30–2, 39, 40
depreciation 277
Detroit Group Project 95
development ix, 3, 6, 12, 25, 30–5, 51–2, 55, 83, 137, 140, 144, 160, 201–02, 208, 212–213, 226, 234, 236–37
development, professional 212–20
diagnostic labels 204
discipline 39, 57–8, 81, 82
discontent 157
disorders, rehabilitation of *see* rehabilitation of disorders
dissociation 192
disturbed children 21, 46, 89, 90, 92–4, 96, 99–100, 107, 114–18, 226, 253, 254, 256
doctors 134, 135, 138

ecology 201–02
economics 3, 5, 10, 37, 76, 136, 210, 253, 271–76, 279, 286, 289–90, 290n2, 295
economies of scale 282–83, 290n6
éducateur 113, 116–17, 118, 232, 233, 234–35
education 2, 4, 7, 8, 73, 121, 209, 228
educational approaches 113–118

effectiveness 180, 206, 251–54, 255–57, 261

effectiveness *v.* efficiency 180–81, 255–57

efficiency 180, 256, 261

emotions, negative 156

empathy 156, 214, 216

'enacted environment' 182–84

energy 157, 159, 160

environment 2, 181–84, 189–93, 202

environments, turbulent 190–93

evaluation 83, 104, 115, 120, 238, 241, 247–66

exercise 162

exhaustion 151, 152, 156–57, 158–59, 162, 165

exosystem of group care 210–11, 217–19, 241–42

expectations 30, 57–8

expenditure 275, 276–77, 287–88

experiences, previous 182–83

experimentation 56

expertise 140, 142, 145, 155, 166, 236–39, 241–42, 272; *see also* skills

expressive approach 215

family viii, 2, 3, 6, 37, 59, 60–1, 80, 107, 122, 142, 145, 185–86, 234, 236

feedback from evaluation 264–65

flexibility 158, 163

flow of clients 135–37

foster care viii, 76, 90

freedom, psychological 23, 24, 30

Fresh Air Camp, Michigan University 119

frustration 152, 153, 170–71, 188

functions of group care work 235

games, therapeutic 23–4, 56

generativity stage 218, 219

government agencies 10, 76, 143, 210–11

group leaders 110–11

group psychology 209

growth *see* self-realization

guided group interaction 108, 109–13, 122n3

Hampstead Child Therapy Clinic 91

handicapped people viii, 75–6, 249, 273–74

Harlesden Community Project 254, 267

Hawthorne Cedar Knolls School, New York 98

Head Start 202, 205

health care 2, 4, 8, 131, 134–35, 137–38, 226

health problems 160, 161

historical perspectives on group care vii–viii, 4–6, 90, 237

holidays 162–63

home 20, 21, 54, 59, 60, 108, 129

hospitals 108, 134–35, 137–38, 174

household functions 37–8

humility, unproductive 214–15, 217

idealism 154

identification with adulthood 216
  with childhood 213–14
  with systems 218
  with the human condition 219

identity, professional 157, 185, 218, 219–20

ideology 83–4, 153, 251

imaginative exercises 163

inadequacy, feelings of 157, 159; *see also* humility, unproductive

incarceration 129

independence 30–1, 36

indifference 192

indirect care *see* exosystem of group care; mesosystem of group care

individual treatment 25–8

individualism 73

Industrial Revolution 5

infants 27, 29, 31, 33

in-patient care 134–35

inspectors 263–65

institutions 2, 3, 5–6, 7, 9, 10, 21, 45, 49, 60, 92, 97–8, 104, 128–30, 135, 139–43, 226, 249, 283, 295

instrumental approach 217, 218, 219–20

integration of programs 141–42

integrity stage 219

interaction 23–30, 31–2, 48, 56, 58, 103, 120, 155, 156, 158, 160, 176, 186, 251

interactional approach 34–5, 50, 51–2; *see also* guided group interaction

interest 19, 24

intimacy stage 216

intolerance 191

intuitive responses 27

isolation rooms 46–7

Jay Report 231–32, *244*
job satisfaction 153–55, 171, 176, 187–88, 194
job stress 151–67, 176, 214
Joint Commission on Mental Health of Children 115, 116, *124*
justice system 3, 4, 7, 8, 129, 136, 137, 144, 226, 243n1

Kingswood Study 258–59, 260

leadership 179, 180–81
learning 39, 55, 58, 73, 107, 114, 215–16, 217, 219
learning experiences 2, 6, 50, 52–4, 144, 234, 256, 262
legislation 79, 172–73, 189, 210, 237
legitimacy of group care *see* acceptability of group care
life issues 213–20
life structure 184–86
life-space interview 95, 96, 97, 113
live-in staff 156, 184
local authorities 89, 229, 264, 272

macrosystem of group care 211–12, 219–20
maladaptive responses 190–92
management 155, 164–65, 166, 210, 241, 242, 256, 273, 277
management perspective 49, 77, 155
managers 180–81
market prices 275, 276
meaning 182–83
mental illness vii
mesosystem of group care 208–10, 216–17, 241–42
microsystem of group care 207–08, 213–16, 239–41
minutiae of residential care 47–8, 119, 120
misjudgement 159
motivation 154
Mulberry Bush 235

NASA 175
National Institute of Child Health and Human Development 31, *68*
National Institute of Mental Health, Bethesda 95, 105, 113, 227
National Training School 102, 105–06
Nazis 91, 92, 180
neurophysiology 195n2

New England Home for Little Wanderers, Boston 98
N. J. Pritzker Children's Hospital and Center, Chicago 152, 168
non-compliance 58
nurturing 2, 31–2, 36, 63–4n3, 138, 214

objectives 253–54, 256, 261–62, 279, 281
occupational stress *see* job stress
off-duty time 158, 164, 165
office tasks 41
offices 42
opportunity costs 84, 274–76, 287
organizational behaviour 179–81, 189–92, 210, 218–19
organizational studies 237–38
orientation 49, 78, 83, 84, 86, 186–88, 201–02, 215, 217, 218
Orthogenic School 108, 235
outcomes 254–55
outputs 281–83, 284–85, 287
'outsiders' and 'insiders' 82–3
Outward Bound Schools 113
overcrowding 43
overestimation 159–60

pain 157–58
parents 20, 27, 33, 43, 59–61, 79, 82–3, 93, 94, 100, 104, 141, 205, 209, 214, 216, 234, 236
partnership with parents 82–3, 205
Peace Corps 113
Peanuts cartoon 64
peer groups 23–5, 54–5, 103, 109–11, 122, 122n3
peers *see* colleagues
personal attributes of workers 11
personal life 158, 161–62, 164, 165, 188
personal problems 157–58
Personal Social Services Council 263, *269*
Personal Social Services Unit 84
personnel deployment 79–80
physical contact 27, 28, 32
physically active temperaments 26–7
physiological influences 177–78
Pioneer House 95, 96
Pittsburgh University 227
play 56
policies 74, 75–7, 85, 143, 153, 164, 172–73, 189, 210, 237–38, 258, 271–72, 286, 289, 295–96

power 42, 50, 54, 57–8, 73, 109, 218
practical arrangements 48
prejudice 191–92
primary prevention of disorders
    203–04, 207, 209–10, 211
privacy 42–5, 64n5, 156
private space 38, 42–5, 46
problems, everyday 19–24, 25–6, 51,
    110, 112, 115, 117, 140, 144, 155–56;
    see also child-care workers, problems
    of; personal problems
process studies 255
professional groups 96
professionalization 10, 152, 227–28,
    231, 232–33
programmed instruction 73
programmes 55–7, 71–86, 241
Project Re-Ed 113–18, 119, 234–35
psychiatry, psychiatrists 96, 98–9, 100,
    108–09, 114, 290n5
psychoanalytic approaches 91–7,
    99–100, 121
psychology, psychologists ix, 50, 85,
    248
psychotic children 92–4, 102
public opinion 153
public space 45–6
public spending 76, 289
punishment 58, 64n8, 81

recidivism 104, 105, 111
recreation 20
Red Wing Institution, Minnesota 111
referrals 135–37, 138, 140, 144
regional variation 280
rehabilitation of disorders 109, 203,
    207
rehearsive practice 53–4, 56
reinforcement 101, 102, 103, 105, 106,
    108, 110, 111
relationships 33, 120, 186
relaxation techniques 162
rescue fantasy 214, 217, 218
research 238–39, 257–59, 287–89
residential care 9, 10, 40, 76, 81, 89,
    129, 272
resources 256, 272–76, 279–80, 289–90
respect 219
responsibility 25, 152, 178–79
restrictiveness 130, 131, 137, 140, 145,
    145–46n3
rhythmic interactions 28–30, 52
rights 73, 128, 129, 144–45, 172, 253

rigidity 153, 157, 158–59, 163
rituals 30, 81
Robert F. Kennedy Youth Center
    105–06
role of institutions 139–40, 141–43
role models 39, 140
Roman Empire 5
rotas 80
routines 30, 52, 55, 56, 80
rules 81

Scandinavia 52, 75
scheduling 165
schools 139–40, 141
scientific methods 260, 264
segmentation 191–92
self-esteem 154, 161, 203–04
self-evaluation 260–62
self-management 39, 40, 53
self-realization 55, 82, 114, 119, 144,
    213, 234
skills 11, 193, 194, 206–12, 239–42; *see
    also* expertise; social skills
sleeping quarters 44
social behaviour 176–78
social control 4, 5, 73, 81, 136, 137
social costs 84, 275, 287
social customs 81–2
social mandate 78–9
social philanthropy 5
social policy *see* policies
social services 2–3, 4, 7, 8, 173, 229–32,
    271, 275
Social Services Research Council 249,
    269
social skills 21, 24, 73, 103, 116, 119,
    120, 203–04
social workers 99, 29n4
socialization 2, 40, 73, 108, 120, 235,
    236
Sonia Shankman Orthogenic School,
    Chicago University 92–3
space, private *see* private space
spatial arrangements 40–7, 60, 79
Special Air Service 175
specialists 75, 134, 135
staff meetings 160, 170–71
stereotyping 159, 160, 163
stimuli 26–8, 51, 177
Stirling University 86
strategy 251
Strathclyde Regional Council 76, *88*
stress *see* job stress

stress in children 33
stress management 158, 160–67
study plans 166
superficiality 191
supervision, supervisors 155, 157, 165–66, 171, 183, 208–09, 216, 241
support, emotional 22, 31–6, 82, 157–58, 159–60, 163–64, 165, 174, 194, 218
synergy 215, 217, 219

task achievement 174–75, 180, 193–94, 206, 252, 254–55, 261, 279
teacher-counselors 113, 114–15, 116–18
team organization 193–94
team psychology 176–77
teamwork 171–72, 173–95, 209
teasing 23–5, 53–4
temperament 25–8
Temple University 105
tensions 19, 43, 46, 51
therapeutic milieu, therapeutic community vii, 92–4, 95–7, 100–1, 119–22, 202, 251, 258, 259
therapy, therapists 88, 96, 97–101, 109, 114, 120, 157
theory 175, 236, 238, 288
togetherness 29–30
token economy 103, 105, 107–08
training for child-care workers vii, ix, 11–12, 90, 112, 151, 152, 157, 158, 161, 166, 170, 202, 203, 206, 224–43, 265
transition 39, 64n9; *see also* worker transition
troubled children *see* disturbed children
trust 159
turnover rate 153, 283–84

values 3, 10, 58, 73–4, 83–4, 187–88, 211, 251, 253–54, 256, 257; *see also* attitudes
visits 60
visual temperaments 26–7
voluntary services 9–10

wages 154, 280
Walker School, Needham 119
Wayne State University 95
Wessex project 249, 257
Whittier State School, California 98
work load 22, 158
work patterns 80, 165, 178, 184–85
work projects for children 55–6
worker transition 158, 162
workplace 181–82
workshops, evaluation 263

Youth Treatment Centre 264